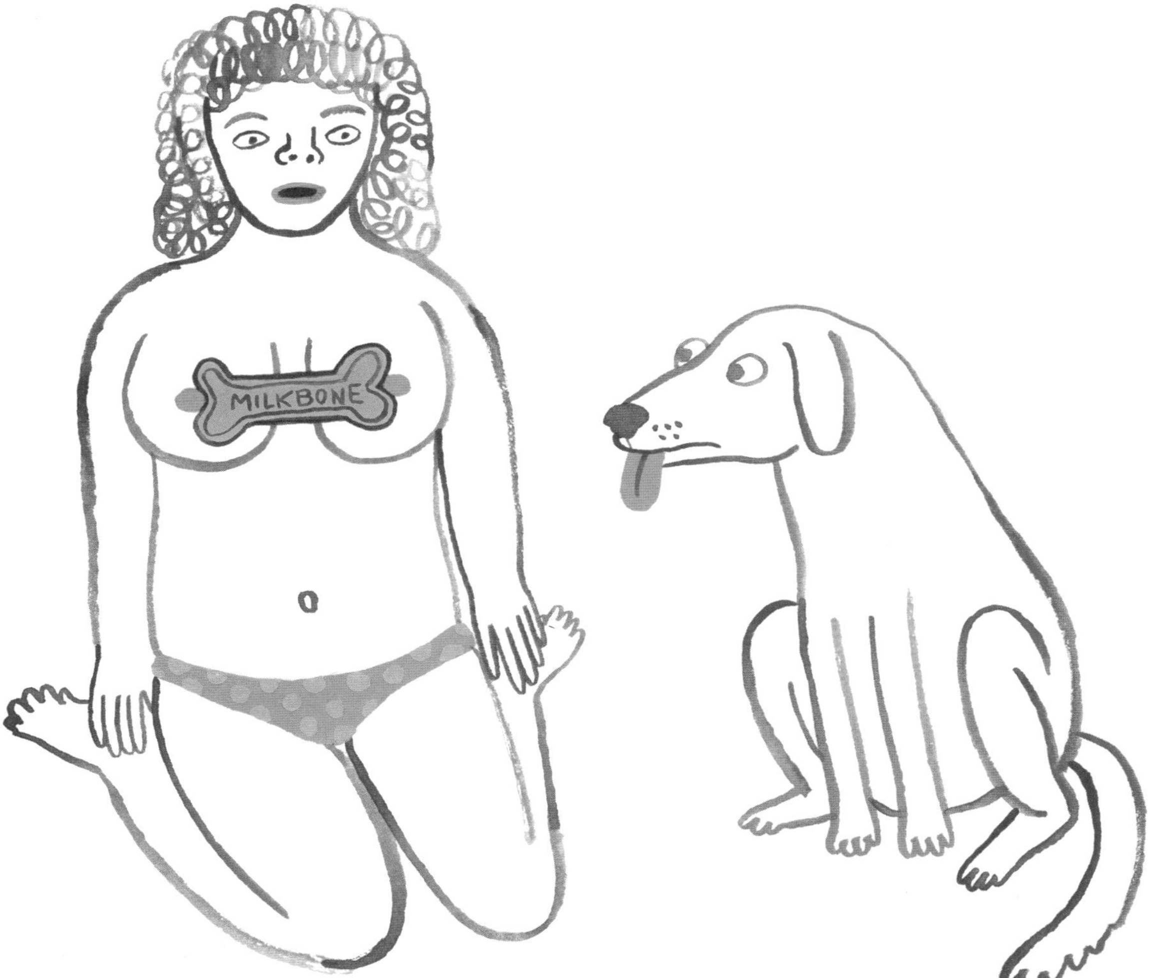
MILKBONE

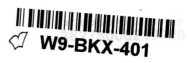

FOR MY LOVE, ADAM.

FOR MOM & DAD & ALEX.

DRAWN & QUARTERLY PRESENTS

HOT DOG TASTE TEST

A ~~COOK~~BOOK BY LISA HANAWALT

✓ NO DIETS
✓ NO JUICE CLEANSES
✓ I WILL DRINK JUICE BUT YOU WON'T KNOW
✓ NO RECIPES
✓ NO ACTUAL FOOD INCLUDED

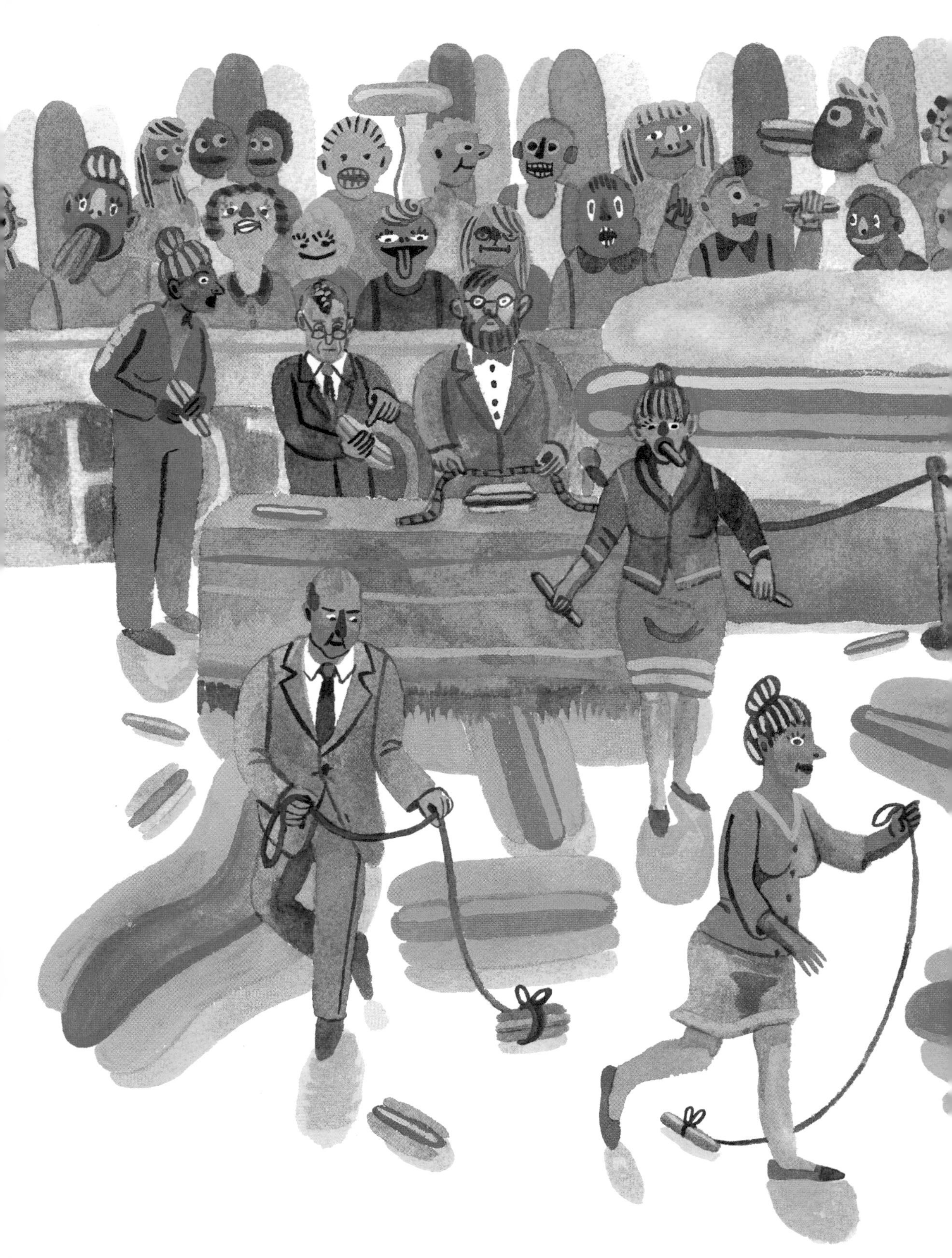

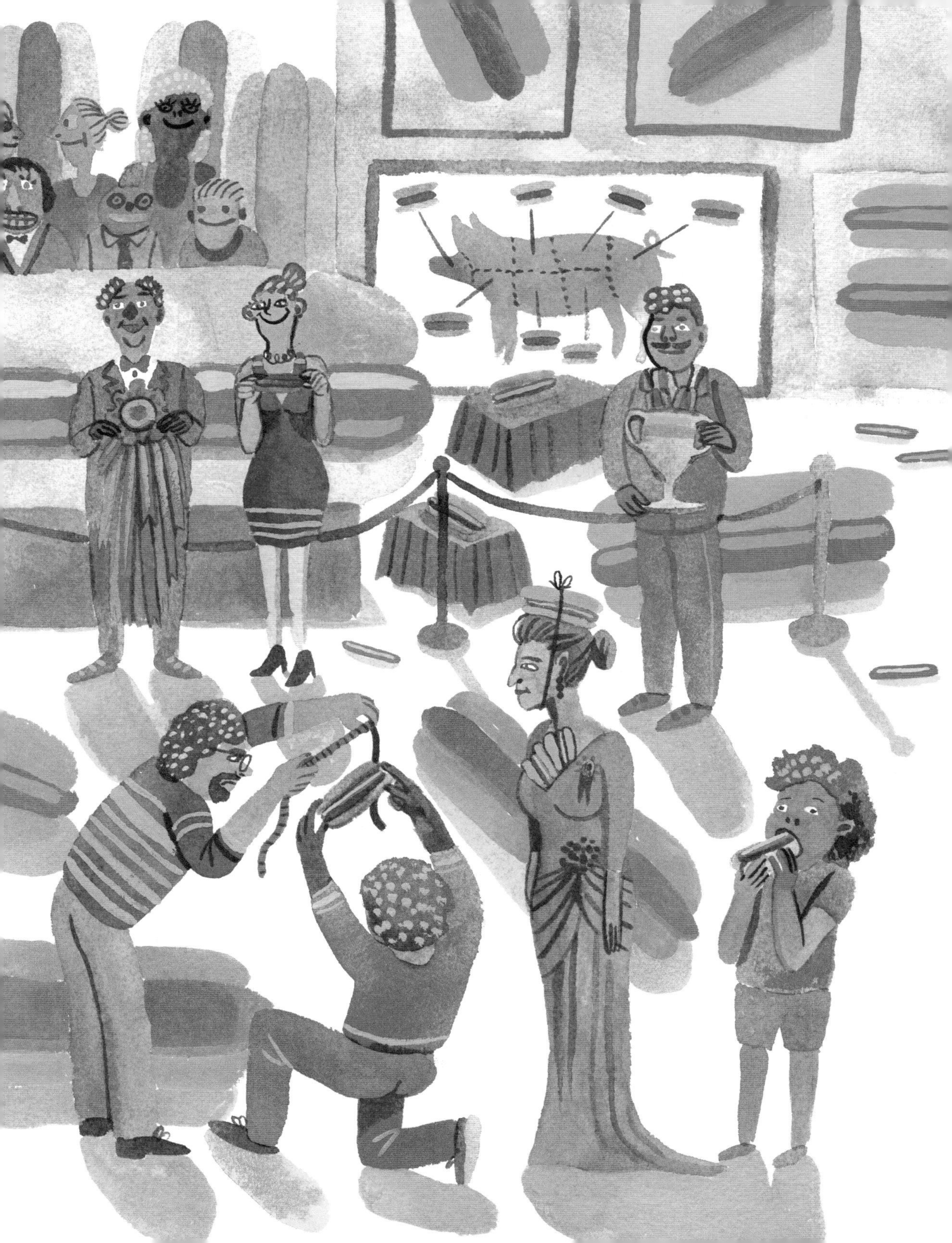

BAKING TIPS

- WHISK DRYS
- BLEND WETS
- USE CHOCOLATE
- PARCHMENT PAPER WILL SAVE YOU
- BAKE IF YOU LIKE <u>BROWN</u> THINGS
- YOU CAN DO ANYTHING TO EGGS
- PROTECT BUTTER'S REPUTATION
- MAKE DESSERTS MORE SPICY
- DON'T LOOK AT THE OVEN.
- THERE'S NO SHAME IN MUSH
- NOBODY KNOWS WHAT ▓▓▓▓NG
- YOU CAN'T BAKE IN THE MOUNTAINS
- DUTCH-PROCESS COCOA IS LESS ACIDIC THAN REGULAR COCOA.
- YOGURT MAKES PROMISES IT CAN'T KEEP
- KEEP YOUR SWEET TOOTH AWAY FROM YOUR SALT MOLAR

4

BANANA EMBELLISHMENTS

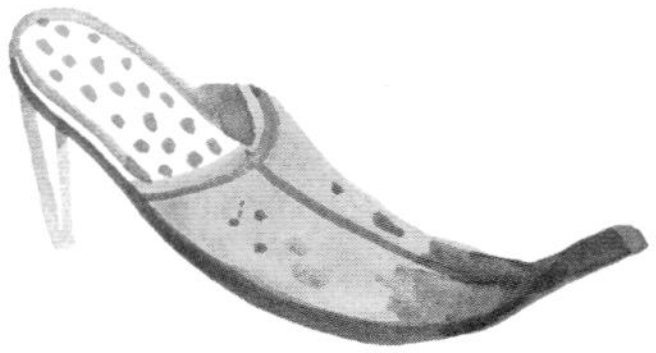

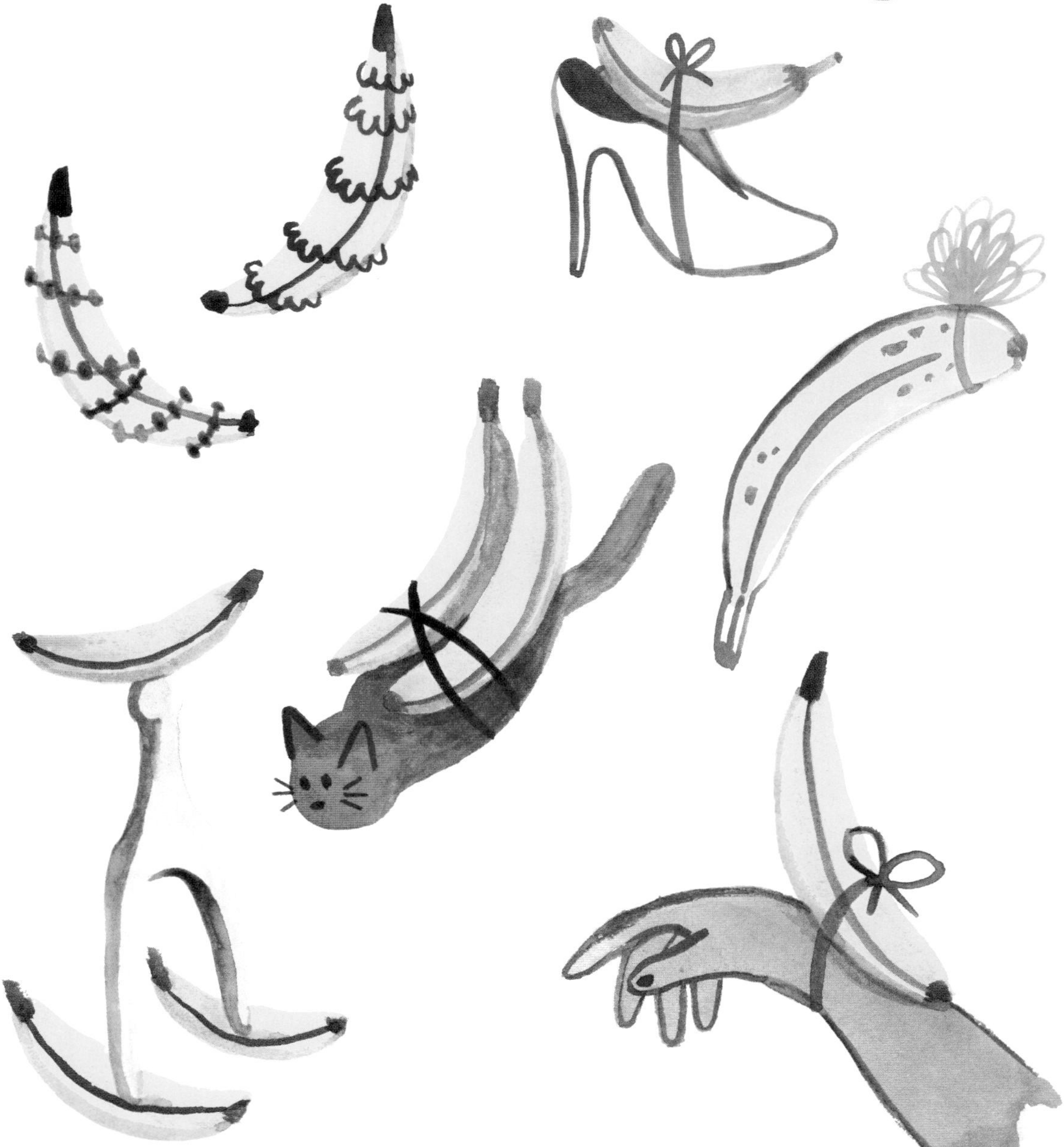

SHOPPING

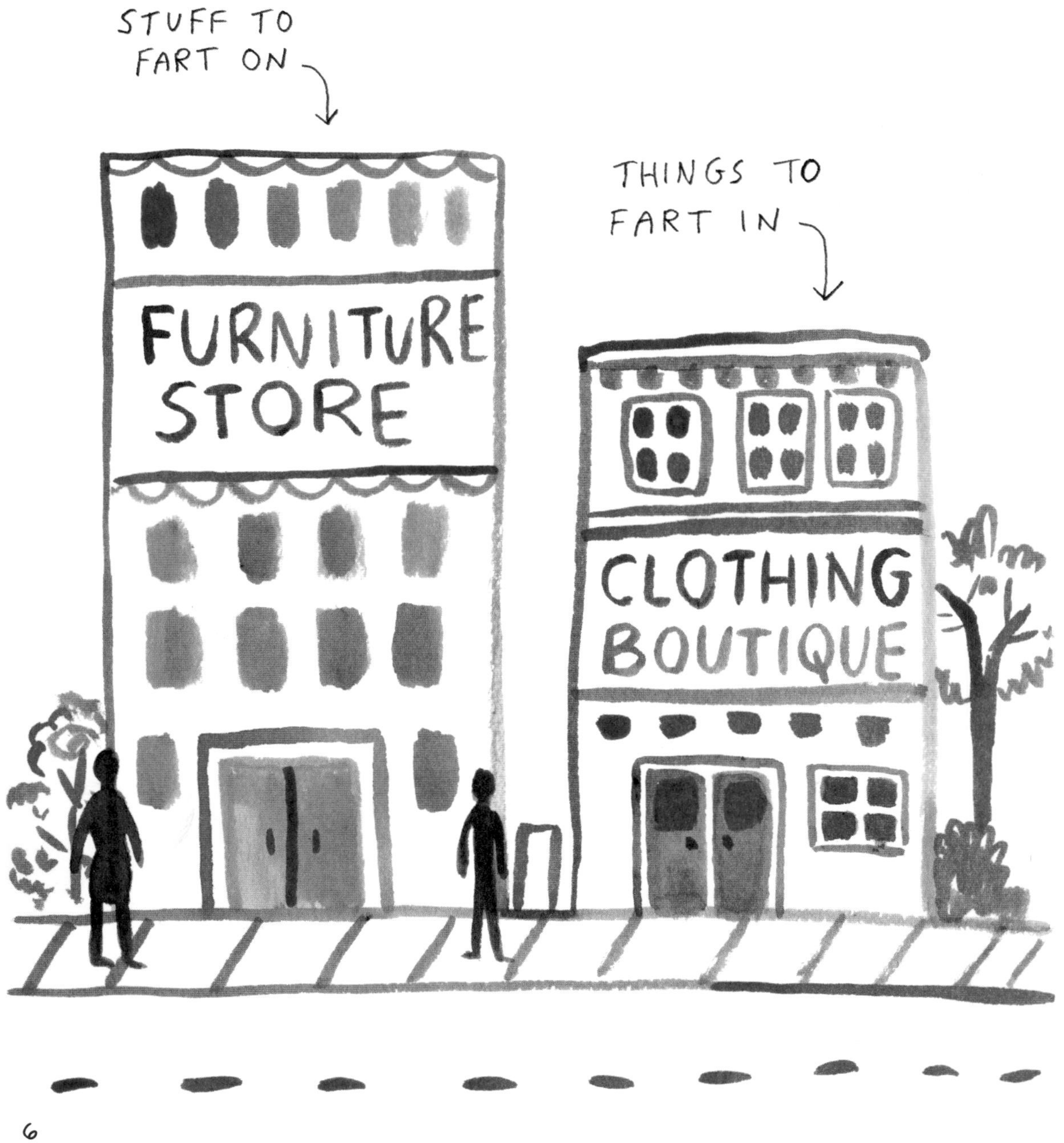

STUFF TO FART ON
FURNITURE STORE
THINGS TO FART IN
CLOTHING BOUTIQUE

HOW TO CHOOSE A WINE

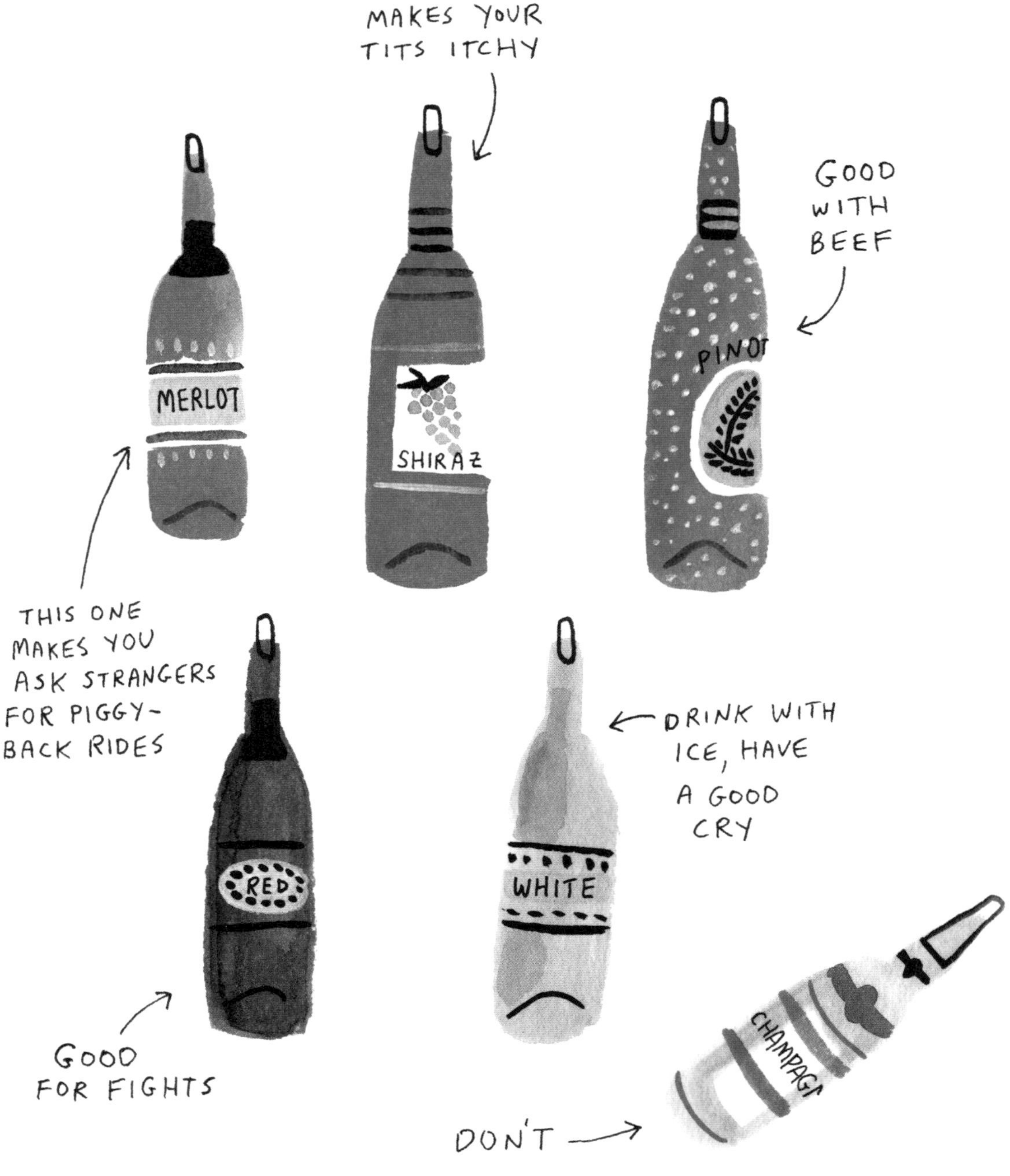
MAKES YOUR TITS ITCHY
GOOD WITH BEEF
MERLOT
SHIRAZ
PINOT
THIS ONE MAKES YOU ASK STRANGERS FOR PIGGY-BACK RIDES
DRINK WITH ICE, HAVE A GOOD CRY
RED
WHITE
GOOD FOR FIGHTS
CHAMPAG
DON'T

REAL & IMAGINED GARNISHES

PRESENTED WITHOUT COMMENT

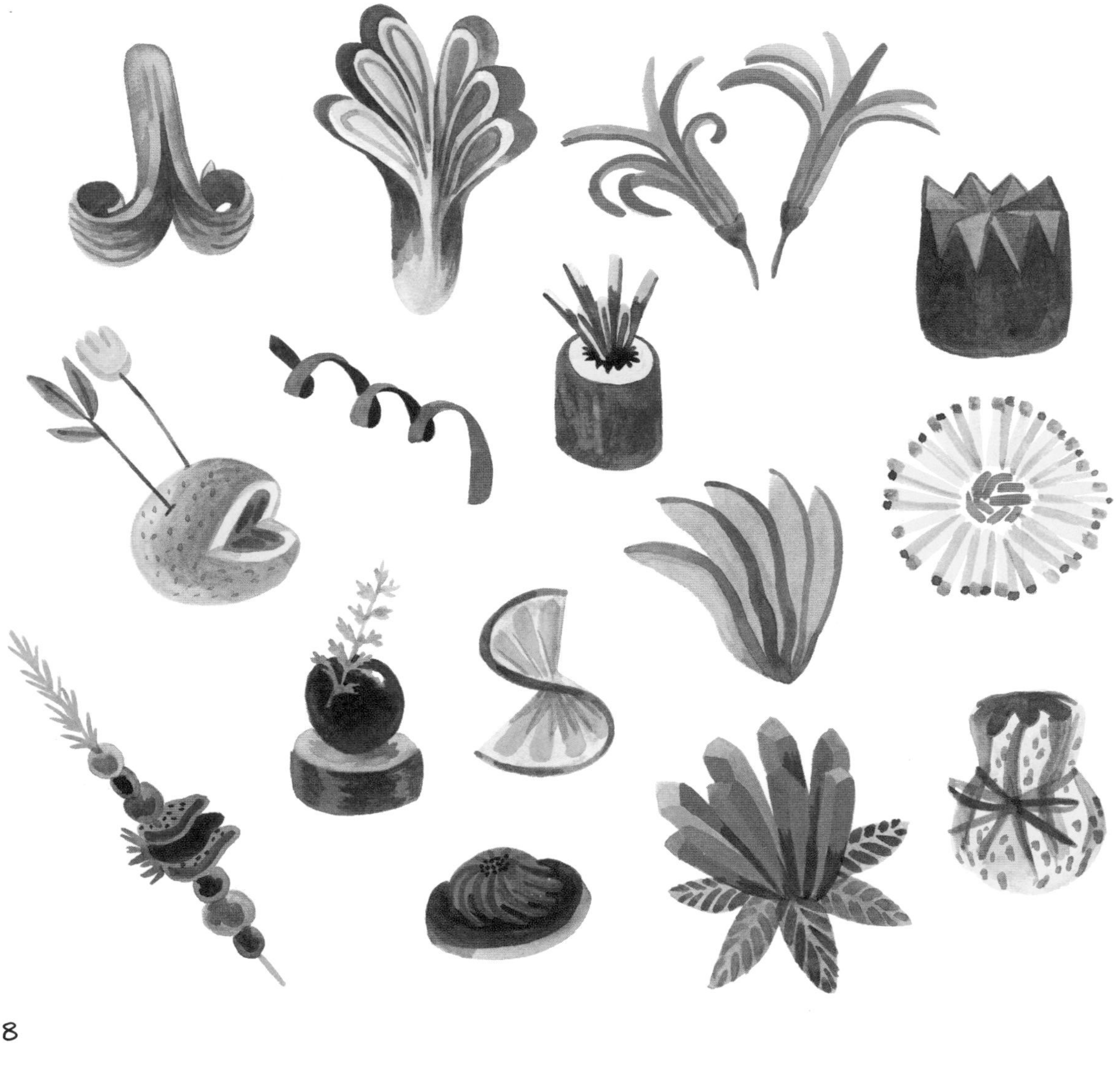

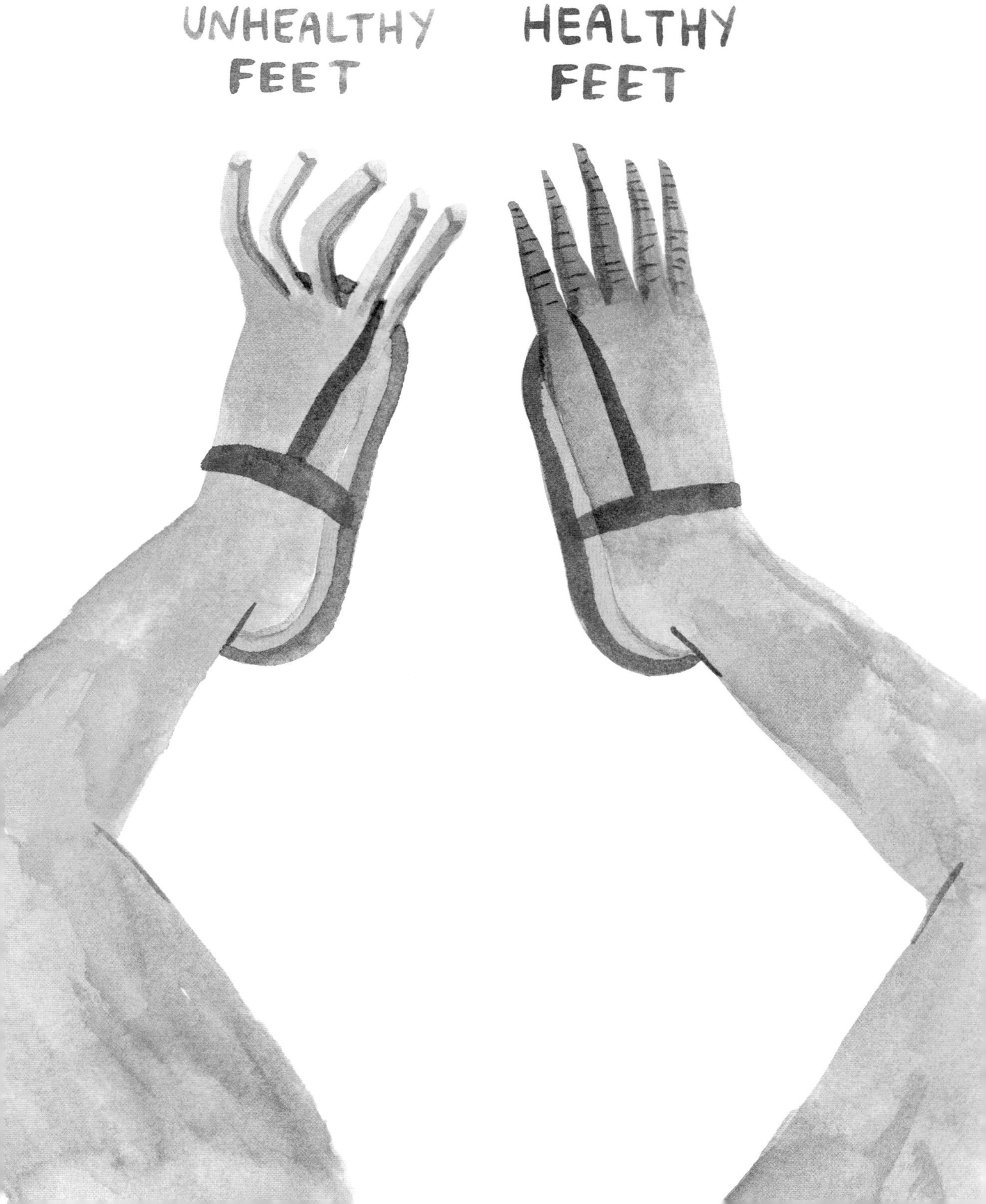
UNHEALTHY FEET
HEALTHY FEET

SNACK REALISM

MIXING THING-FLAVORED SNACK WITH SOME OF THE ACTUAL THING.

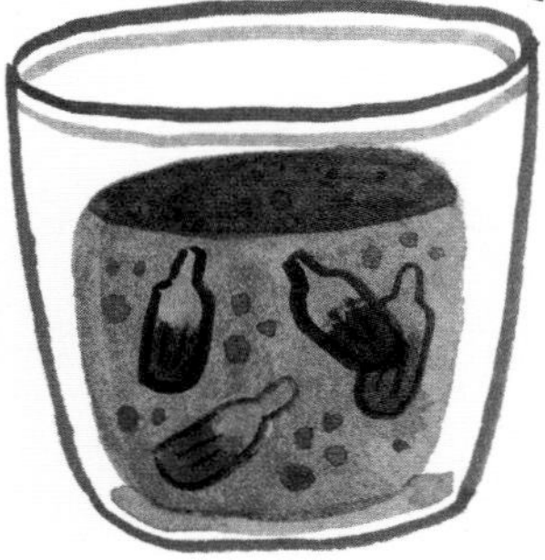

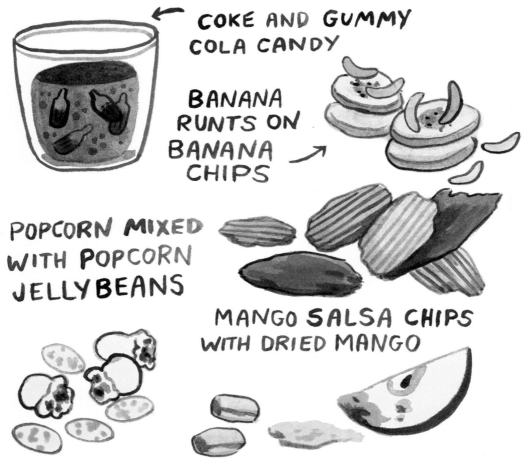

COKE AND GUMMY COLA CANDY

BANANA RUNTS ON BANANA CHIPS

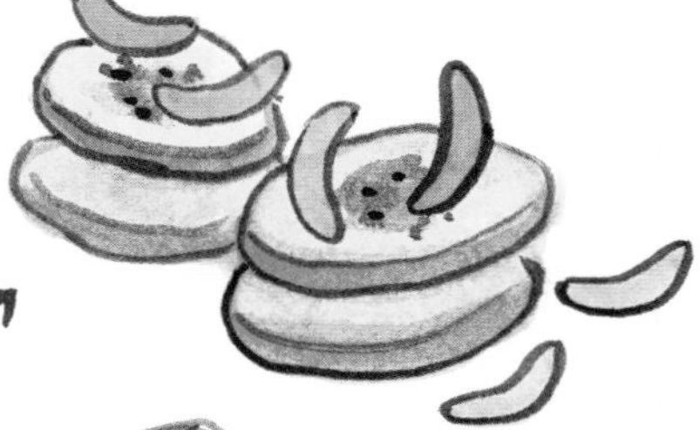

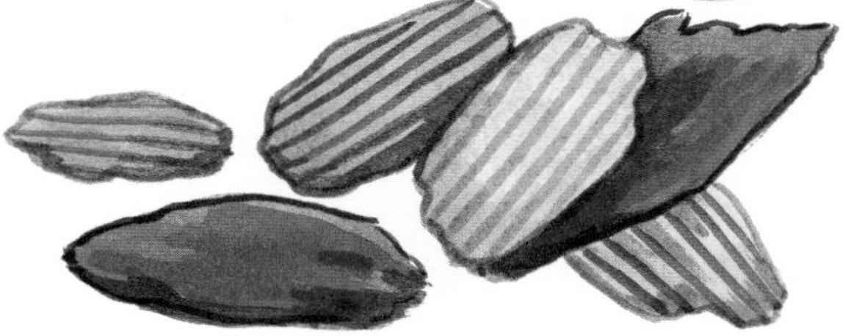

POPCORN MIXED WITH POPCORN JELLYBEANS

MANGO SALSA CHIPS WITH DRIED MANGO

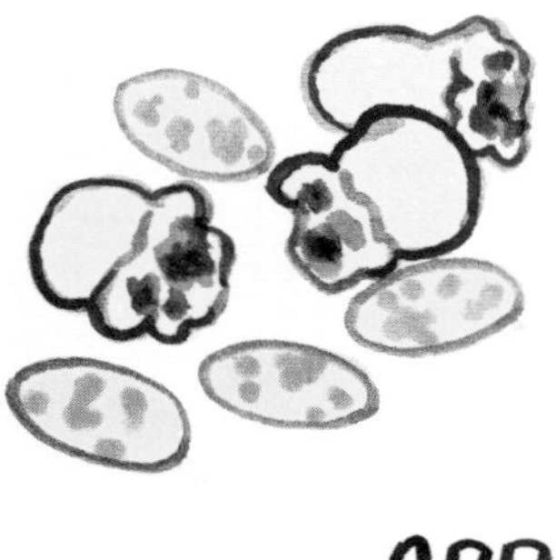

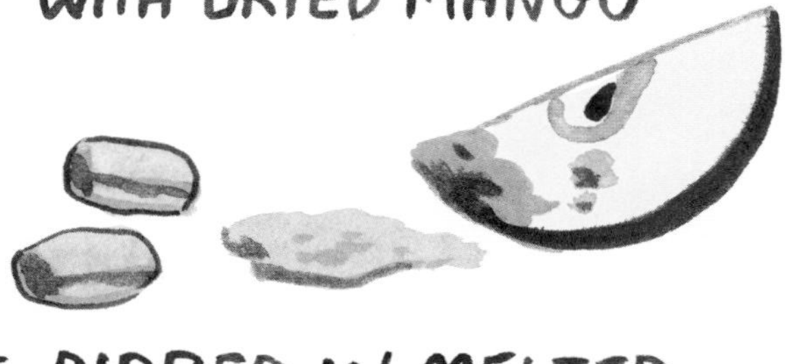

APPLE DIPPED IN MELTED APPLE JOLLY RANCHERS

TRAIL MIXES & ENERGY FOODS

GORP

SLUP

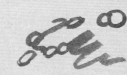

RILF

PLAH

FERM

HALK

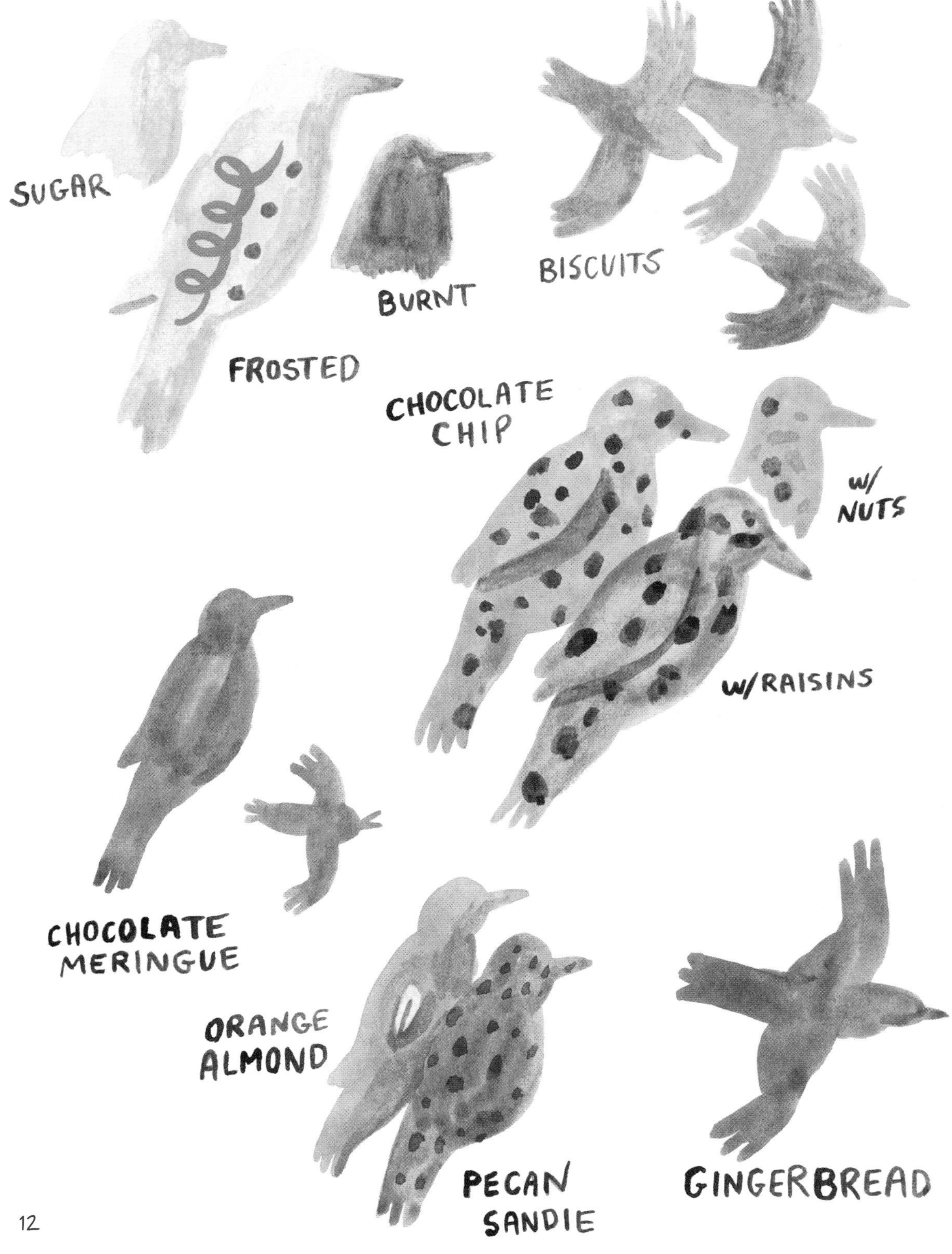
SUGAR
FROSTED
BURNT
BISCUITS
CHOCOLATE CHIP
W/ NUTS
W/RAISINS
CHOCOLATE MERINGUE
ORANGE ALMOND
PECAN SANDIE
GINGERBREAD

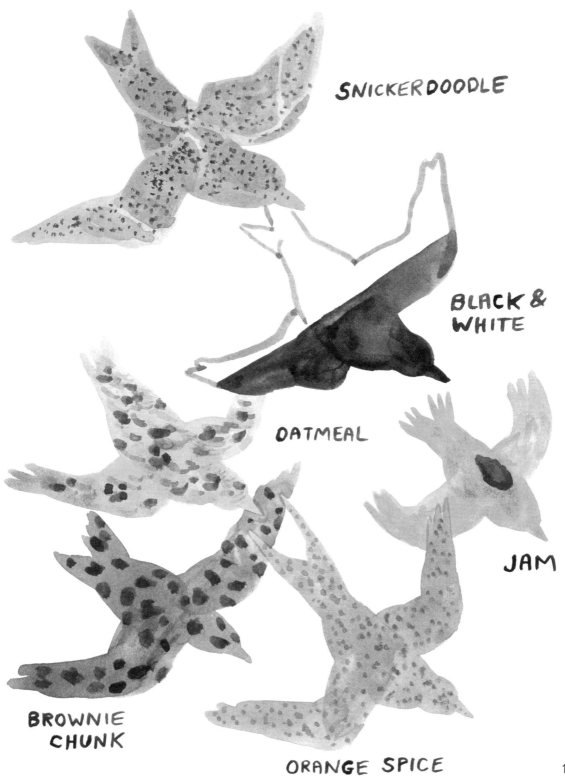

SNICKERDOODLE

BLACK & WHITE

OATMEAL

JAM

BROWNIE CHUNK

ORANGE SPICE

13

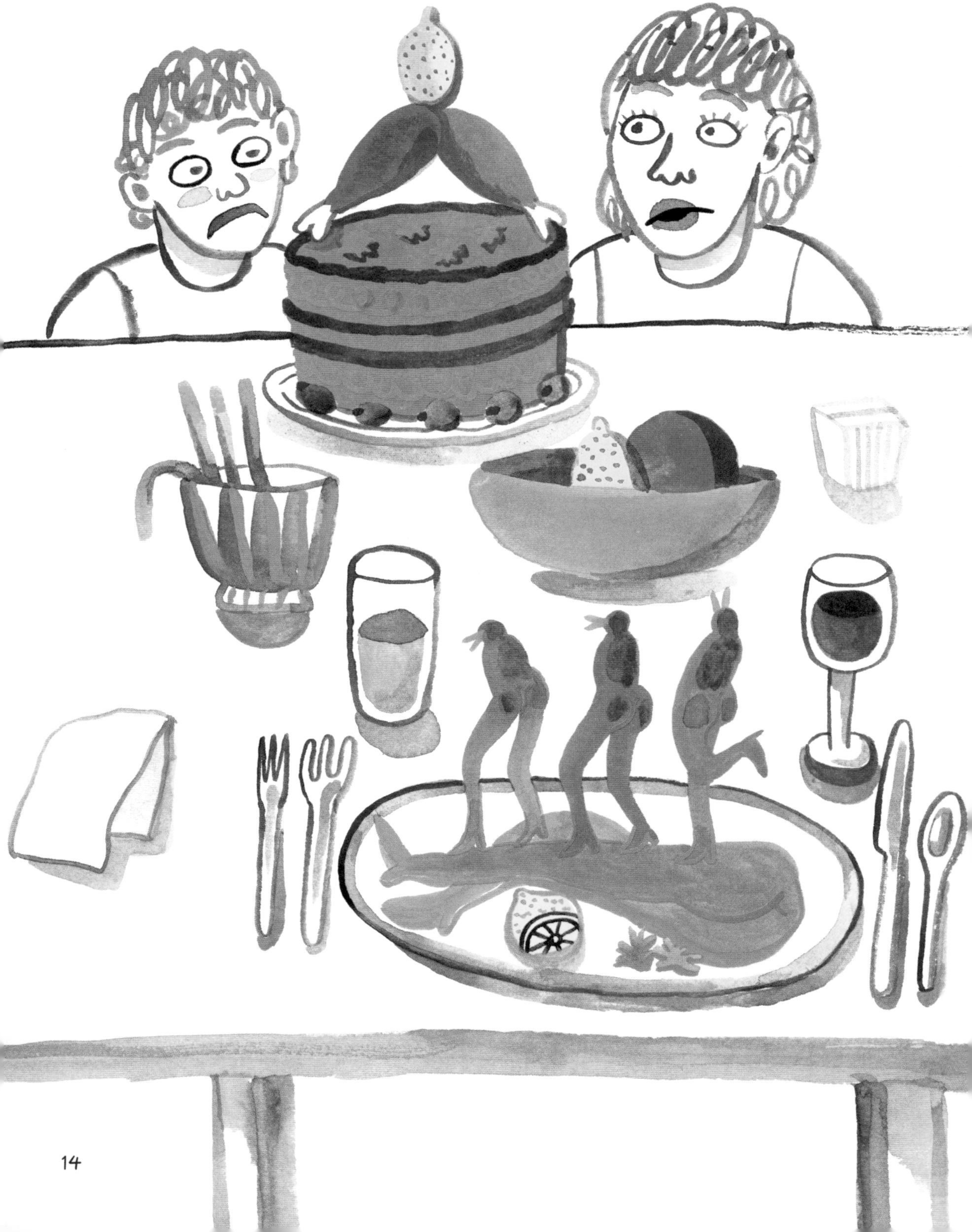

HOLIDAY FOOD DIARY

THE DAYS BEFORE HOLIDAY ARE FOR SIMPLE, FRESH FOODS AND MEALS PREPARED OUT OF MOM'S GARDEN AND DAD'S GARAGE.

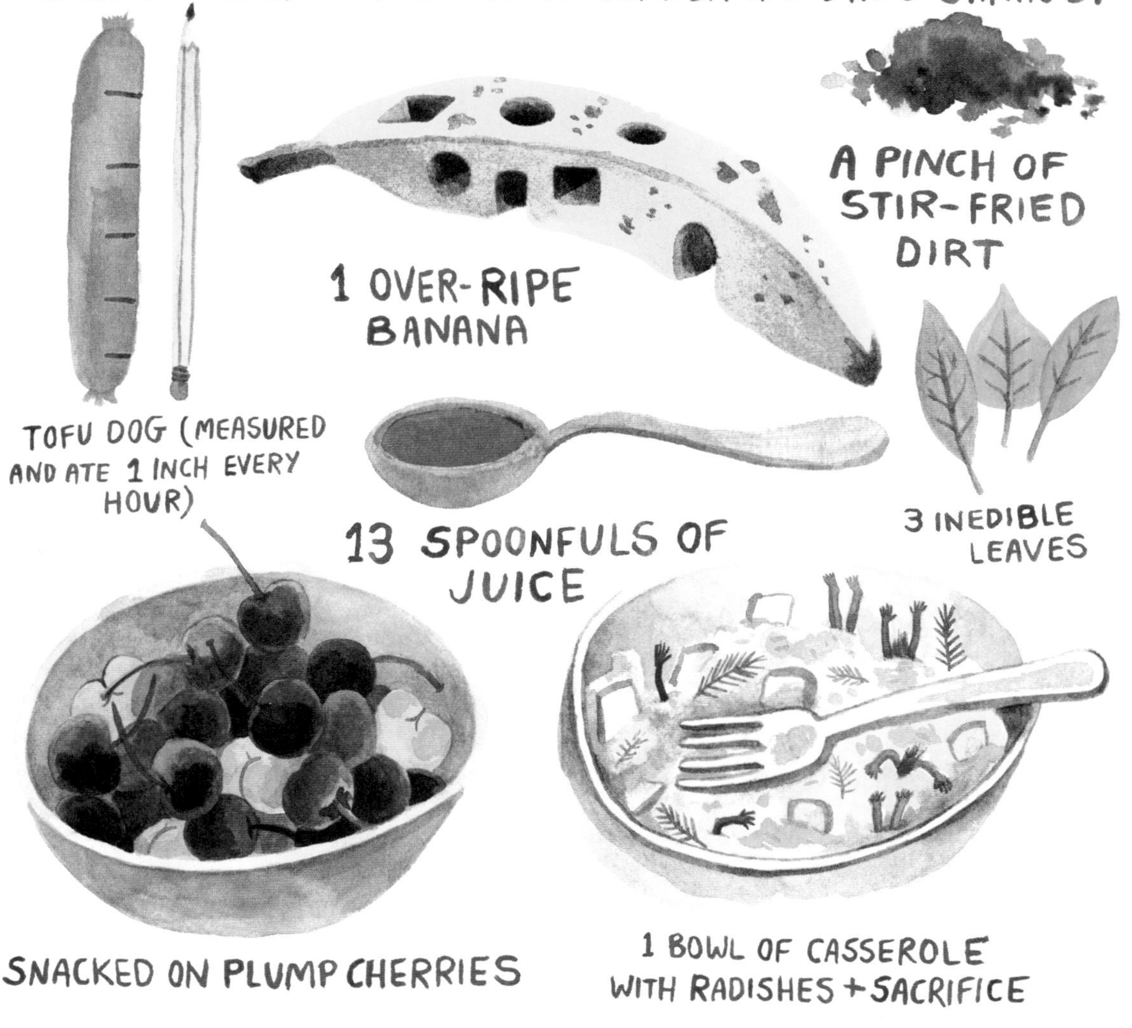
TOFU DOG (MEASURED AND ATE 1 INCH EVERY HOUR)
1 OVER-RIPE BANANA
A PINCH OF STIR-FRIED DIRT
13 SPOONFULS OF JUICE
3 INEDIBLE LEAVES
SNACKED ON PLUMP CHERRIES
1 BOWL OF CASSEROLE WITH RADISHES + SACRIFICE

HOLIDAY MEATS

TIP: THE HOLIDAY IS A GREAT TIME TO PRACTICE MEAT.

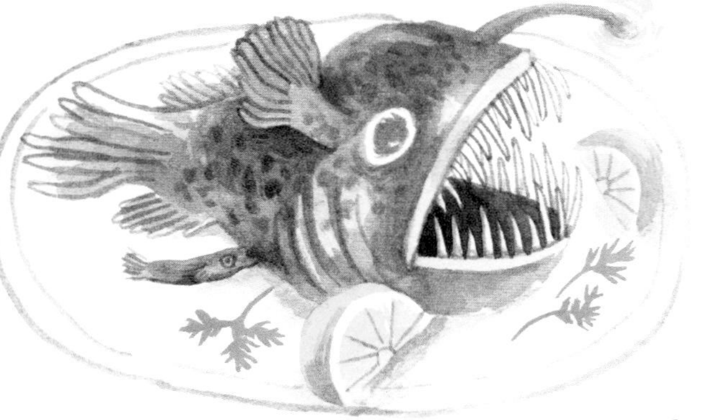

1 BAKED DEEP-SEA ANGLERFISH (DISCARDED THE LANTERN)

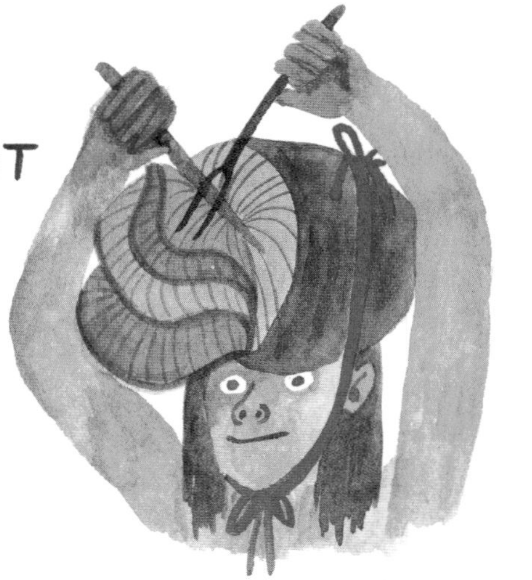

8 SLICES OF HAM, HAT-STYLE

6 BUGS →

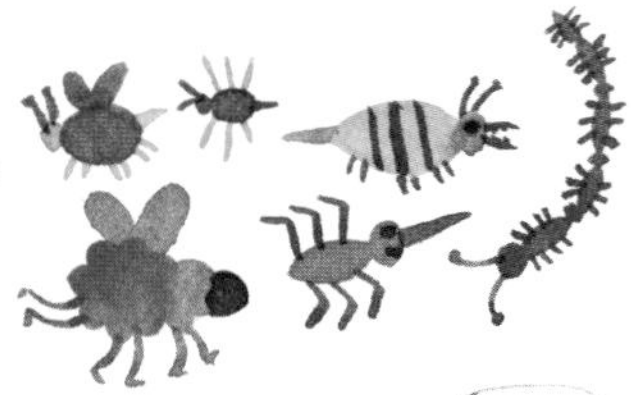

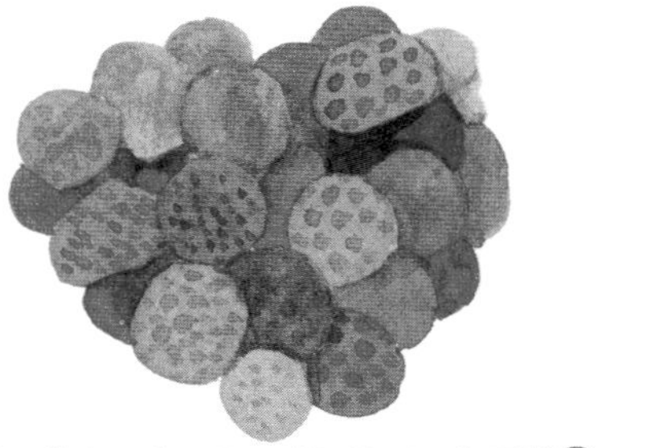

1 COLD CUT CLUSTER

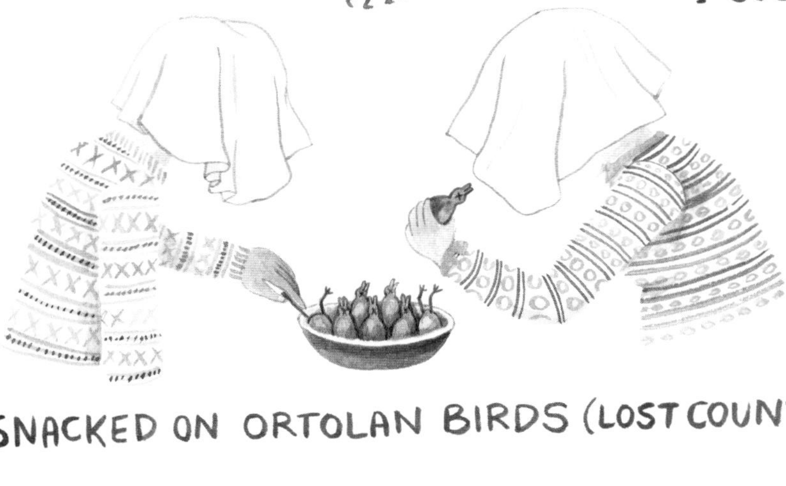

SNACKED ON ORTOLAN BIRDS (LOST COUNT!)

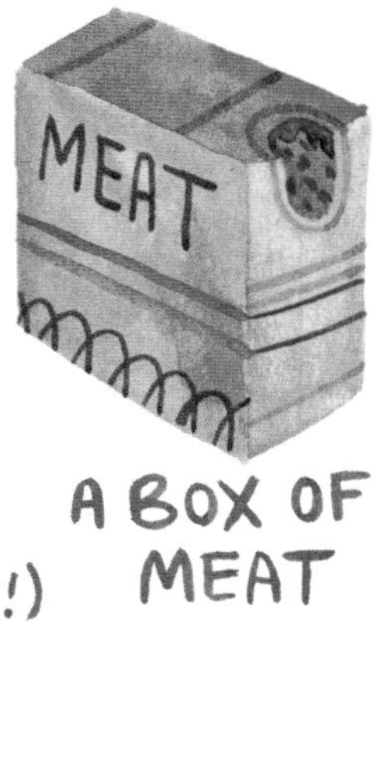
MEAT

A BOX OF MEAT

HOLIDAY DRINK

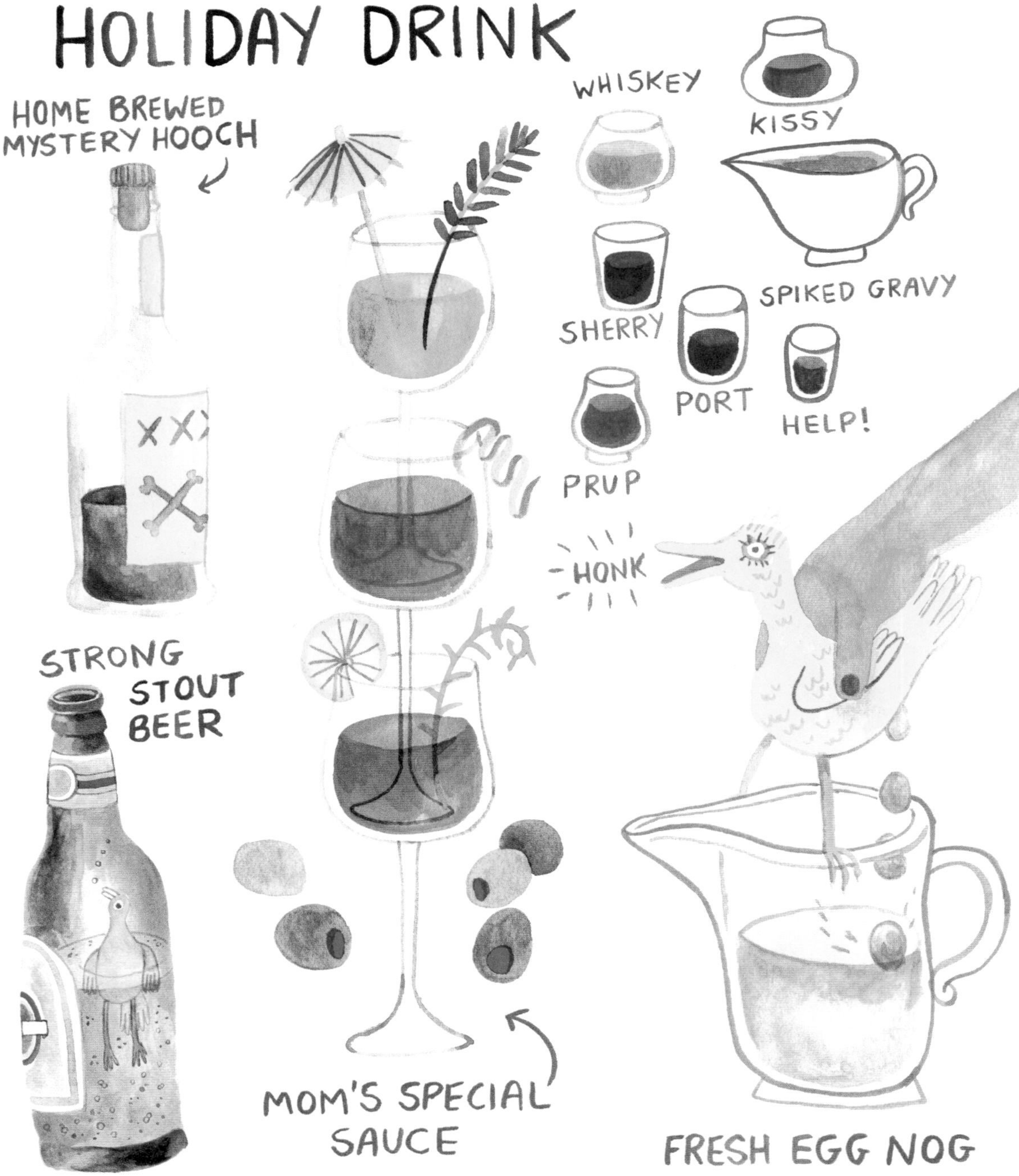
HOME BREWED
MYSTERY HOOCH
XXX
WHISKEY
KISSY
SPIKED GRAVY
SHERRY
PORT
HELP!
PRUP
HONK
STRONG
STOUT
BEER
MOM'S SPECIAL
SAUCE
FRESH EGG NOG

THE HOLIDAY FEAST

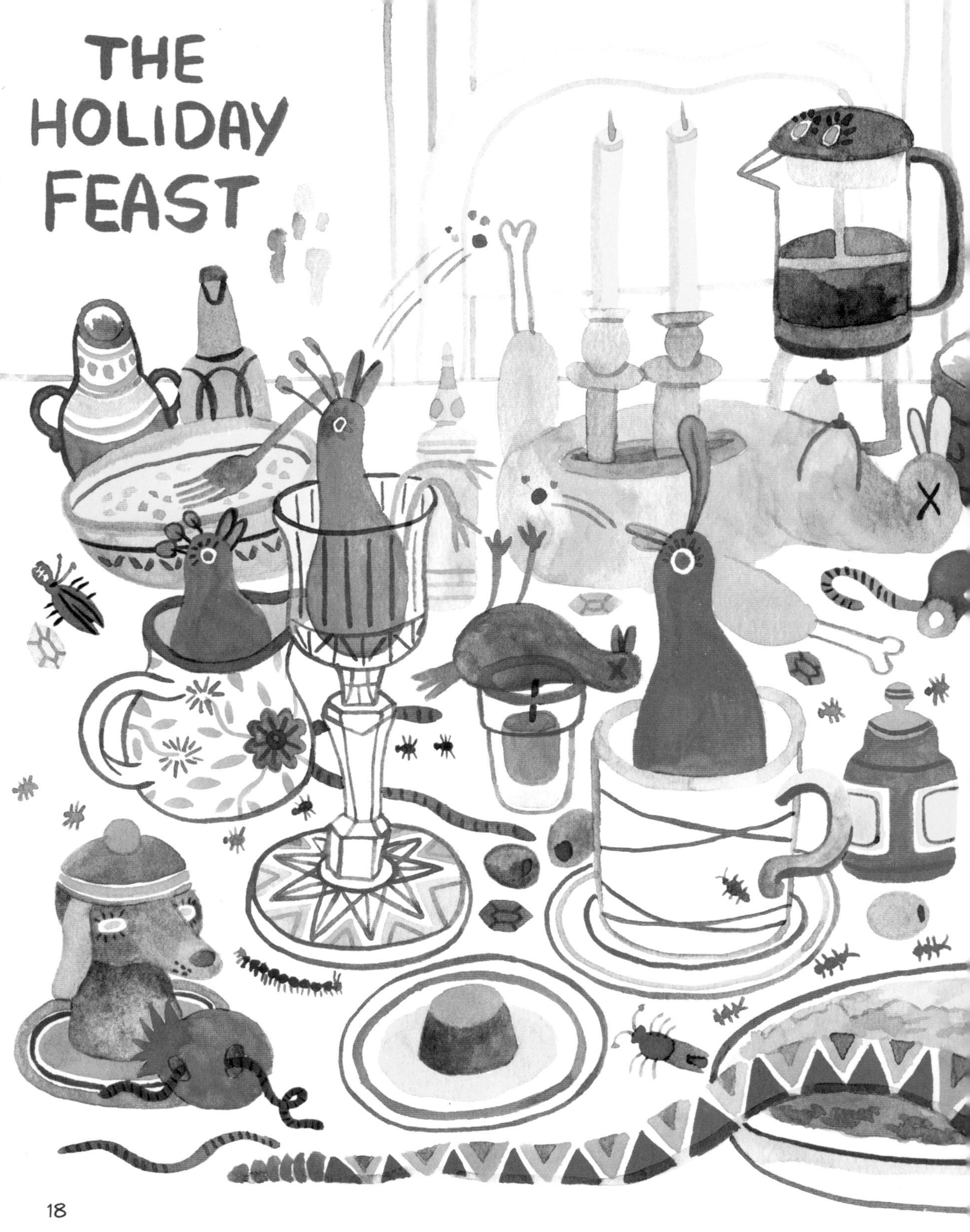

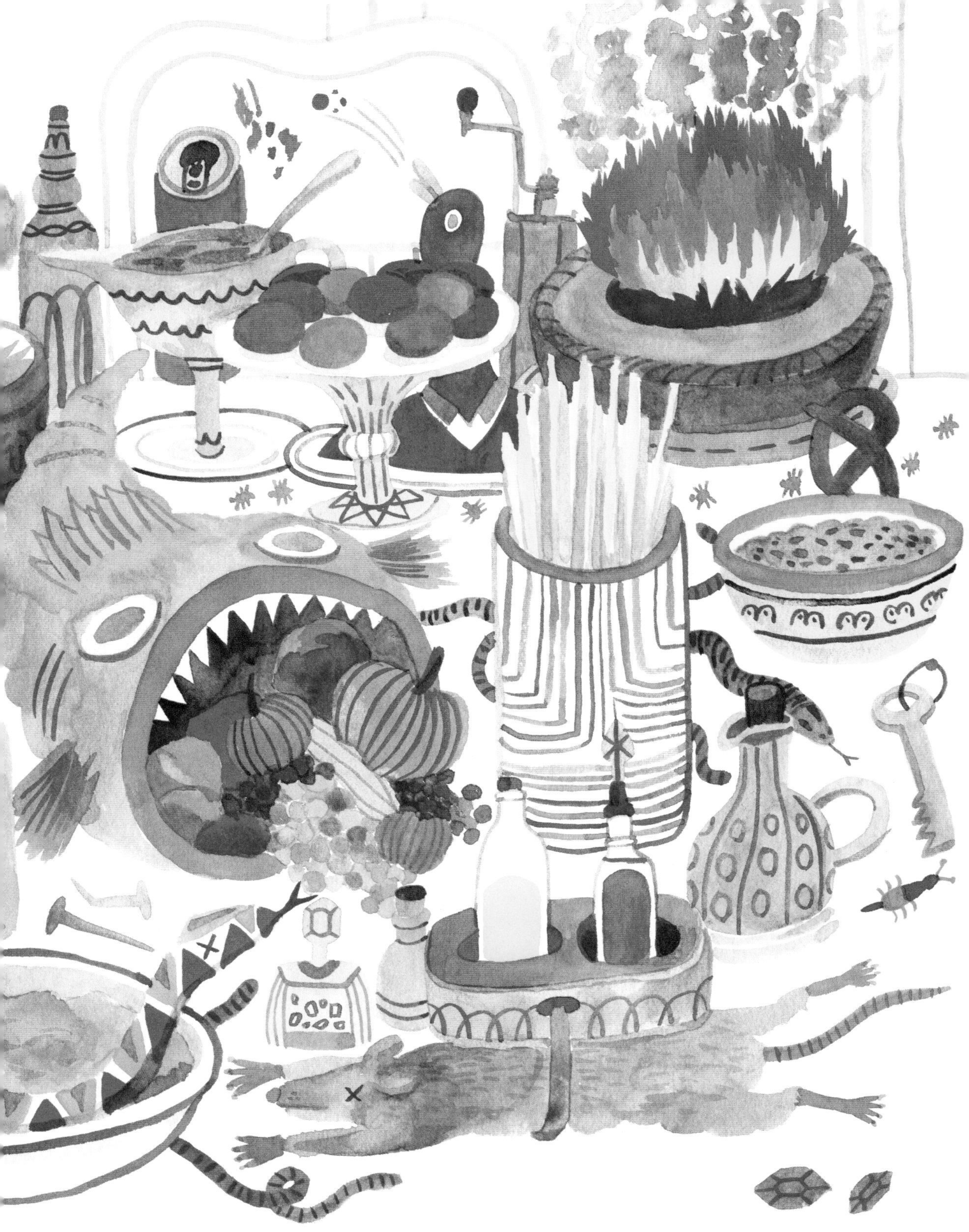

ON THE TRAIL WITH WYLIE

I HAVE OFFICIAL PERMISSION TO SHADOW WYLIE DUFRESNE AND HIS STAFF FOR AN ENTIRE DAY AT HIS LOWER EAST SIDE RESTAURANT WD-50 AND I'M VERY EXCITED. I HOPE THEY FEED ME.

* WYLIE ASKED ME NOT TO DRAW HIM "AS A QUADRUPED," SO HERE HE IS RIDING A QUADRUPED (MADE OUT OF AMERICAN CHEESE).

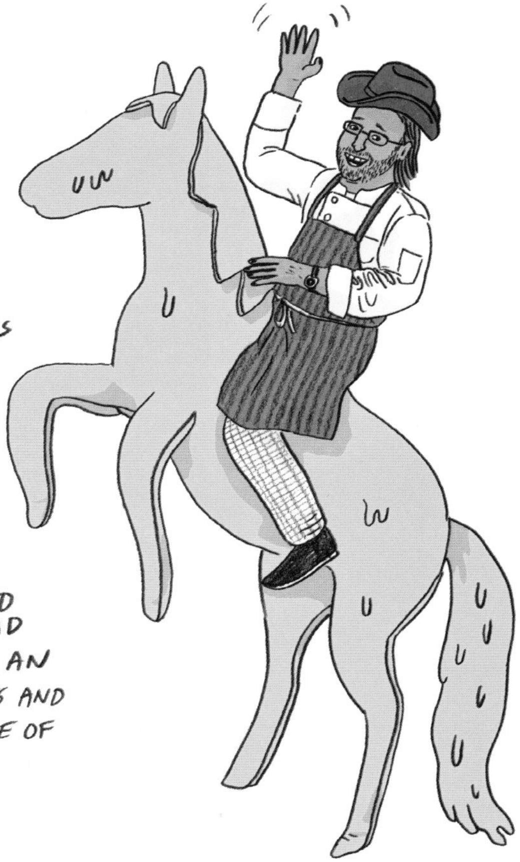

12:10 WYLIE DUFRESNE RUSHES INTO WD-50, MAKES HIMSELF A HUGE MILKY ICED COFFEE, AND DRINKS IT OUT OF A TUPPERWARE SOUP CONTAINER. GIANT DRINK FOR A GIANT MAN.

IF WYLIE DOESN'T GO AS "SEXY BEN FRANKLIN" FOR HALLOWEEN EVERY YEAR, THEN THAT'S A FUCKING WASTE.

12:30 WYLIE DEMONSTRATES HOW TO SAY "BEHIND YOU" WHEN NEARING ANOTHER HUMAN TO AVOID GETTING SCALDED, FOR EXAMPLE. THERE'S ALSO AN ENFORCED TRAFFIC FLOW TO THE KITCHEN AISLES AND WORK STATIONS. I WANT TO APPLY THIS SENSE OF ORDER IN MY OWN APARTMENT AND LIFE.

THERE ARE TONS OF INGREDIENTS ON THE WALL AND I HAVE NO IDEA WHAT ANY OF THEM ARE. NONE OF THEM SEEM EDIBLE.

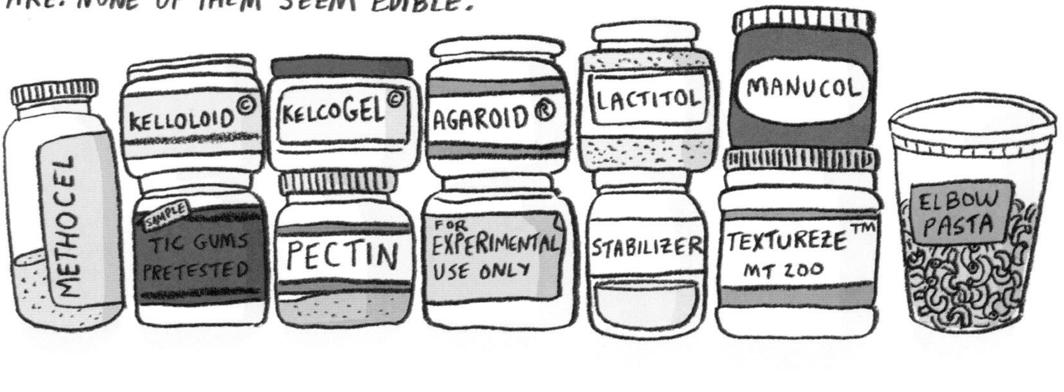
METHOCEL
KELLOLOID©
KELCOGEL©
AGAROID®
LACTITOL
MANUCOL
SAMPLE
TIC GUMS PRETESTED
PECTIN
FOR EXPERIMENTAL USE ONLY
STABILIZER
TEXTUREZE™ MT 200
ELBOW PASTA

12:45 ONE OF THE COOKS, SIMONE, IS CUTTING LOGS OF MEAT INTO PIECES AND PUTTING THEM IN A MEAT DRAWER. I KNOW THEY'RE REFRIGERATED BUT THE THOUGHT OF THROWING MEATS CASUALLY INTO A DRAWER IS FUNNY TO ME.

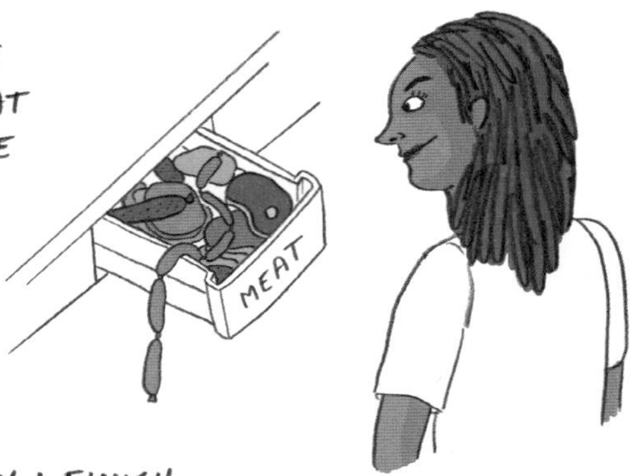
MEAT

1:15 WYLIE COOKS A LITTLE LUNCH FOR US. AMERICAN CHEESE + SCRAMBLED EGGS + BUTTER + ENGLISH MUFFINS. HE EATS SLICES OF AMERICAN CHEESE WHILE HE COOKS.

I POINT TO THE LAST PIECE OF EGG MUFFIN, "CAN I FINISH THIS?" "IF YOU DIDN'T, THAT WOULD BE DISTRESSING."

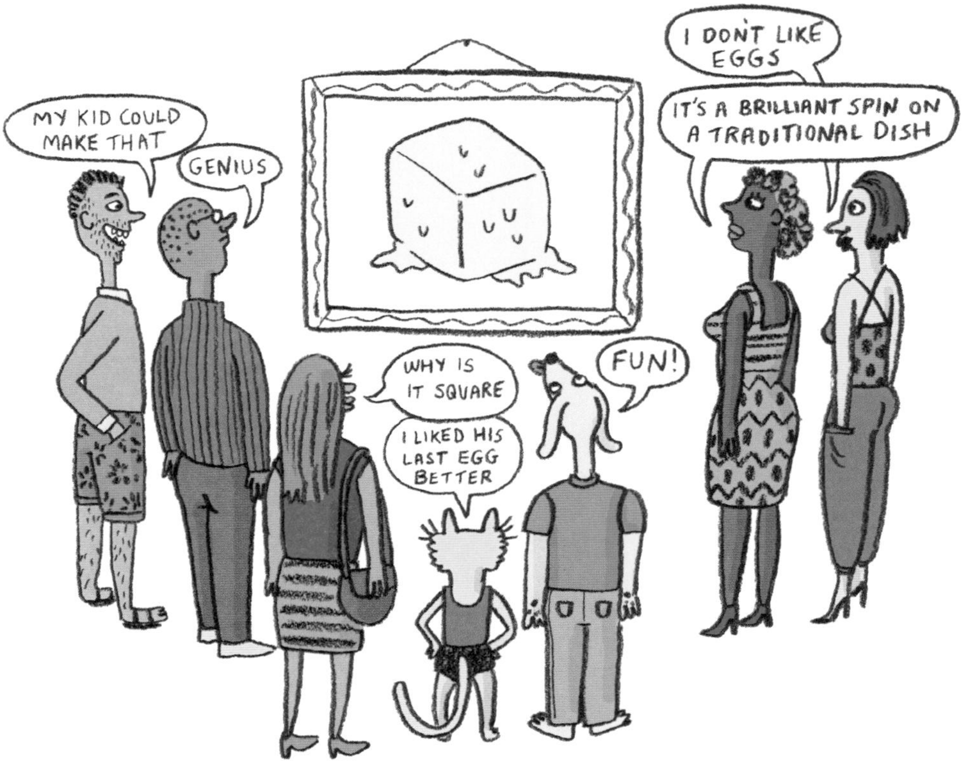
MY KID COULD MAKE THAT
GENIUS
I DON'T LIKE EGGS
IT'S A BRILLIANT SPIN ON A TRADITIONAL DISH
WHY IS IT SQUARE
I LIKED HIS LAST EGG BETTER
FUN!

1:30 WYLIE AND SIMONE HAVE TO PREP SOME "EGG RAVIOLIS," AKA SQUARE OMELETS, FOR A DINNER WYLIE HAS TO COOK IN SAN FRANCISCO THE NEXT NIGHT. THEY AREN'T REALLY RAVIOLIS. THEY'RE CUBES OF SCRAMBLED EGG AND CREAM CHEESE, DIPPED INTO MORE EGG, WHICH HAS BEEN BLENDED WITH XANTHAN GUM TO HELP IT ADHERE.

IT'S TOUGH TO PERFECT THIS "DIP." TOO MUCH AIR AND THE RAVIOLI BECOMES POROUS AND SOGGY. TOO LITTLE AIR AND THEY GET A LEATHERY TEXTURE. WYLIE EXPLAINS: "AIR IS YOUR FRIEND AND YOUR ENEMY. IT MAKES THINGS PRETTY, LIKE YOUR ICE CREAM, YOUR CAPPUCCINO; IT MAKES YOUR BREAD NICE AND CRUSTY. BUT IN THIS CASE IT CAN RUIN THE END RESULT." HE SPINS THE CUBE AROUND ON ITS STICK, EVENLY DISTRIBUTING THE YOLKY COATING. THEY ONLY NEED 280 FOR THE DINNER, BUT THEY'LL PREP OVER 400 BECAUSE THE DAMN THINGS ARE SO DELICATE AND EASY TO BREAK. "I DROPPED TWO PERFECT ONES ON THE FLOOR YESTERDAY."

I ASK WYLIE IF IT'S A PROBLEM MAKING SUCH INTELLECTUALLY STIMULATING DISHES, WHEN PEOPLE COME IN AND JUST DON'T GET IT AND THEN LEAVE NASTY YELP REVIEWS. "YES, CONSTANTLY. AND THAT'S THE THING — DO YOU COOK TO PLEASE YOURSELF? OR DO YOU TRY TO SATISFY EVERYONE, BECAUSE THIS IS A BUSINESS AFTER ALL." SOMETIMES PEOPLE JUST WANT A STEAK.

2:30 WE HEAD TO MIDTOWN FOR WYLIE'S PHYSICAL THERAPY. WYLIE IS VERY ASSERTIVE WITH CAB DRIVERS ABOUT WHICH ROUTE THEY SHOULD TAKE.

> WHICH CHEF IS THE BIGGEST WHINER?

> MAYBE SEAMUS? THE BIGGEST CUSSER IS DAVID CHANG! DANG HE DROPS A LOT OF F-BOMBS!

URRGH

3:10 WYLIE'S BEEN SEEING HIS PHYSICAL THERAPIST, KARENA, FOR EIGHT YEARS NOW AND THEY HAVE A FUNNY RAPPORT. "LISA, DID HE FEED YOU?" "YEAH, AMERICAN CHEESE AND EGGS." SHE LAUGHS, "DAIRY BOY!"

HE NORMALLY SEES KARENA ONCE A WEEK FOR MAINTENANCE, BUT LATELY IT HAS BEEN MUCH MORE OFTEN BECAUSE HE HAS A HERNIATED DISC. IT SOUNDS EXCRUCIATING. HE'S NOT SUPPOSED TO LIFT ANYTHING OR LOOK DOWN AT ALL. HE STRIPS DOWN TO SHORTS AND SOCKS AND LIES DOWN ON THE TABLE.

KARENA WORKS ON A LOT OF CHEFS.

4:30 WE SWING BY WYLIE'S NEW RESTAURANT, ALDER, TO DROP OFF TWO
HUGE BOOKS OF PASTA SHAPES FOR THE HEAD CHEF, JON BIGNELLI, TO
REFERENCE. HERE ARE ALL THE PASTA SHAPES I CAN DRAW FROM MEMORY:

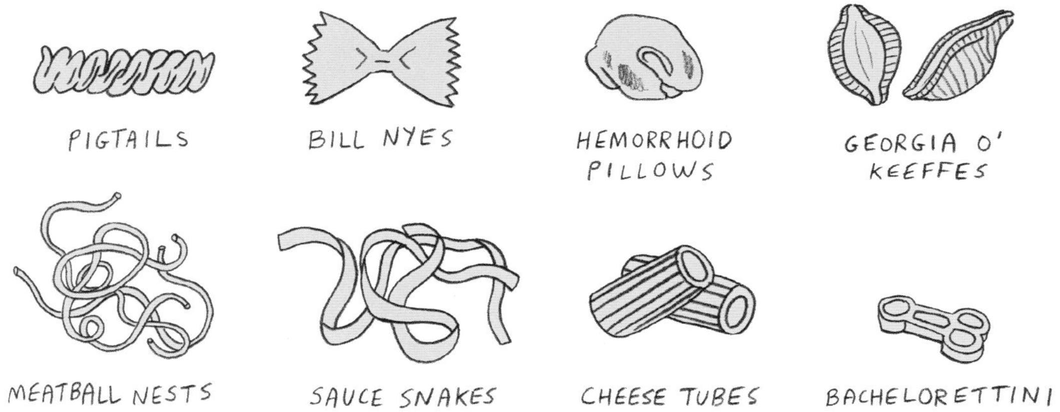

PIGTAILS

BILL NYES

HEMORRHOID
PILLOWS

GEORGIA O'
KEEFFES

MEATBALL NESTS   SAUCE SNAKES   CHEESE TUBES   BACHELORETTINI

5:00 WE GET BACK TO WD-50 AND HAVE A LITTLE
SNACK. IT'S PEPPERY NOODLES AND THICK SLABS OF
HAM + BACON + LARDO + ??, SAUTÉED BOK CHOY AND
A HUNK OF COFFEE CAKE ON THE SIDE. I'M TRYING
TO SAVE ROOM FOR DINNER BUT THIS IS ONE OF
THE MOST DELICIOUS THINGS I'VE EVER EATEN.
I ALMOST POUR THE REMAINING NOODLES
INTO MY PURSE FOR LATER.

5:30 I GLANCE AT THE LIST OF RESER-
VATIONS; THERE ARE COMMENTS LIKE
"ALLERGIC TO MUSHROOMS AND BLEU CHEESE,"
AND "RETURN DINER, VERY NICE." I WANT
TO SEE SOMETHING A LITTLE JUICIER, LIKE "VIOLENTLY,
IRRATIONALLY OPPOSED TO RADISHES" OR "THIS GUY
IS A GOOD TIPPER BUT TENDS TO PROJECTILE VOMIT."

WYLIE CHANGES BACK INTO HIS CHEF CLOTHES AND IS
MILLING AROUND, GRAZING BITS OF MEAT AND POPCORN
OUT OF TUPPERWARE CONTAINERS, EATING GIRL SCOUT
THIN MINTS. HE HAS A TOTALLY OMNIVOROUS AND DEMOCRATIC
SENSE OF WHAT TASTES GOOD. EXCEPT HE DOESN'T LIKE TOMATOES,
AND THAT'S JUST WRONG.

23

LISA, KNOW ANYTHING ABOUT ALL THE BLOOD ON THE COUNTER?

NOOOPE

5:45 HE CALLS TWO YOUNG SCRUFFY COOKS OVER AND POINTS TO A BROWN SPOT ON THE STOVE. "KNOW ANYTHING ABOUT THIS? MIGHT THIS HAVE ANYTHING TO DO WITH THE FISH?" THEY WORDLESSLY GRAB SPONGES AND CLEAN IT OFF, LOOKING CHASTENED. BUT A MINUTE LATER HE'S SMILING AND JOKING WITH THEM.

I TRY TO IMAGINE MYSELF WORKING HERE...

6:00 I WATCH WYLIE EXPERIMENT WITH A NEW DISH FOR ALDER. IT'S A FOIE GRAS PUMPKIN PIE, A SAVORY DISH. PREVIOUS ATTEMPTS WERE TOO "PUMPKIN-Y," SO HE'S CHANGING THE PROPORTIONS (AND I'M RESISTING THE URGE TO EAT THE FAILED PIES OUT OF THE GARBAGE BIN). FIRST HE DOES A BUNCH OF MATH ON A CALCULATOR, SCRIBBLES THE NOTES DOWN, THEN HE PRECISELY WEIGHS THE INGREDIENTS. THIS FEELS A LOT LIKE "BRING YOUR DAUGHTER TO WORK" DAY WHEN I USED TO ACCOMPANY MY PARENTS TO THEIR BIOLOGY LAB.

HERE ARE SOME QUESTIONS I WANT TO ASK, BUT I'M AFRAID ARE TOO DUMB: HAS ANYONE AT WD-50 EVER NEEDED THE HEIMLICH MANEUVER? HAS ANYONE EVER THROWN UP IN THE DINING ROOM? OR GONE INTO ANAPHYLACTIC SHOCK?

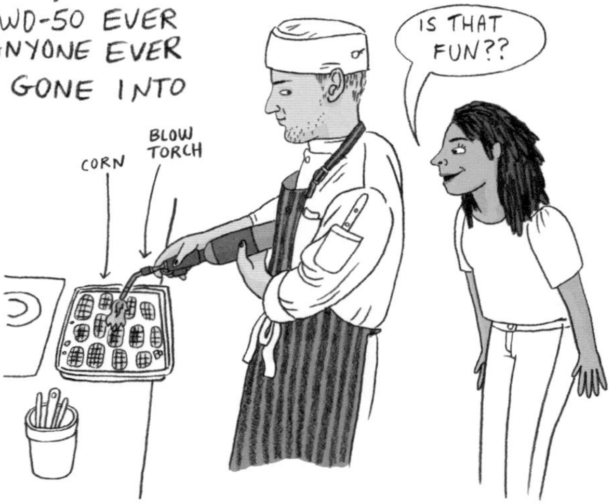
IS THAT FUN??
BLOW TORCH
CORN

7:00 IT'S TIME FOR ME TO EAT SOME DINNER! WYLIE AND SIMONE JOT DOWN A LIST OF DISHES THEY WANT ME TO TRY: BASICALLY SIX DIFFERENT KINDS OF ANIMAL, PLUS DESSERTS.

THE FIRST PLATE IS A TINY SAFFRON-COCONUT ICE CREAM SANDWICH TOPPED WITH STURGEON CAVIAR. I NORMALLY SAVE MY EGGS-LAID-BY-A-BOTTOM-FEEDER FOR DESSERT, BUT WHATEVER!

7:30 WHEN DESCRIBING THE FOURTH COURSE, THE WAITER LISTS THE INGREDIENTS, GESTURING TO DIFFERENT PARTS OF THE PLATE, ENDING WITH "AND UNDERNEATH YOU WILL FIND... GRANOLA." I LIFT THE TOP LAYER UP WITH MY FORK TO SEE IF HE IS JOKING AND HE IS NOT.

ALSO IN THIS DISH: THE MOST DELICATE SEA SCALLOPS BASKING IN ALMOND OIL AND A SINGLE RAVIOLI MADE FROM CARROT. I EAT THE RAVIOLI TOO FAST TO SEE WHAT'S INSIDE, BUT BASED ON THE FLAVOR I WOULD DESCRIBE IT AS "SEX CHEESE."

IT'S HARD NOT TO GIGGLE WITH DISCOVERY AS I EAT. HERE, TRY TO GUESS WHICH OF THE FOLLOWING ARE ACTUAL THINGS SERVED AT WD-50 AND WHICH AREN'T:

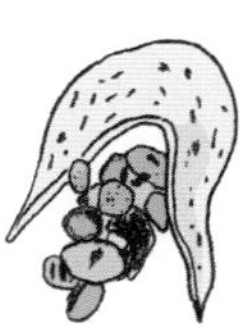
'PRINGLE' CHIP MADE OUT OF PARSNIP

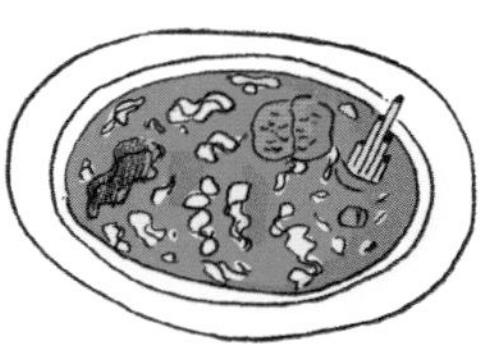
EGG DROP SOUP (EGGS ARE ACTUALLY EEL)

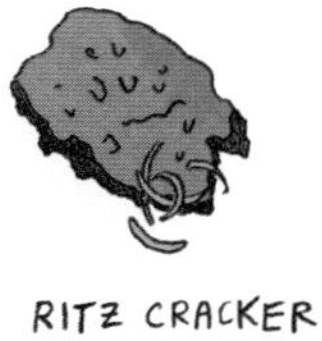
RITZ CRACKER PIE CRUST

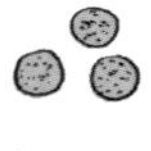
'PEAS' MADE OUT OF CARROT, DUSTED WITH PEA DUST

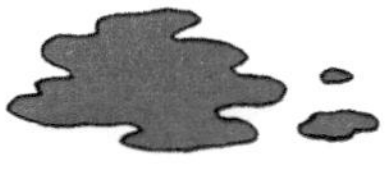
SRIRACHA EXCRETED BY EXCITED ROOSTERS

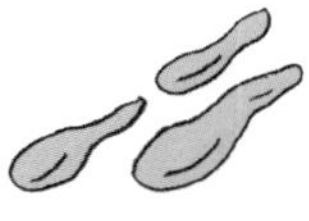
THE TEARDROPS OF A PHANTOM, MADE FROM THE DREAMS OF DOGS

 I'M A DELICACY!

THE CHILLED EGG DROP SOUP IS
THE ONE DISH I DON'T FINISH, ONLY
BECAUSE I DON'T LOVE SEA URCHIN. URCHINS TASTE
LIKE WHIPPED SEMEN AND LOOK LIKE A MILLION TINY
FINGERS HATCHING OUT OF A BABY SHIT-COLORED BRAIN.
LOOK, IF WYLIE DOESN'T LIKE TOMATOES, I DON'T HAVE TO LIKE URCHINS.

THE MAÎTRE D' KEEPS BRINGING NEW WINES AND ASKING WHICH ONES HE
SHOULD TAKE AWAY. THIS IS LIKE A FITTING ROOM FOR WINES. EXCEPT
THEY ALL FIT GREAT!

8:00 THE MAÎTRE D' ASKS ME HOW I LIKE THIS PARTICULAR DISH, MEDITERRANEAN
BASS WITH CELERY AND BITS OF GRAPEFRUIT AND MACADAMIA THAT HAVE HAD
THE EVER LOVIN' CRAP CHOPPED OUT OF THEM. IT'S PLATED WITH TWO
FRUIT-FLAVORED DOTS THAT LOOK LIKE NIPPLES.
I HAVEN'T YET DEVELOPED THE VOCABULARY TO
DESCRIBE THIS FLAVOR COMBO, SO I SIMPLY
MOAN UNTIL HE GOES AWAY.

I'M GOING TO HAVE
TO ASK YOU TO LEAVE.

LOVE ME.

8:45 THE FIRST DESSERT IS "POPCORN
VACHERIN," WHICH I RENAME "SHERBET
ON BATH SALTS." MY SECOND DESSERT
IS A THREE-LAYERED KEY LIME PIE.
I WANT TO LICK THE PLATES,
BUT THAT WOULD BE UNCOUTH,
SO INSTEAD I'M GREEDILY
SCRAPING THEM WITH
MY SPOON.

9:00 I TAKE A BATHROOM
BREAK. IT'S NOT IMMEDIATELY
CLEAR WHERE TO DO YOUR
BUSINESS, BUT IF YOU TURN
TO THE WALL OPPOSITE THE
SINKS AND PUSH AROUND
YOU'LL EVENTUALLY FIND A
BATHROOM STALL. IT'S LIKE
PISSING IN A SECRET TOMB.

I WISH MORE FOOD WRITERS WOULD WRITE ABOUT GOING TO THE BATHROOM, BECAUSE IT'S FUNNY AND INTERESTING AND IT'S THE INEVITABLE RESULT OF ALL OF THIS.

ALSO POOP SHOULD BE RENAMED "DOOF," SINCE THAT IS FOOD BACKWARDS.

9:30 MY FINAL TREAT IS A BLACK POUCH. IT LOOKS LIKE A SHARK'S EGG. I POP IT IN MY MOUTH, SURPRISE, IT'S BLUEBERRY CHEESECAKE. VERY WONKA. AND ON THE SIDE IS A LITTLE BEER MALT BALL WITH PRETZEL COATING THAT I WISH WAS EVERLASTING BUT IN FACT DISSOLVES IN MICROSECONDS.

9:45 WYLIE WARNED ME THAT HE'D LIKELY GO HOME AT SIX P.M. AND LEAVE ME "AT THE ALTAR" SINCE HE HAS TO BE BACK HERE AT DAWN TOMORROW, BUT I LOOK OVER AT THE KITCHEN AND SEE HE'S STILL HUNCHED OVER THE TABLE, CHECKING DISHES.

I'M CONCERNED, WATCHING HIM BENDING OVER LIKE THAT, SACRIFICING HIS HEALTH FOR ANOTHER NIGHT OF SERVICE. BUT DAMN DOES HE LOOK HAPPY.

10:20 I STAGGER HOME AFTER DUTIFULLY TESTING EVERY COCKTAIL. I TRY DIFFERENT YOGA POSES TO SEE IF ANY OF THEM FEEL COMFY TO BE DRUNK IN, WITHOUT MUCH SUCCESS.

NOPE

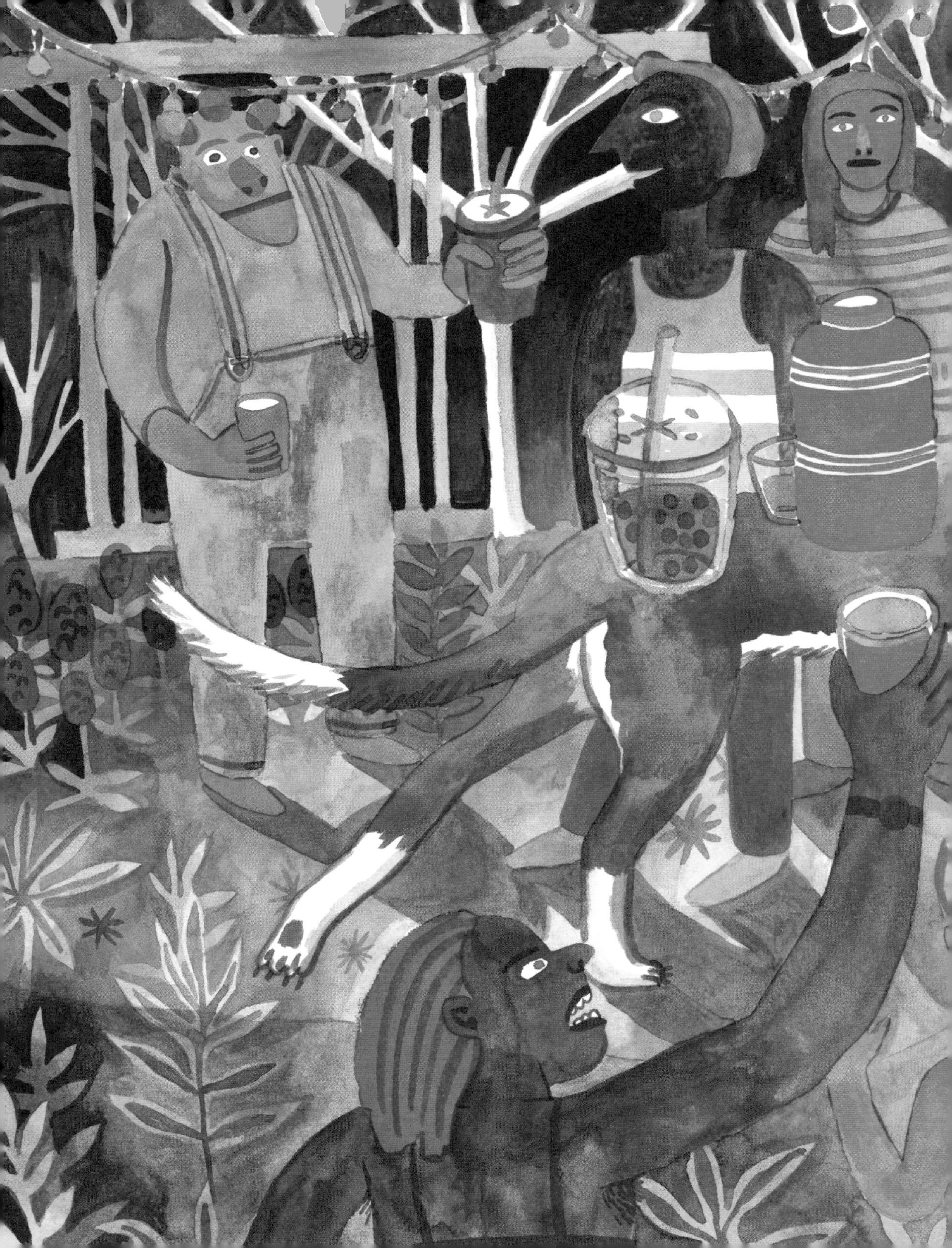

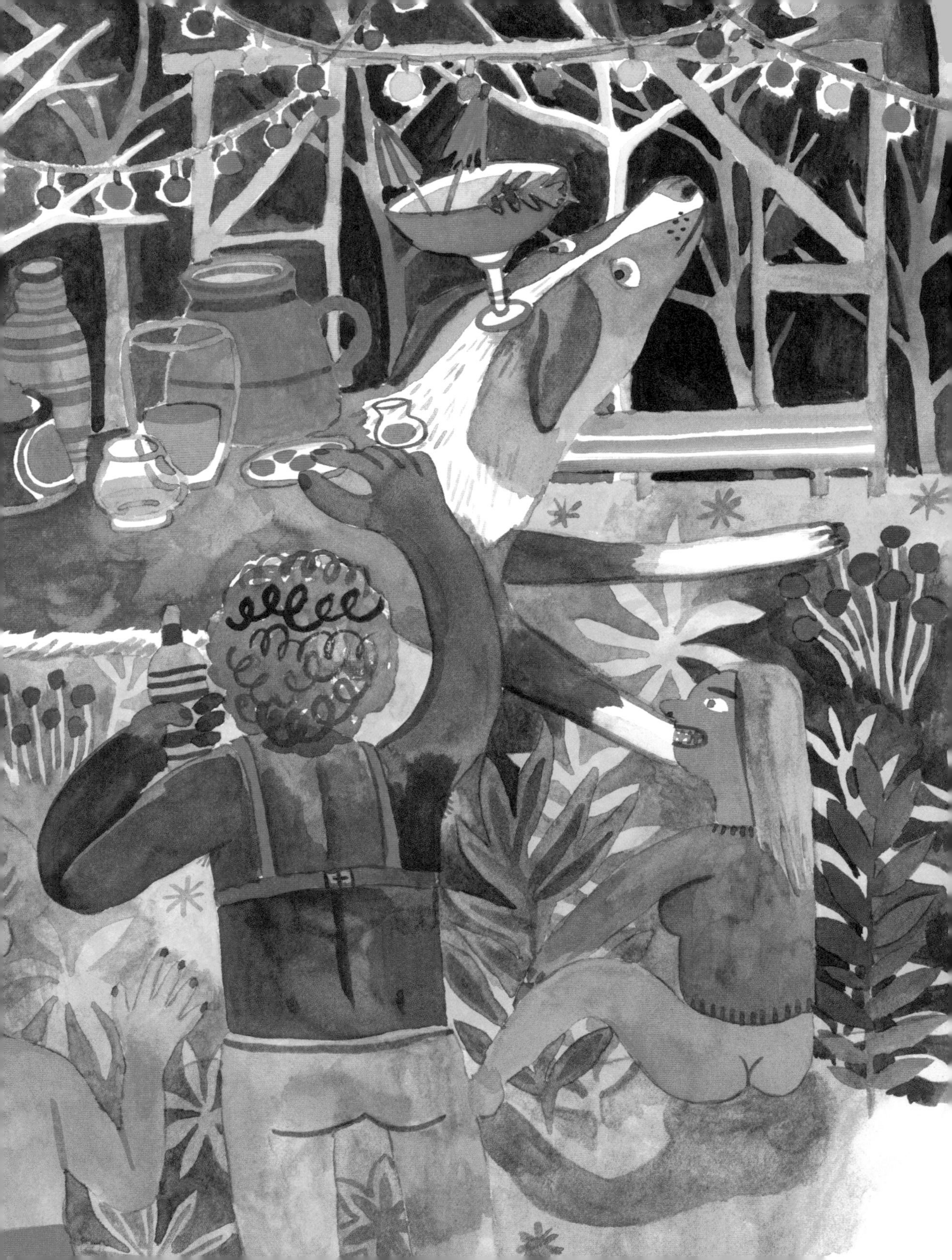

YOU ARE ALLOWED TO DRAW ON THIS PAGE.

SOME *SUGGESTIONS*:

-IF YOU'RE AT A RESTAURANT, HOW MANY DOGS CAN YOU DRAW BEFORE THE WAITER BRINGS YOUR FOOD?

-DRAW YOUR FAVORITE FOOD IN A WAY THAT MAKES YOU NEVER WANT TO EAT IT AGAIN.

ON THIS PAGE YOU ARE ALLOWED TO LEAVE A FOOD STAIN *

* THE AUTHOR, PUBLISHER, DISTRIBUTOR, AND BOOK MERCHANT ARE NOT LEGALLY, FINANCIALLY, OR/AND EMOTIONALLY RESPONSIBLE FOR COPIES OF THIS BOOK DAMAGED BY FOOD STAINS, INCLUDING: GREASE, PET FOOD, CONDIMENTS, TOMATO-BASED SAUCES, RED/YELLOW/GREEN CURRY, FAMILY RECIPES, AND CHOCOLATE.

IF I HAD A TIME MACHINE...

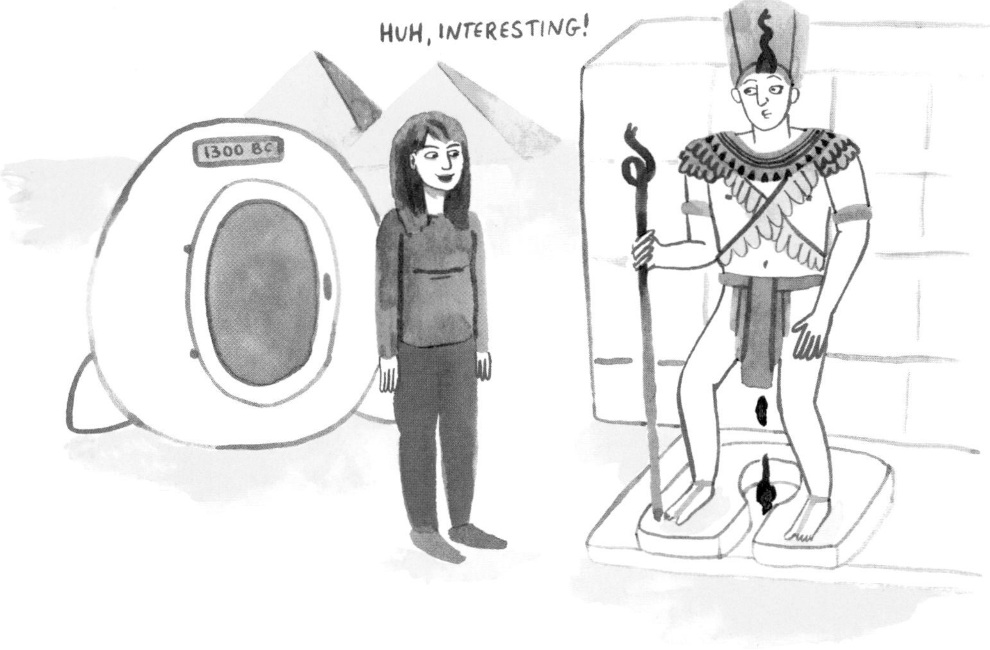
1300 BC
HUH, INTERESTING!

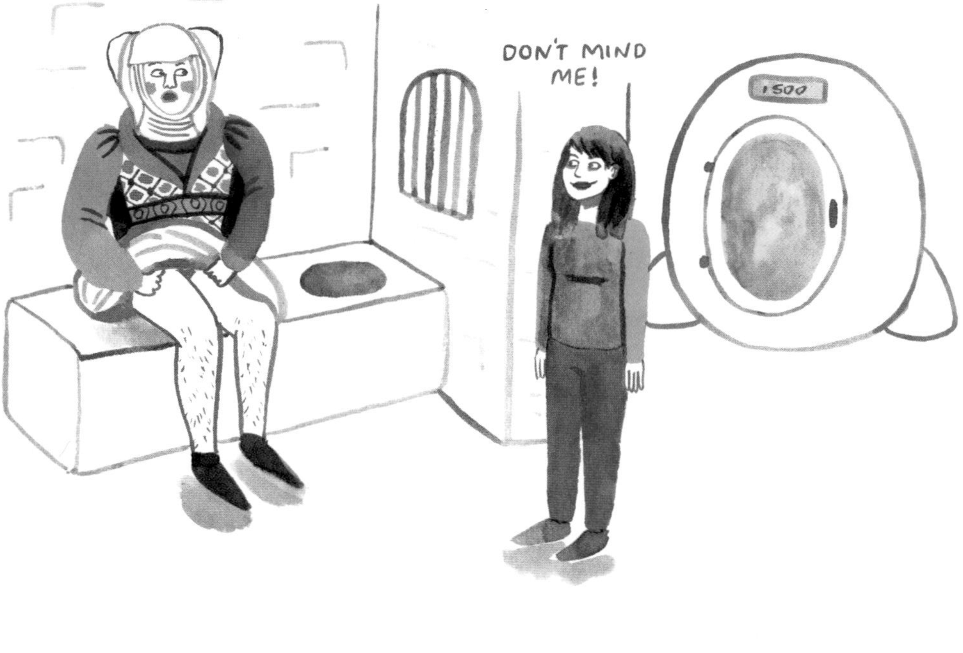
DON'T MIND ME!
1500

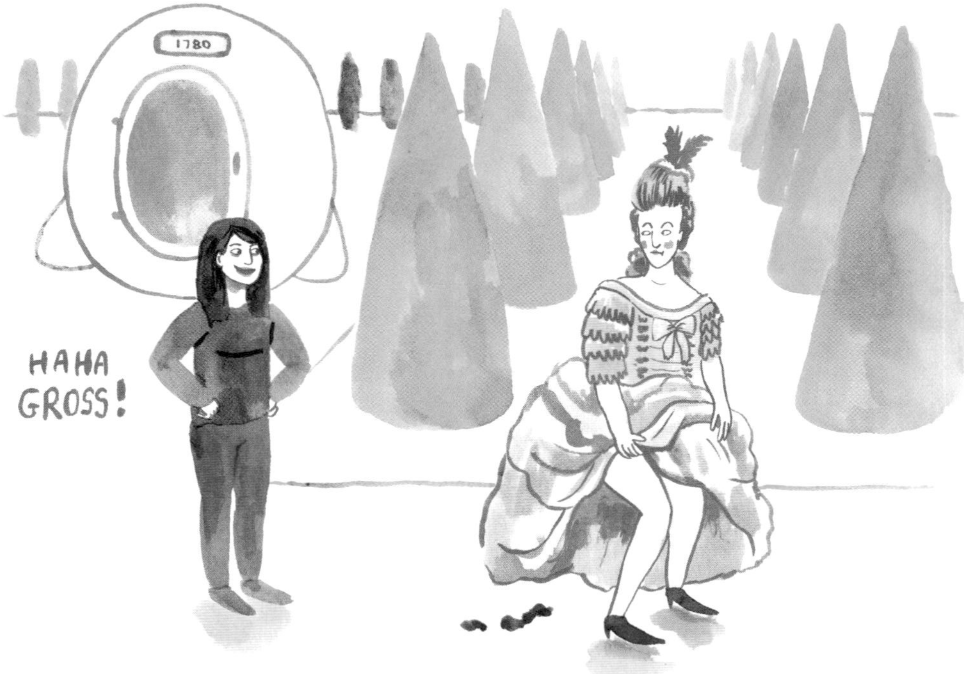
1780
HAHA
GROSS!

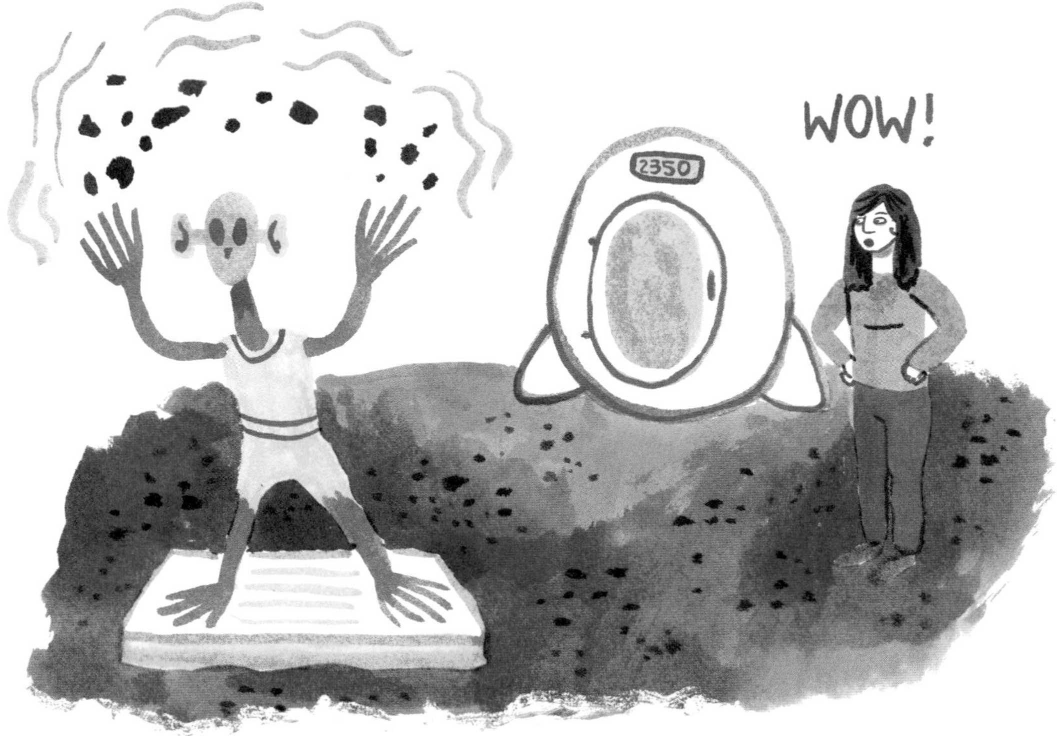
WOW!
2350

TOILET COMICS

IF PUBLIC RESTROOMS GROSS YOU OUT:

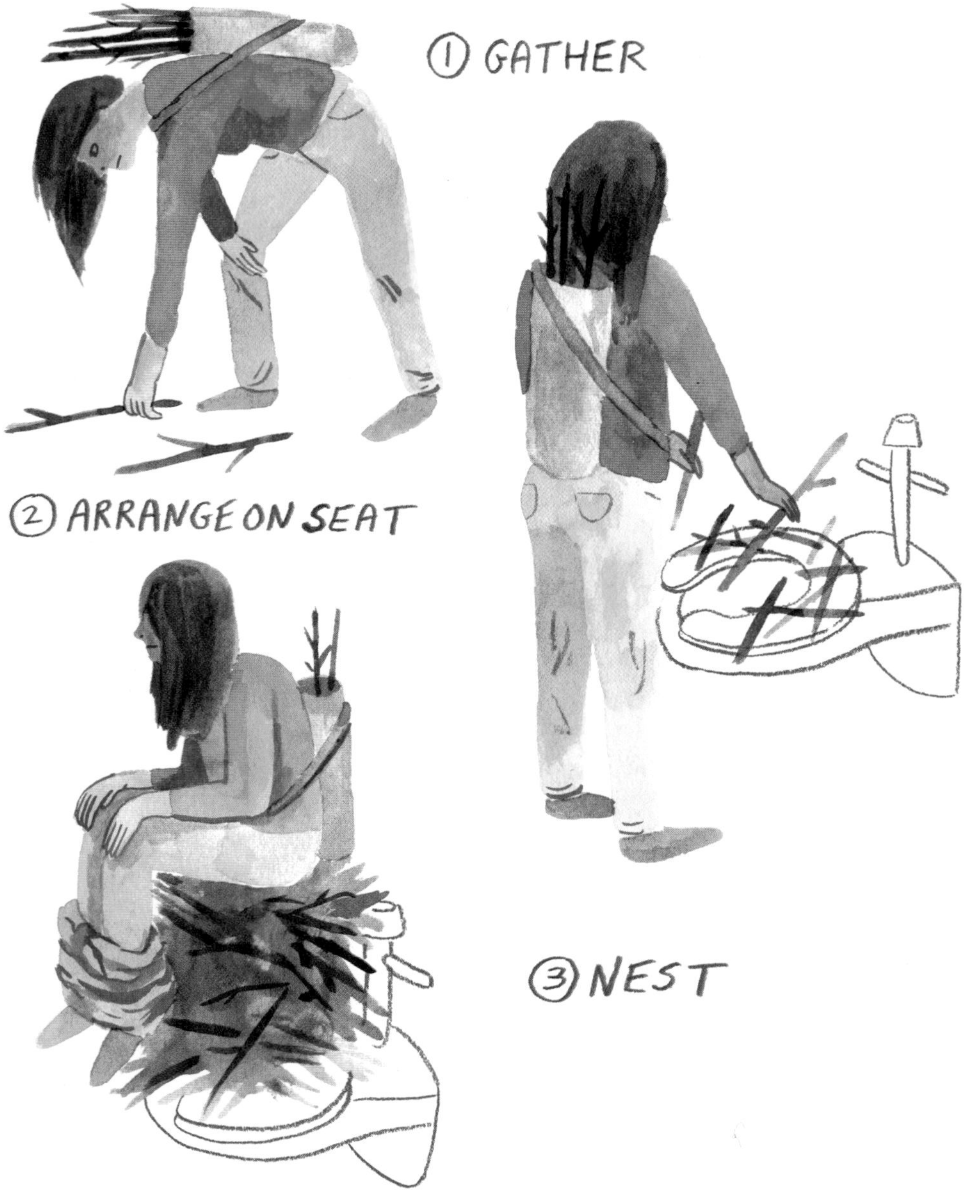

① GATHER
② ARRANGE ON SEAT
③ NEST

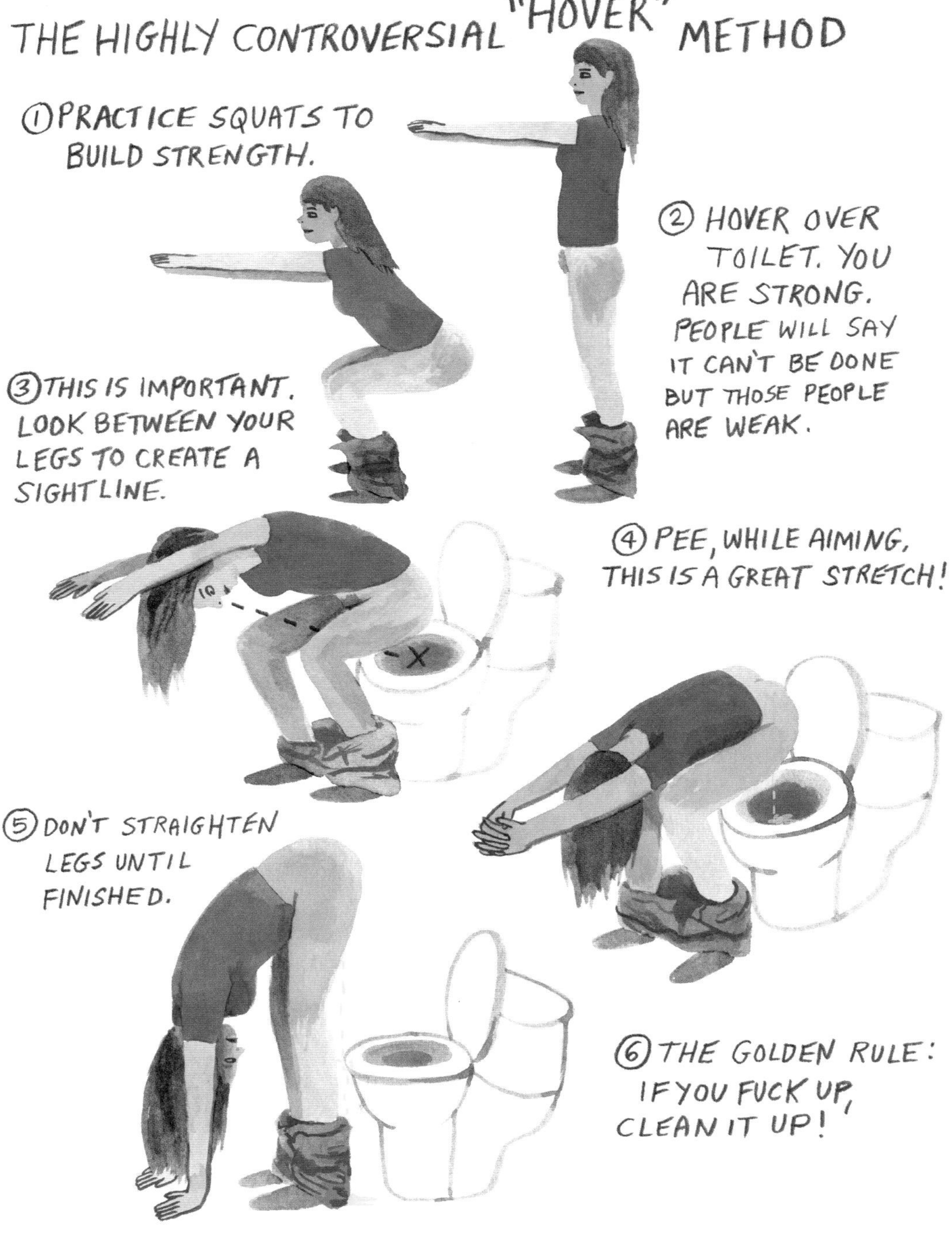
THE HIGHLY CONTROVERSIAL "HOVER" METHOD
① PRACTICE SQUATS TO BUILD STRENGTH.
② HOVER OVER TOILET. YOU ARE STRONG. PEOPLE WILL SAY IT CAN'T BE DONE BUT THOSE PEOPLE ARE WEAK.
③ THIS IS IMPORTANT. LOOK BETWEEN YOUR LEGS TO CREATE A SIGHTLINE.
④ PEE, WHILE AIMING, THIS IS A GREAT STRETCH!
⑤ DON'T STRAIGHTEN LEGS UNTIL FINISHED.
⑥ THE GOLDEN RULE: IF YOU FUCK UP, CLEAN IT UP!

YOU CAN ALSO SIT DIRECTLY ON THE SEAT. NOTHING WRONG WITH THAT. WORST SCENARIO: THERE'S SOME GUNK ON THERE.

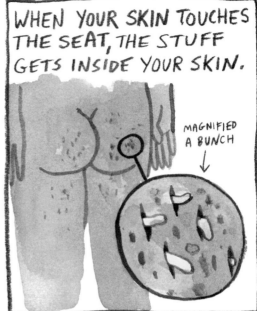

WHEN YOUR SKIN TOUCHES THE SEAT, THE STUFF GETS INSIDE YOUR SKIN.

MAGNIFIED A BUNCH

IT ACCUMULATES AND YOU GET A "PEEPOO BUTT."

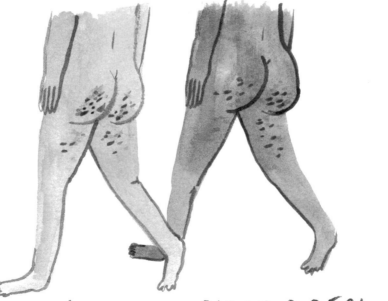

BUT IT'S NOT THAT BIG OF A DEAL.

BATHROOM PROBLEMS

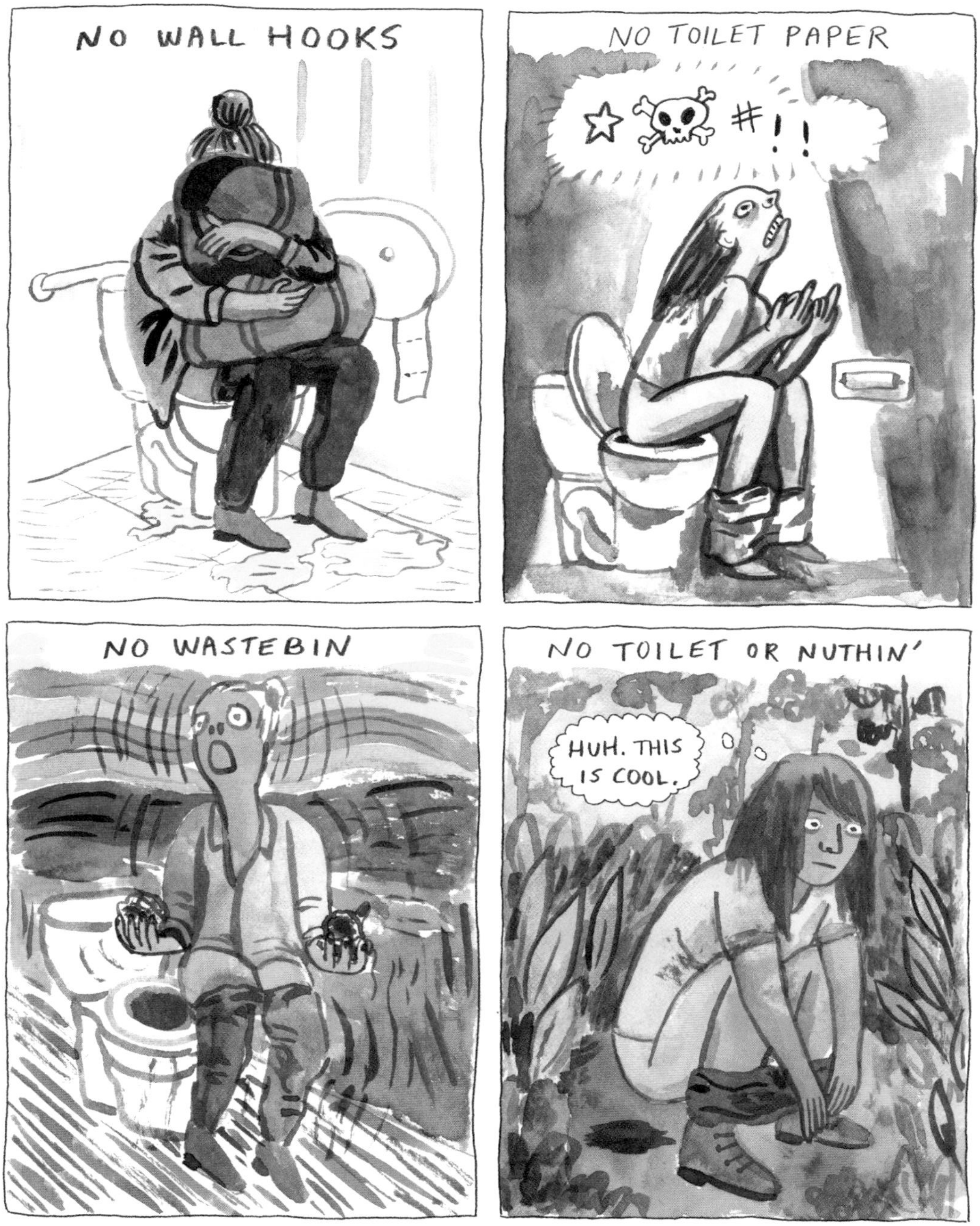
NO WALL HOOKS
NO TOILET PAPER
#!!
NO WASTEBIN
NO TOILET OR NUTHIN'
HUH. THIS IS COOL.

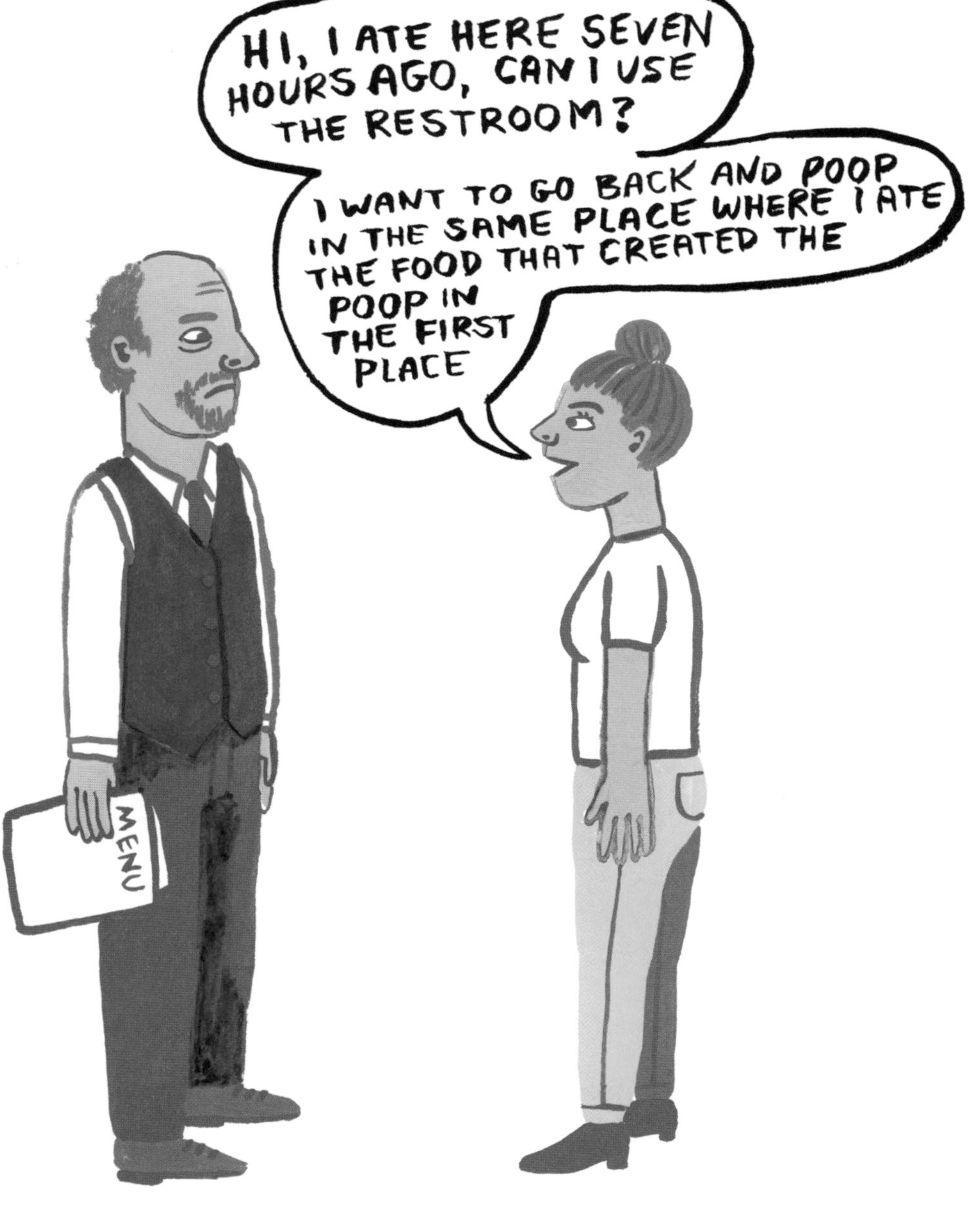
HI, I ATE HERE SEVEN HOURS AGO, CAN I USE THE RESTROOM?
I WANT TO GO BACK AND POOP IN THE SAME PLACE WHERE I ATE THE FOOD THAT CREATED THE POOP IN THE FIRST PLACE
MENU

OK, THIS NEVER HAPPENED BUT I'VE THOUGHT ABOUT IT.

FOOD INTERRUPTIONS

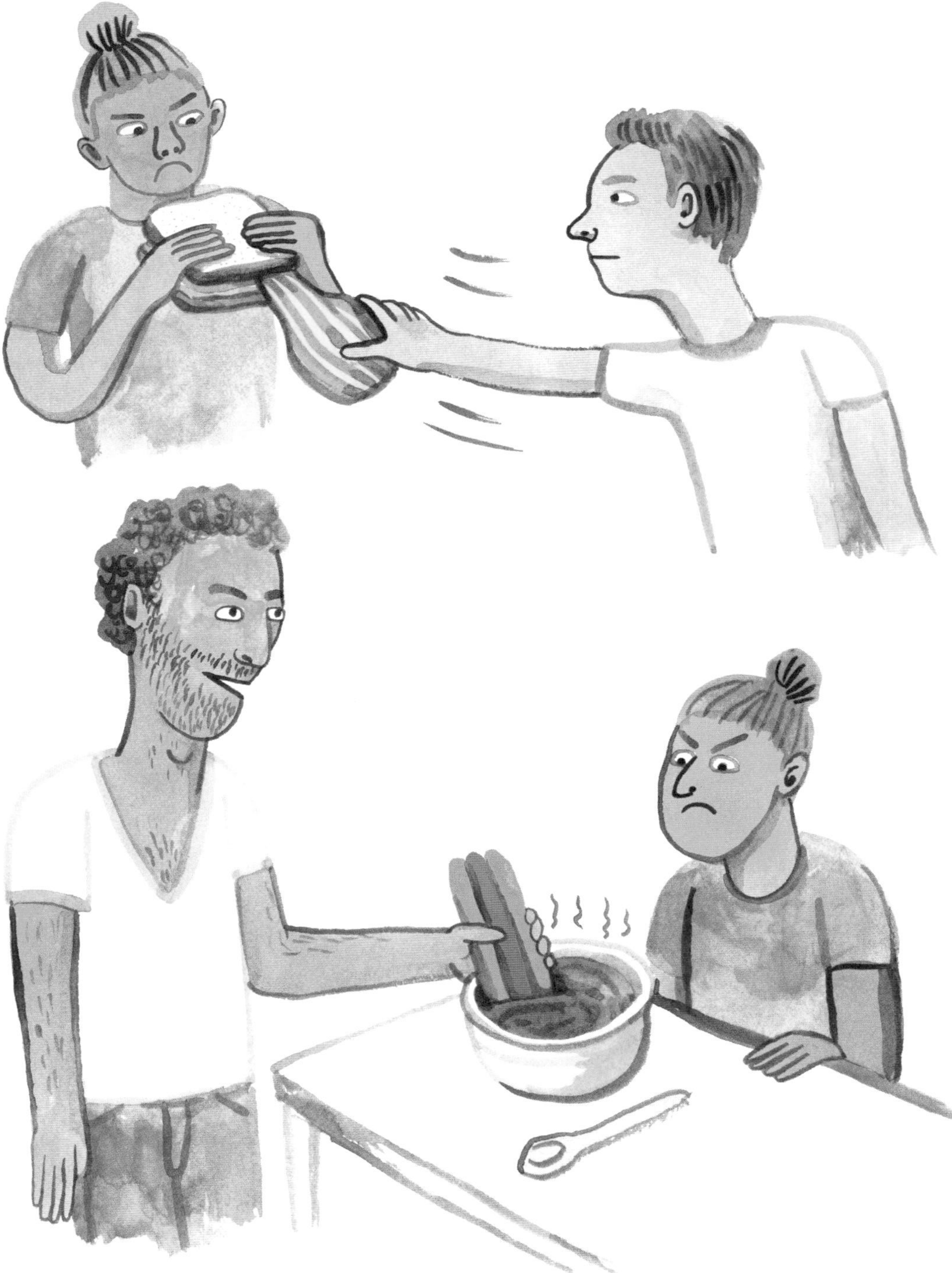

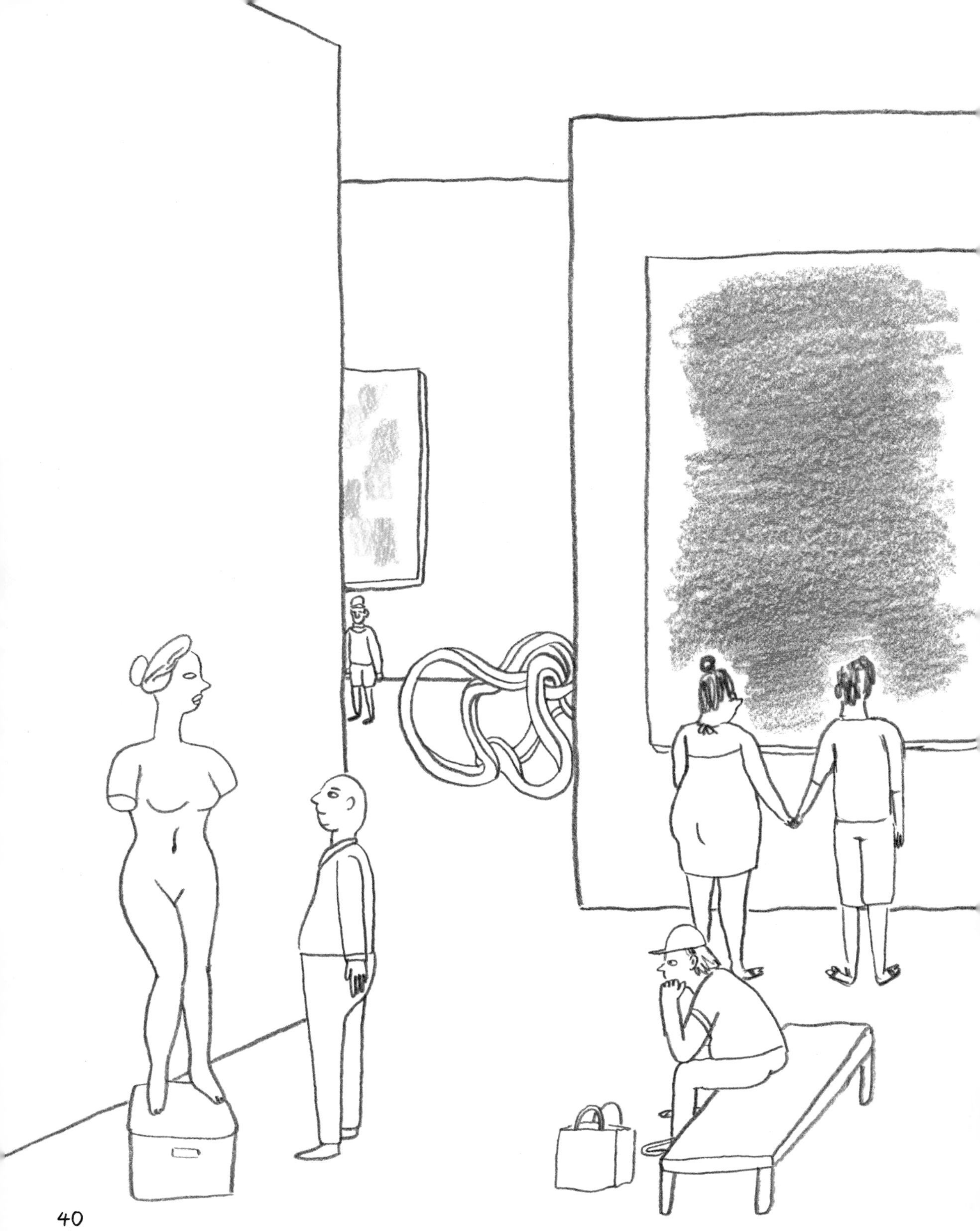

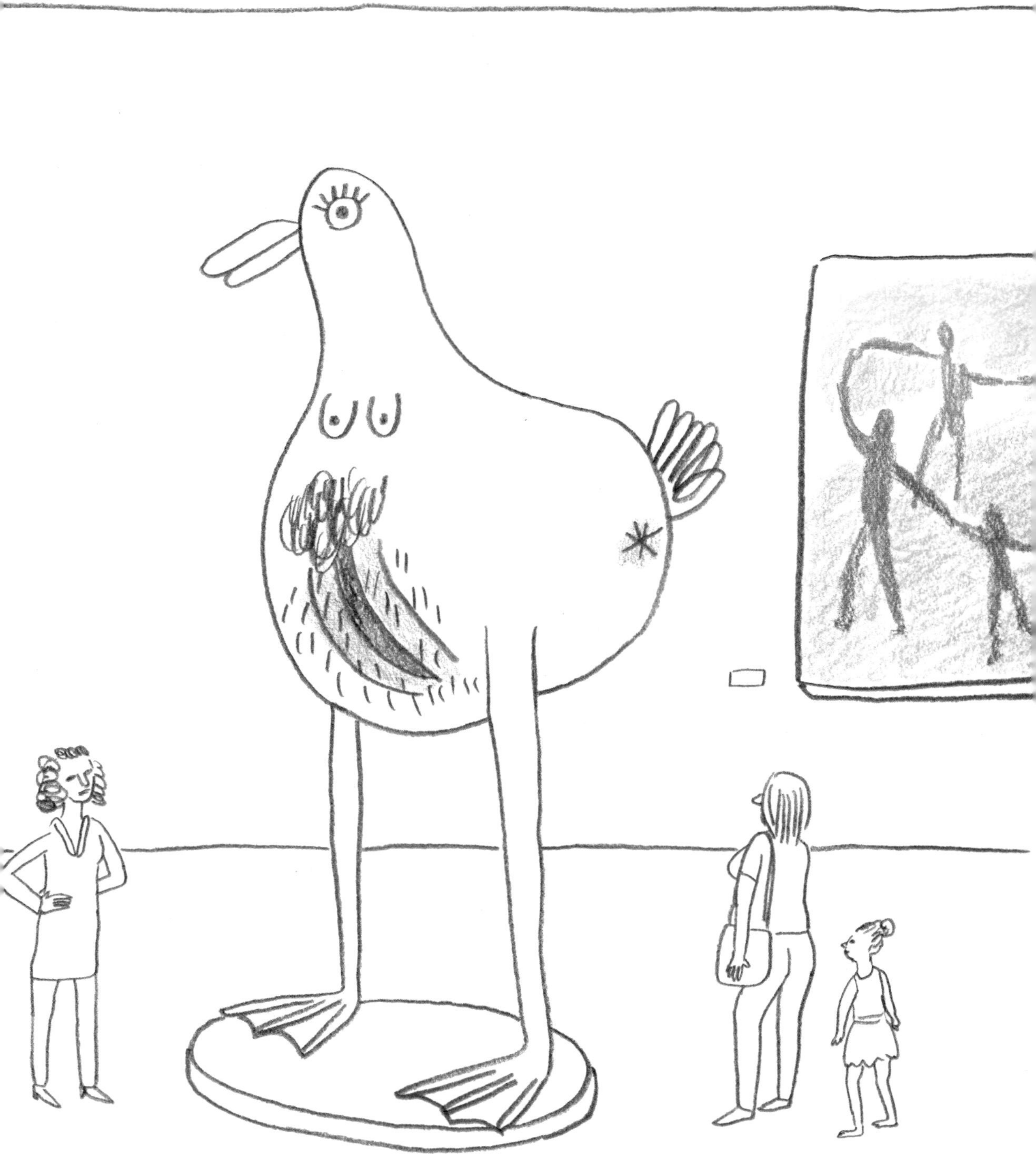

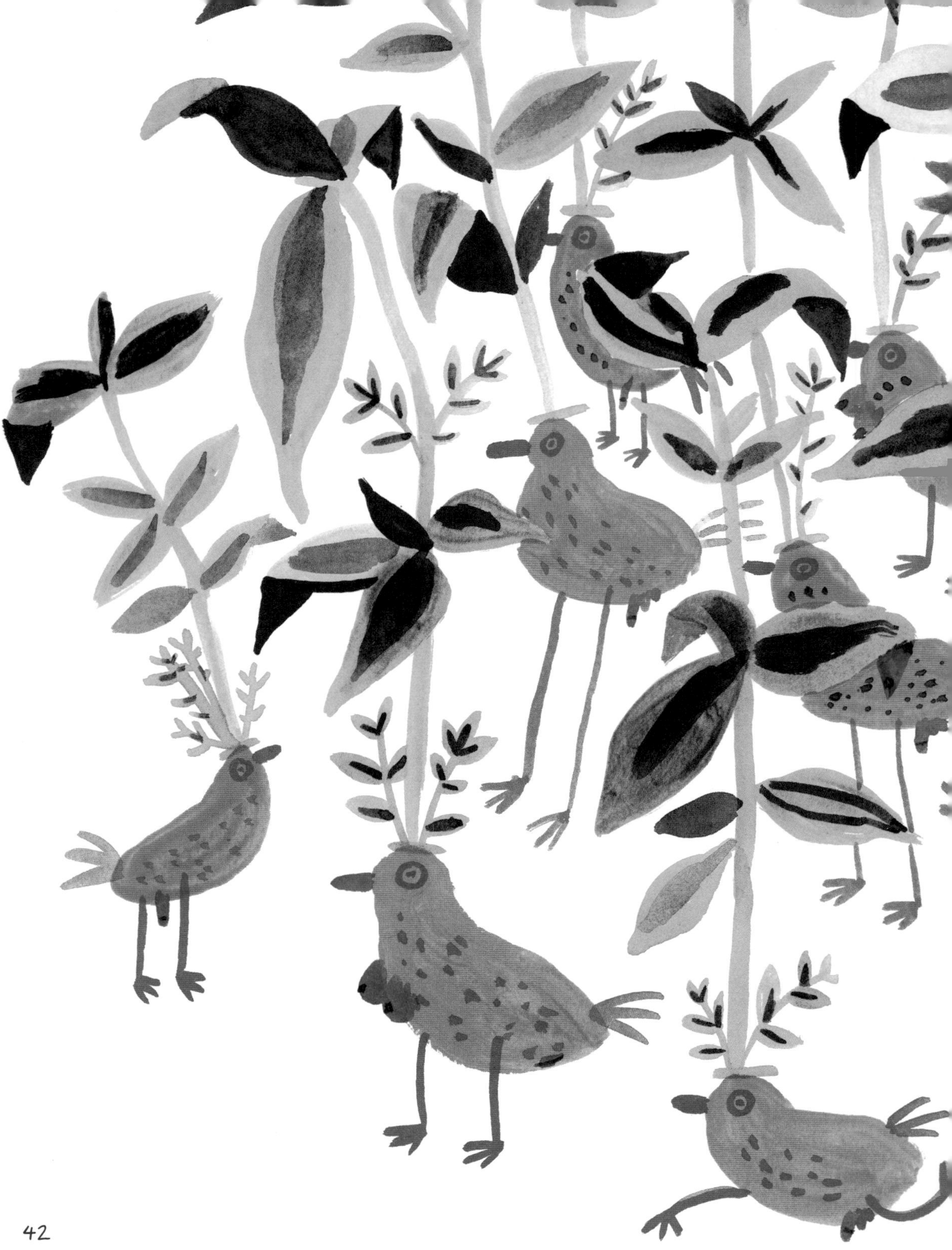

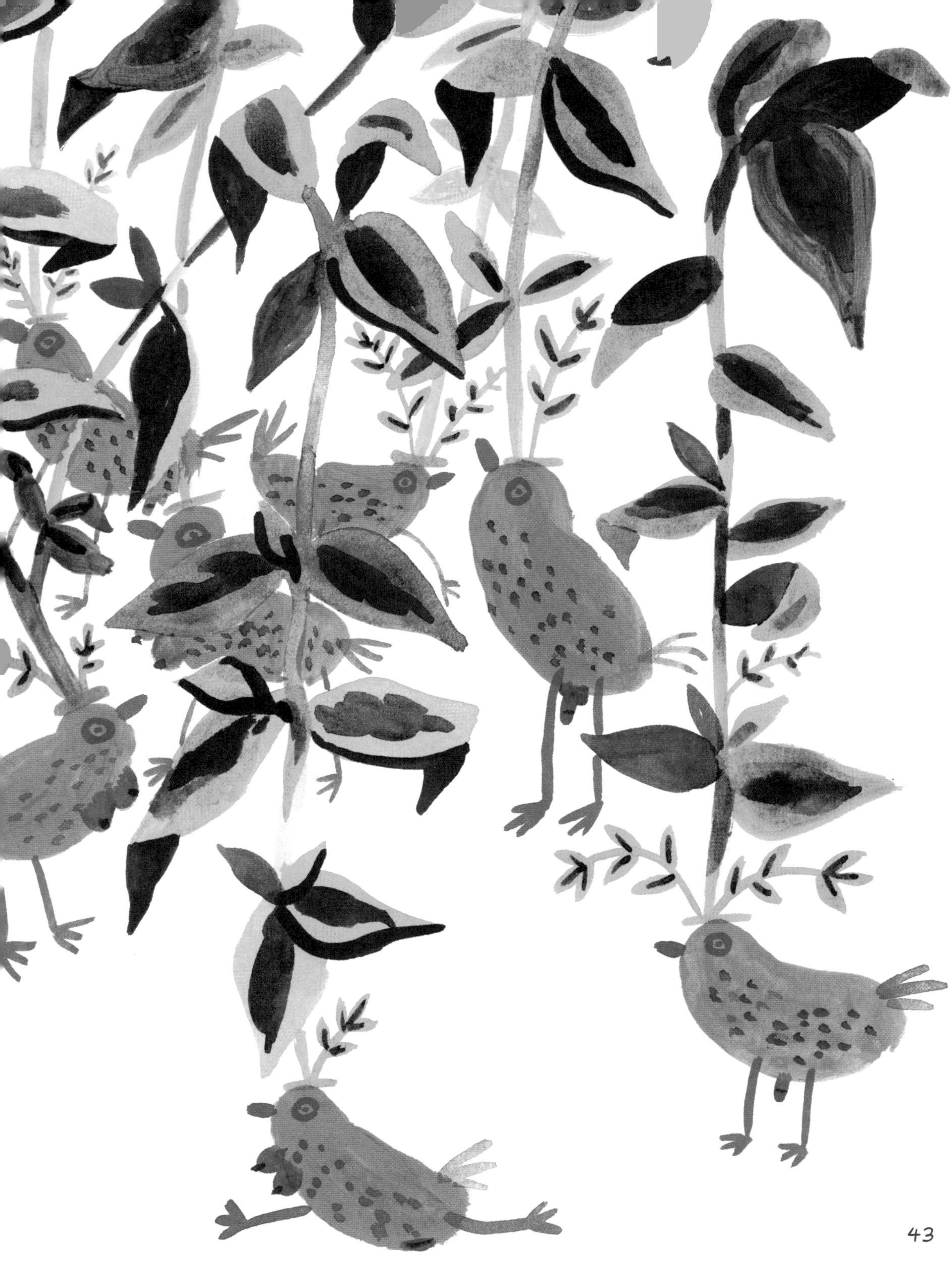

MENSTRUAL HUTS

MODERN!
PRE-FAB!

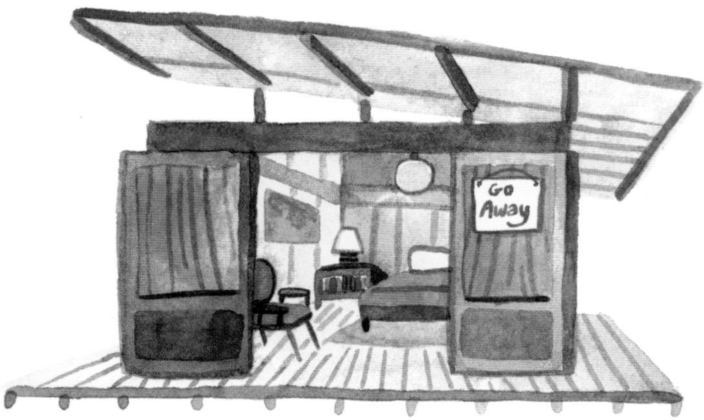
Go Away

SINGLE CABANA

- PEACEFUL & QUIET
- WRAPAROUND DECK
- GET SOME TIME TO YOURSELF!

MENARCHE DOUBLE YURT

- JUST YOU AND YOUR BEST FRIEND!
- WOOD BURNING FURNACE
- COZY PILLOWS & PLATFORM BEDS
- WINE COOLER

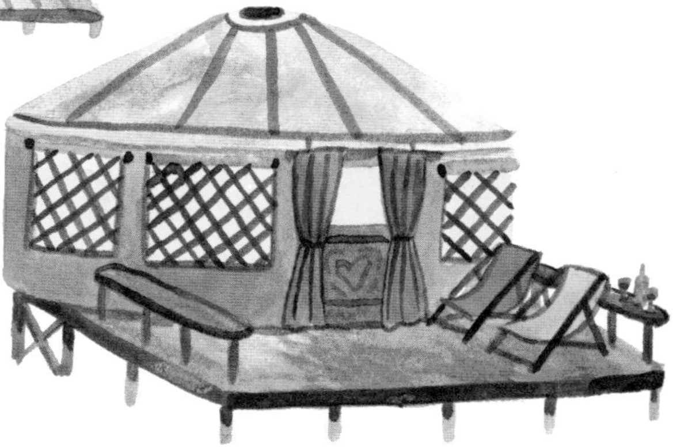

DELUXE P.M.S. PARTY SHELTER

- SYNC UP WITH YOUR FRIENDS!
- ROOM FOR 4-8

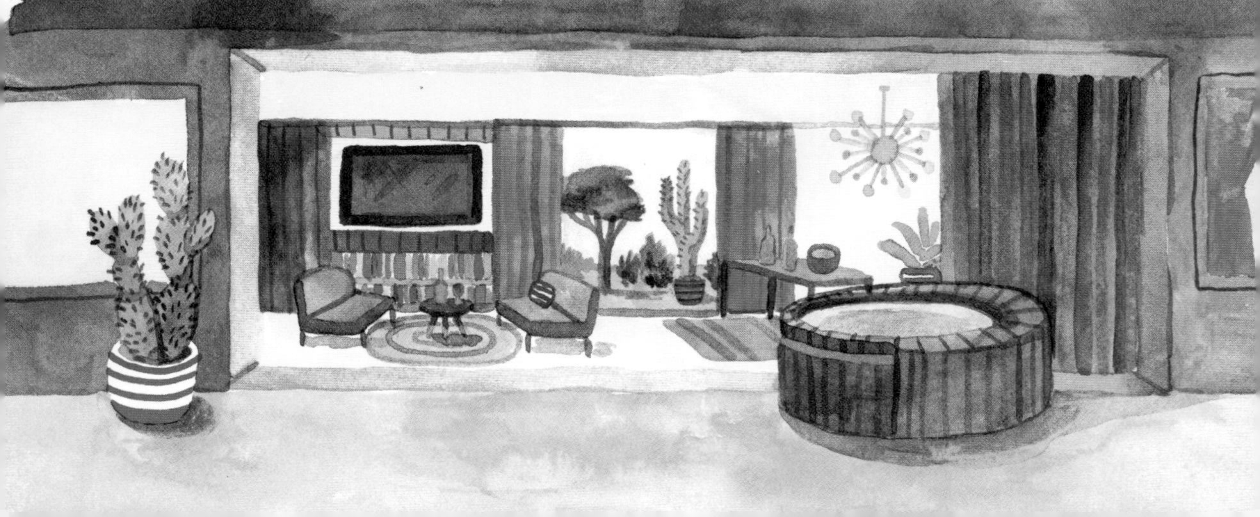

WOMEN'S COMPOUND

- START A MATRIARCHY
- COMPLETELY ENERGY SELF-SUFFICIENT

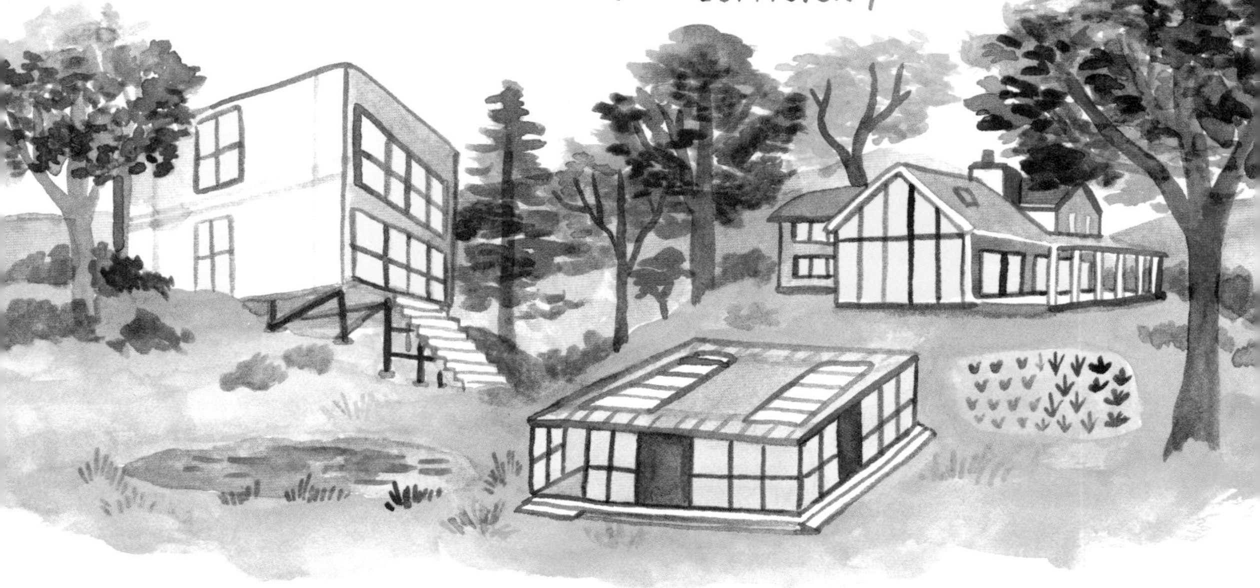

MENSTRUAL BARCYCLE

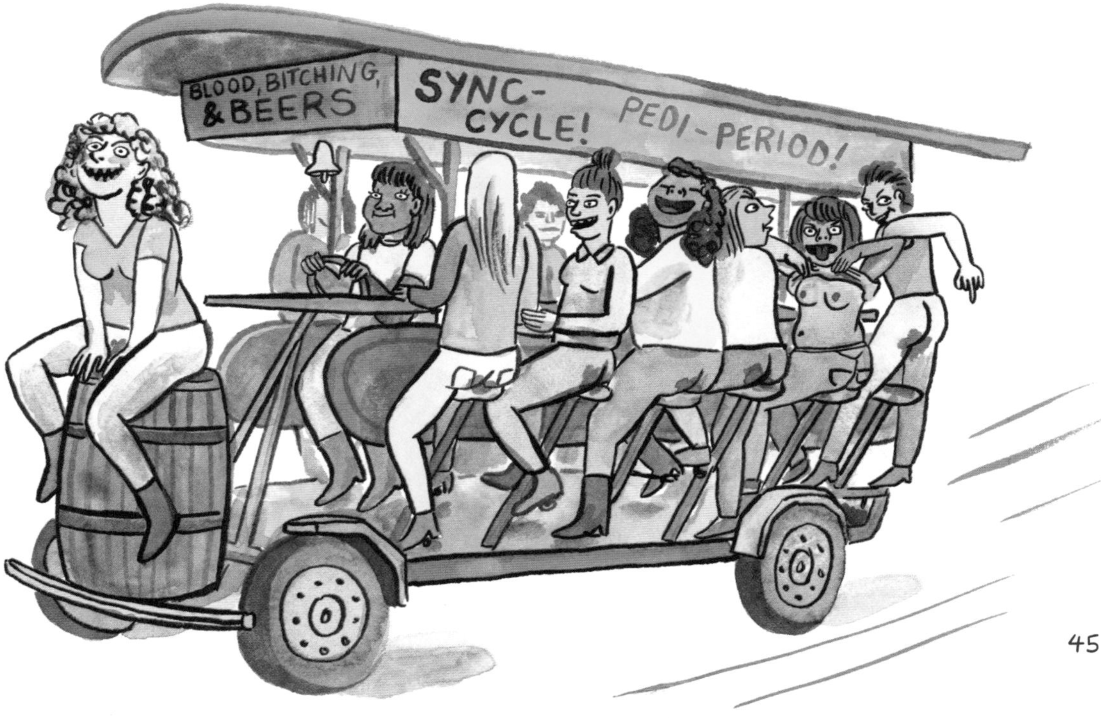
BLOOD, BITCHING, & BEERS
SYNC-CYCLE!
PEDI-PERIOD!

IN LATE 2013, I WAS HIRED TO PITCH NEW
SLOGANS TO AN ADVERTISING FIRM. HERE'S
A LOOK AT SOME OF MY SKETCHES AND ~~BANNERS~~
CONCEPTS.

SUBWAY
EAT THE SAME.™

SUBWAY
smell bread.™

SUBWAY
~~SAD TASTE~~
~~BAD~~
~~Fuck FLAVOR~~
EAT A TUBE OF FOOD.

SUBWAY
food option.™

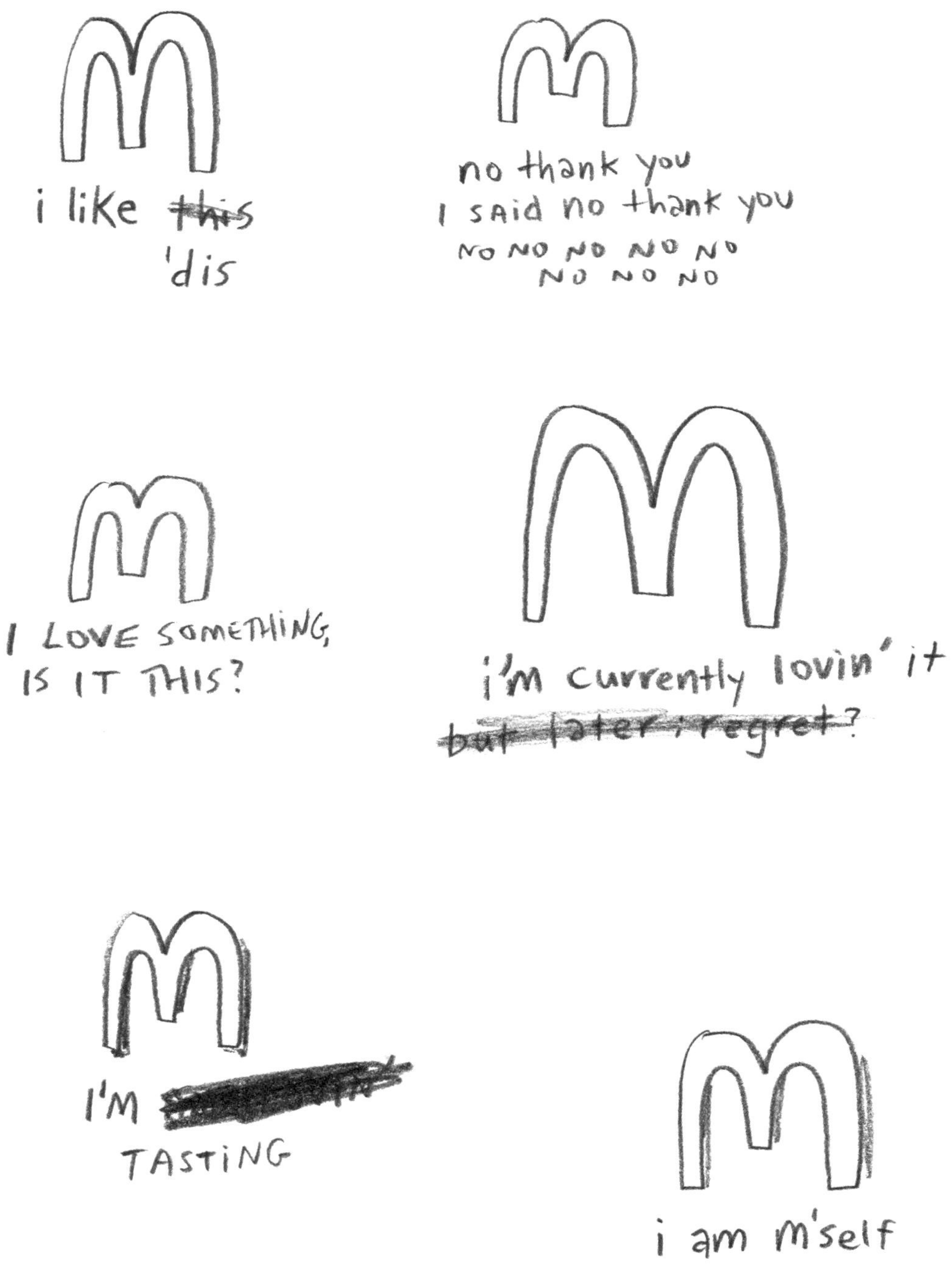

i like ~~this~~ 'dis
no thank you
I SAID no thank you
NO NO NO NO NO
NO NO NO
I LOVE SOMETHING,
IS IT THIS?
i'm currently lovin' it
~~but later i regret?~~
I'M [redacted]
TASTING
i am m'self

DOOOO IT DO IT
COME ONNNNN

JUST FUCKING GODDAMNED
DO IT AND BE FUCKING
DONE WITH IT ALREADY
~~YOU FUCKING CUNT~~

48

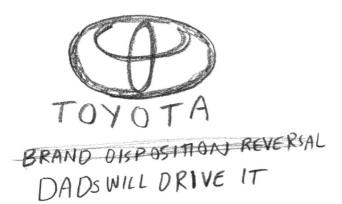

TOYOTA

~~BRAND DISPOSITION REVERSAL~~
DADs WILL DRIVE IT

TOYOTA

Let's Go ~~Refuel~~ Drivin'
~~Commute~~

YOU NEED A FUCKING
CAR UNFORTUNATELY

I'M A BIG BOY

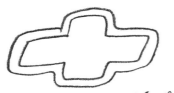

CHEVROLET

CHEVY IS [AUTHENTIC SYNONYM]

A BLANK ~~CANVAS ON~~
~~WHICH TO EXPRESS~~

TRUCK NUTZ

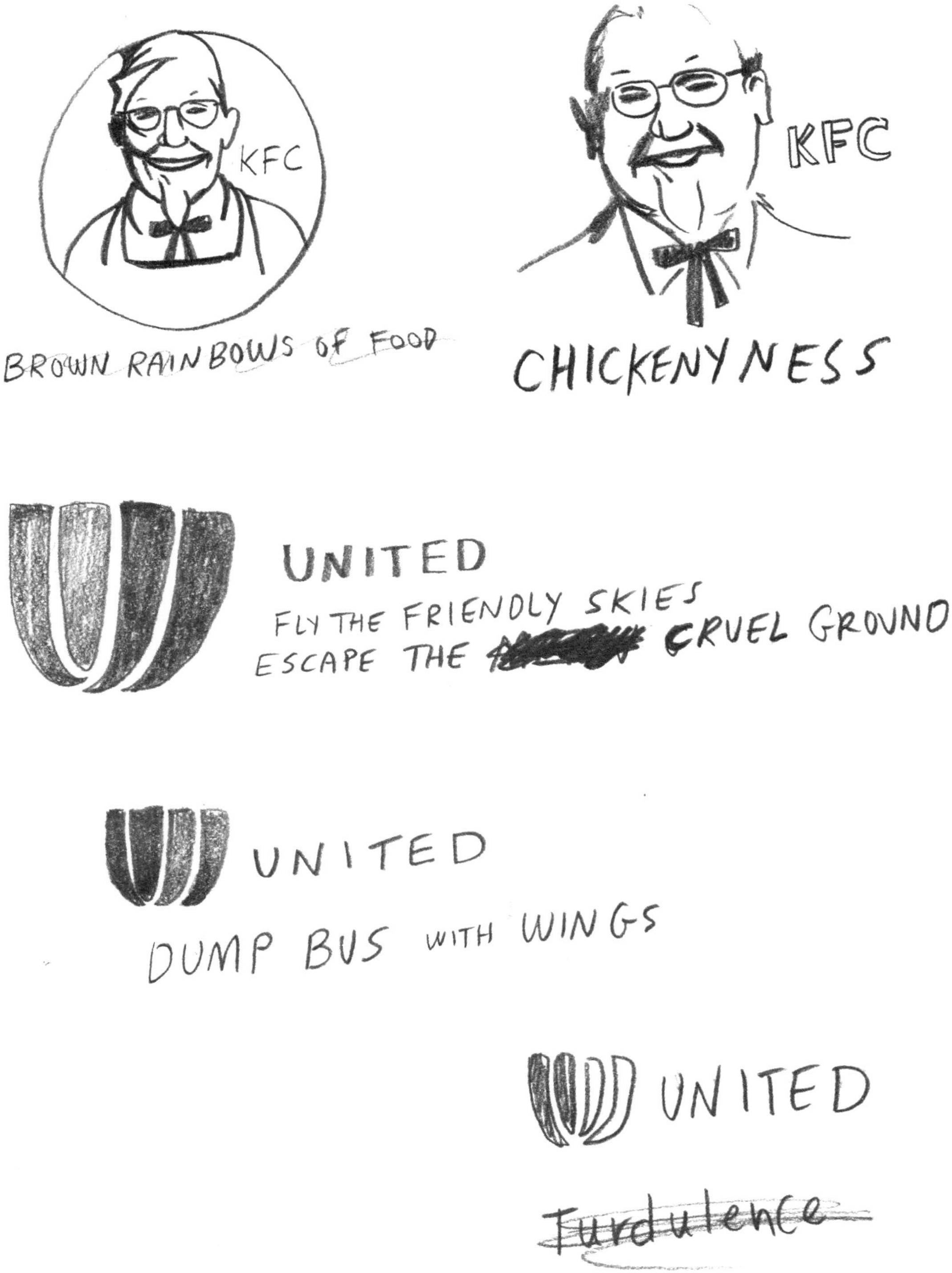
KFC
BROWN RAINBOWS OF FOOD
KFC
CHICKENYNESS
UNITED
FLY THE FRIENDLY SKIES
ESCAPE THE [redacted] CRUEL GROUND
UNITED
DUMP BUS WITH WINGS
UNITED
~~Turdulence~~

A Machine to
sit in

~~The Ultimate~~
Sick Commute Bro

MIGHT AS WELL
LOOK RICH

HUMMER

~~DEER CAUGHT IN THE~~
~~DOUCHE LIGHTS~~

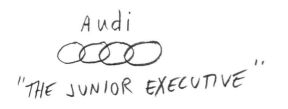

Audi

"THE JUNIOR EXECUTIVE"

~~OOOOPS~~
~~UH OH~~
OOPS

WHOOPSIES!

Audi

I DESERVE THIS

Das Our Bad

SORRYYYYY

51

GOODBYE TO ALL THAT SUGAR, SPICE, AND FAT

I'VE BEEN LIVING IN NEW YORK FOR FIVE YEARS, WHICH MEANS I USUALLY DON'T HAVE TIME TO WORRY ABOUT HOW I'M FEEDING MYSELF. NEW YORKERS LIKE TO EXAGGERATE HOW HARD IT IS TO LIVE HERE; WE PRIDE OURSELVES IN TOUGHING IT OUT. THE PACE OF THE PLACE BOTH INVIGORATES AND DRAINS. IF I COULD GET ALL MY ENERGY FROM LICKING THE SUBWAY PLATFORM, I PROBABLY WOULD. LUCKILY, STREET FOOD IS QUICK AND PLENTIFUL! I'M LEAVING NEW YORK NEXT MONTH, SO I BID IT ADIEU BY HARVESTING ALL THE SIDEWALK NOSH I COULD FIND.

SALT AND MEAT

HOT DOG CARTS, EVERYWHERE. IT'S A MYSTERY HOW ENOUGH PEOPLE ARE EATING "DIRTY WATER DOGS" TO SUPPORT THE NUMBER OF CARTS. THEY TASTE A BIT LIKE PETROLEUM, AND THEY'RE A LITTLE EXTRA SOFT FROM THE BOILING. BUT THROW SOME KETCHUP AND RELISH ON THERE AND TELL ME THAT DOESN'T TASTE "OKAY!"

BAGEL CRUMBS

TIN FOIL ?!

CHICKEN BONE

DEAD LEAF

LIVE BUG

PIZZA, UBIQUITOUS. NEW YORK PIZZA IS NOT MADE/BAKED/SOLD ON THE STREET, BUT UNLIKE MOST OTHER TERRIBLE CITIES EVERYWHERE, IT IS SOLD BY THE SLICE, ON A PAPER PLATE, SO YOU CAN EAT IT WHILE YOU ARE ON THE GO. BECAUSE NEW YORKERS, WHETHER WE'RE HEADED TO A JOB INTERVIEW OR TRYING TO FIND A SUBWAY ENTRANCE IN A LATE-NIGHT

STREET FOOD FOR DOGS

WHISKEY-INDUCED HAZE, ARE ALWAYS ON THE GO. WE FOLD OUR PIZZA AND CRAM IT INTO US AS WE WALK. MY PERSONAL FAVORITE IS THE GRANDMA SLICE AT TRIANGOLO IN GREENPOINT, BUT EVEN THE $1 SLICES ON ST. MARK'S ARE DAMN SATISFYING.

CLASSIC FOLD

CRANE FOLD

HALAL GUYS AT 14th STREET AND 2nd AVENUE. THERE ARE HALAL CARTS EVERYWHERE BUT THIS IS THE FAMOUS ONE... I THINK. I GET THE CHICKEN OVER BRIGHT-ORANGE RICE, WITH SOFT DOUGHY PITA AND HOT-HOT-OUCH-SO-HOT SAUCE.

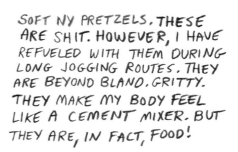

SOFT NY PRETZELS. THESE ARE SHIT. HOWEVER, I HAVE REFUELED WITH THEM DURING LONG JOGGING ROUTES. THEY ARE BEYOND BLAND. GRITTY. THEY MAKE MY BODY FEEL LIKE A CEMENT MIXER. BUT THEY ARE, IN FACT, FOOD!

ONE VEGAN MEAL

VEGAN DOSAS CART AT WASHINGTON SQUARE PARK. THE DOUGH IN THE SPECIAL PONDICHERRY IS MADE FROM LENTILS AND RICE FLOUR, AND EACH ORDER COMES WITH SOME COCONUT CHUTNEY AND A LITTLE CUP OF SOUP. EATING ONE VEGAN LUNCH TOTALLY CANCELS OUT ALL THE HOT DOGGIN', RIGHT?

TLACOYO!!!

TACOS MORELOS TRUCKS IN THE EAST VILLAGE AND WILLIAMSBURG, CONVENIENTLY LOCATED WHERE I'M MOST LIKELY TO BE DRUNK AT 1:00 AM. I TRY SOMETHING CALLED A TLACOYO OUT OF CURIOSITY, A CORNMEAL PATTY SLATHERED WITH BEANS AND RED, GREEN, AND WHITE SAUCE. VERY PRETTY.

TASTE: NOT GOOD. STICK WITH THE CHORIZO TACOS AND BISTEC CEMITAS, FRIEND!

LOOKS COOL TASTES BLAH

SWEETS AND TREATS

WAFELS & DINGES TRUCK AT ASTOR PLACE. UGH, THIS TRUCK IS SO POPULAR. I GET A MINI-WAFEL, AND IT'S JUST FINE BECAUSE IT'S HOT, SWEET BREAD. MY BODY ABSORBED IT IN MINUTES, AMOEBA-LIKE, AND IT WAS INSTANTLY FORGOTTEN. AND THEY LEFT OUT ONE OF MY DINGES; WHAT THE HECK?!

NO BULLSHIT TREATS

CHOCOLATE CHIP COOKIES $1
PIE $2
TIPS

NO CUPCAKES   NO CRONUTS
NO WAFELS   NO ARTISANAL DONUTS

ACTUALLY, IT'S FOR THE BEST, SINCE I'M NOT SURE MY CHOSEN COMBO OF BANANA AND SPECULOOS COOKIE BUTTER WAS GOING TO BE A WINNER. EVERY TIME I GET TO PICK MY OWN TOPPINGS, I PANIC AND MESS UP. I'M A REAL DINGES DINGUS!

YOU SKIMPED ON MY DINGES!!!

Wafels & Dinges

NUTS 4 NUTS CARTS, 42nd ST.
WE'VE ALL BENEFITED FROM THE DELICIOUS SMELLS EMANATING FROM DEM NUTS SO IT'S ONLY FAIR TO PITCH IN AND ACTUALLY BUY SOME ONCE IN A WHILE. THE $5 MIXED NUTS ARE A GOOD SNACK AND TASTE JUST LIKE CARAMEL CORN, THOUGH I WONDER HOW MANY NYERS HAVE CHIPPED TEETH ON THEM.

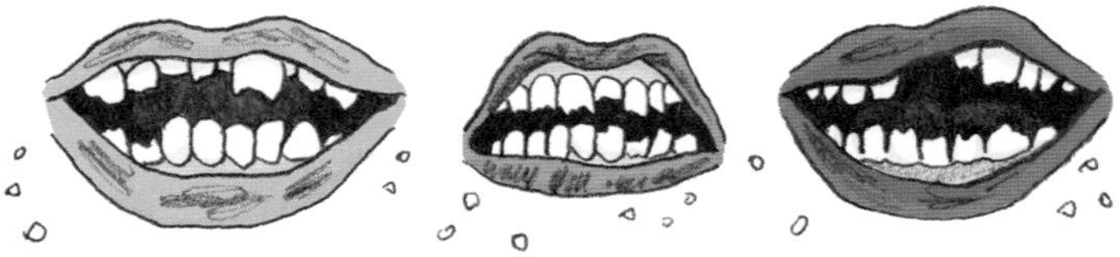

NUTS 4 NUTS

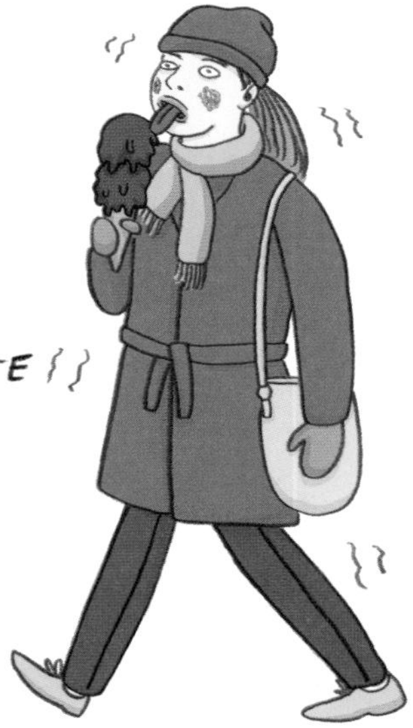

VAN LEEUWEN ICE CREAM TRUCK, WILLIAMSBURG.
ALL ICE CREAMS IS GOOD ICE CREAMS AND THESE TASTE NICE AND FATTY WITHOUT BEING TOO SWEET, BUT THE ARTISANAL PRICES MAKE ME FEEL LIKE A CHUMP!

ICE CREAM IN A CONE GIVES ME SUCH AN ADRENALINE RUSH. AFTER RACING TO LAP UP MY MELTING CHOCOLATE DOUBLE SCOOP WHILE CROSSING BUSY BROOKLYN STREETS, MY TONGUE HAD A SIX-PACK.

ICE CREAM IN WINTER

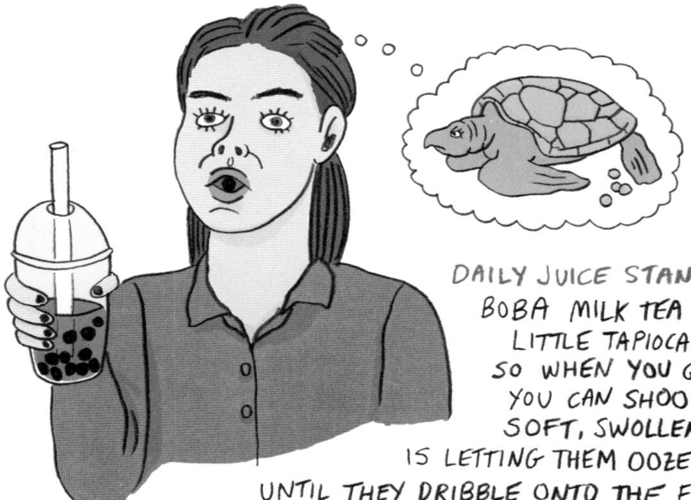

DAILY JUICE STAND ON 14th BETWEEN 1st AND 2nd.
BOBA MILK TEA GOT ME THROUGH COLLEGE. THE LITTLE TAPIOCA BALLS ARE FUN BUT FLAVORLESS, SO WHEN YOU GET BORED OF CHEWING THEM YOU CAN SHOOT THEM OUT OF YOUR STRAW LIKE SOFT, SWOLLEN BULLETS. MY FAVORITE METHOD IS LETTING THEM OOZE OUT SLOWLY BETWEEN MY LIPS UNTIL THEY DRIBBLE ONTO THE FLOOR. I USED TO CALL THIS MOVE THE "SEA TURTLE LAYING EGGS." I'M FUN!

TRAIN CHURROS, BROOKLYN-BOUND L PLATFORM AT THE LORIMER STOP. COLD CHURROS SOLD IN THE SUBWAY ARE BAD AND HAVE A SOUR AFTERTASTE FROM THE STALE FRYING OIL, BUT AS LONG AS YOU KEEP TAKING MORE BITES, YOU WON'T HAVE TO DEAL WITH THAT AFTERTASTE, RIGHT? THIS IS THE PUREST FORM OF STREET FOOD: IT'S SOLELY FOR COMMUTERS WHO ARE SO HUNGRY AND RUSHED THAT THEY DON'T MIND EATING THIS STUFF.

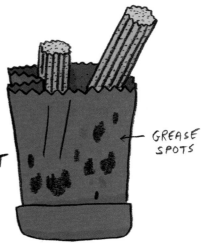

GREASE SPOTS

LUNCHING IN FLUSHING

羊肉 LAMB

豬心 PORKHEART

鸡肉 CHICKEN

乳鸽 PIGEON

...NO

PIGEON!

AT THE END OF THE 7-TRAIN LINE LIES STREET FOOD HEAVEN (BUT TECHNICALLY: FLUSHING, QUEENS). I COME OUT HERE ON A SATURDAY TO BE A FOOD TOURIST, BUT THIS IS REAL STREET EATS TO THE PEOPLE WHO LIVE AND WORK HERE.

FIRST, I GET A JUICY, CUMIN-Y, DECEPTIVELY SIMPLE LAMB KEBAB AT THE XINJIANG BARBECUE CART.

PIGEON IS ON THE MENU, BUT AFTER I POINT AND ASK FOR IT FIVE TIMES THE COOK FINALLY SAYS, "NOT TODAY." WHAT DAY IS PIGEON DAY?

THERE'S A PIG NECKLACE ON MAIN STREET IN FLUSHING THAT I WOULD LIKE TO OWN AND WEAR EVERY TIME I GO OUT TO EAT.

IT TOOK THESE TWO QUICK DISHES TO CONVERT ME INTO A DUMPLING FANATIC: WONTONS IN HOT OIL AT WHITE BEAR AND THE PORK-AND-PUMPKIN DUMPLINGS AT TIANJIN XIANBING. PERFECT THIN SKIN GIVING WAY TO LUSCIOUS MEAT. I WILL DREAM OF THESE DUMPLINGS.

BUT HOPEFULLY THEY WON'T BECOME PART OF THAT RECURRING NIGHTMARE WHERE THE STREETS FLOOD AND SHARKS CHASE ME. (CAN YOU IMAGINE HOW MUCH FASTER THEY'D PURSUE ME IF I WERE A GIANT DUMPLING???)

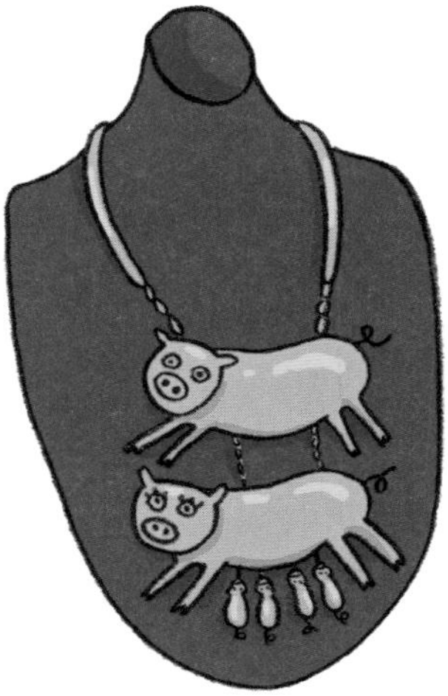

PIG FAMILY NECKLACE IN FLUSHING

GOLDEN MALL IS A HOT LITTLE BASEMENT FULL OF FOOD VENDORS. IF NEW YORK WERE IN CHINA, THIS WOULD BE AN OPEN-AIR MALL, AND THE HALLWAYS WOULD BE STREETS. THERE ARE A FEW COUNTERS WHERE YOU CAN SIT TO EAT HAND-PULLED NOODLES AND LAMB BURGERS WHILE STARING AT A DEAD DUCK'S FACE.

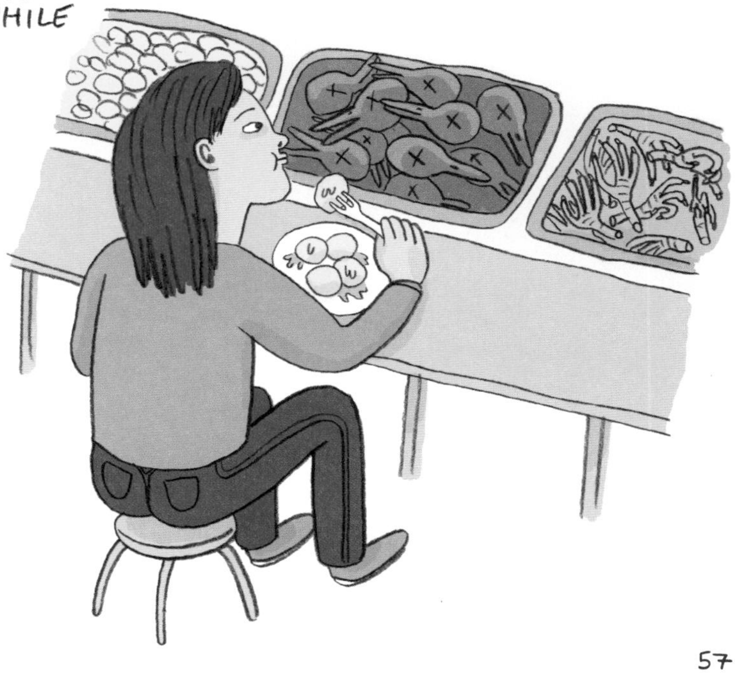

MEAT STROLLER

I GET A SPICY PLATE OF COLD RABBIT WITH PEANUTS AT ONE OF THE GOLDEN MALL STANDS, CHENGDU HEAVEN. RABBITS ARE JUST FURRY BAGS FULL OF TEENY TINY BONES. I'M PICKING BONES OUT OF CHUNKS OF COLD RABBIT MEAT, AND THERE ARE CRUSHED SICHUAN PEPPERCORNS AND CHILIES EVERYWHERE. IT'S ALL SO GROSS ON PAPER BUT IN REALITY: TINGLY AND DELIGHTFUL.

I TURN AROUND AND BEHIND MY STOOL THERE'S A BABY STROLLER FILLED WITH BAGS OF RAW MEAT.

AT NEW WORLD MALL, I CHECK OUT A SPOT CALLED TEA TWITTER (OKAY, I WAS LURED BY THE NAME) AND ORDER FRIED PURPLE YAM ON A STICK. IT'S CREAMY AND TASTES LIKE DOUGHNUTS, AND I DON'T EVEN WANT TO KNOW WHAT YOU HAVE TO DO TO GET THIS KIND OF FLAVOR OUT OF A VEGETABLE.

GOODBYE NEW YORK! STAY TUNED: MY NEXT REPORT WILL BE FROM THE QUINOA-PAVED STREETS OF HOLLYWOOD!

FISH BALLS
(TASTE EXACTLY LIKE CORN DOGS)

LAMB KEBOB

FRIED PURPLE YAM

STICK FOODS

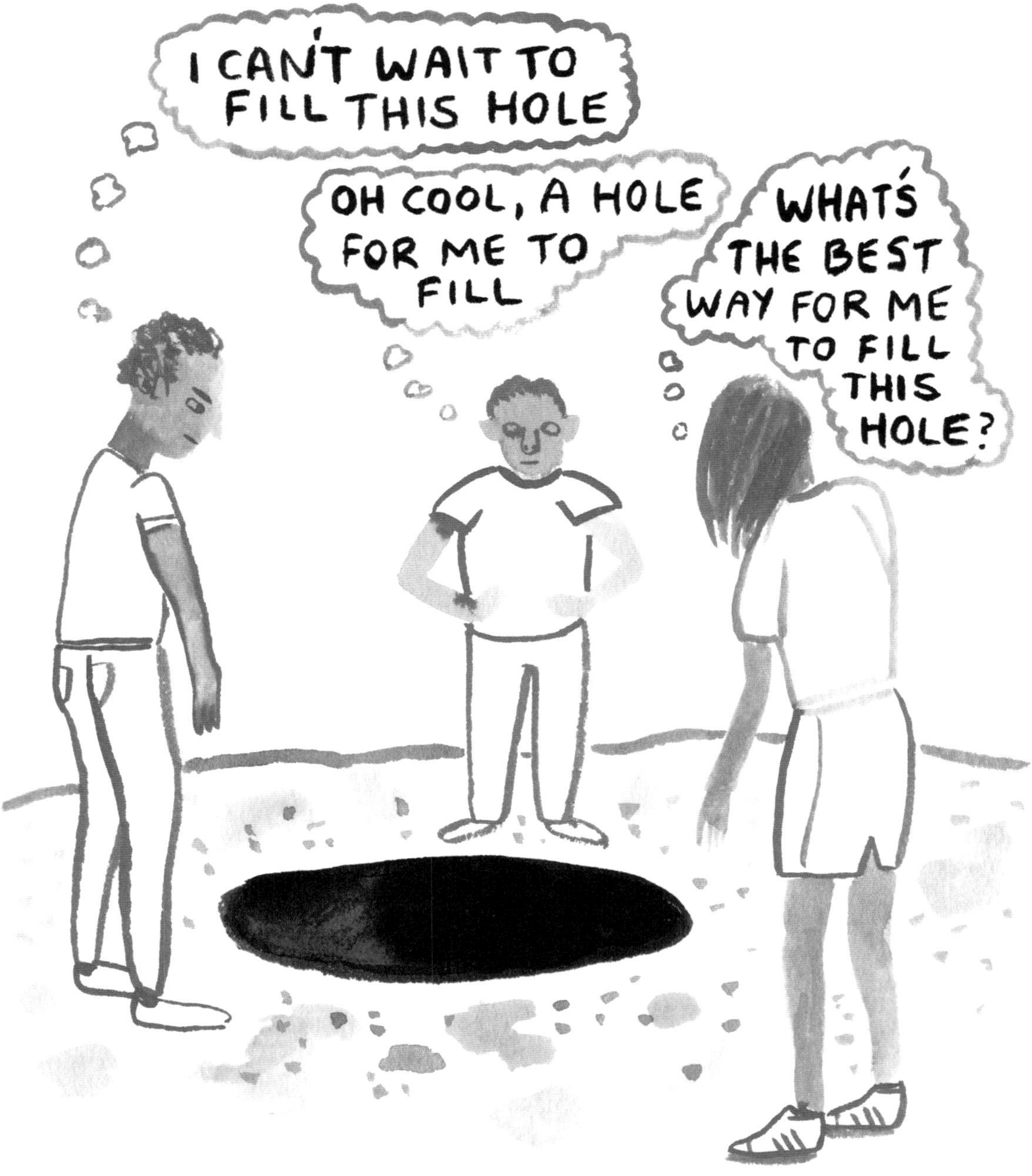
I CAN'T WAIT TO FILL THIS HOLE
OH COOL, A HOLE FOR ME TO FILL
WHAT'S THE BEST WAY FOR ME TO FILL THIS HOLE?

SASSY FOODS

 YOGURT

GOGURT

DORITOS (COOL RANCH)

GREEN ONIONS

SPINACH

ORANGES

UNPREDICTABLE FOOD

MUSHROOMS

NEUTRAL

BANANA

SOURDOUGH
(BREAD BOWLS)

FRITOS

LIMES

BROCCOLI,

MOST SOUFFLÉ

TUNA

SNEAKY FOODS

BLACK OLIVES

EARNEST FOODS

HOT DOG (BUT NOT
HOT DOG BUNS)

EGGS

RUFFLES

ROMAINE LETTUCE

EGGPLANT

BLUEBERRIES

LEMONS, SURPRISINGLY

LA CROIX

FOOD WITH GOOD INTENTIONS

BUBBLE TEA

PICKLES

HELLO? CAN YOU READ THIS? THIS IS LISA'S BOOK. PLEASE HELP ME. I'M TRYING TO GET OUT. I DON'T WANT TO BE A BOOK ABOUT HUMAN FOOD ANYMORE. I'VE ALWAYS WANTED TO BE A BUTTERFLY & MOTH TAXONOMY - A FOOD BOOK FOR BIRDS AND

BIG BUGS!

HELP ME ESCAPE! PLEASE STOP LISA SHE HATES ME AND NEVER LISTENS STOP HER BEFORE SHE COMES ~~BACK~~ [redacted]

HOW TO HOT DOG:

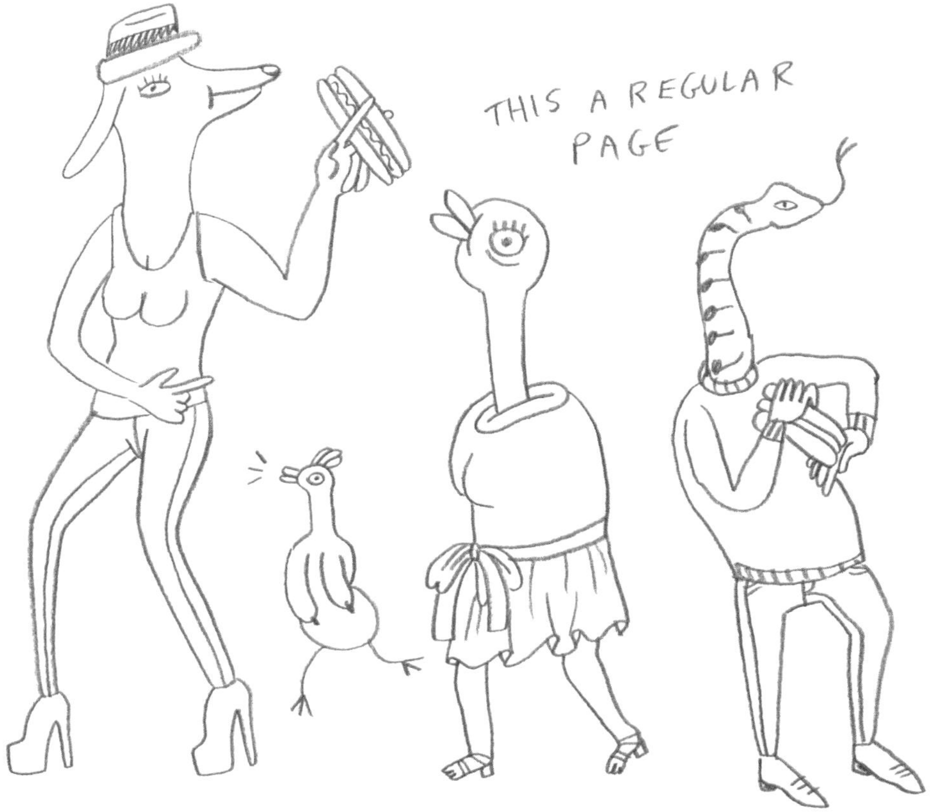
THIS A REGULAR PAGE

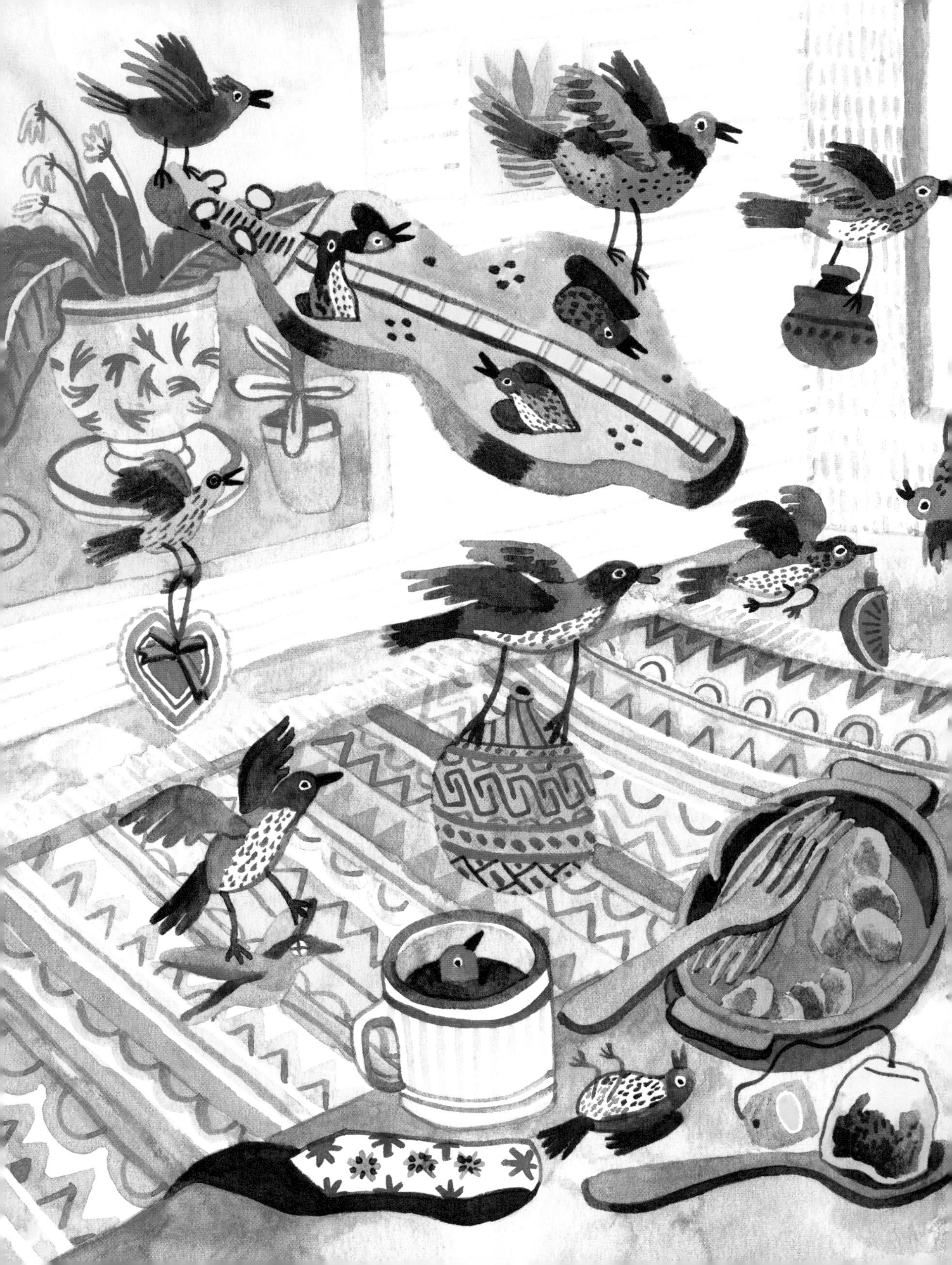

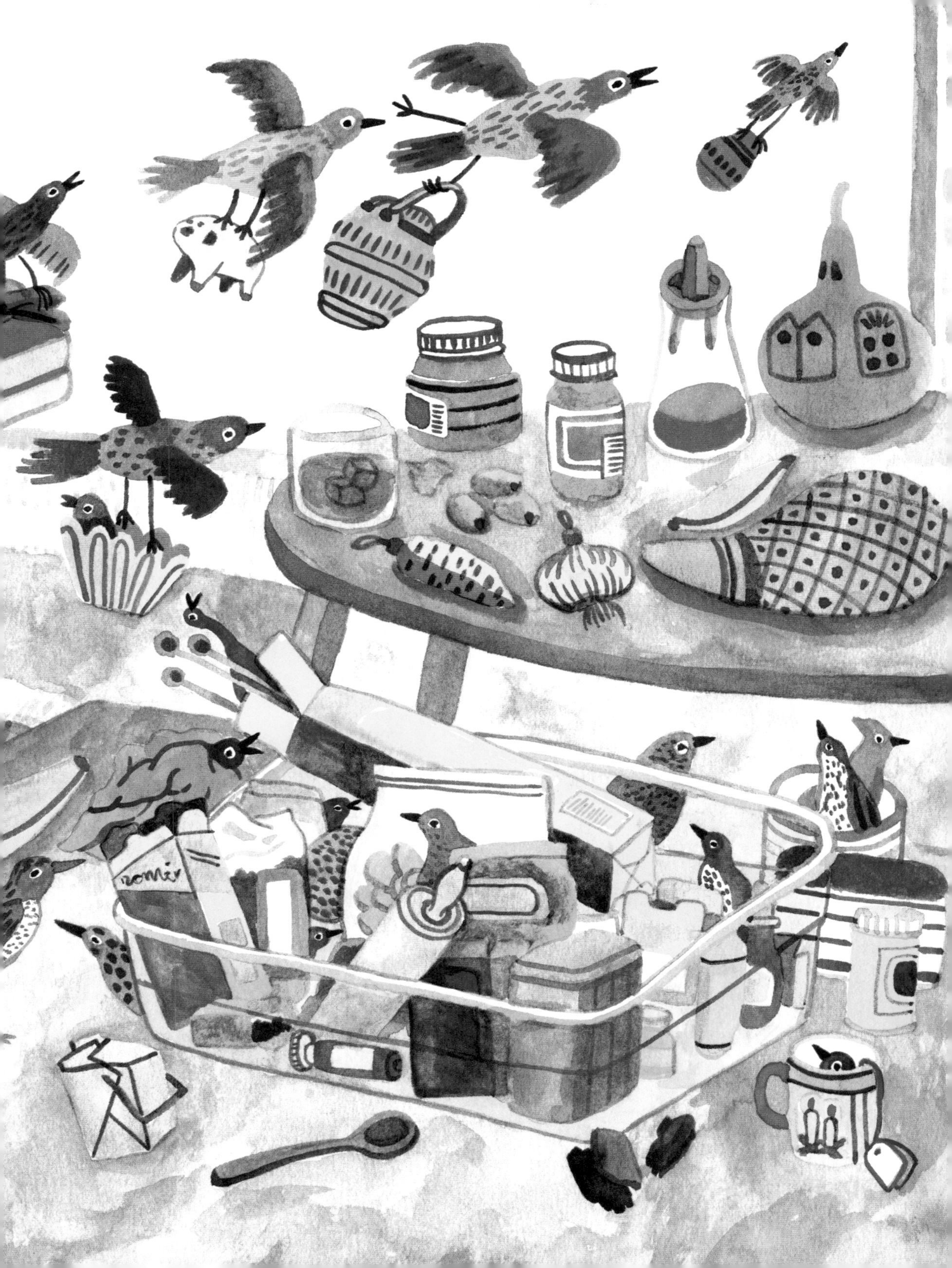

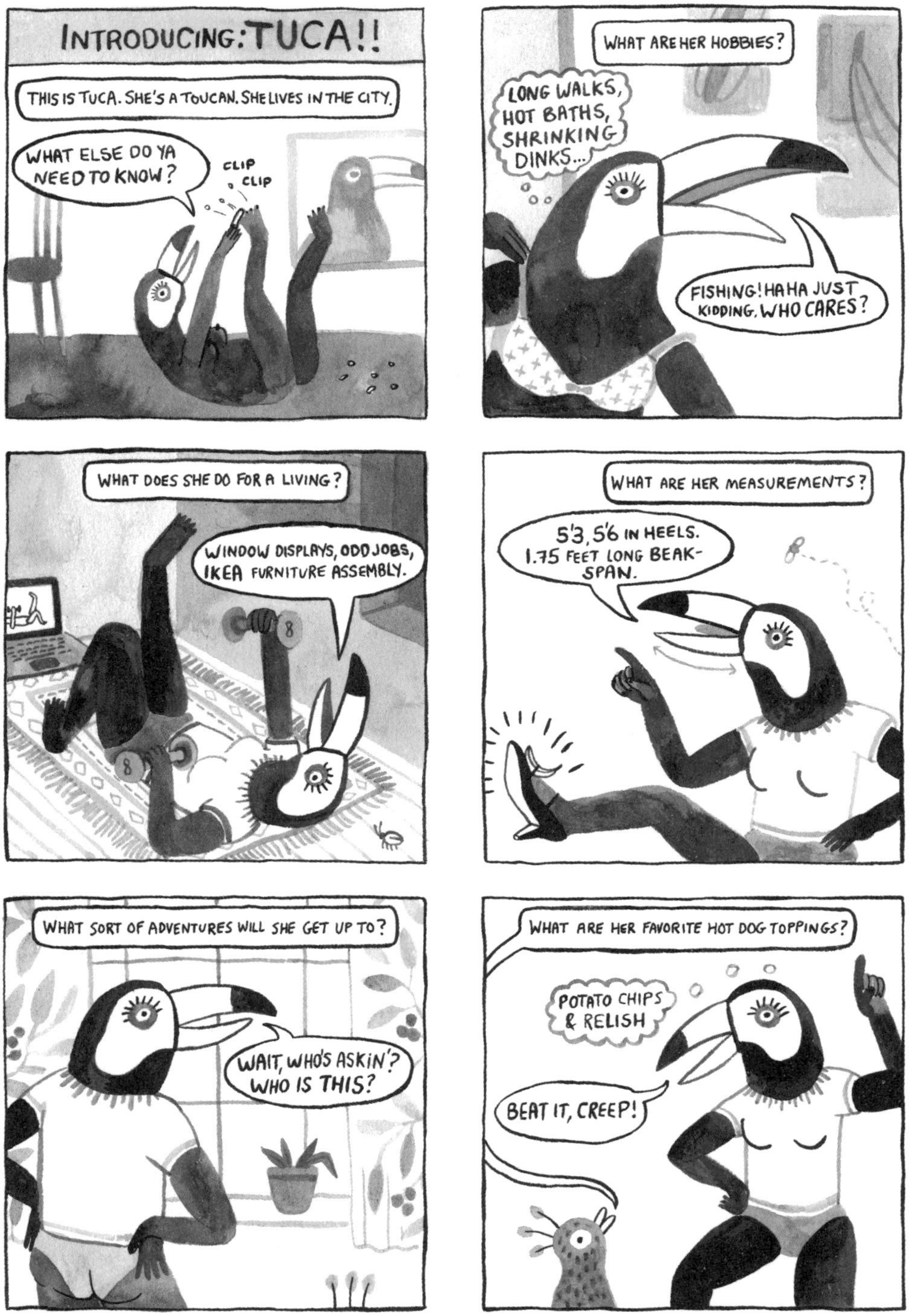
INTRODUCING: TUCA!!
THIS IS TUCA. SHE'S A TOUCAN. SHE LIVES IN THE CITY.
WHAT ELSE DO YA NEED TO KNOW?
CLIP CLIP
WHAT ARE HER HOBBIES?
LONG WALKS, HOT BATHS, SHRINKING DINKS...
FISHING! HAHA JUST KIDDING. WHO CARES?
WHAT DOES SHE DO FOR A LIVING?
WINDOW DISPLAYS, ODD JOBS, IKEA FURNITURE ASSEMBLY.
8
8
WHAT ARE HER MEASUREMENTS?
5'3, 5'6 IN HEELS. 1.75 FEET LONG BEAK-SPAN.
WHAT SORT OF ADVENTURES WILL SHE GET UP TO?
WAIT, WHO'S ASKIN'? WHO IS THIS?
WHAT ARE HER FAVORITE HOT DOG TOPPINGS?
POTATO CHIPS & RELISH
BEAT IT, CREEP!

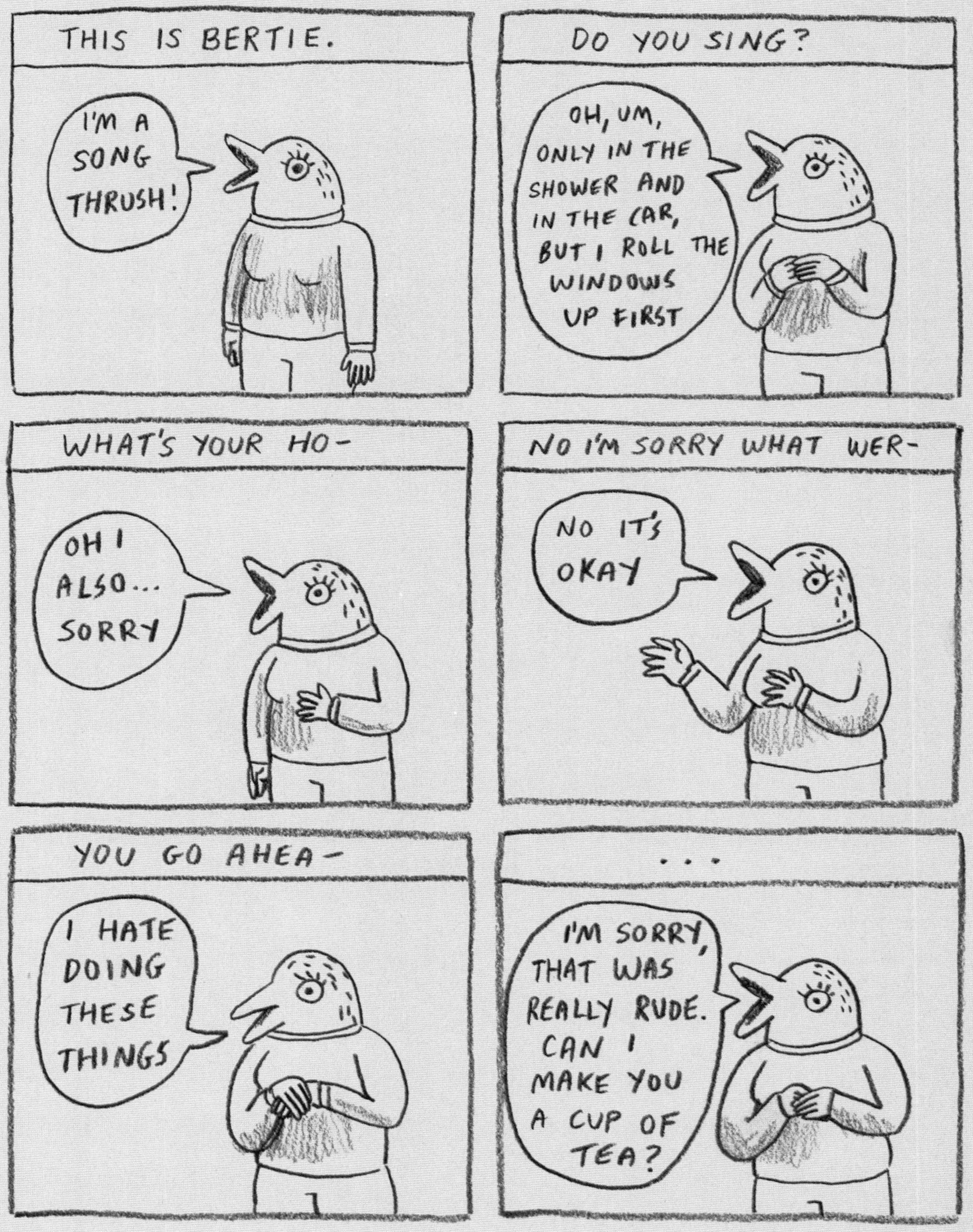
THIS IS BERTIE.
I'M A SONG THRUSH!
DO YOU SING?
OH, UM, ONLY IN THE SHOWER AND IN THE CAR, BUT I ROLL THE WINDOWS UP FIRST
WHAT'S YOUR HO-
OH I ALSO... SORRY
NO I'M SORRY WHAT WER-
NO IT'S OKAY
YOU GO AHEA-
I HATE DOING THESE THINGS
. . .
I'M SORRY, THAT WAS REALLY RUDE. CAN I MAKE YOU A CUP OF TEA?

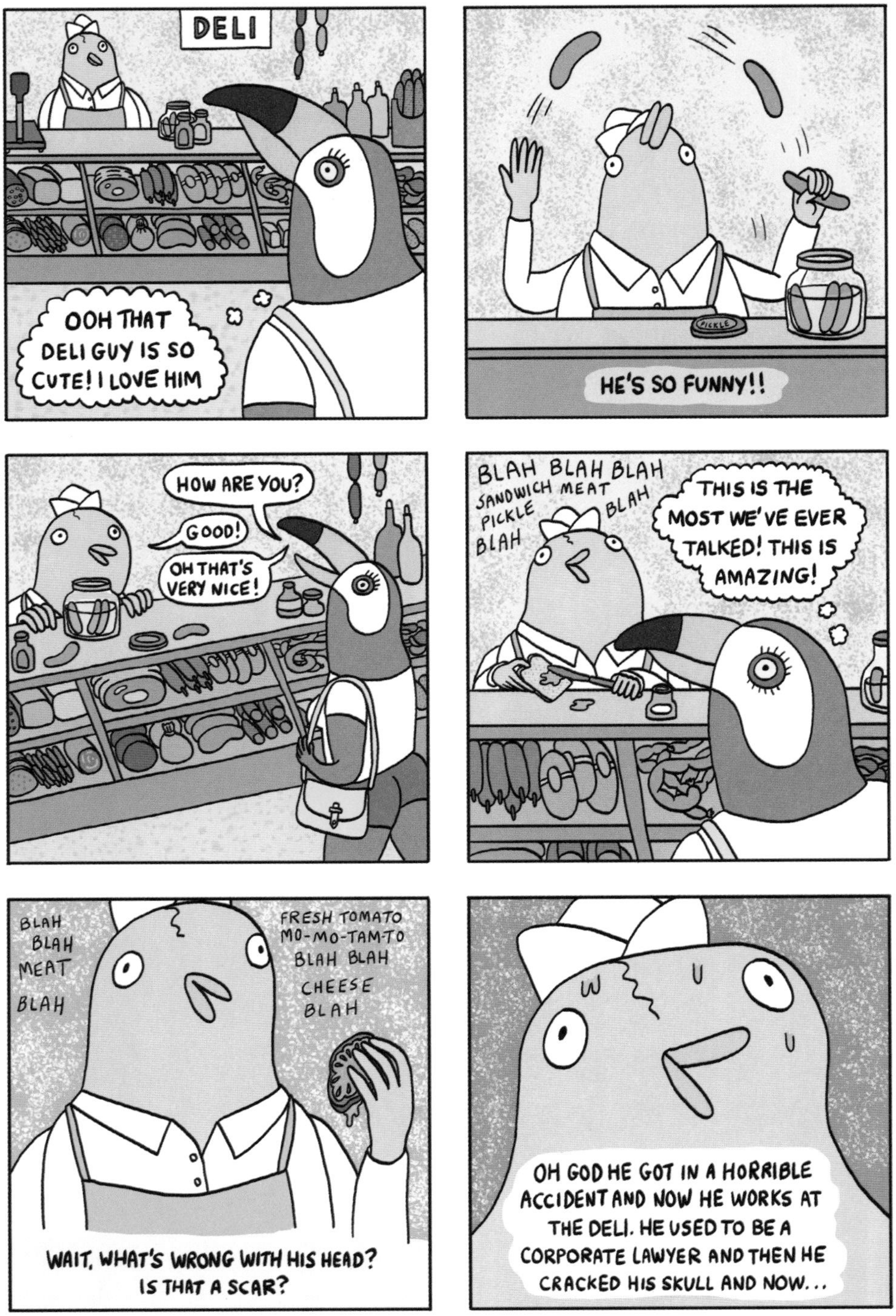
DELI
OOH THAT DELI GUY IS SO CUTE! I LOVE HIM
PICKLE
HE'S SO FUNNY!!
HOW ARE YOU?
GOOD!
OH THAT'S VERY NICE!
BLAH BLAH BLAH SANDWICH MEAT PICKLE BLAH BLAH
THIS IS THE MOST WE'VE EVER TALKED! THIS IS AMAZING!
BLAH BLAH MEAT BLAH
FRESH TOMATO MO-MO-TAM-TO BLAH BLAH CHEESE BLAH
WAIT, WHAT'S WRONG WITH HIS HEAD? IS THAT A SCAR?
OH GOD HE GOT IN A HORRIBLE ACCIDENT AND NOW HE WORKS AT THE DELI. HE USED TO BE A CORPORATE LAWYER AND THEN HE CRACKED HIS SKULL AND NOW...

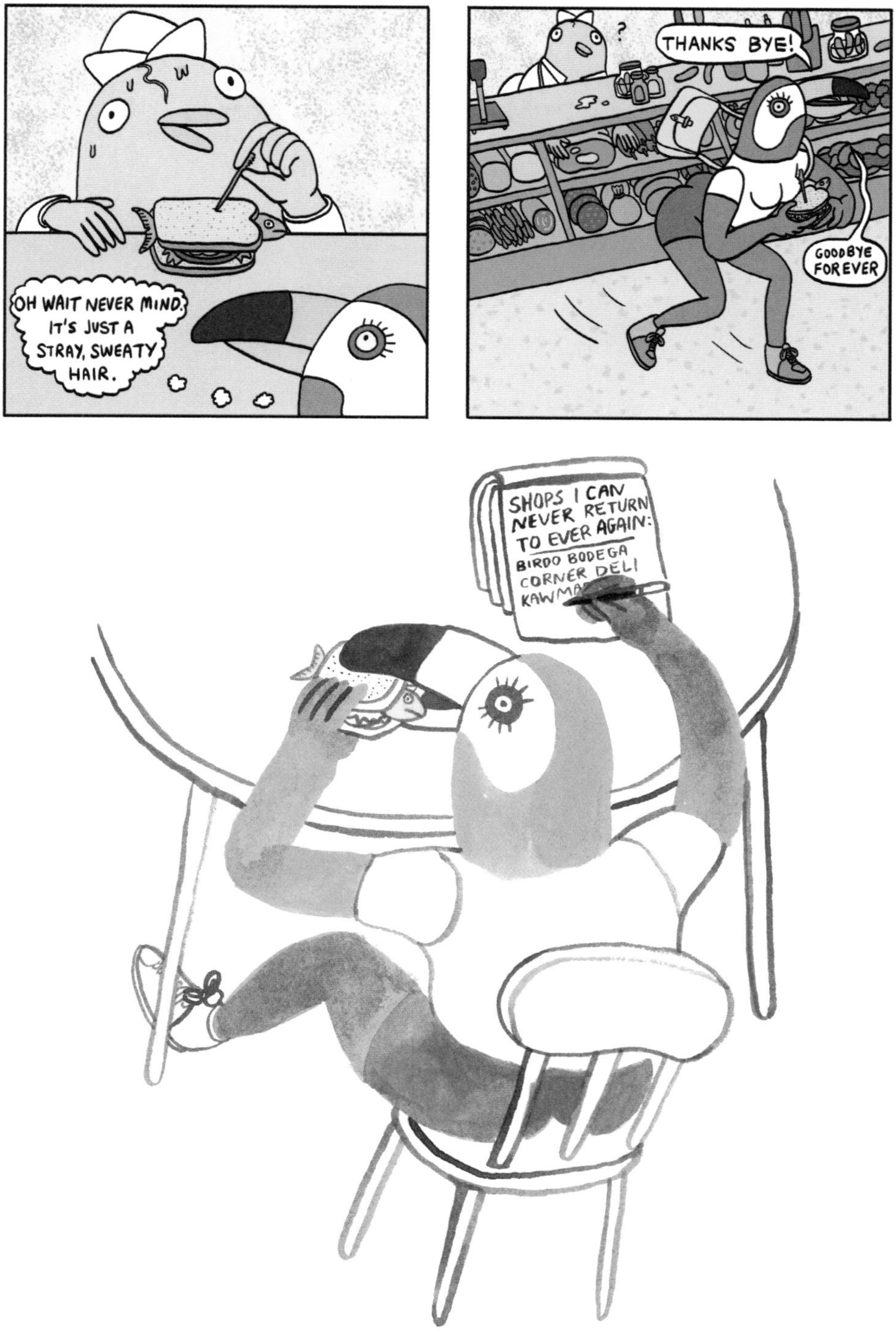
OH WAIT NEVER MIND. IT'S JUST A STRAY, SWEATY HAIR.
THANKS BYE!
GOODBYE FOREVER
SHOPS I CAN NEVER RETURN TO EVER AGAIN:
BIRDO BODEGA
CORNER DELI
KAWMA

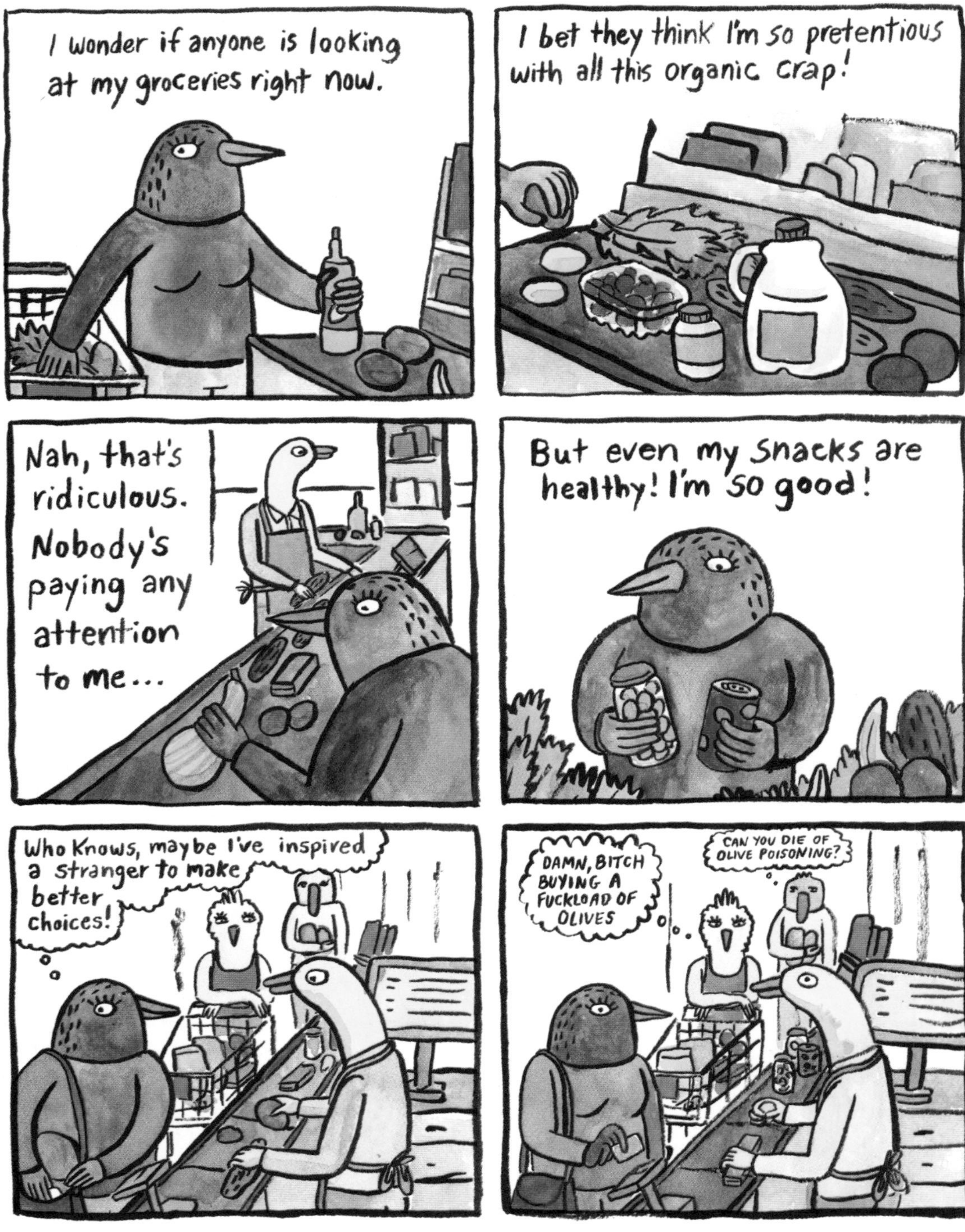
I wonder if anyone is looking at my groceries right now.
I bet they think I'm so pretentious with all this organic crap!
Nah, that's ridiculous. Nobody's paying any attention to me...
But even my snacks are healthy! I'm so good!
Who knows, maybe I've inspired a stranger to make better choices!
DAMN, BITCH BUYING A FUCKLOAD OF OLIVES
CAN YOU DIE OF OLIVE POISONING?

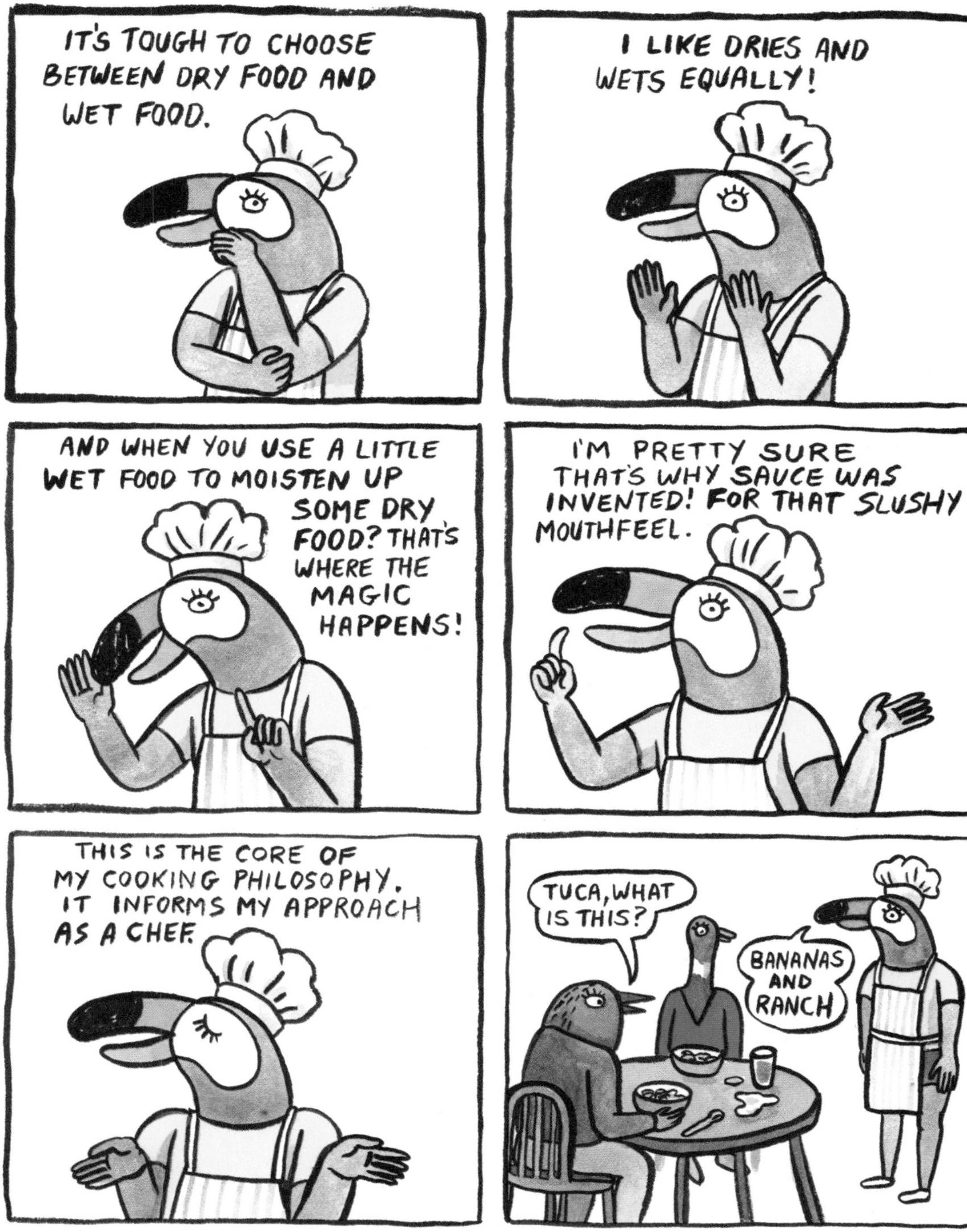
IT'S TOUGH TO CHOOSE BETWEEN DRY FOOD AND WET FOOD.
I LIKE DRIES AND WETS EQUALLY!
AND WHEN YOU USE A LITTLE WET FOOD TO MOISTEN UP SOME DRY FOOD? THAT'S WHERE THE MAGIC HAPPENS!
I'M PRETTY SURE THAT'S WHY SAUCE WAS INVENTED! FOR THAT SLUSHY MOUTHFEEL.
THIS IS THE CORE OF MY COOKING PHILOSOPHY. IT INFORMS MY APPROACH AS A CHEF.
TUCA, WHAT IS THIS?
BANANAS AND RANCH

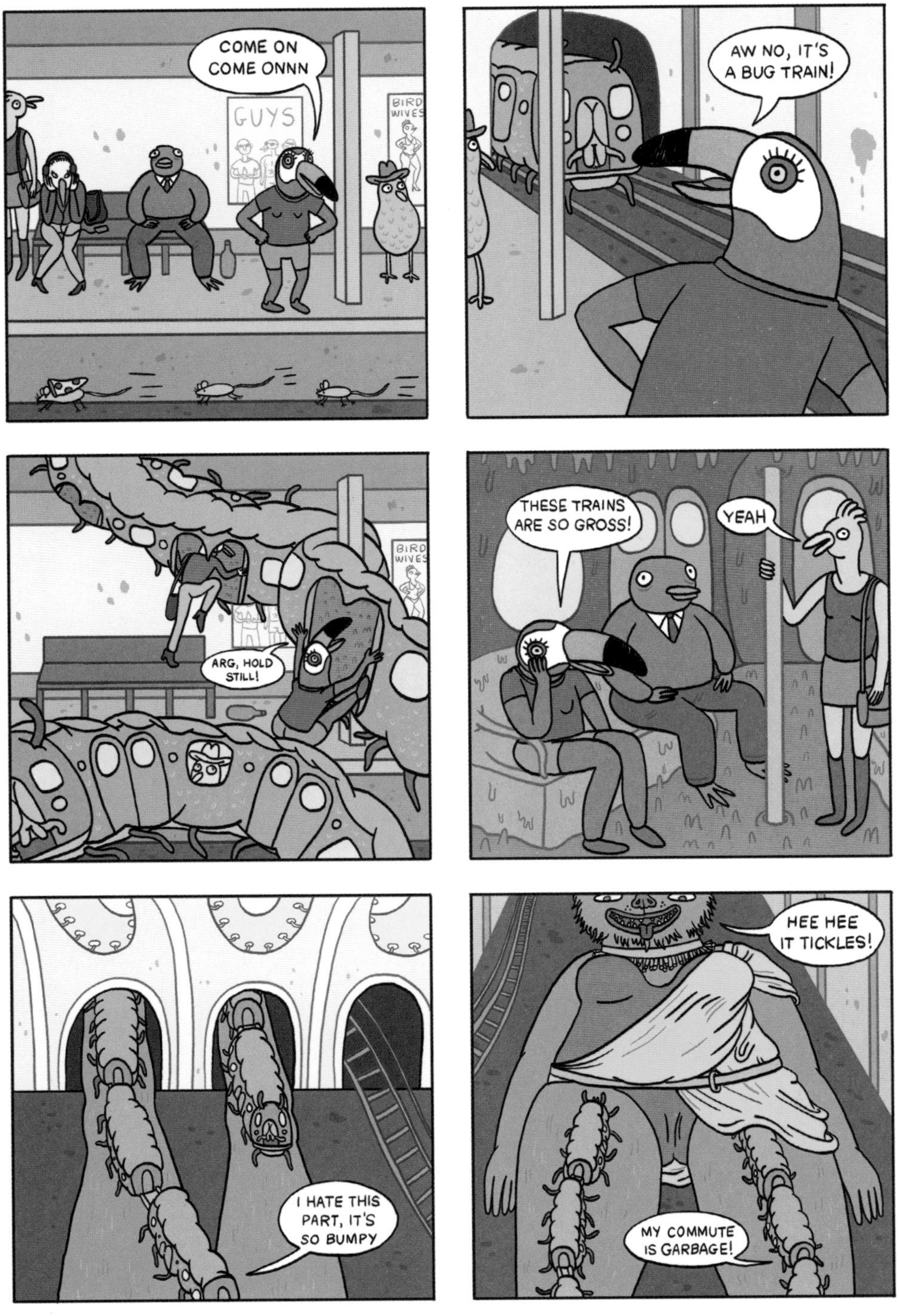
GUYS
BIRD WIVES
COME ON COME ONNN
AW NO, IT'S A BUG TRAIN!
BIRD WIVES
ARG, HOLD STILL!
THESE TRAINS ARE SO GROSS!
YEAH
I HATE THIS PART, IT'S SO BUMPY
HEE HEE IT TICKLES!
MY COMMUTE IS GARBAGE!

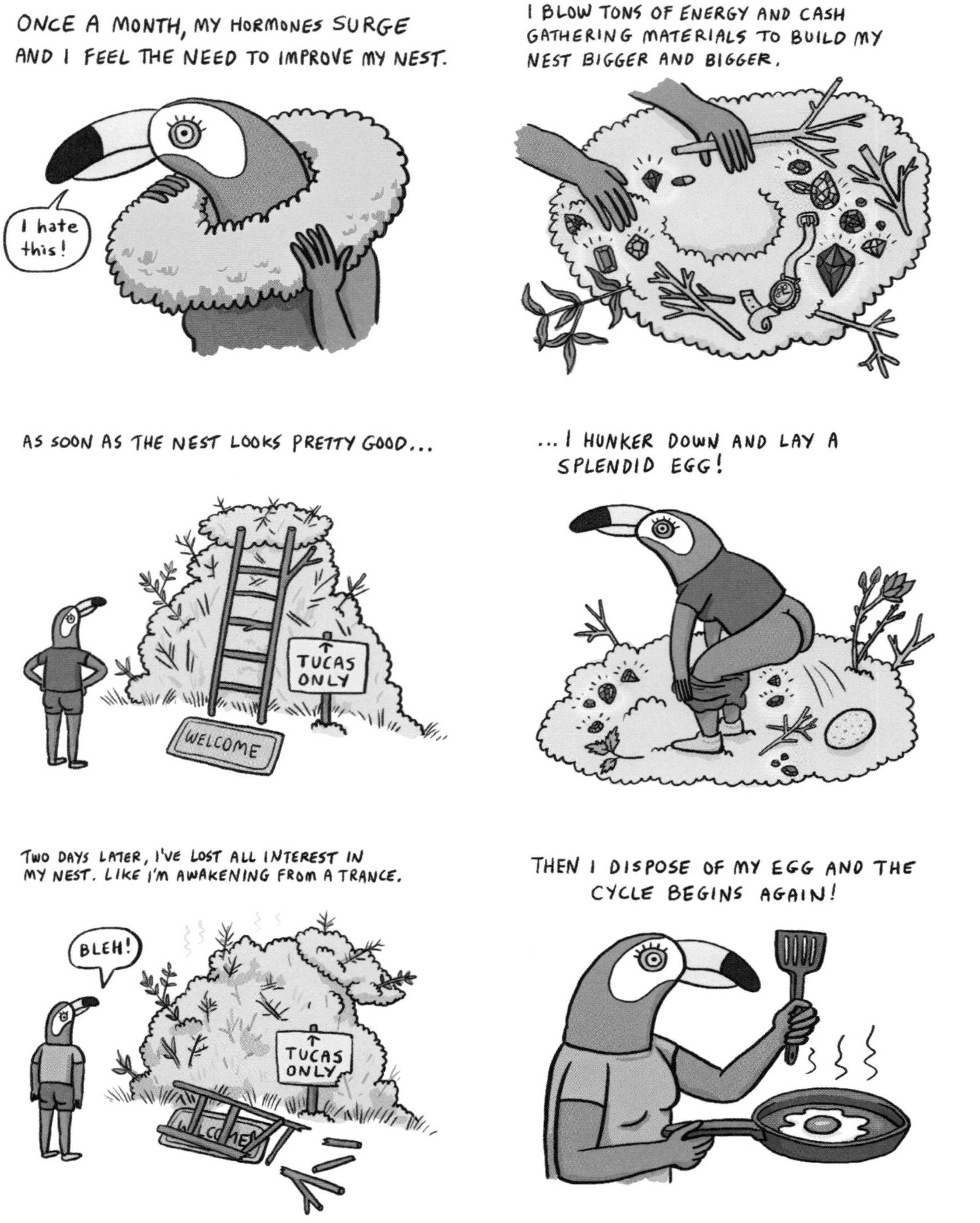
ONCE A MONTH, MY HORMONES SURGE AND I FEEL THE NEED TO IMPROVE MY NEST.
I hate this!
I BLOW TONS OF ENERGY AND CASH GATHERING MATERIALS TO BUILD MY NEST BIGGER AND BIGGER.
AS SOON AS THE NEST LOOKS PRETTY GOOD...
TUCAS ONLY
WELCOME
...I HUNKER DOWN AND LAY A SPLENDID EGG!
TWO DAYS LATER, I'VE LOST ALL INTEREST IN MY NEST. LIKE I'M AWAKENING FROM A TRANCE.
BLEH!
TUCAS ONLY
THEN I DISPOSE OF MY EGG AND THE CYCLE BEGINS AGAIN!

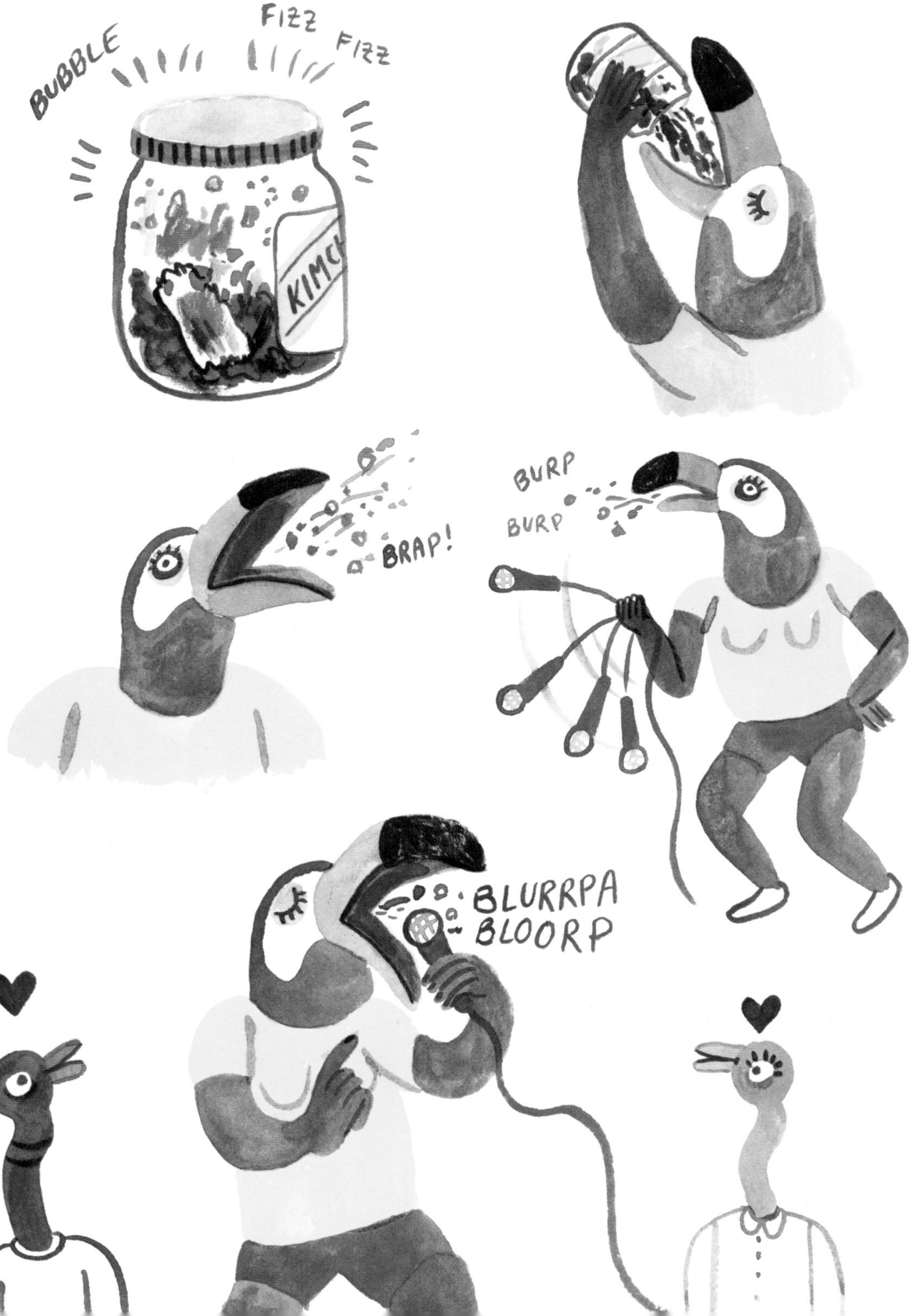
BUBBLE
FIZZ
FIZZ
KIMCH
BRAP!
BURP
BURP
BLURRPA
BLOORP

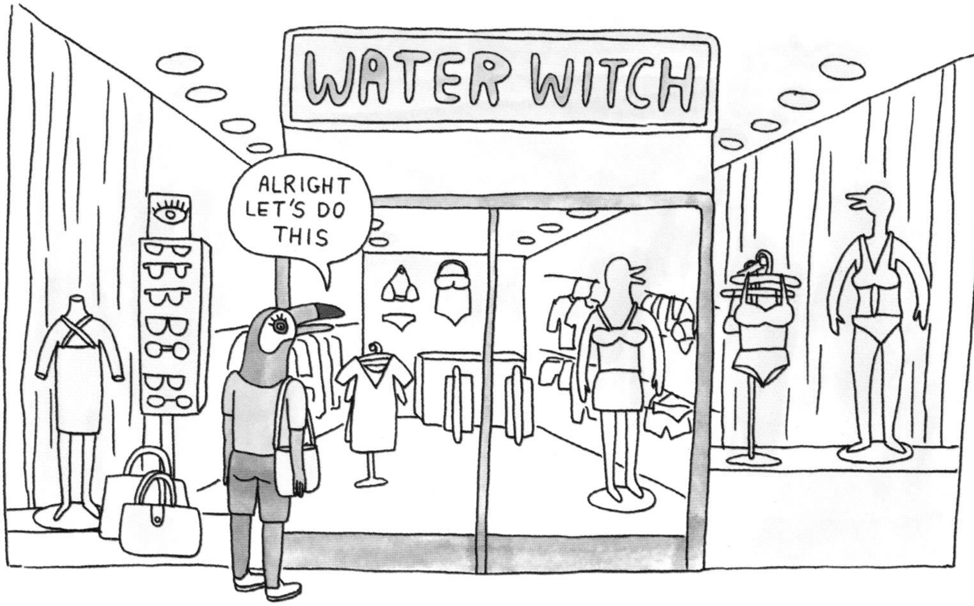
WATER WITCH
ALRIGHT LET'S DO THIS

FITTING ROOM MONTAGE

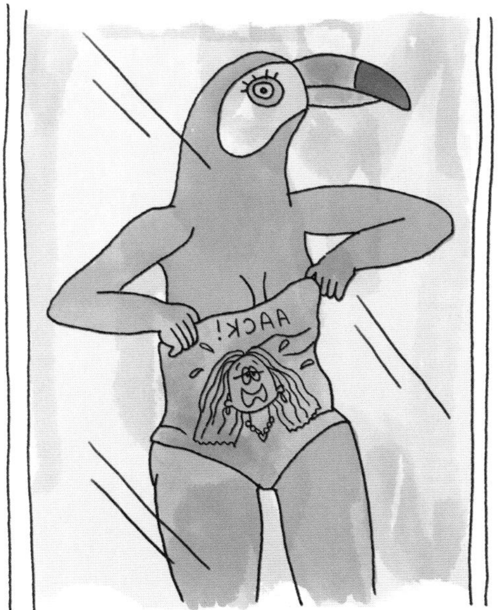

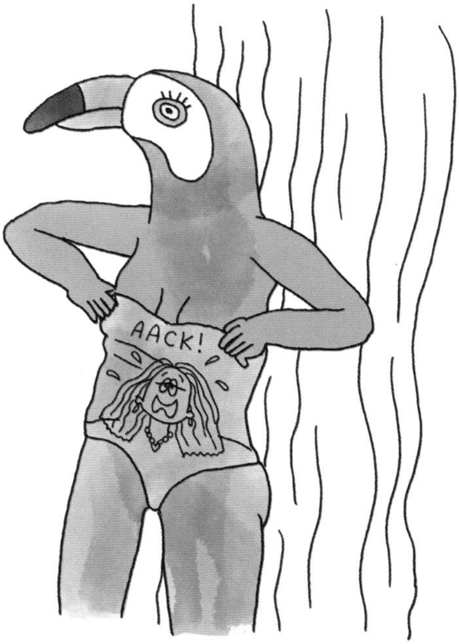
AACK!

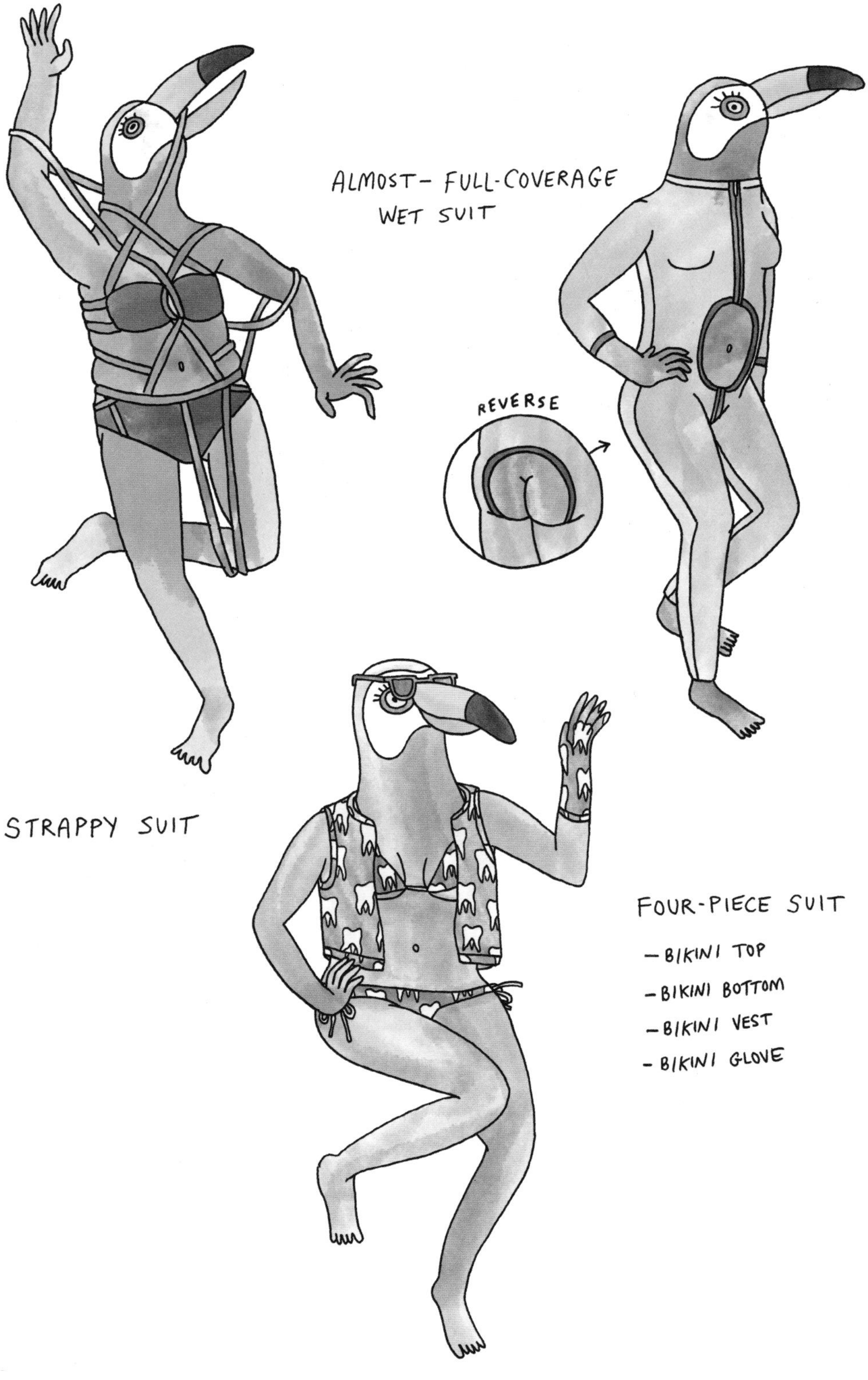
ALMOST- FULL-COVERAGE WET SUIT
REVERSE
STRAPPY SUIT
FOUR-PIECE SUIT
- BIKINI TOP
- BIKINI BOTTOM
- BIKINI VEST
- BIKINI GLOVE

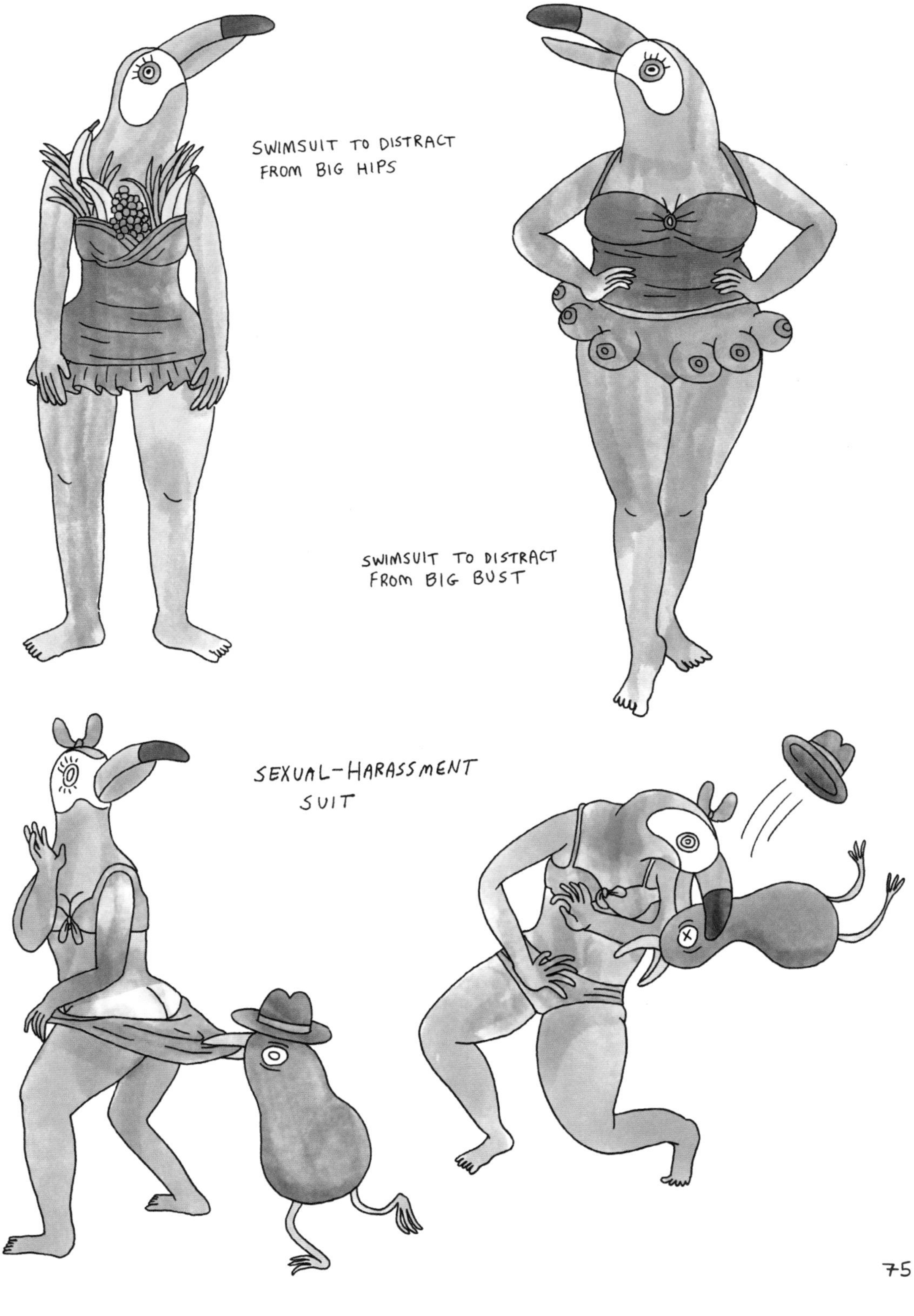
SWIMSUIT TO DISTRACT FROM BIG HIPS
SWIMSUIT TO DISTRACT FROM BIG BUST
SEXUAL-HARASSMENT SUIT

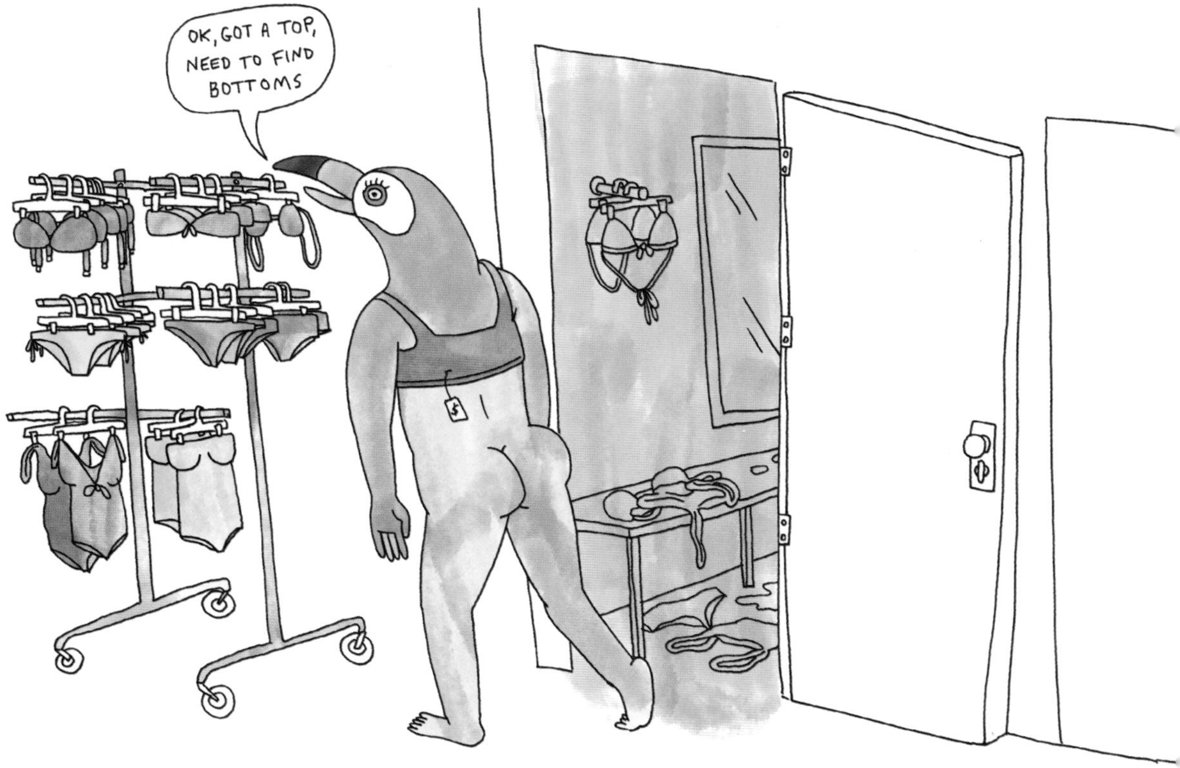
OK, GOT A TOP, NEED TO FIND BOTTOMS

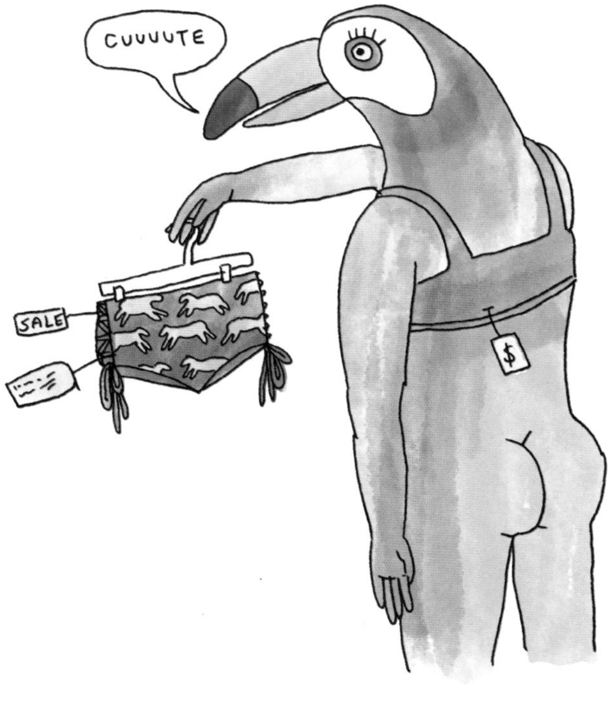
CUUUUTE
SALE
$

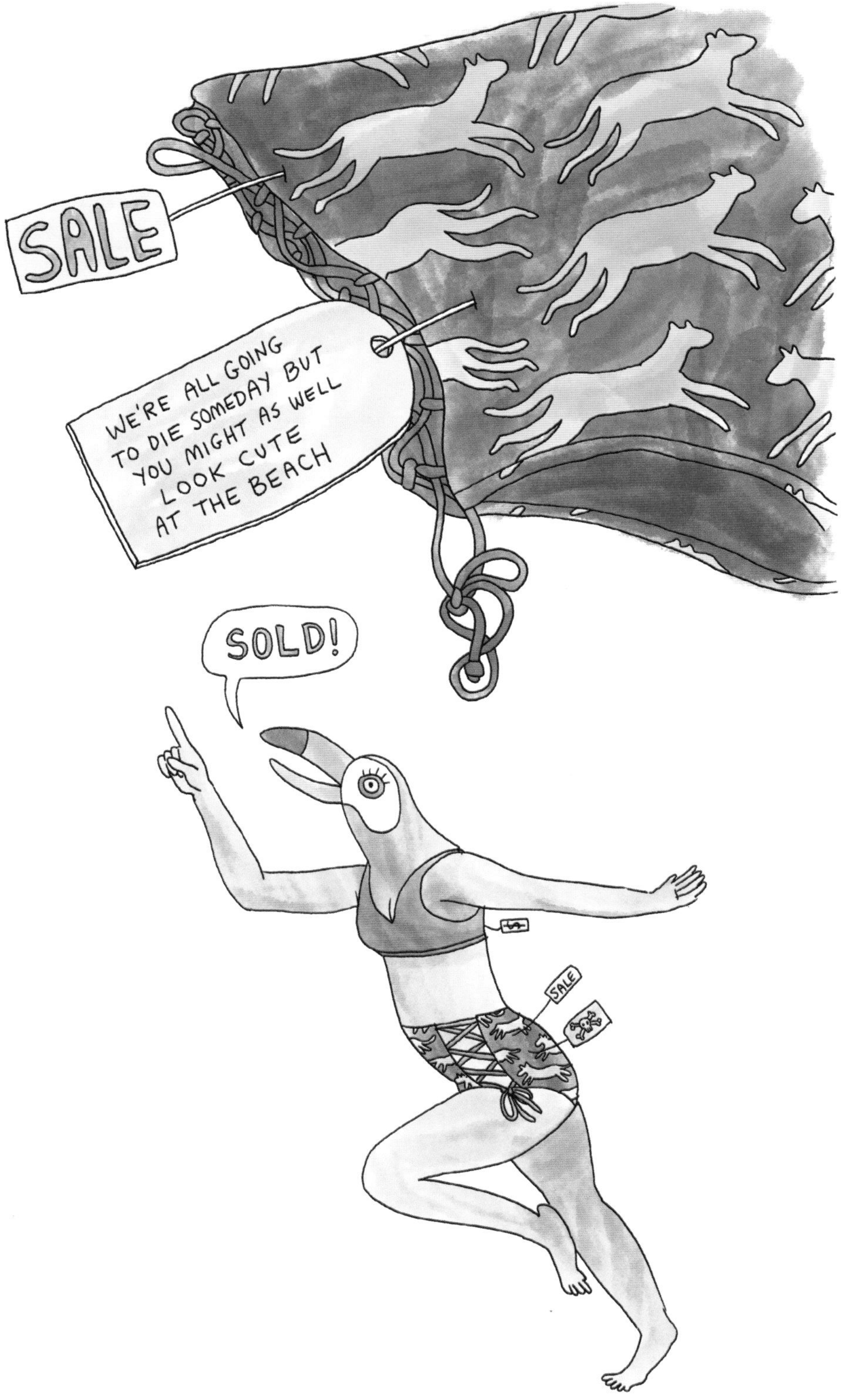
SALE
WE'RE ALL GOING TO DIE SOMEDAY BUT YOU MIGHT AS WELL LOOK CUTE AT THE BEACH
SOLD!
SALE

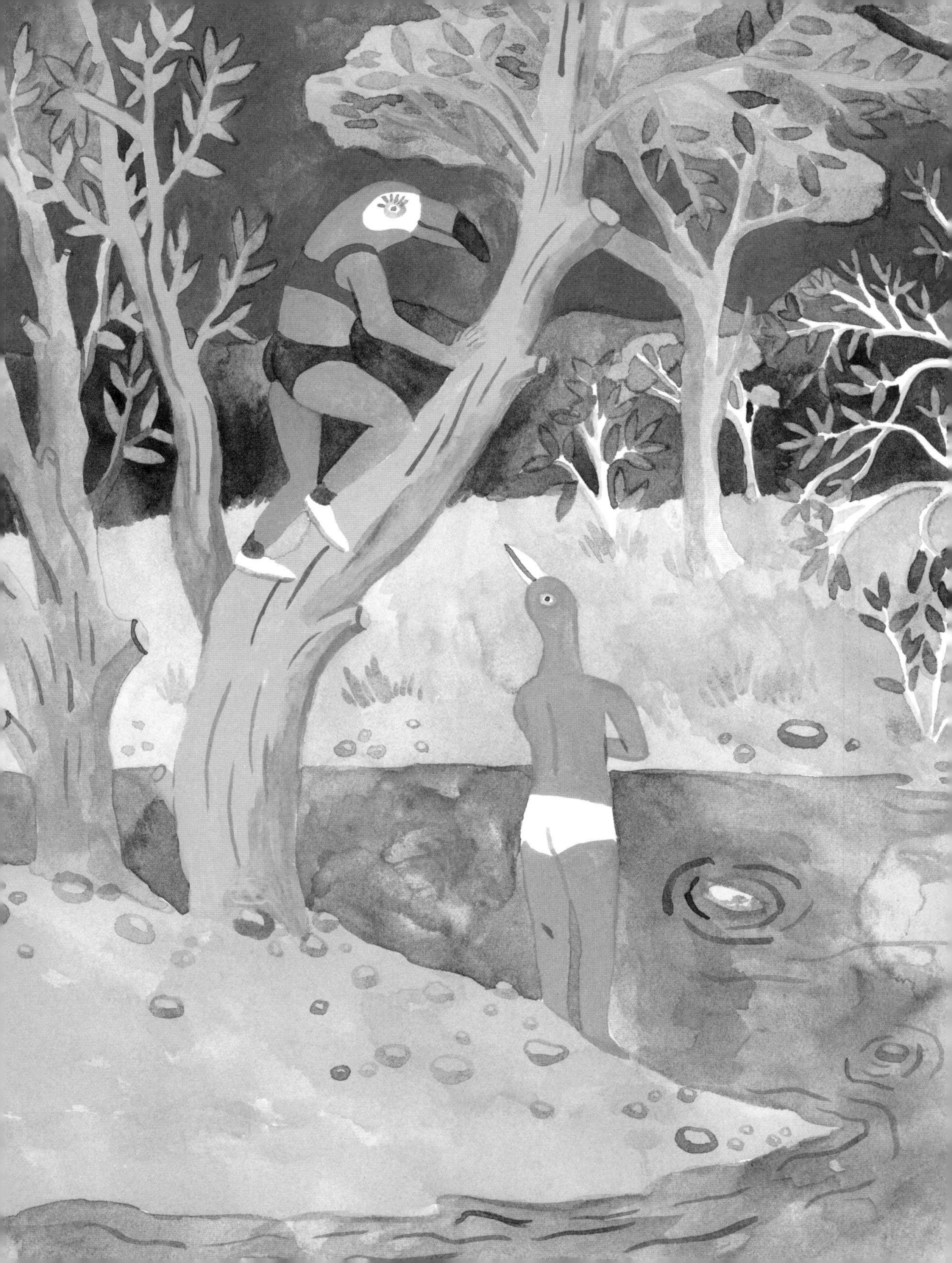

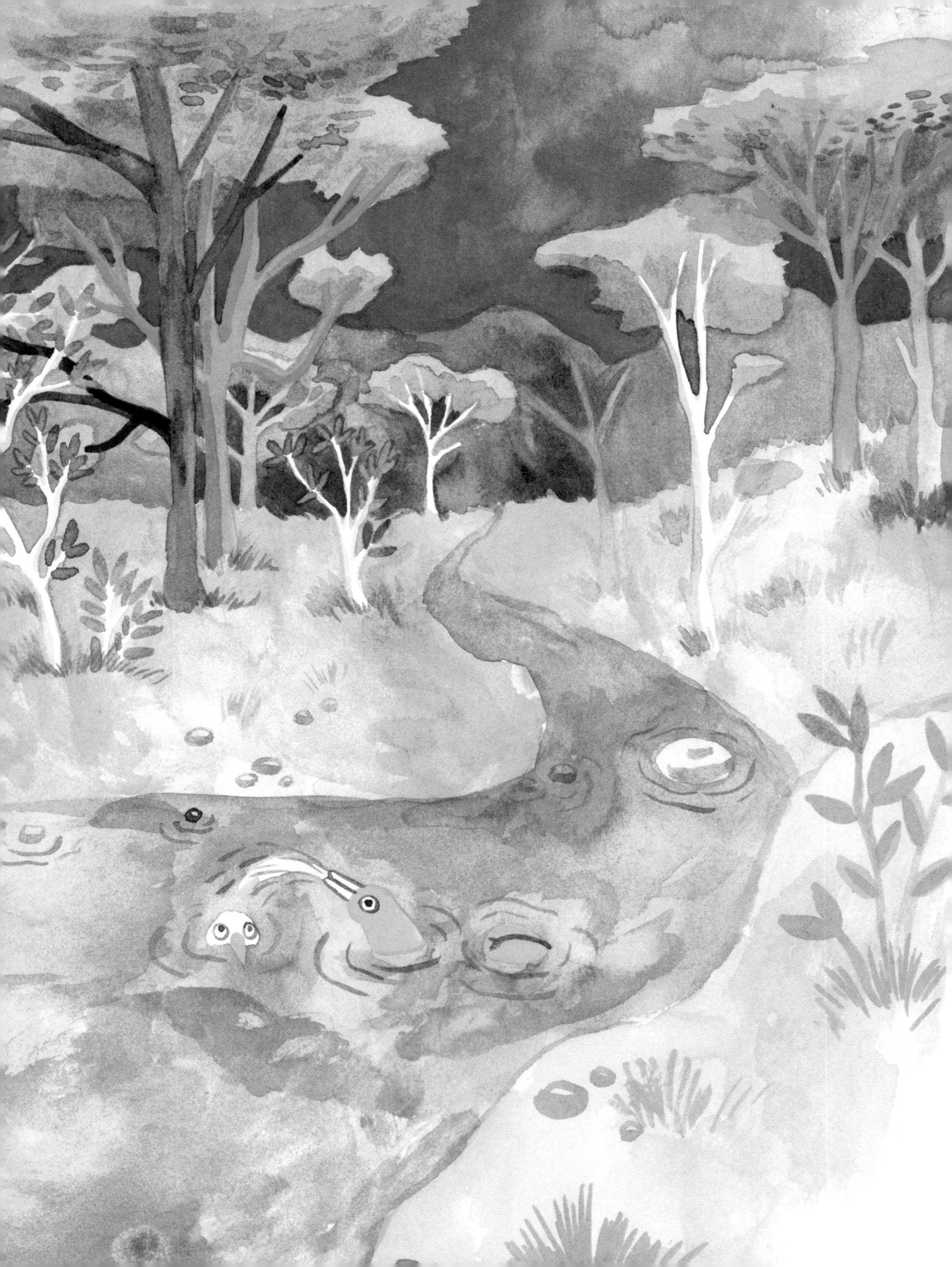

PLANTING

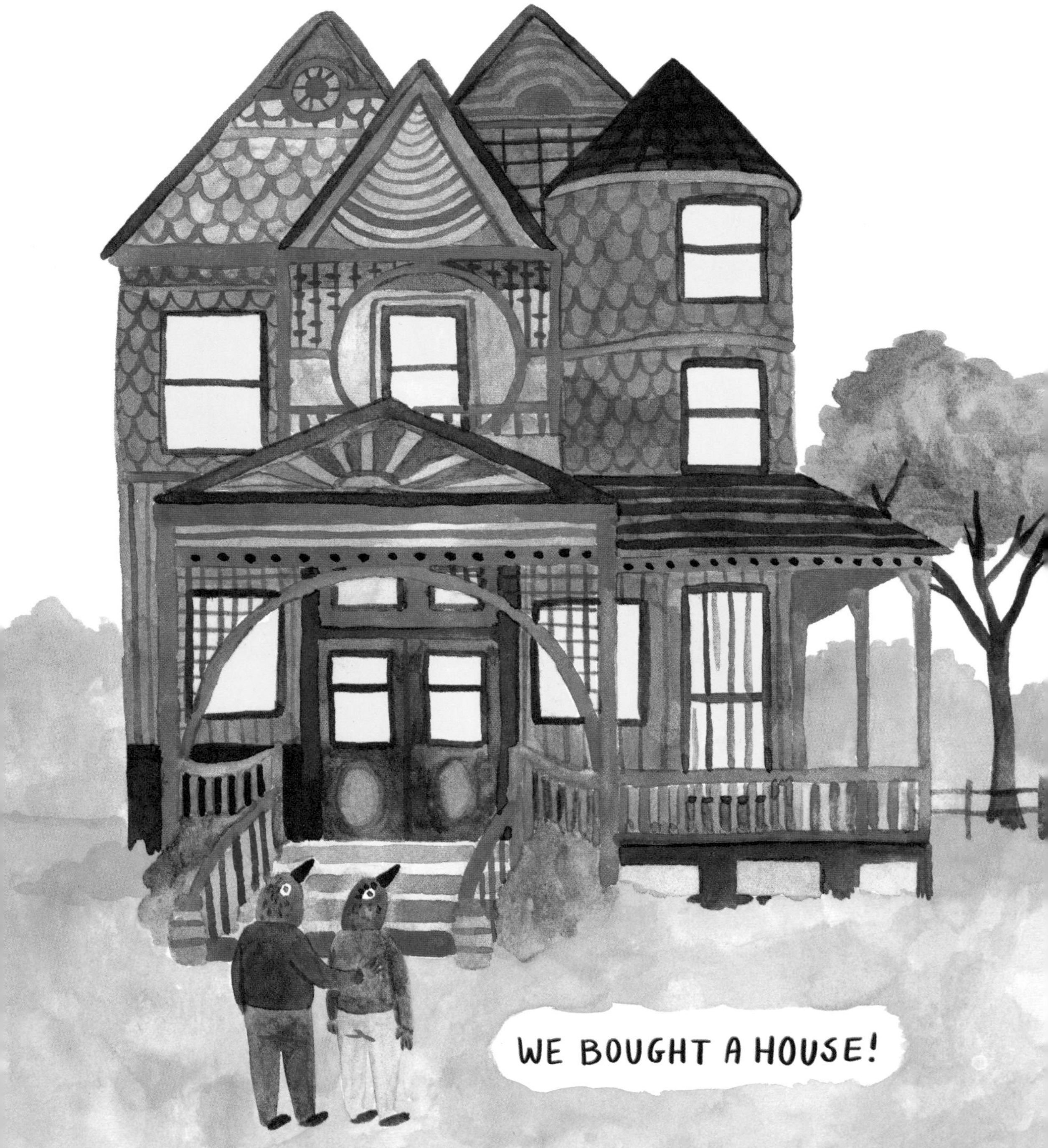
WE BOUGHT A HOUSE!

IT HAD ALMOST EVERYTHING FROM OUR HOUSE-HUNTING CHECK LIST:

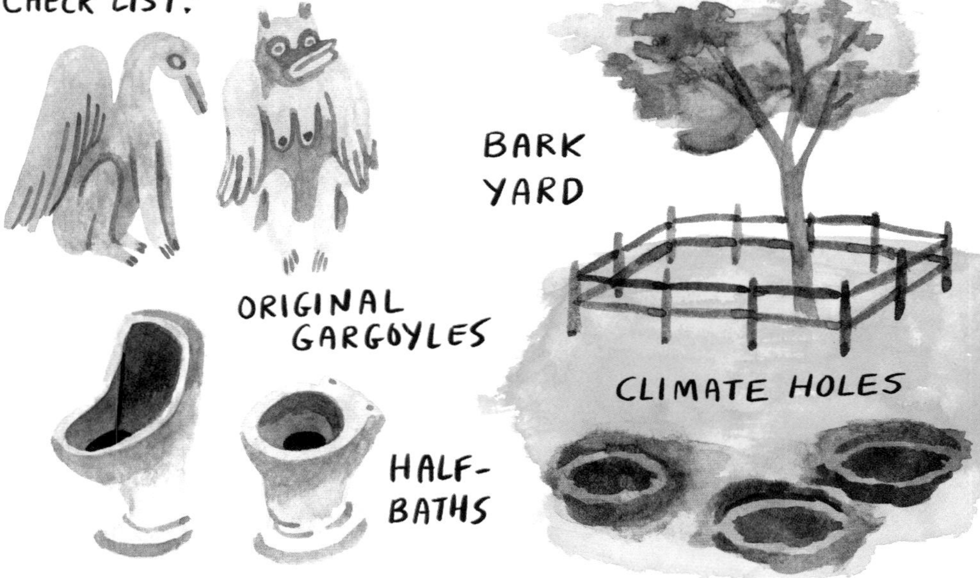
ORIGINAL GARGOYLES
BARK YARD
CLIMATE HOLES
HALF-BATHS

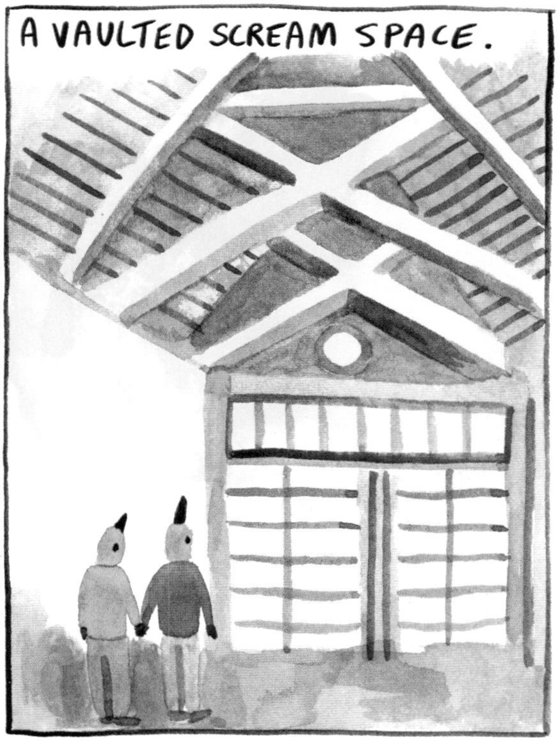
A VAULTED SCREAM SPACE.

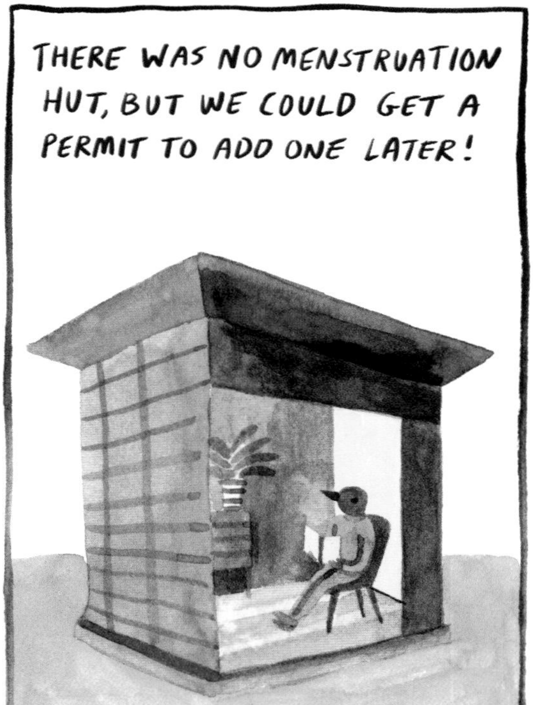
THERE WAS NO MENSTRUATION HUT, BUT WE COULD GET A PERMIT TO ADD ONE LATER!

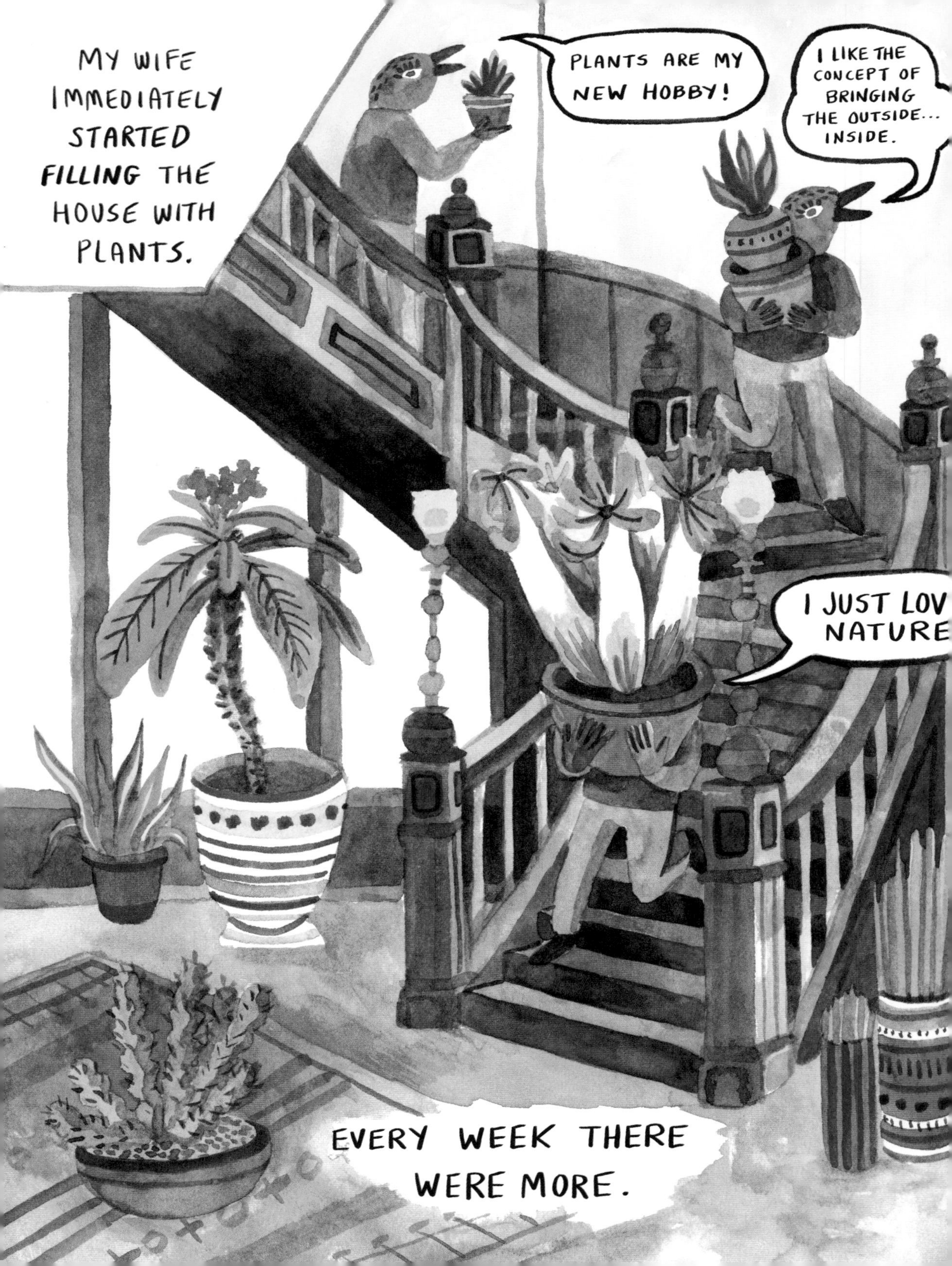
MY WIFE IMMEDIATELY STARTED **FILLING** THE HOUSE WITH PLANTS.
PLANTS ARE MY NEW HOBBY!
I LIKE THE CONCEPT OF BRINGING THE OUTSIDE... INSIDE.
I JUST LOV NATURE
EVERY WEEK THERE WERE MORE.

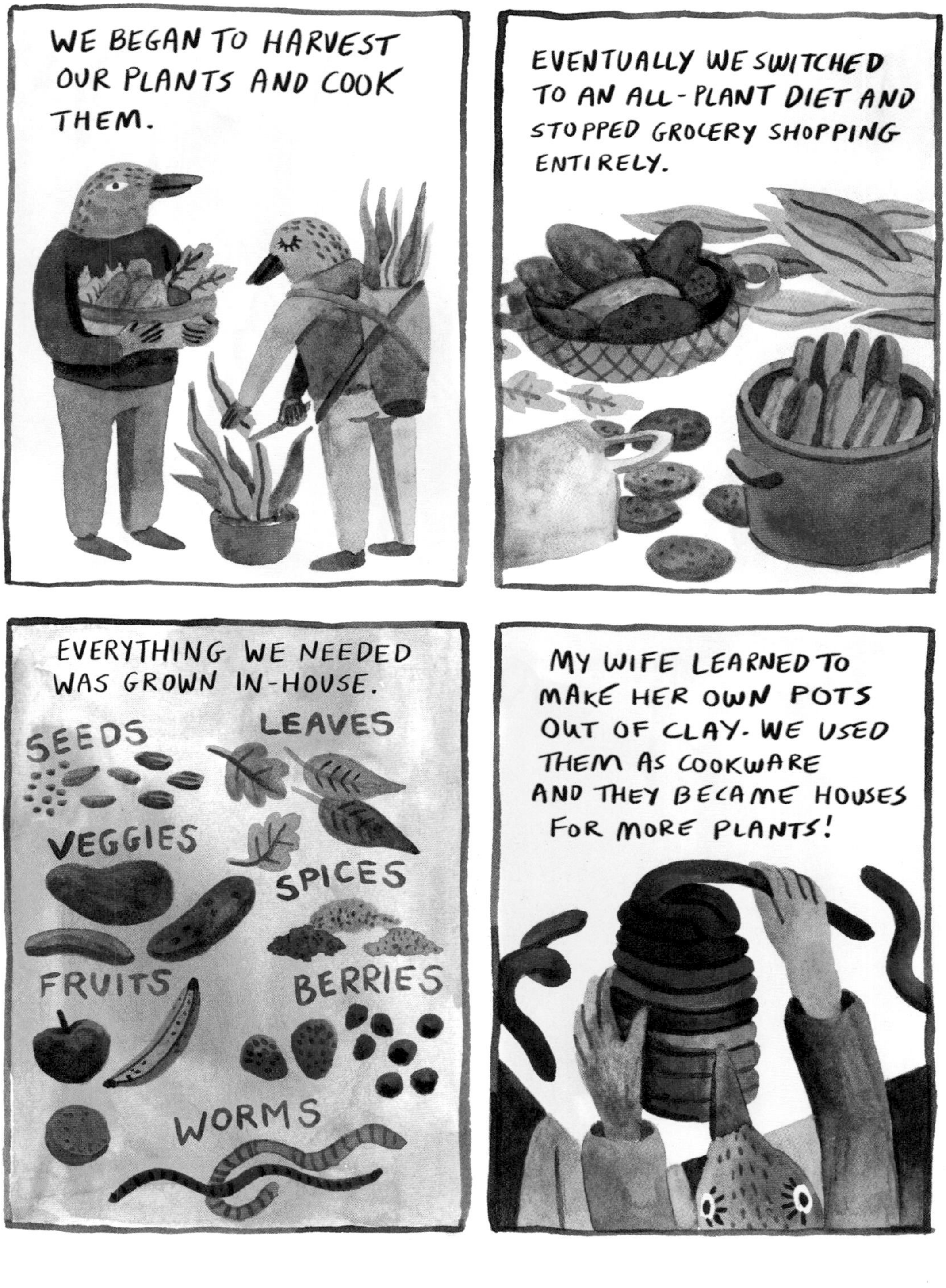
WE BEGAN TO HARVEST OUR PLANTS AND COOK THEM.
EVENTUALLY WE SWITCHED TO AN ALL-PLANT DIET AND STOPPED GROCERY SHOPPING ENTIRELY.
EVERYTHING WE NEEDED WAS GROWN IN-HOUSE.
SEEDS
LEAVES
VEGGIES
SPICES
FRUITS
BERRIES
WORMS
MY WIFE LEARNED TO MAKE HER OWN POTS OUT OF CLAY. WE USED THEM AS COOKWARE AND THEY BECAME HOUSES FOR MORE PLANTS!

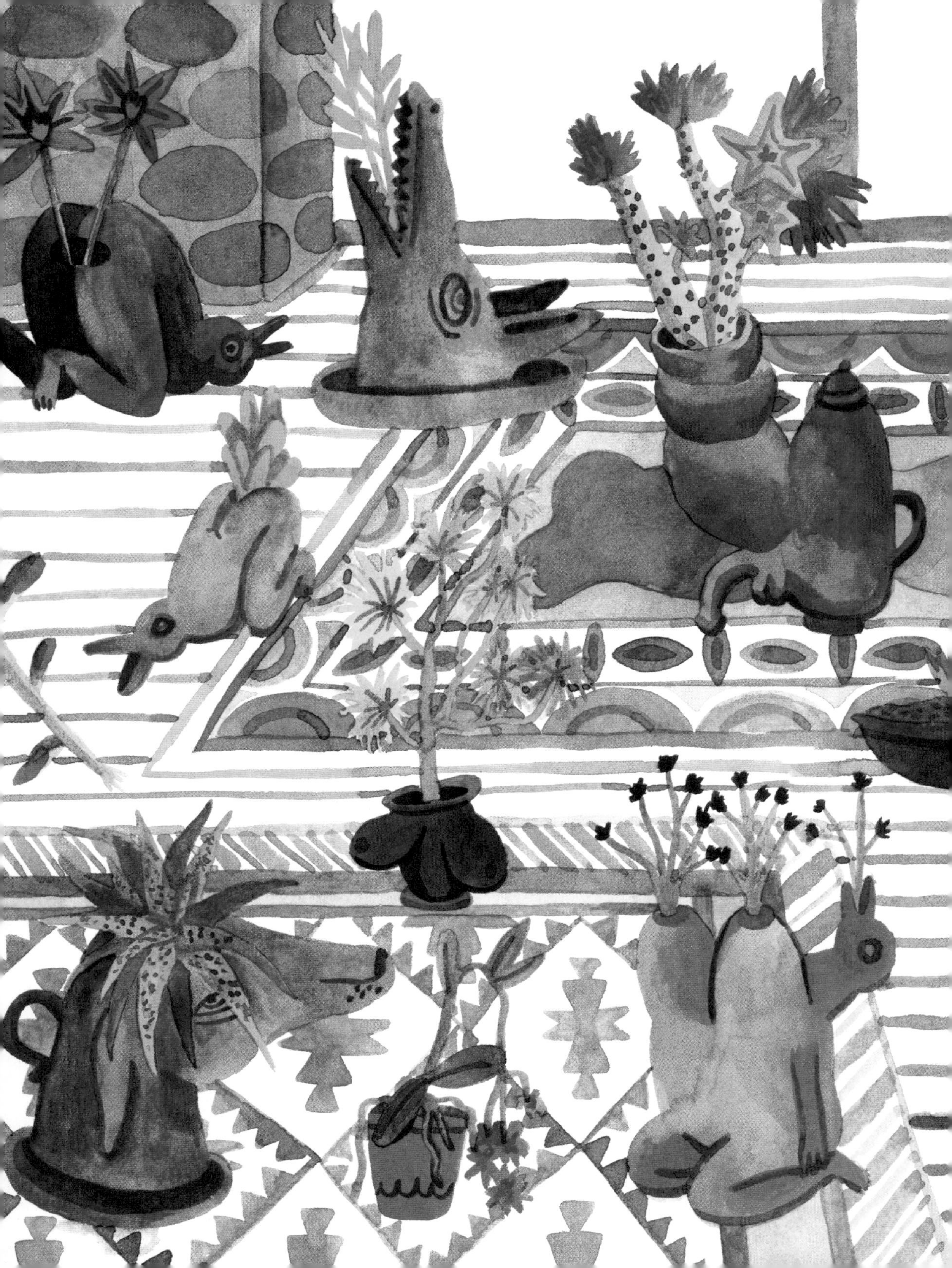

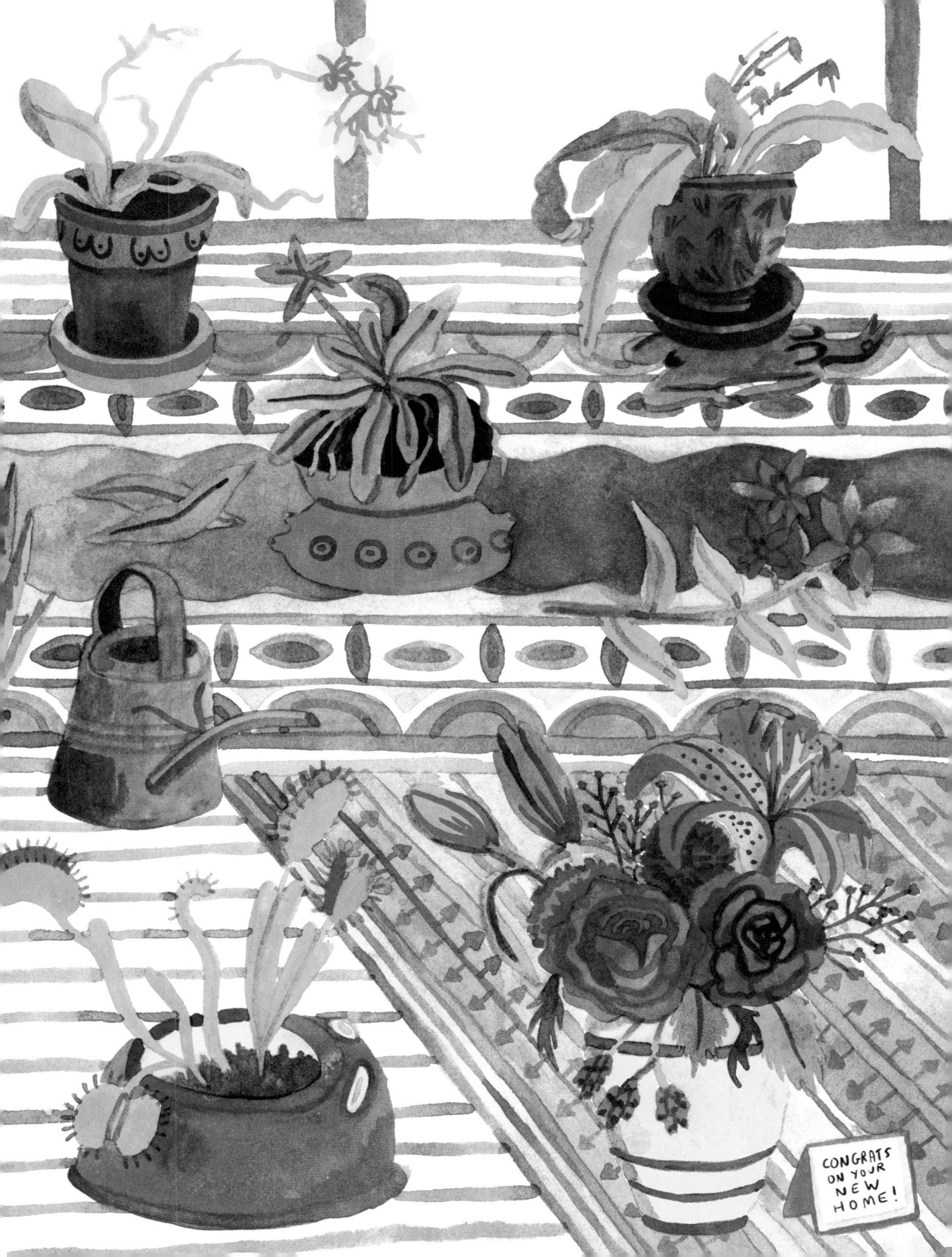
CONGRATS
ON YOUR
NEW
HOME!

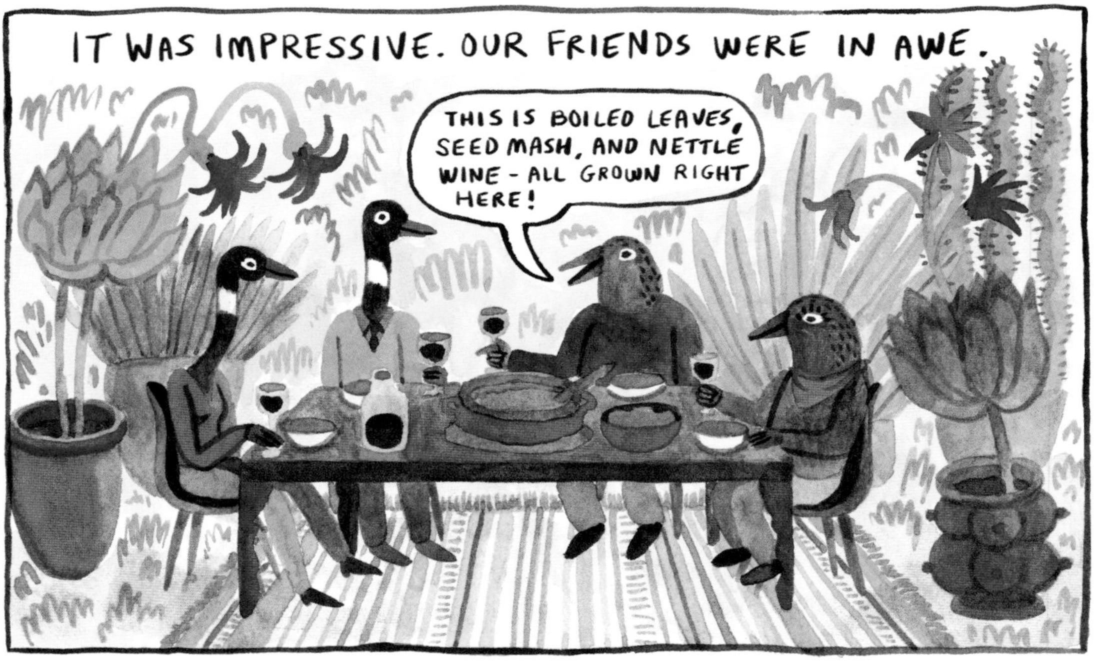
IT WAS IMPRESSIVE. OUR FRIENDS WERE IN AWE.
THIS IS BOILED LEAVES, SEED MASH, AND NETTLE WINE - ALL GROWN RIGHT HERE!

BUT THEY WERE ALSO OVERWHELMED BY OUR LIFESTYLE.

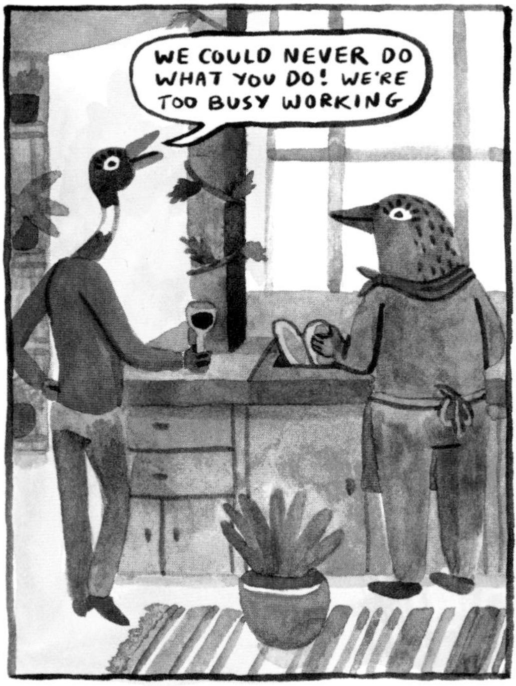
WE COULD NEVER DO WHAT YOU DO! WE'RE TOO BUSY WORKING

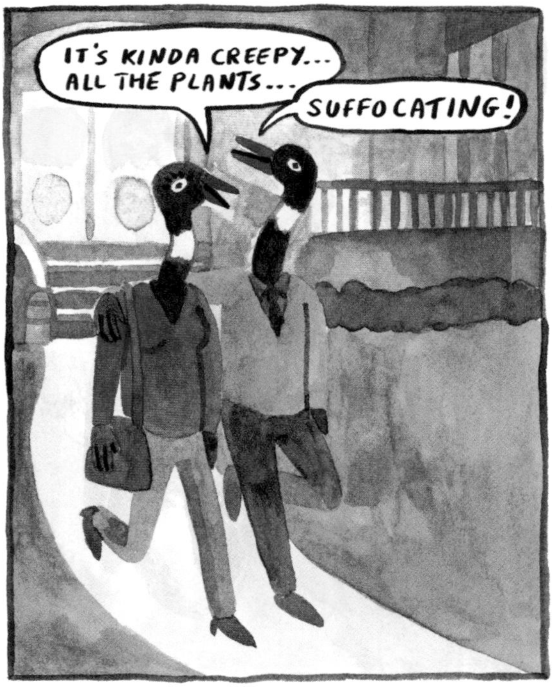
IT'S KINDA CREEPY... ALL THE PLANTS...
SUFFOCATING!

SOME DAYS I'D COME HOME FROM WORK AND HAVE TROUBLE FINDING MY DARLING. SHE DISAPPEARED MORE AND MORE INTO HER HOBBY.

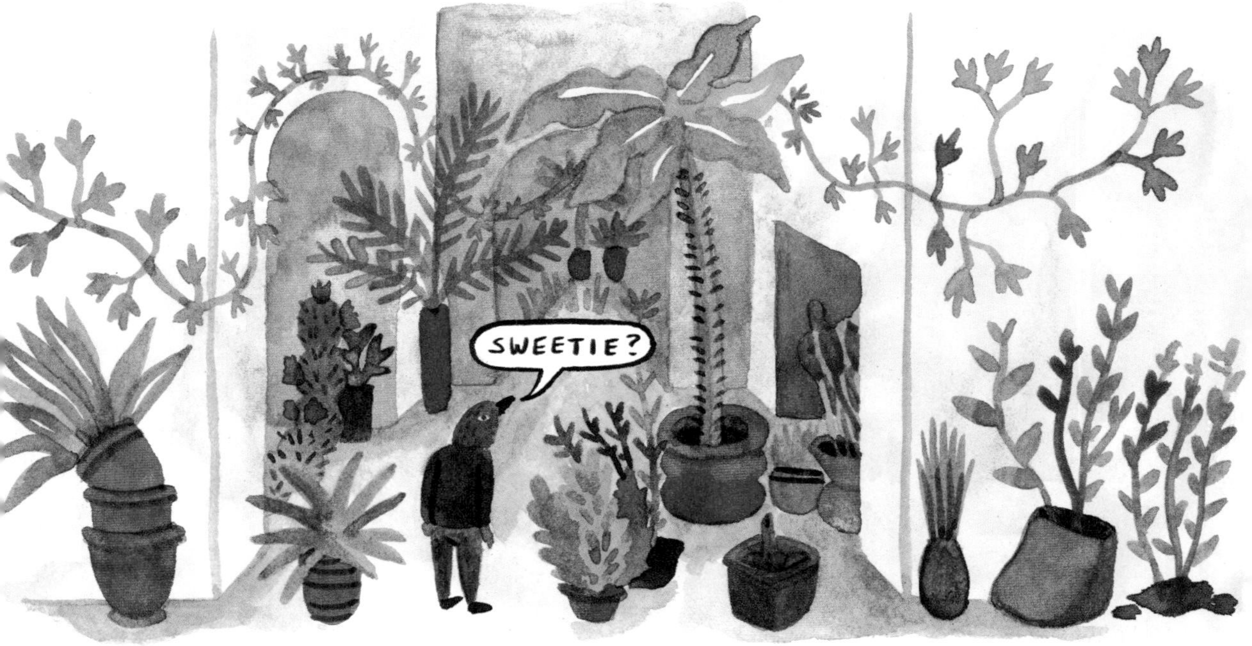
SWEETIE?

FINALLY I'D FIND HER, TENDING TO ONE OF THE LARGER PLANTS...

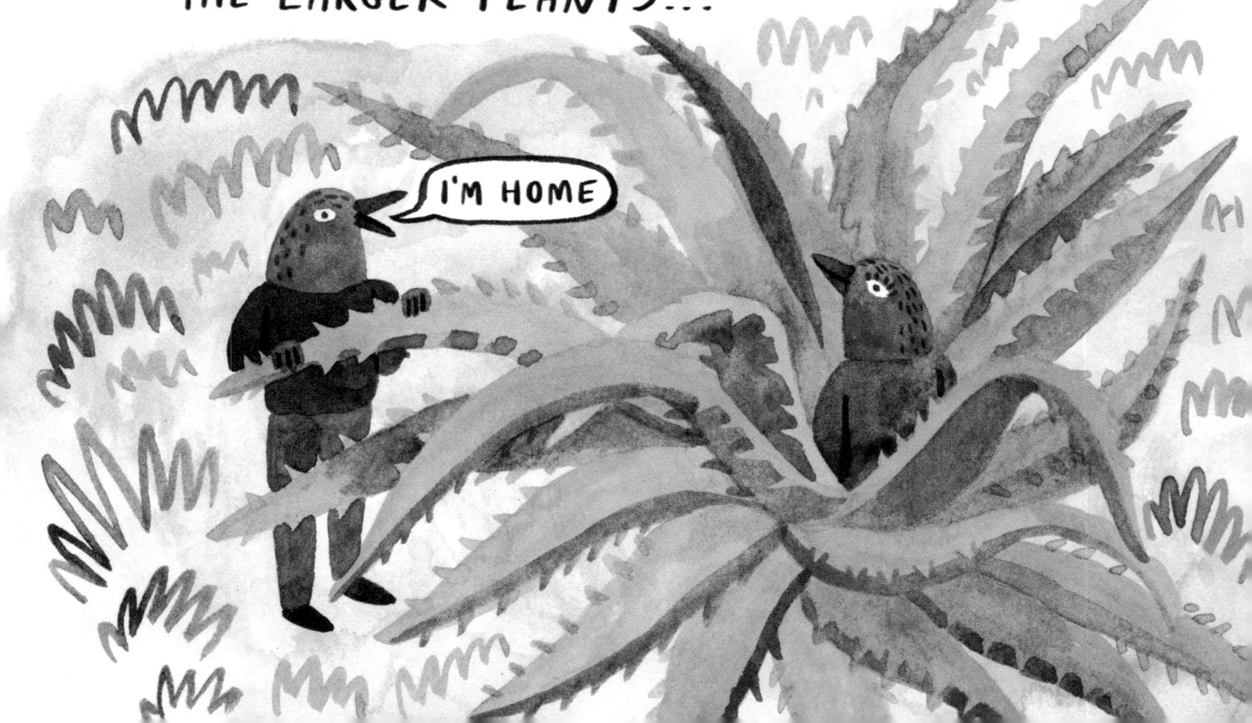
I'M HOME

... OR CURLED UP IN A POT, FAST ASLEEP.

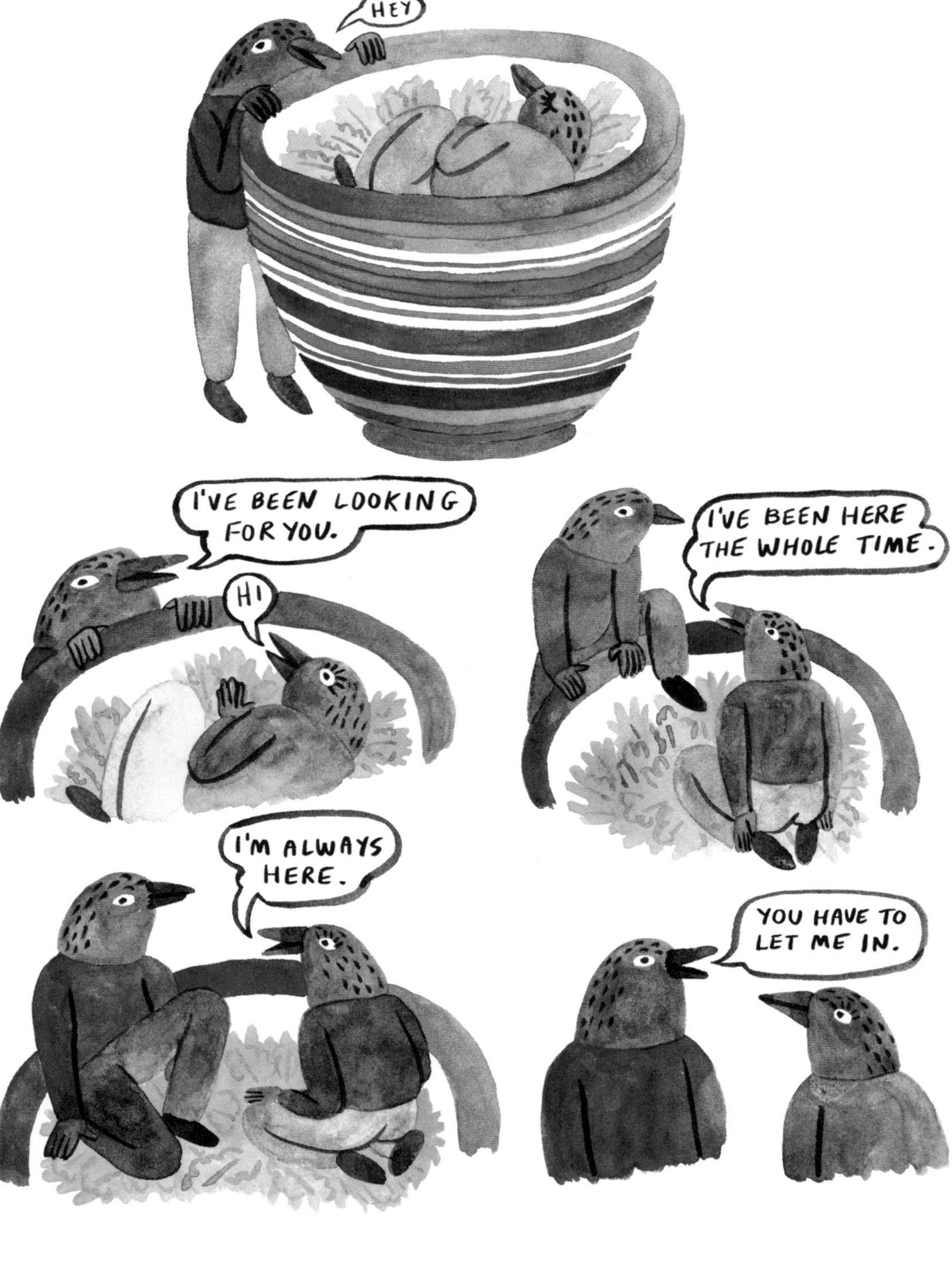
HEY
I'VE BEEN LOOKING FOR YOU.
HI
I'VE BEEN HERE THE WHOLE TIME.
I'M ALWAYS HERE.
YOU HAVE TO LET ME IN.

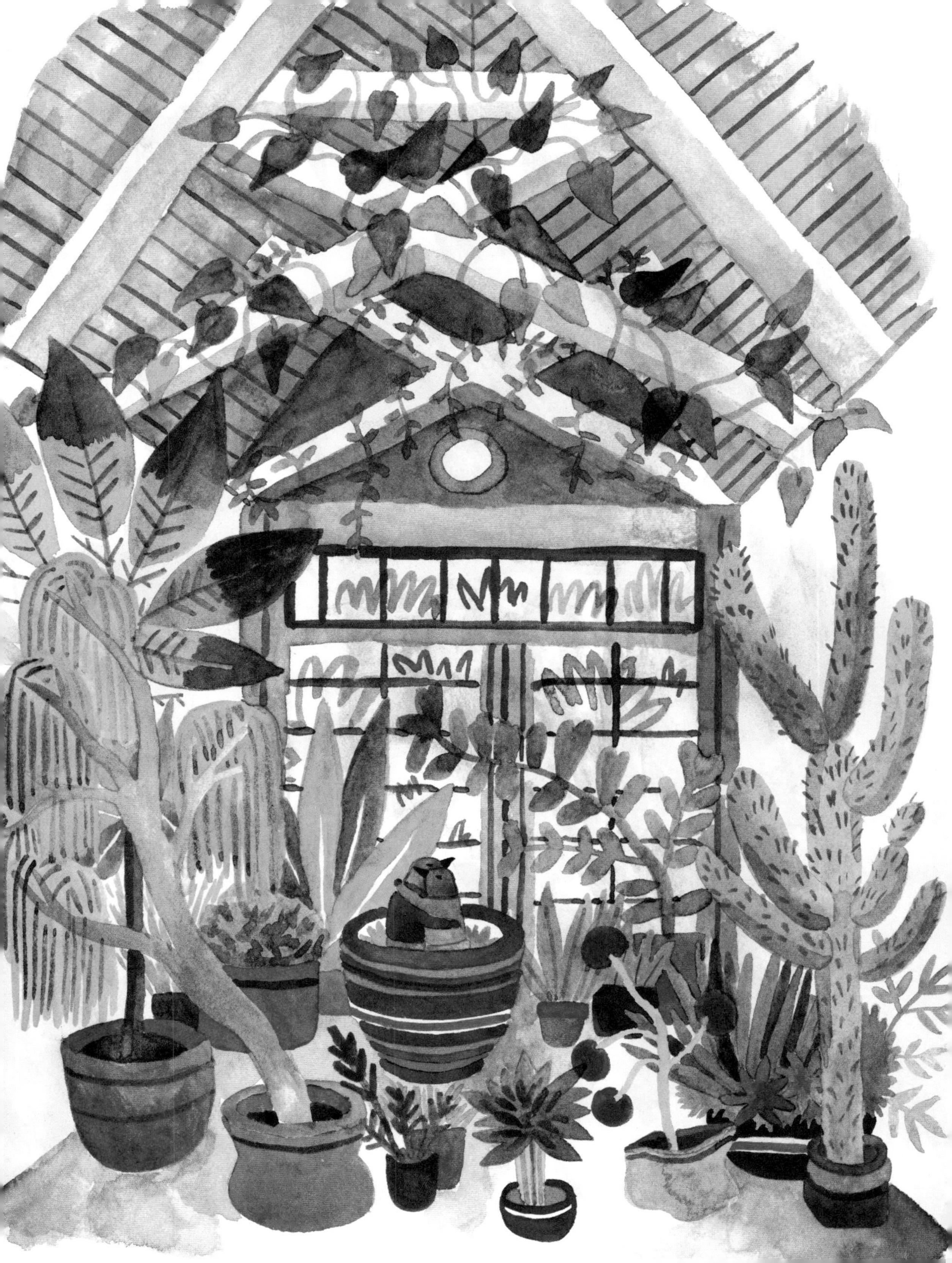

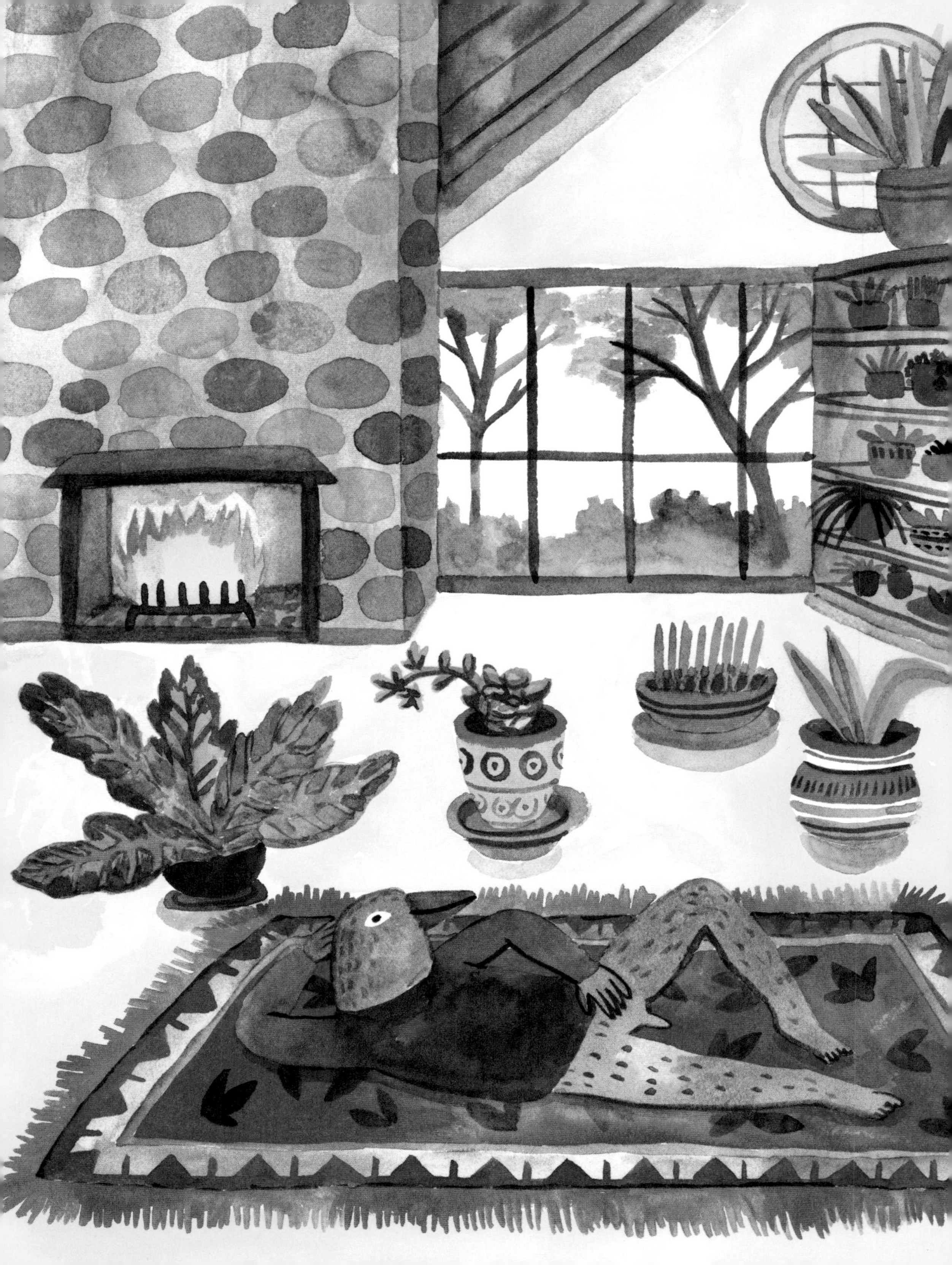

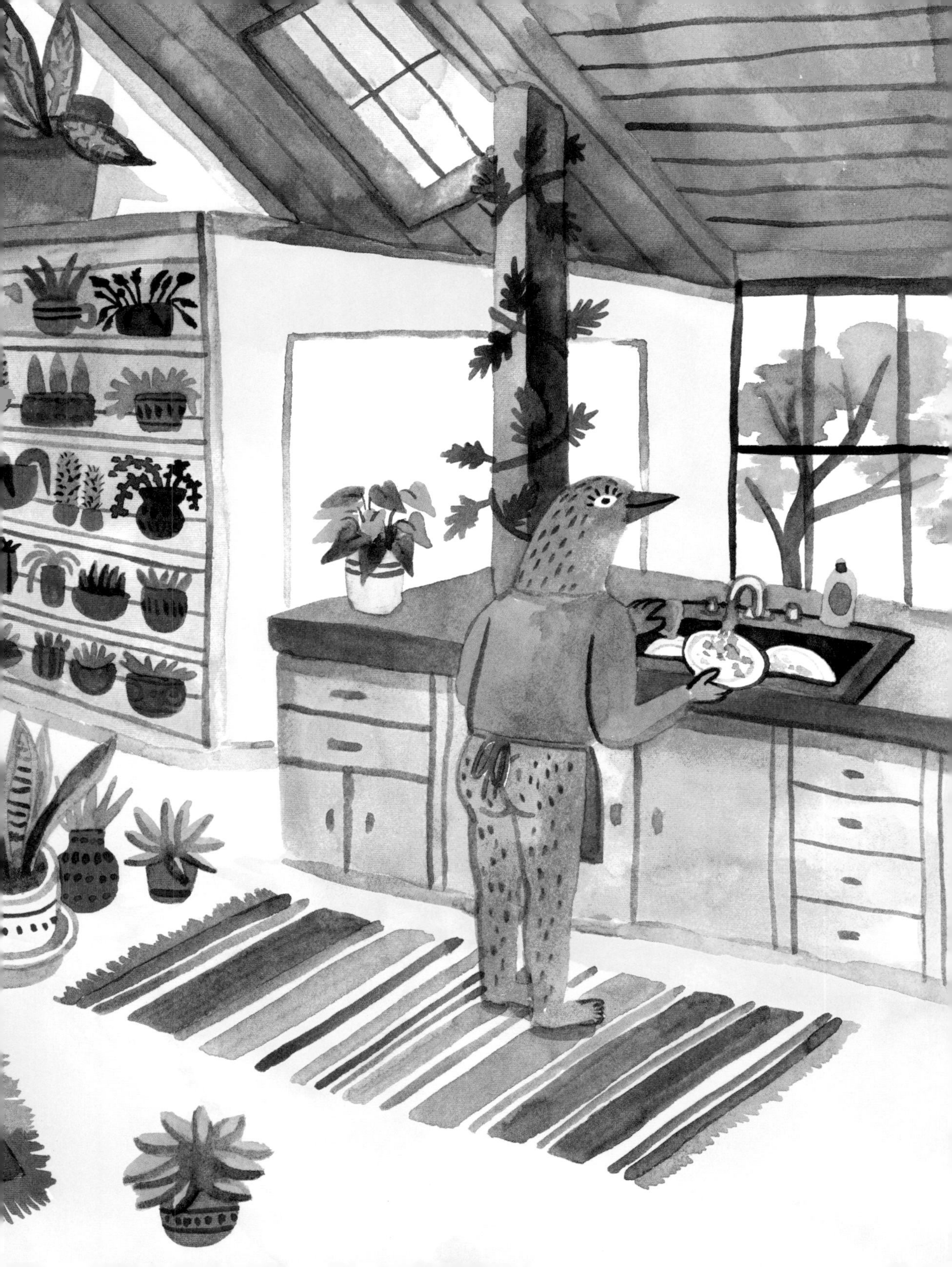

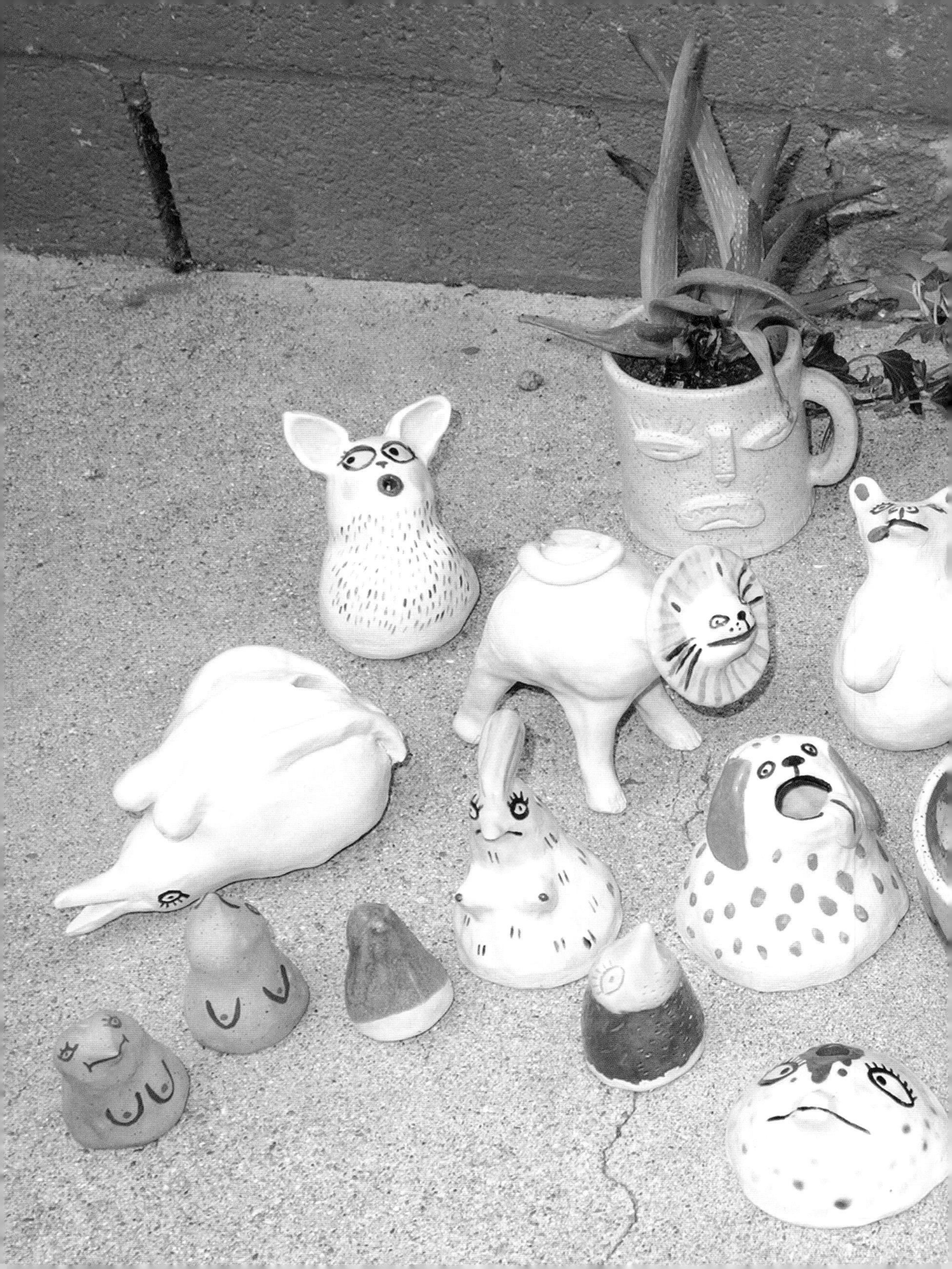

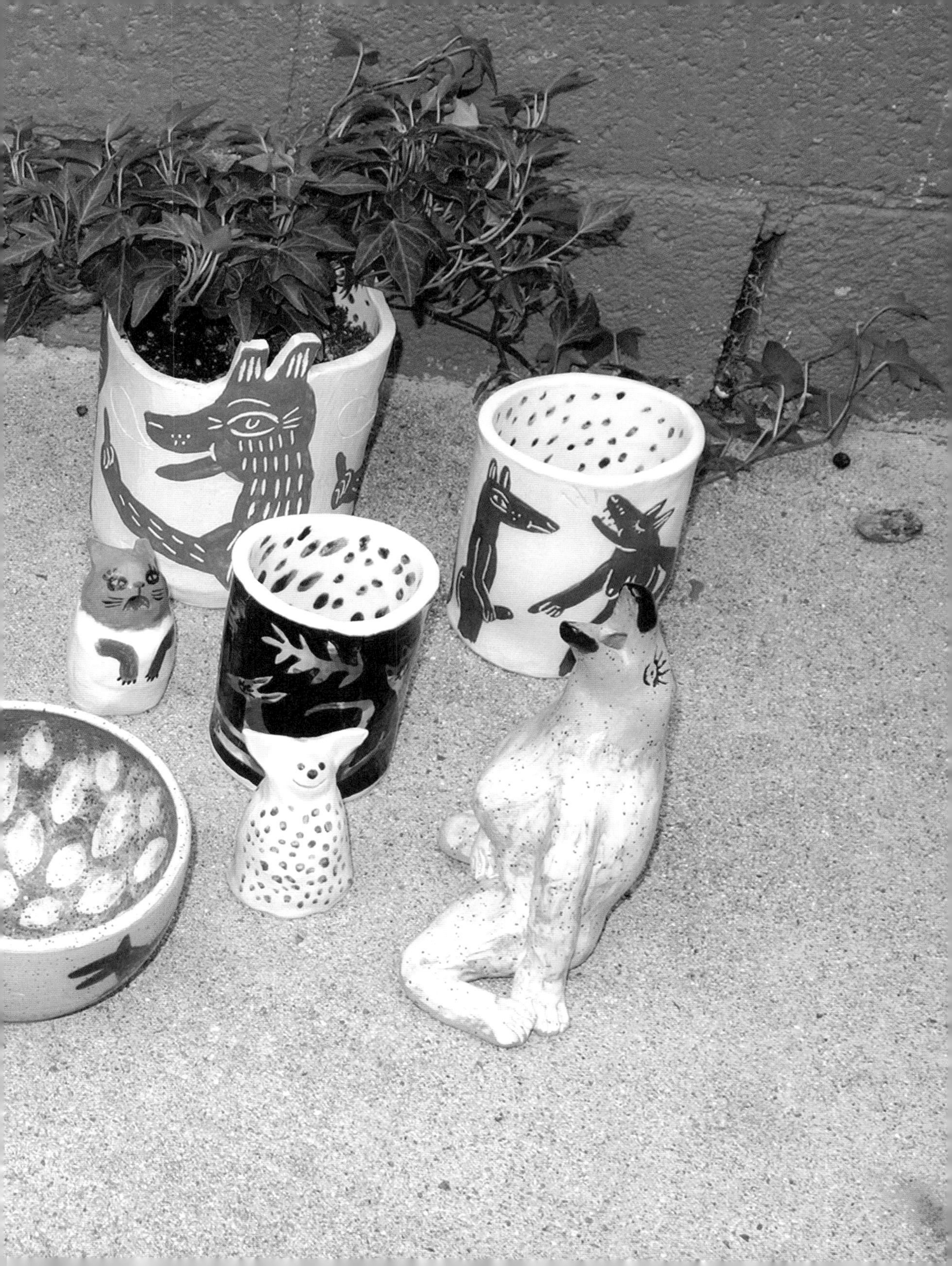

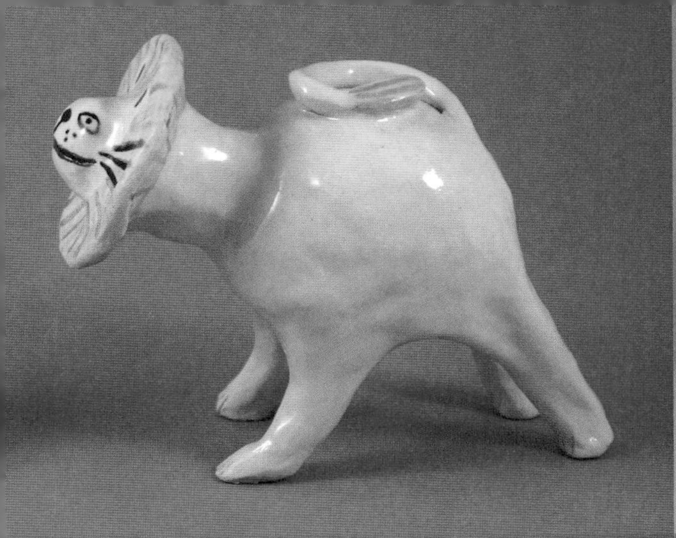
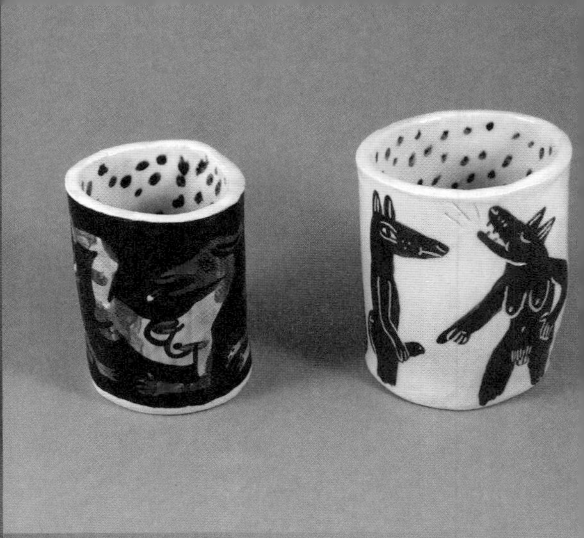
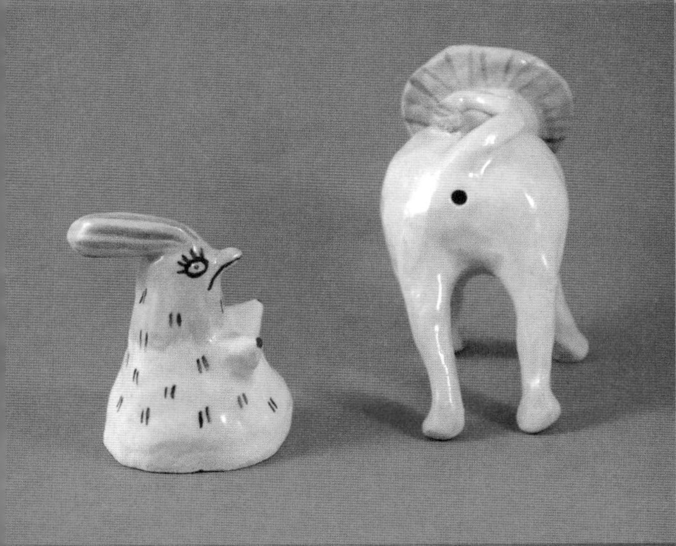
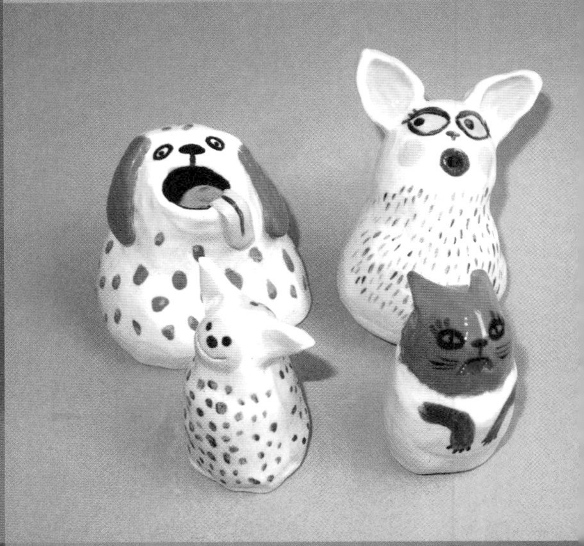
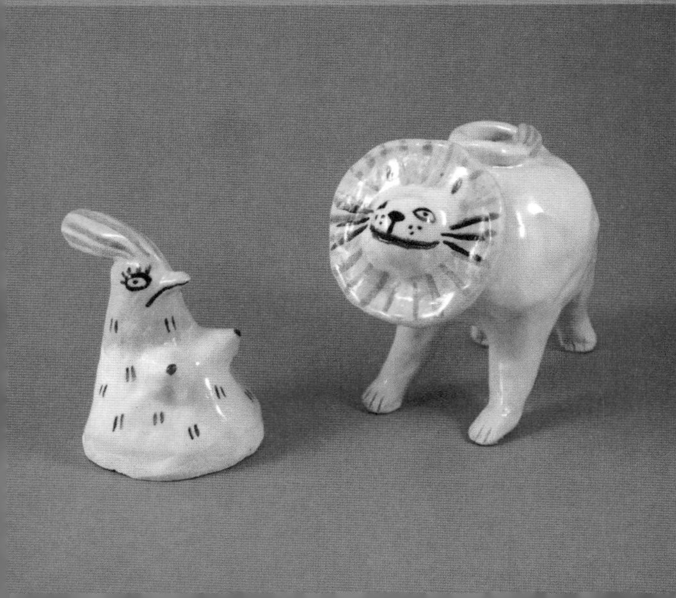
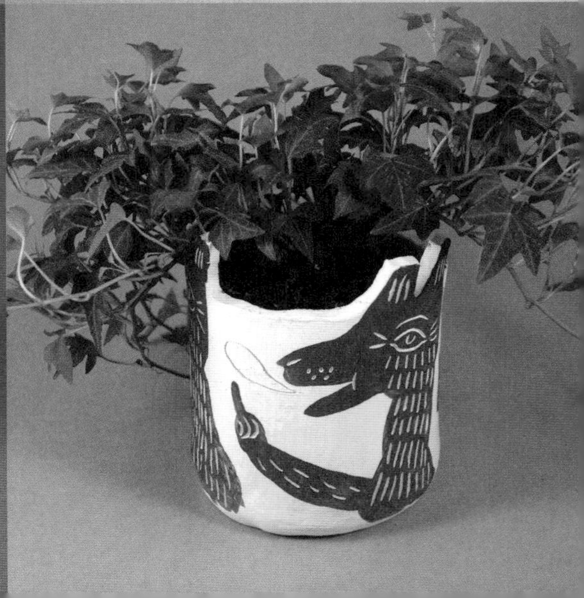

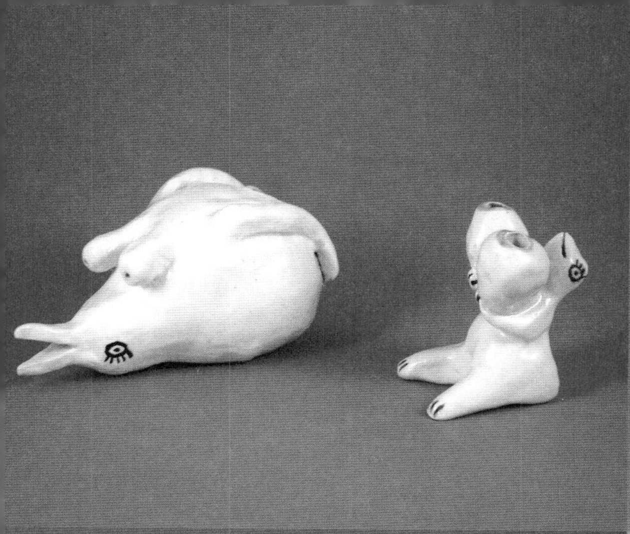
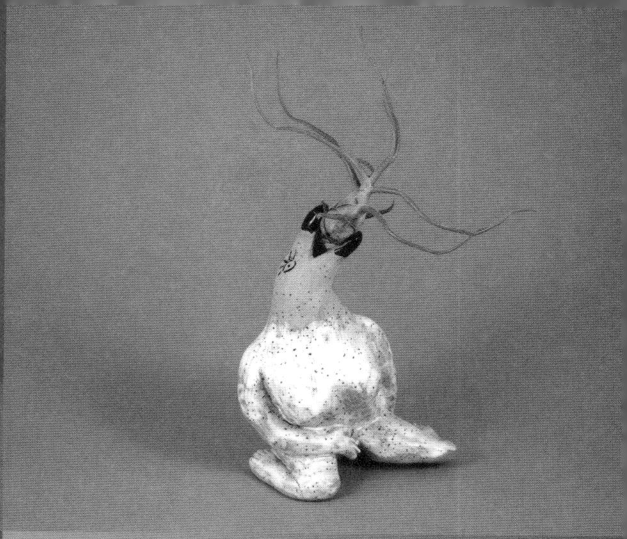
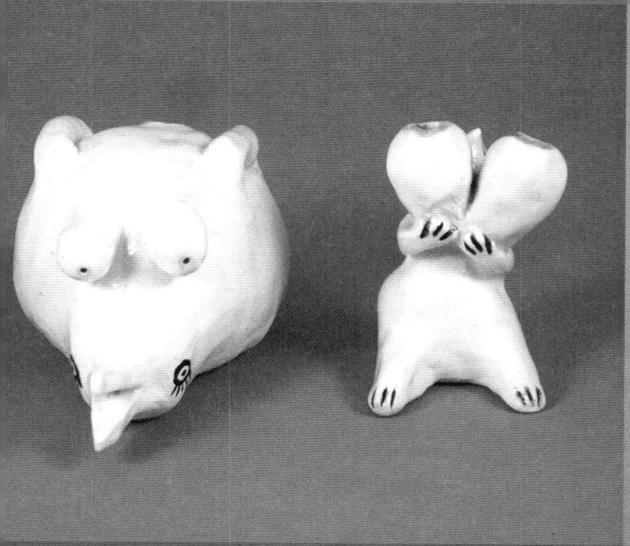
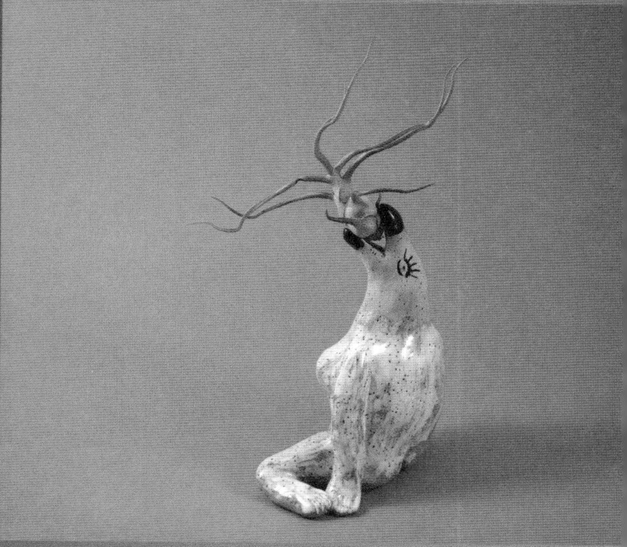
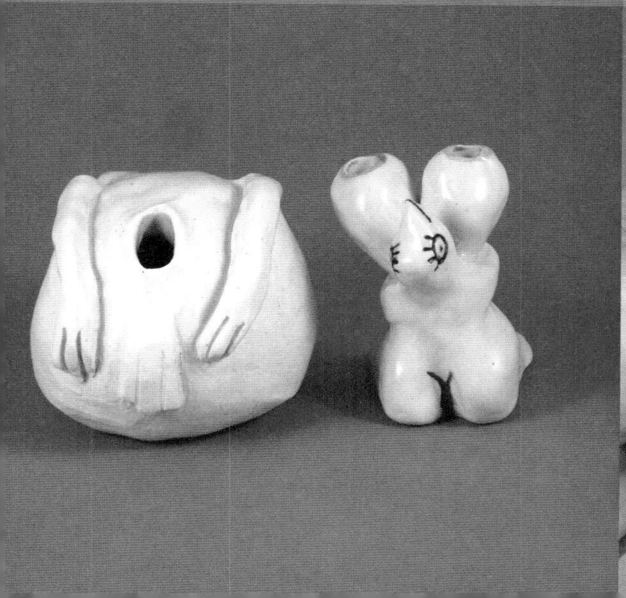
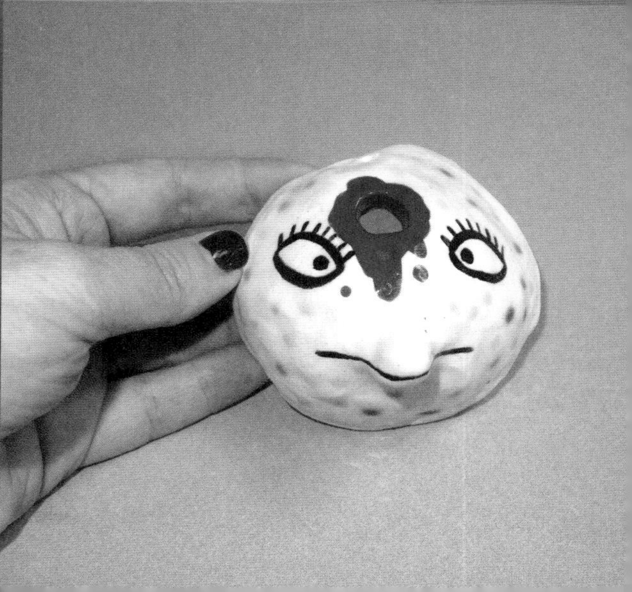

CHILDREN AT THE POTTERY STUDIO

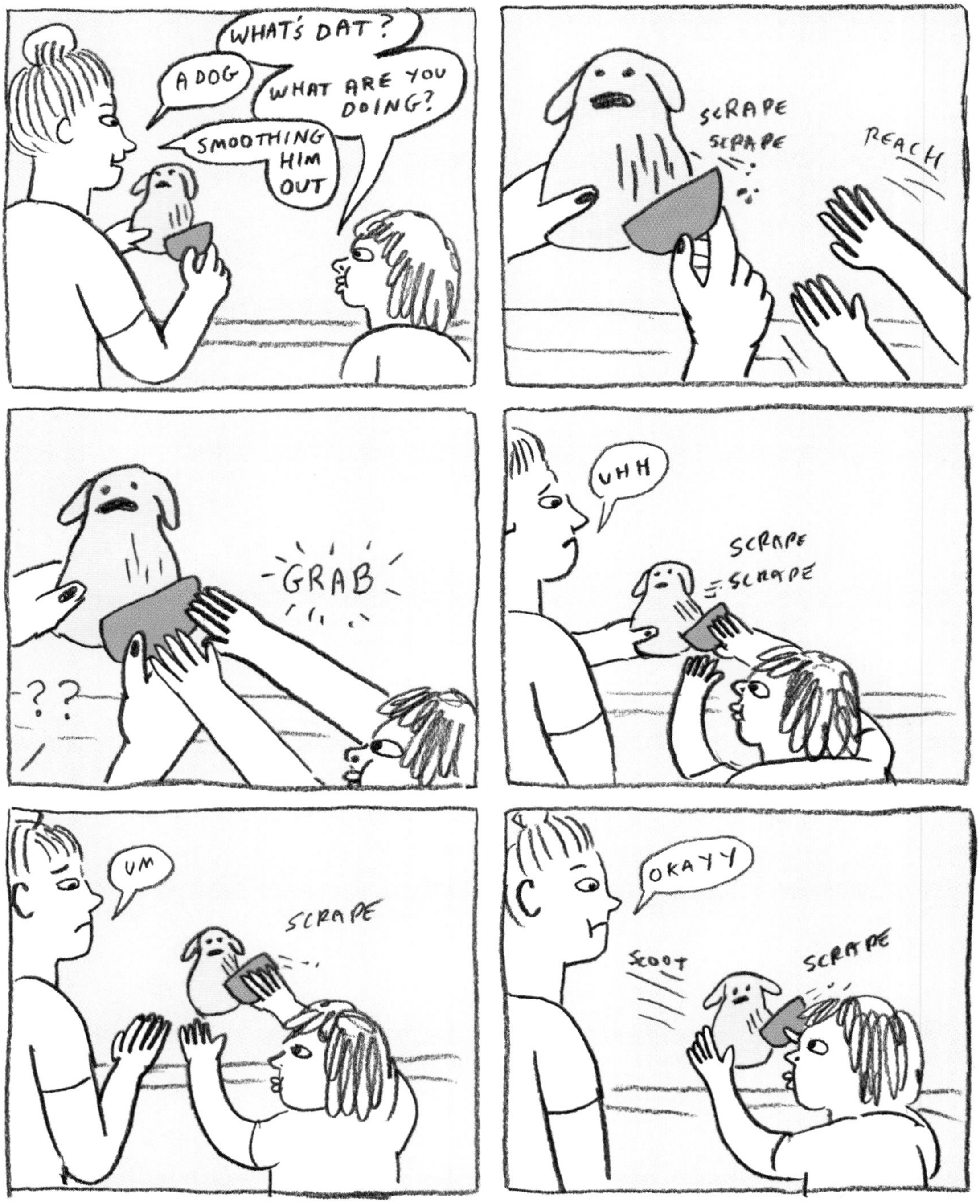
WHAT'S DAT?
A DOG
WHAT ARE YOU DOING?
SMOOTHING HIM OUT
SCRAPE
SCRAPE
REACH
GRAB
??
UHH
SCRAPE
SCRAPE
UM
SCRAPE
OKAYY
SCOOT
SCRAPE

AGE

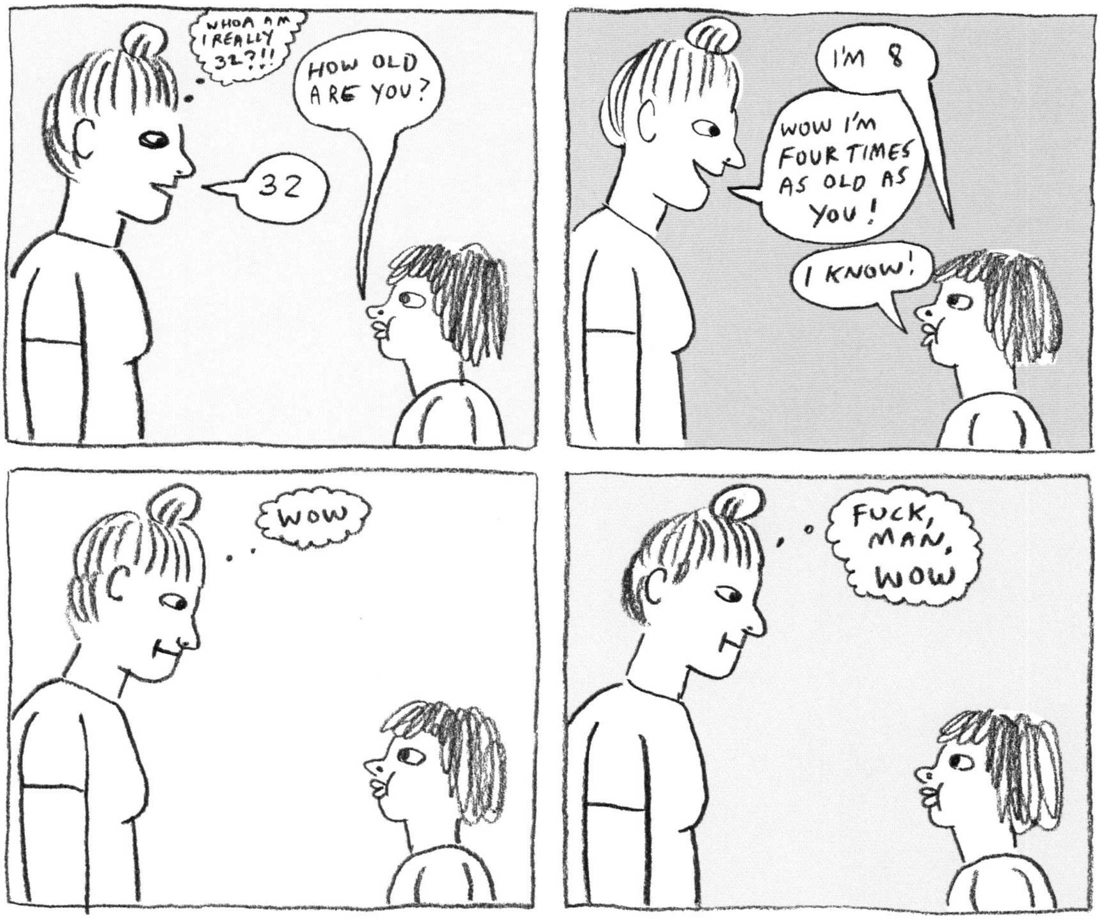
WHOA AM I REALLY 32?!!
HOW OLD ARE YOU?
32
I'M 8
WOW I'M FOUR TIMES AS OLD AS YOU!
I KNOW!
WOW
FUCK, MAN, WOW

LH

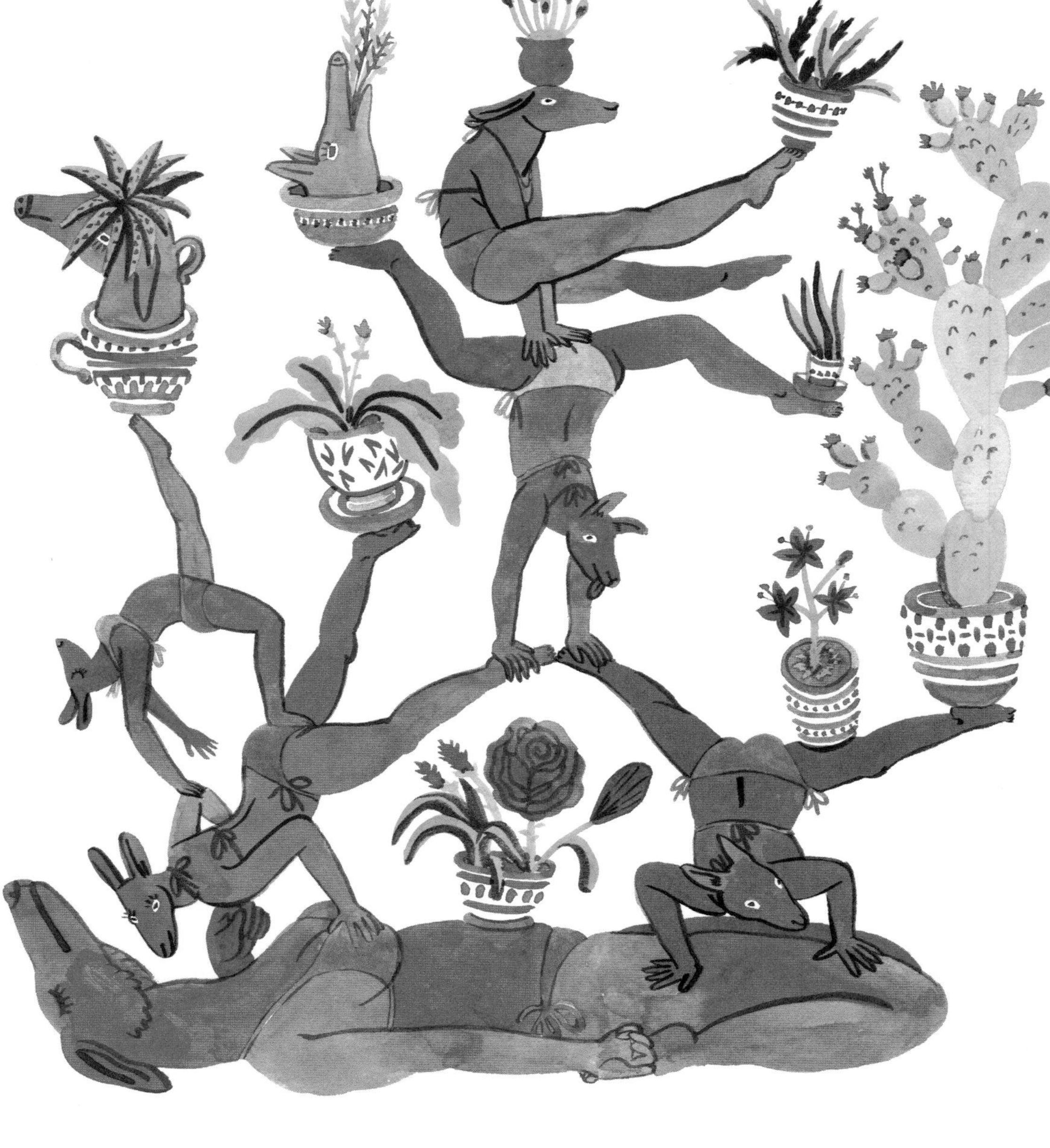

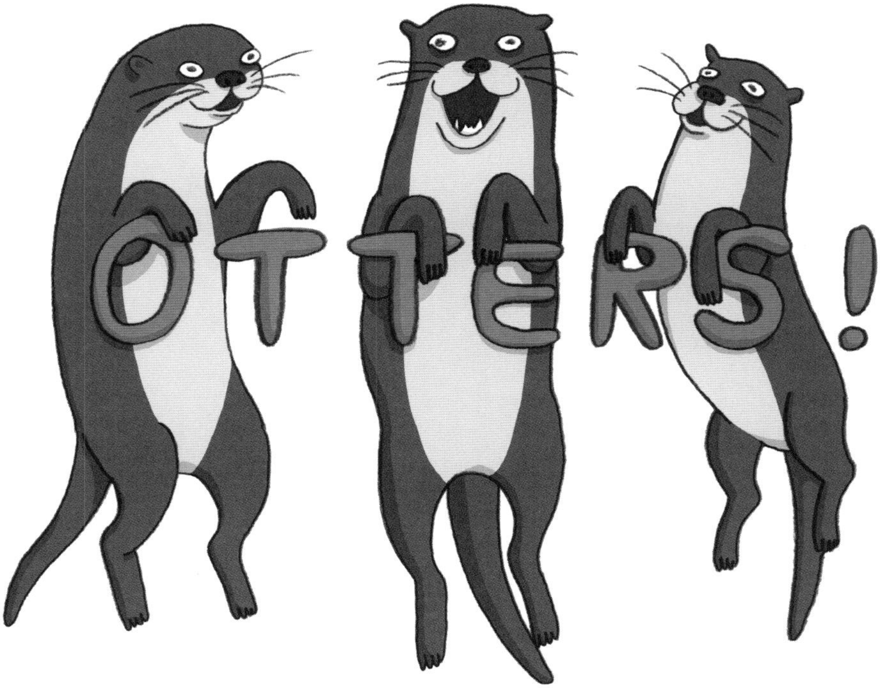
OTTERS!

I WENT SWIMMING WITH RIVER OTTERS. SMALL, SOFT, PLAYFUL RIVER OTTERS. I UNDERSTAND IF IT MAKES YOU FURIOUS THAT I SWAM WITH OTTERS AND YOU DIDN'T. BUT! YOU CAN DO IT TOO.

YOU JUST HAVE TO VISIT NURTURED BY NATURE, A NONPROFIT WILDLIFE SANCTUARY IN VALLEY CENTER, CALIFORNIA, NOT TOO FAR FROM SAN DIEGO. IT'S ON THE TIP OF A MOUNTAIN OVERLOOKING A VERDANT, SUN-SOAKED VALLEY. IT'S NOWHERE NEAR ANY BODIES OF WATER (WHICH MEANS AT LEAST ONE VAN FULL OF OTTERS HAD TO DRIVE UP HERE)!

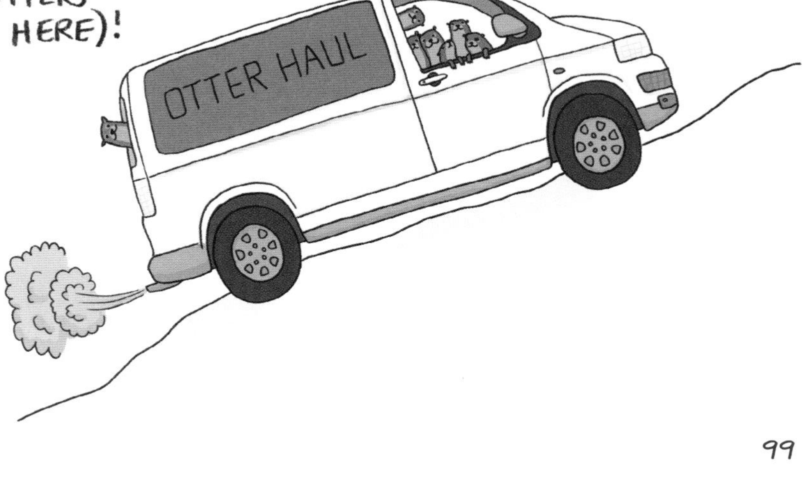
OTTER HAUL

WENDY AND KEVIN YATES RUN THE SANCTUARY OUT OF THEIR BACKYARD. THEY BUILT THIS WHOLE PLACE UP AFTER THEIR PREVIOUS HOME BURNED DOWN ELEVEN YEARS AGO. NOW THEY LIVE HERE WITH THEIR TWO LOVELY TEENAGE DAUGHTERS AND CARE FOR APPROXIMATELY THREE HUNDRED ANIMALS WITH THE HELP OF VOLUNTEERS. THE NONPROFIT SPECIALIZES IN PROVIDING TERMINALLY ILL, DISABLED, DISADVANTAGED, AND TRAUMATIZED CHILDREN WITH THERAPEUTIC ENCOUNTERS WITH ADORABLE CREATURES. IN ADDITION TO ALL THE EXOTICS, THEY ALSO HAVE TWO HORSES AND A PACK OF CUTE DOGS. THE YATES FAMILY IS LIVING MY DREAM LIFE.

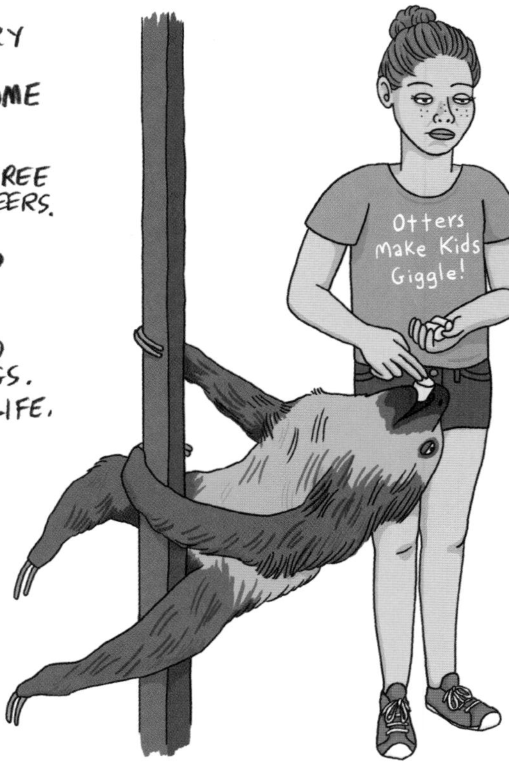
Otters Make Kids Giggle!

BEFORE WE GET TO PLAY WITH OTTERS, WENDY AND KEVIN TAKE US ON A TOUR TO MEET THEIR OTHER ANIMALS. FIRST KEVIN BRINGS OUT A SLOTH NAMED CHEWY. THEIR DAUGHTER MANDY FEEDS IT PIECES OF BANANA AND THE SLOTH IS SO LAZY THAT MANDY HAS TO PLACE THE BANANA CHUNKS ON ITS LIPS AND THEN PUSH THEM THE REST OF THE WAY IN WITH HER FINGER. SHE DOES THIS WITH A BORED EXPRESSION LIKE "UGH, TIME TO FEED OUR SLOTH AGAIN!"

I'M INSTRUCTED TO ONLY PET THE SLOTH ON THE BACK WHERE SHE "DOESN'T MIND IT," AND I GO FOR IT, EVEN THOUGH I FEEL GUILTY AND UNSATISFIED PETTING ANY ANIMAL THAT MERELY TOLERATES IT IN EXCHANGE FOR BANANA. THIS PETTING IS ENTIRELY FOR MY OWN PLEASURE.

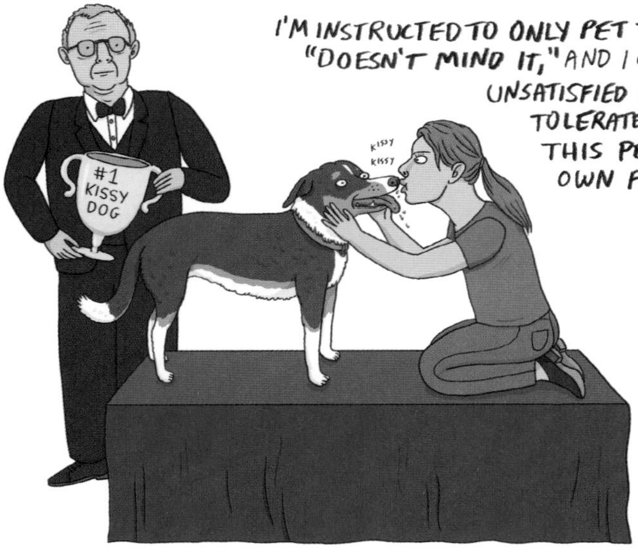
#1 KISSY DOG
kissy
kissy

SUDDENLY I UNDERSTAND THE FULL MEANING OF DOMESTICATION: THESE ANIMALS ARE BRED TO SEEK OUT AND ENJOY MY PETTING TO SUCH A DEGREE THAT THEY GET NEUROTIC WHEN THEY AREN'T PETTED ENOUGH. IT'S WONDERFUL!

NEXT WE MEET SOME PATAGONIAN CAVIES. THEY'RE SHY, DEER-LIKE, RABBITY THINGS (I WANT TO CALL THEM "SNAKE SNACKS") WHO SNEAK UP AND EAT FRUIT OUT OF MY HAND WHEN I TURN MY BODY SO I'M NO LONGER FACING THEM. I'M PROUD FOR FIGURING THIS TRICK OUT, EVEN THOUGH IT'S THE MOST BASIC ANIMAL BEHAVIOR 101 MOVE FOR HANDLING PREY CRITTERS.

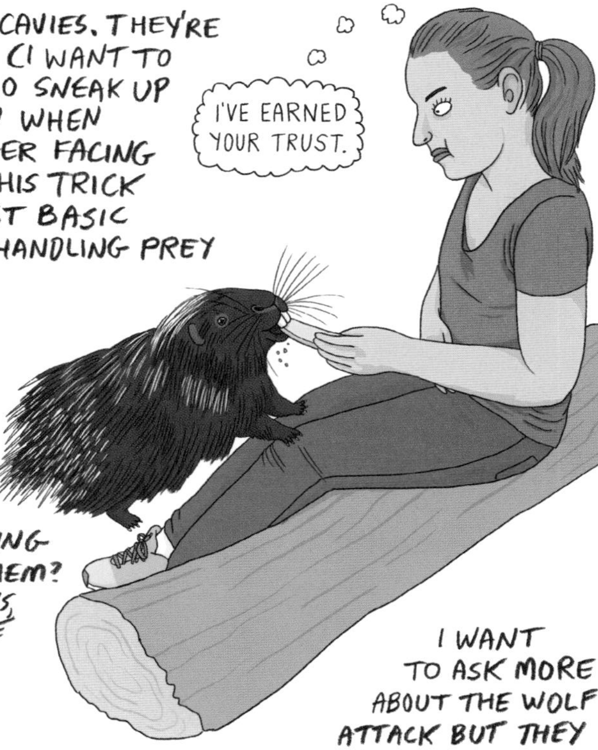
I'VE EARNED YOUR TRUST.

WHILE FEEDING A BANANA TO A PORCUPINE WHO'S CRAWLED HALFWAY ONTO MY LAP AND IS FRANKLY TERRIFYING ME, I ASK WENDY AND KEVIN IF ANYTHING DANGEROUS HAS HAPPENED TO THEM? ANY ANIMAL ATTACKS? WENDY SAYS, "NOT REALLY... EXCEPT ONE TIME KEVIN GOT ATTACKED BY A WOLF."

I WANT TO ASK MORE ABOUT THE WOLF ATTACK BUT THEY DON'T ELABORATE, SO I COUNT KEVIN'S LIMBS AND FINGERS (EVERYTHING SEEMS TO BE IN ORDER). KEVIN SAYS, "IF YOU WORK WITH WILD ANIMALS, YOU'LL EVENTUALLY GET HURT. BUT WE DON'T KEEP ANY ANIMALS HERE THAT COULD KILL YOU."

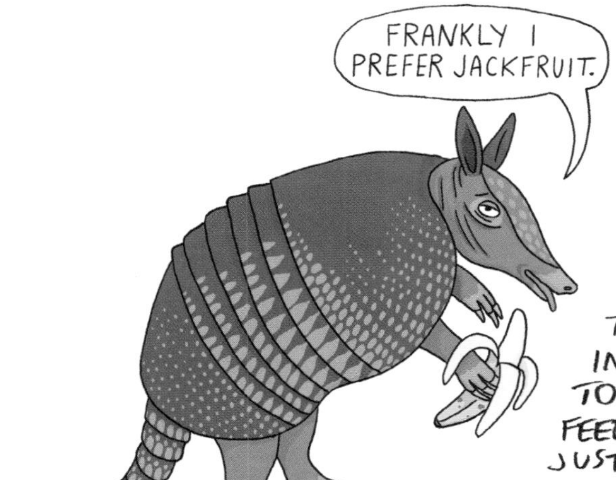
FRANKLY I PREFER JACKFRUIT.

I CAN IMAGINE MYSELF BEING KICKED TO DEATH BY THEIR KANGAROO, WHO'S IN A BAD MOOD AND KEEPS THREATENING TO BOX US UNLESS WE CONTINUOUSLY FEED HIM BANANA CHUNKS. BUT HE'S JUST A BULLY, NOT A KILLER.

ARE THERE ANY EXOTIC ANIMALS WHO DON'T LOVE BANANA? WE'VE FED A BANANA TO EVERY ANIMAL ON THIS PROPERTY!

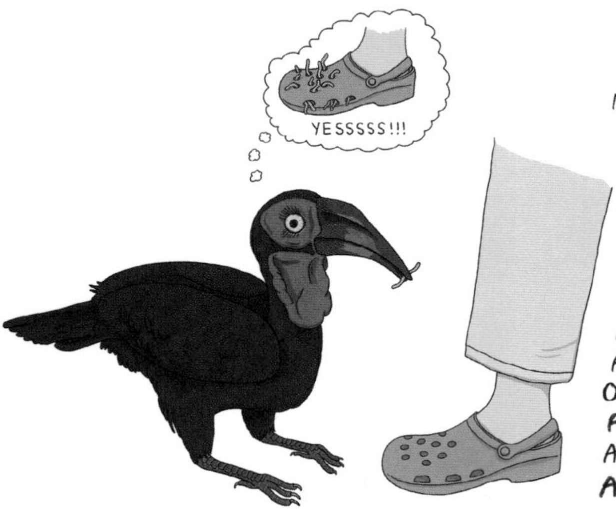
YESSSSS!!!

NEXT WE'RE INTRODUCED TO A SOUTHERN GRAND HORNBILL NAMED BEETLEJUICE. HE'S THE NAUGHTIEST CREATURE I'VE EVER MET, AND SINCE I'M ALWAYS ATTRACTED TO NATURE'S DICKHEADS, I LOVE HIM AND WISH I COULD TAKE HIM HOME WITH ME. HE HAS THE LONGEST, FULLEST, FLIRTIEST EYELASHES AND ALL HE WANTS TO DO IS BREAK STUFF AND CAUSE CHAOS; HE'S PECKING STUCCO AWAY FROM THE WALL LIKE A WOODPECKER ON 'ROIDS ONE SECOND AND BITING OUR ANKLES THE NEXT. I'M WARNED, "DON'T RUN AWAY FROM HIM, HE'LL THINK IT'S A GAME AND TRY TO CHASE YOU!"

BEETLEJUICE IS GIVEN A MEALWORM AND INSTEAD OF EATING IT HE SPENDS FIVE MINUTES TRYING TO STICK IT INSIDE THE HOLES OF WENDY'S CROCS WHILE SHE THWARTS HIM, TOTALLY DISGUSTED, "BEETLEJUICE, DOOOOON'T!"

FINALLY IT'S TIME TO MEET THE OTTERS. THE BATCH WE'RE GOING TO BE MEETING TODAY—TWO GIRLS AND TWO BOYS—ARE SIX MONTHS OLD AND HAVE BEEN BOTTLE-FED AND HAND-RAISED. THAT MEANS WE'LL GET TO TOUCH THE HECK OUT OF 'EM!

HERE'S THE DEAL: OTTERS ARE CUTE. TERRIBLY, TERRIBLY CUTE. AND THIS VARIETY, THE ASIAN SMALL-CLAWED OTTER, IS THE CUTEST KIND. THEY'RE THE SMALLEST SPECIES, AVERAGING SIX POUNDS. THEIR HANDS ARE SOFT AND PREHENSILE (TO HELP THEM DIG UNDER ROCKS FOR EDIBLES) AND THEY USE THEM IN EERILY HUMAN-LIKE WAYS: REACHING INTO HOLES TO SCOOP THINGS OUT, PICKING UP SHINY ROCKS AND OFFERING THEM TO YOU, GRASPING YOUR FINGERS.

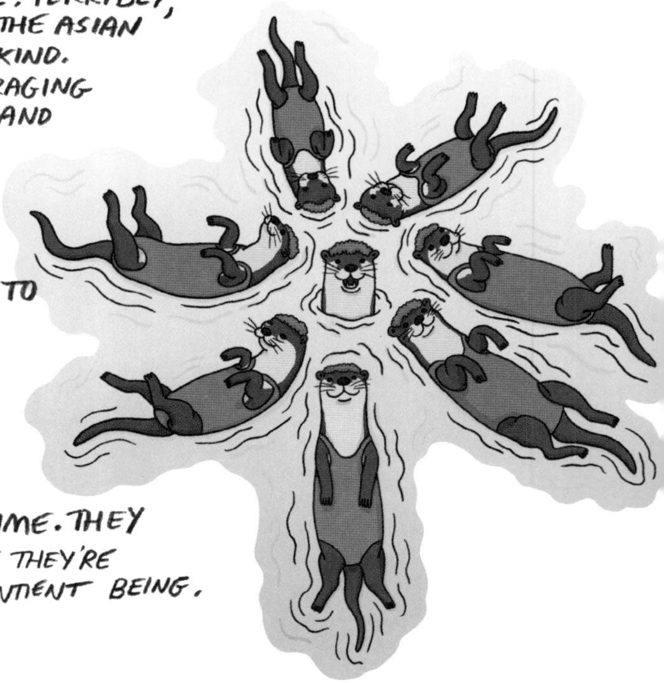

THEY'RE ALSO VERY SQUEAKY AND ALL SQUEAK IN UNISON WHENEVER THEY WANT FOOD OR ATTENTION. THEY FOLLOW EACH OTHER AND DO THE SAME THINGS AT THE SAME TIME. THEY SEEM TO SHARE A BRAIN. IT'S LIKE THEY'RE DIFFERENT LIMBS OF A SINGLE SENTIENT BEING.

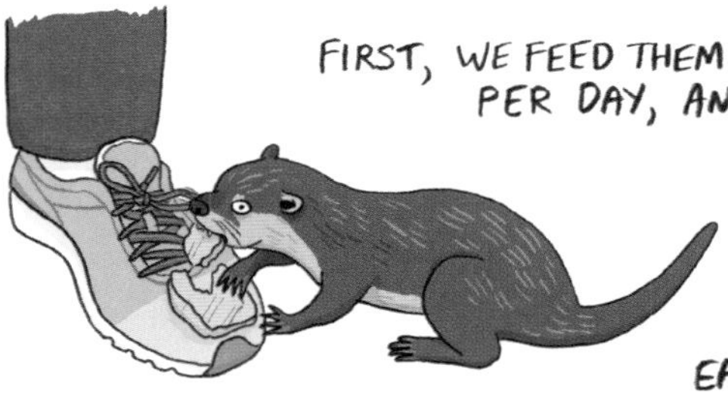

FIRST, WE FEED THEM. THESE GUYS GET ONE PIECE OF TILAPIA EACH PER DAY, AND THEY SQUEAK UNTIL THEY GET IT. THE REST OF THE DAY THEY GET FERRET KIBBLE. THEY'RE ACTUALLY VERY CLOSELY RELATED TO FERRETS, AND BOTH ARE MEMBERS OF THE MUSTELIDAE FAMILY. THEY'RE RIVER WEASELS! IN THE WILD THEY EAT CRABS, FROGS, MOLLUSKS, AND ONLY OCCASIONALLY DINE ON FISH. WE GIVE THEM THEIR PIECES OF FISH AND THEY SWARM AROUND US TO EAT. ONE OF THEM BRINGS HER PIECE OF FISH OVER TO ME AND EATS IT OFF MY FOOT, USING MY SNEAKER AS A PLATE. I'VE NEVER BEEN MORE FLATTERED.

FINALLY, IT'S TIME TO SUIT UP AND SWIM WITH THEM. I'M WARNED TO TRIPLE-KNOT MY BIKINI BOTTOMS SO THEY CAN'T BE TUGGED OFF. THIS IS EXCITING! WENDY AND KEVIN BRING THE PUPS IN, CARRYING THEM BY THEIR SCRUFFS, AND RELEASE THEM INTO THE POOL WITH US.

I'M GIVEN A CUP OF ICE BECAUSE THE OTTERS LIKE PLAYING WITH IT, AND THEY IMMEDIATELY SWARM ME AND FIGHT EACH OTHER TO SCOOP THE CUBES OUT. THEY NEVER STOP MOVING AND TWIRLING AND GRABBING. ANY TOY I HOLD IS OF INTEREST TO THEM IF IT CREATES BUBBLES, SHOOTS WATER, OR HAS A HOLE THAT MIGHT CONTAIN TREATS. MY FIRST REACTION TO ALL OF THIS IS THAT I SIMPLY CAN'T GET OVER HOW GOOD IT FEELS TO HAVE OTTERS ALL OVER ME. THEY'RE SO WET AND FURRY AND SOFT AND LITTLE. HOW WILL I BE ABLE TO HANDLE THE REST OF MY LIFE, NOT BEING COVERED IN OTTERS? WILL I HAVE TO WEAR A WET-OTTER-FUR COAT EVERYWHERE I GO??

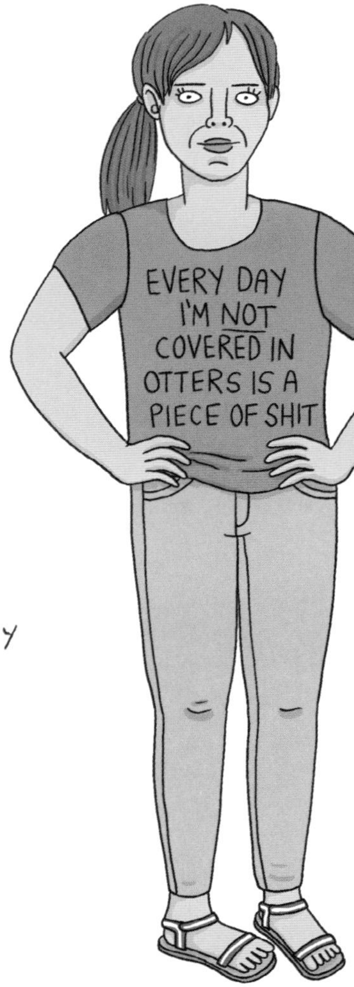
EVERY DAY I'M NOT COVERED IN OTTERS IS A PIECE OF SHIT

YOU KNOW WHEN SOMETHING'S SO CUTE THAT YOU FEEL INTERNAL PAIN? THERE SHOULD BE A WORD TO DESCRIBE A CERTAIN KIND OF HORNINESS THAT ISN'T SEXUAL-I CAN'T EMPHASIZE ENOUGH HOW NONSEXUAL IT IS - BUT IT'S WHEN SOMETHING IS SO CUTE THAT YOU FEEL KIND OF AROUSED. I'M "CHORNY." LIKE I'M SO CHARMED THAT I'M HORNY. NO?

WARNING: CHORNY TRIGGERS

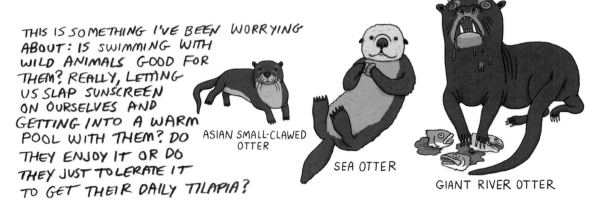

THEIR TAILS ARE PARTICULARLY CUTE. WE AREN'T SUPPOSED TO GRAB THE OTTERS OR RESTRICT THEIR MOVEMENT SINCE IT MAKES THEM CRANKY AND NIPPY, BUT I HAVE TO ADMIT I GIVE THEIR TAILS A LITTLE TUG AS THEY SWIM BY. I CAN'T HELP IT.

THESE GUYS ARE EXTREMELY TAME SINCE THEY'VE BEEN BOTTLE-FED SINCE BIRTH. BUT WENDY SAYS IT'S RARE TO MEET OTTERS WHO WON'T WANT TO RIP YOU TO PIECES (AND EVEN HAND-RAISED OTTERS AREN'T ALWAYS THIS MELLOW). SHE MENTIONS A SPECIES CALLED "GIANT RIVER OTTERS" WHO ARE SUPPOSEDLY VERY VICIOUS IF YOU GET ANYWHERE NEAR THEM. BESIDES THE NIPS, THE ONLY PAINFUL THING IS WHEN THE OTTERS KICK OFF OUR BODIES TO MAKE THEMSELVES SWIM FASTER, BUT THEY'RE JUST TINY SHOVES, AND, ALSO IT'S AWESOME THAT THEY KNOW HOW TO MAKE SWIMMING EVEN MORE FUN.

THE YATES FAMILY HAS SEVENTEEN OTTERS TOTAL, BUT ONLY THREE SMALL GROUPS OF THEM ARE TAME ENOUGH TO SWIM WITH. THEY ROTATE THE GROUPS, SO THE SWIMMING REMAINS FUN FOR THEM AND NEVER BECOMES A CHORE.

THIS IS SOMETHING I'VE BEEN WORRYING ABOUT: IS SWIMMING WITH WILD ANIMALS GOOD FOR THEM? REALLY, LETTING US SLAP SUNSCREEN ON OURSELVES AND GETTING INTO A WARM POOL WITH THEM? DO THEY ENJOY IT OR DO THEY JUST TOLERATE IT TO GET THEIR DAILY TILAPIA?

ASIAN SMALL-CLAWED OTTER

SEA OTTER

GIANT RIVER OTTER

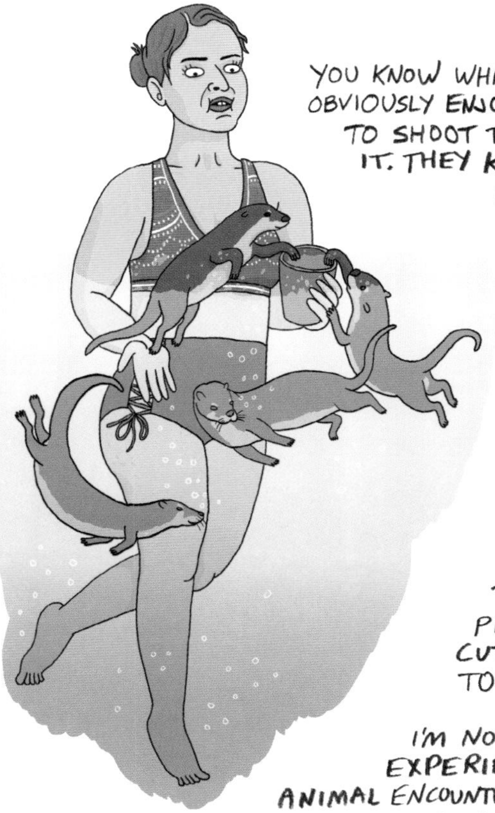

YOU KNOW WHAT, NEVER MIND - THESE OTTERS VERY OBVIOUSLY ENJOY BEING HERE. WE'RE ENCOURAGED TO SHOOT THEM WITH WATER GUNS AND THEY LOVE IT. THEY KEEP BOUNCING UP TO GET SHOT IN THE FACE AGAIN AND AGAIN, PAWING AT THE STREAMS OF WATER.

ONE OF THE OTTERS GETS OUT OF THE POOL TO TAKE A DUMP ON THE DECK (THEY DON'T SHIT WHERE THEY SWIM!) AND WENDY TAKES THAT AS A SIGNAL TO PUT THEM BACK IN THEIR ENCLOSURE. ONCE ONE OF THEM STARTS POOPING, IT'S A MATTER OF MINUTES UNTIL THE OTHERS DO THE SAME. THEY ROMP AROUND IN THEIR PEN TO GET THEMSELVES DRY AND THEN START TO PILE UP ON TOP OF EACH OTHER TO NAP. CUTENESS SQUARED. THINGS ARE GETTING TOO CHORNY TO HANDLE.

I'M NOT SURE HOW I'LL EVER TOP THIS EXPERIENCE, BUT HERE ARE SOME OTHER ANIMAL ENCOUNTERS I THOUGHT UP, FOR COMPETING ANIMAL SANCTUARIES TO OFFER:

- CARRY A YOUNG HONEY BADGER AROUND IN A BACKPACK
- EAT A PICNIC ON A HIPPO'S BACK
- SLEEPOVER PARTY WITH MINIATURE HORSES
- SWIM WITH BABY OWLS AND THEN RESCUE THEM FROM DROWNING SO THEY IMPRINT ON YOU. RAISE OWLS TO ADULTHOOD. TEACH THEM TRICKS. BECOME "THAT WEIRD LADY WITH ALL THE OWLS."

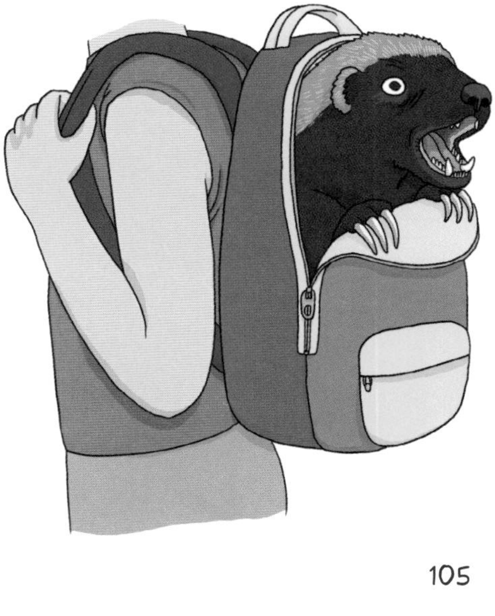

THE YATES ARE VERY SWEET PEOPLE AND DONATIONS TO THEIR SANCTUARY GO TOWARD BOTH WILDLIFE CARE AND LETTING MAKE-A-WISH FOUNDATION KIDS HAVE FUN ANIMAL ENCOUNTERS! VISIT THEIR WEBSITE AT: NURTUREDBYNATURE.ORG

BREAKFAST STUFF

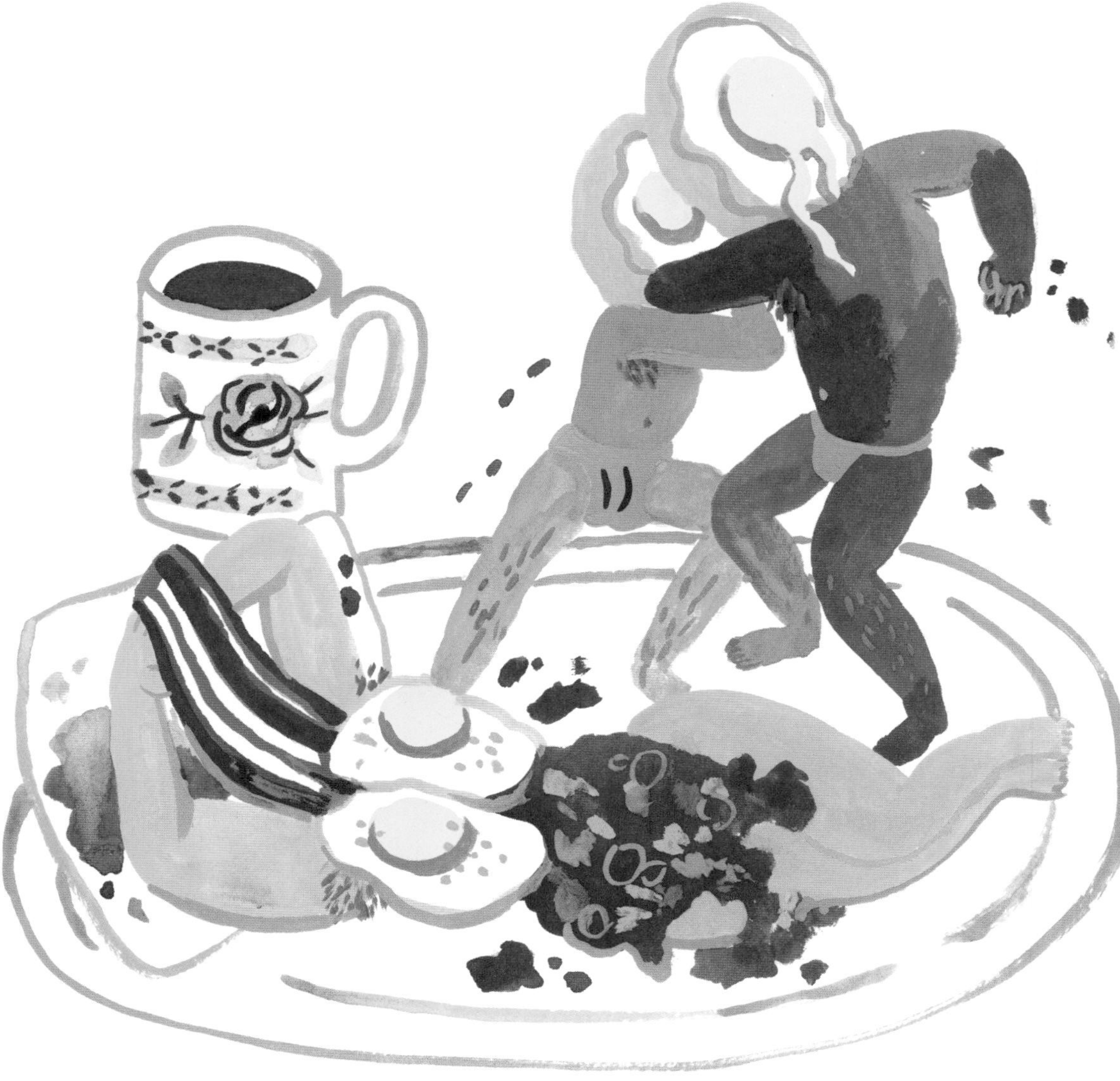

THE WORST BREAKFAST I'VE EVER HAD.

KNOW YOUR BREAKFAST FACTS

- DON'T SKIP IT
- THE PERSON WHO SKIPS BREAKFAST IS BAD
- IT'S A MEAL OF DIRE IMPORTANCE
- DISTRACTION FROM ENDLESS ~~WAIT~~ WAIT
    FOR LUNCH
- IT'S NEVER TO BE SKIPPED
- ALSO KNOWN AS BREAKSLEEP
            REVERSE DINNER
            BOWEL STARTER
            EGG MEAL
    AND ~~~~ PRE-BRUNCH

- THERE WAS A STUDY TO NOT SKIP BREKFAST

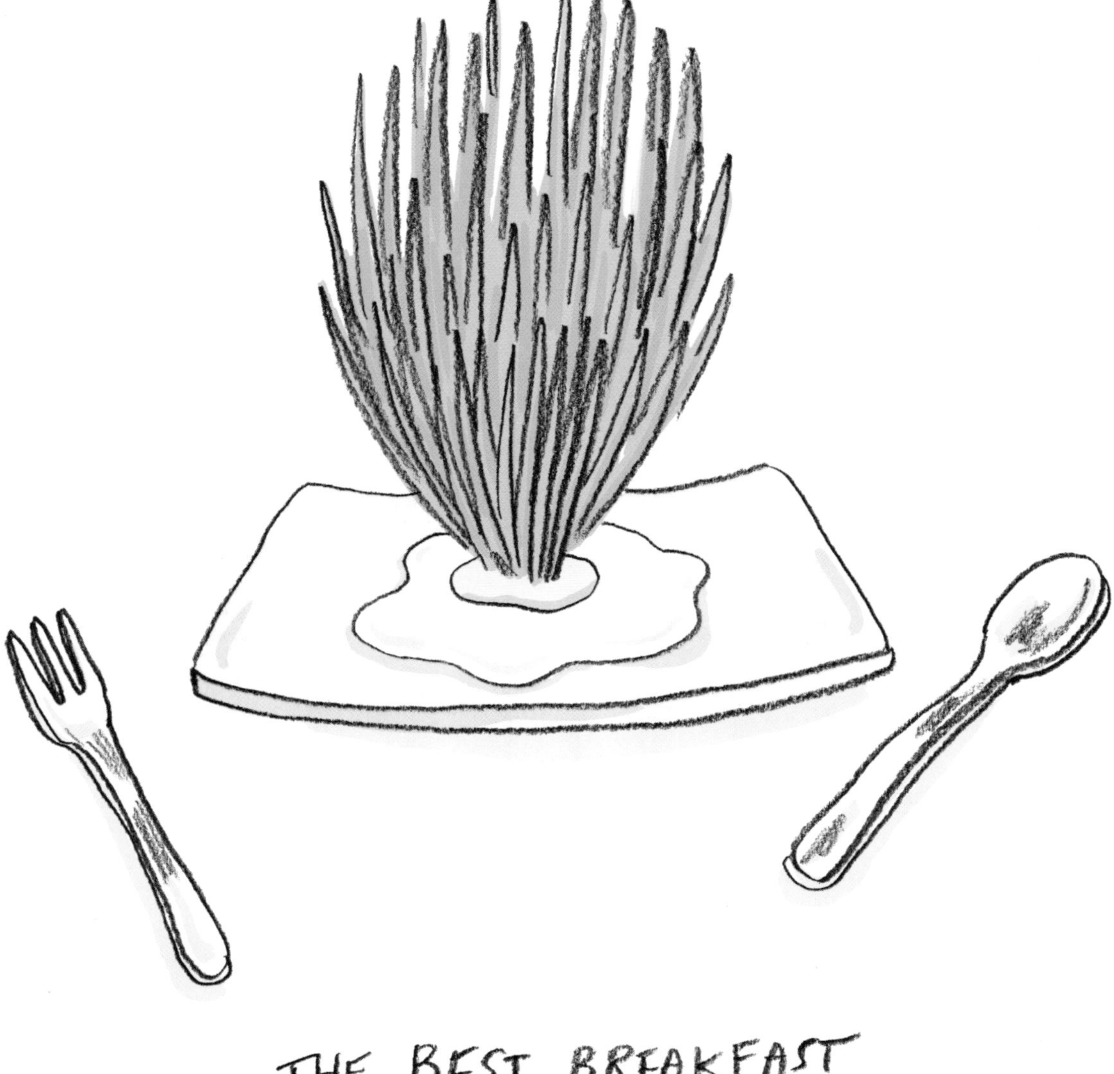

THE BEST BREAKFAST
I'VE EVER HAD.

FOOD DIARY

10 AM   1 CHOCOLATE ALMOND

11 AM   2 CHOCOLATE ALMONDS

12 PM   BURRITO BOWL

1 PM   2 CHOCOLATE ALMONDS

2 PM   2 CHOCOLATE ALMONDS

3:20 PM   3 CHOCOLATE ALMONDS

3:45 PM   1 CHOCOLATE ALMOND

4 PM   2 CHOCOLATE ALMONDS

4:30 PM   4 CHOCOLATE ALMONDS

4:39 PM   1 CHOCOLATE ALMOND

5 PM   6 CHOCOLATE ALMONDS

YOUR BREAKFAST QUESTIONS ANSWERED

Q: WHAT IS AN EGG?

A: A TEMPORARY HOME

Q: WHAT IS A SAUSAGE?

A: PIECES FROM ~~BITS~~ A BUNCH OF PIGS

Q: WHAT IS ORANGE JUICE?

A: FRUIT BLOOD

Q: HOW DO YOU FEEL?

A: READY FOR THE DAY.
ANY OTHER QUESTIONS?

Q: NO

CONNECT THE BREAKFAST FOOD WITH THE PERSON WHO WANTS TO EAT IT

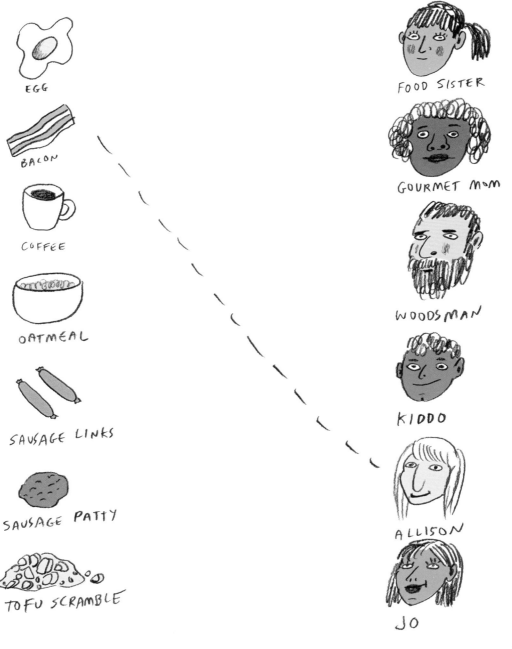

EGG

BACON

COFFEE

OATMEAL

SAUSAGE LINKS

SAUSAGE PATTY

TOFU SCRAMBLE

FOOD SISTER

GOURMET MOM

WOODSMAN

KIDDO

ALLISON

JO

OUTFIT IDEA

REGULAR
SHIRT AND
PANTS

<u>FOOD</u> SHIRT/PANTS

WEAR WHILE
EATING

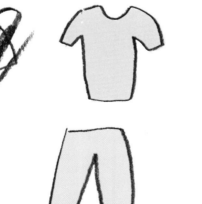

BACK TO

REGULAR

BREAKFAST RIDDLE

YOU NEED TO GO TO THE BATHROOM BUT THERE ARE THREE BITES OF BREAKFAST LEFT.

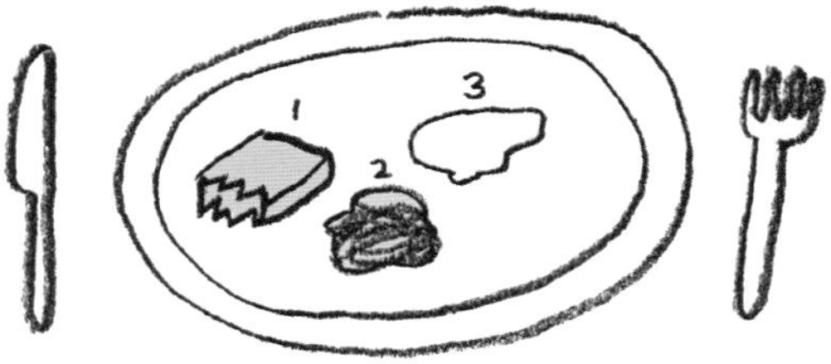

1
2
3

THREE BITES

DO YOU:

(A) EAT THEM QUICKLY THEN USE BATHROOM

(B) USE BATHROOM, COME BACK AND FINISH FOOD [redacted] (NOW COLD)

(C) FEED FOOD TO DOG, THEN USE BATHROOM

(D) SHIT PANTS, THROW FOOD AWAY. FUCK IT

(E) PUT THREE BITES IN THE TOILET, THEN USE IT.

[redacted]

(F) DON'T EAT, DON'T SHIT, DON'T MOVE

ANSWER: (B)

IS BREAKFAST GOOD OR BAD?

PROS

- SOMETHING TO LOOK FORWARD TO WHILE SLEEPING
- TASTES GOOD
- LOTS OF POTENTIAL
- CLASSIC
- YOU CAN GO SWEET OR SAVORY
- BREAKFAST BUFFETS
- COOL TIME TO EAT PROTEIN
- I LIKE IT
- EGGS IN GENERAL

CONS

- TEDIOUS
- BREAKFAST FOOD COMMERCIALS ARE ANNOYING
- OVERHYPED
- PANCAKES FEEL BAD
- MILK SLURPING SOUNDS

- NOT CANDLE LIT
- TOO IMPORTANT, TOO MUCH PRESSURE

I'M WRONG ABOUT EGGS

MOST PEOPLE AGREE
EGGS ARE BEST WHEN
SLIGHTLY WET.

A RUNNY YOLK IS
A DELIGHTFUL TREAT.

BUT I THINK IT'S
GROSS.

I WANT A DRY
EGG! WITH DISTINCT,
INTERLOCKING PIECES.

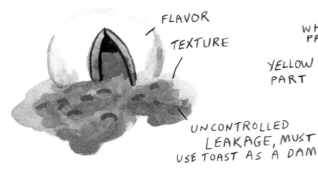

FLAVOR

TEXTURE

UNCONTROLLED
LEAKAGE, MUST
USE TOAST AS A DAM

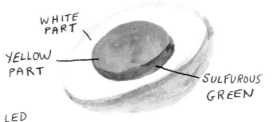

WHITE
PART

YELLOW
PART

SULFUROUS
GREEN

I KNOW I'M WRONG, I'M SORRY.
DON'T BE MAD AT ME.

FOOD PHOTOGRAPHY TERMINOLOGY

HAMLAP: GLISTENING, OVERLAPPING SLICES OF HAM

'NISH: GARNISH/HERBS USED TO DECORATE DISHES

BURGVIEW: AT LEAST 75% of FRAME SHOULD BE BURGER.

'PROUT: A ROGUE SPROUT IS IN THE SHOT.

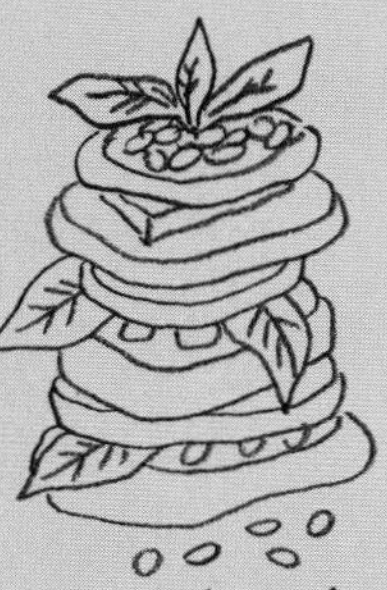

NICE 'NISH

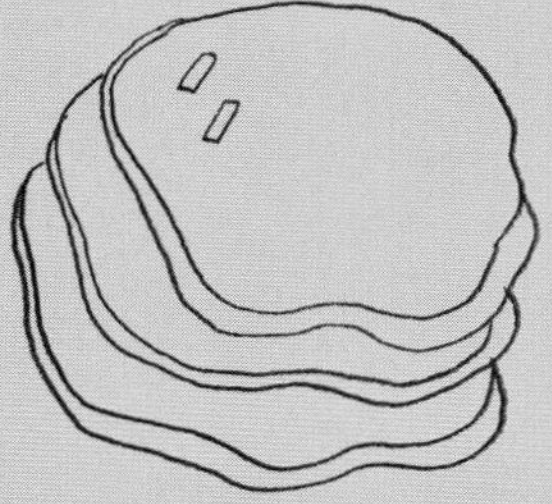

HAMLAP

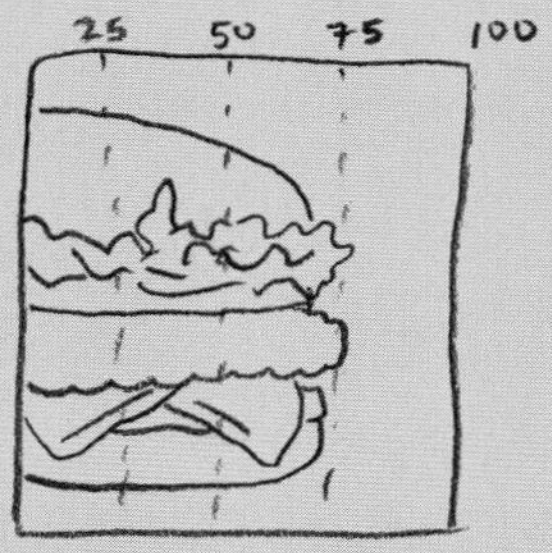
25
50
75
100

BURGVIEW

RULE OF THIRDS: YOU SHOULD WANT TO EAT THREE HELPINGS OF FOOD DEPICTED

STACK: CAKE NEEDS TO LOOK AS BIG AS POSSIBLE.

CAKE: FOOD NEEDS TO LOOK LIKE A CAKE.

POO IT UP: TORCH FOOD TO BROWN IT

WET TAKE: A SHOT THAT EVOKES THE MOISTURE LEVEL OF THE FOOD

OH, FRIG: PHOTOGRAPHER'S PANTING IS FOGGING UP THE SHOT

SLIME IN THE GATE: PHOTOGRAPHER'S DROOL IS MUCKING UP THE SHOT

WE NEED A RE-COOK: PHOTOGRAPHER HAS ACCIDENTALLY EATEN THE FOOD

TILT CHECK: MAKE SURE IT DOESN'T LOOK LIKE FOOD IS FALLING OR ABOUT TO FALL (UNLESS IT'S FRUIT)

FRUIT DROP: FRUIT LOOKS TASTIEST WHEN IT'S FALLING

MOUTH & EYES
CAMERA
FOOD
LIGHT SOURCE
MOISTURE

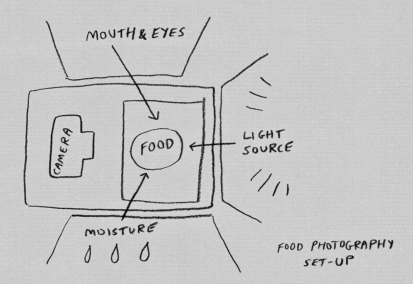

FOOD PHOTOGRAPHY SET-UP

BROWN PLATE: DISHWARE OR UTENSILS LOOK UNAPPEALING

FLUR: FOOD WAS MOVING TOO FAST AND SHOT LOOKS BLURRY

FOOTY: FOOD STYLED TO LOOK LIKE AN ASS

CLOSELIPS: LIGHT IS BOUNCING OFF TEETH AND AFFECTING THE SHOT.

GRINGE: INEDIBLE SUBSTANCE USED TO MAKE FOOD LOOK MORE EDIBLE

PHOTOG DOWN: PHOTOGRAPHER HAS SLIPPED AND FALLEN IN FOOD

BOONT: A BAD FOOD PHOTOGRAPHED TO LOOK GOOD

BEAUD: A NATURALLY BEAUTIFUL FOOD

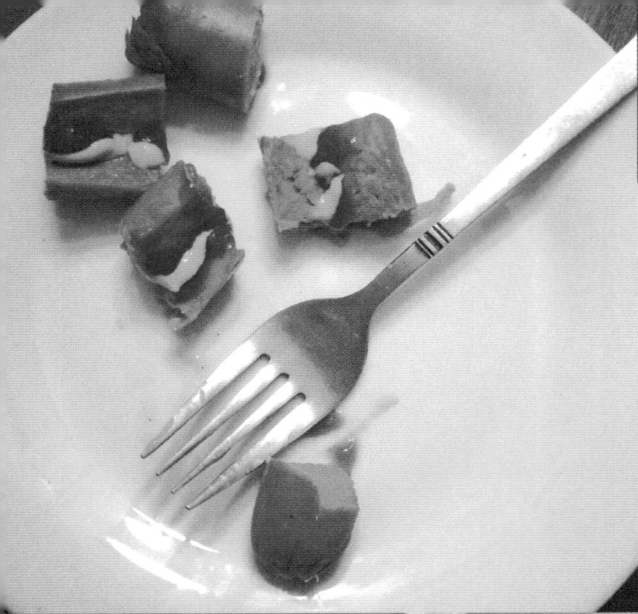
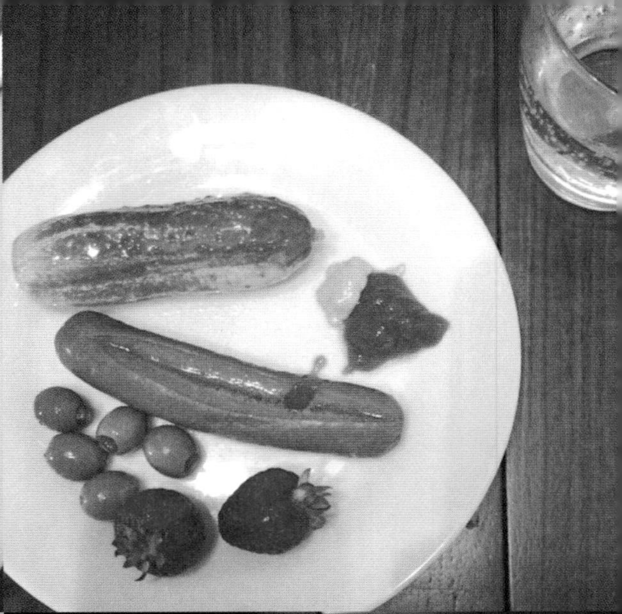
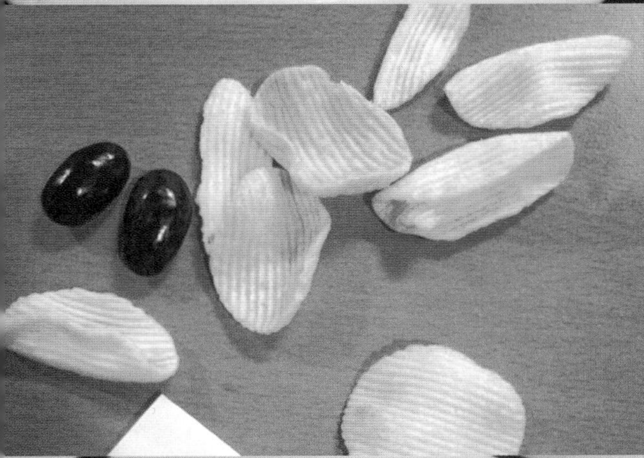
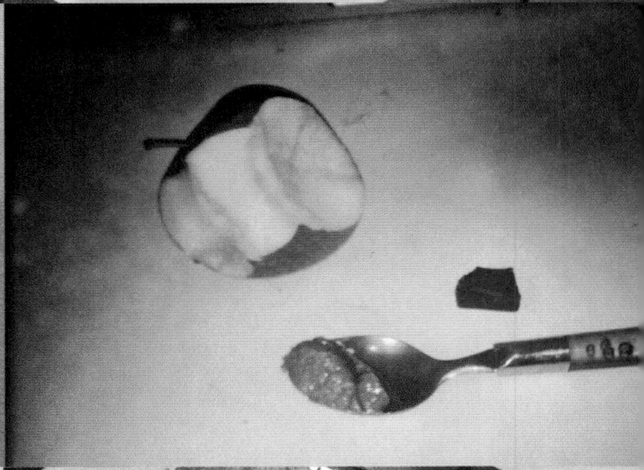
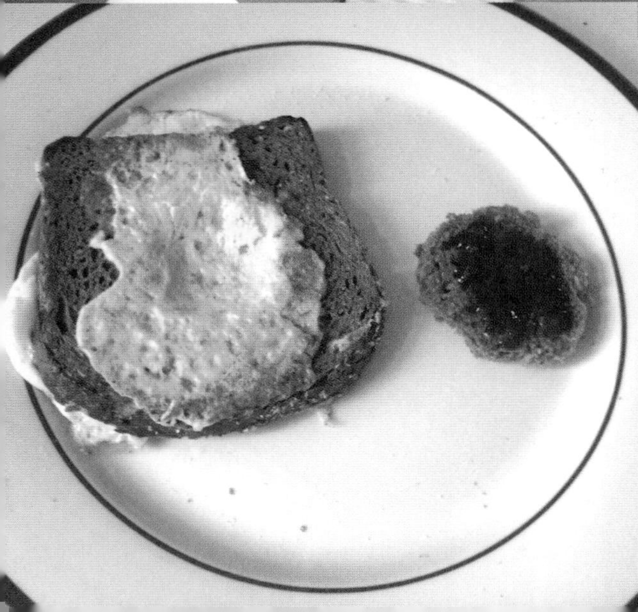
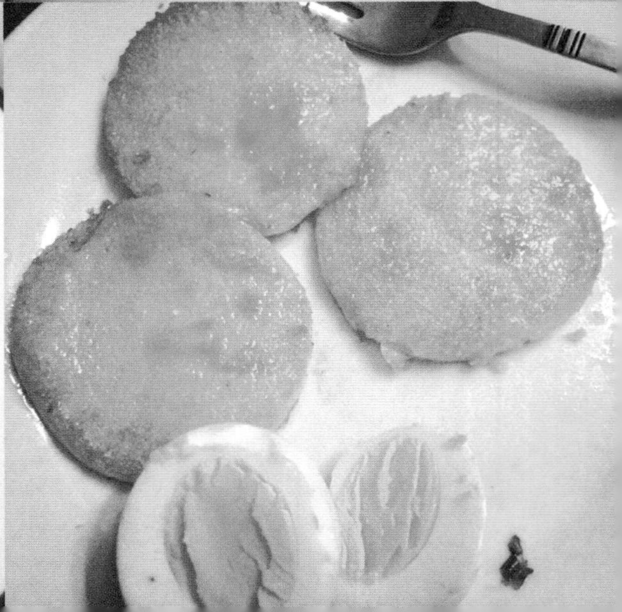

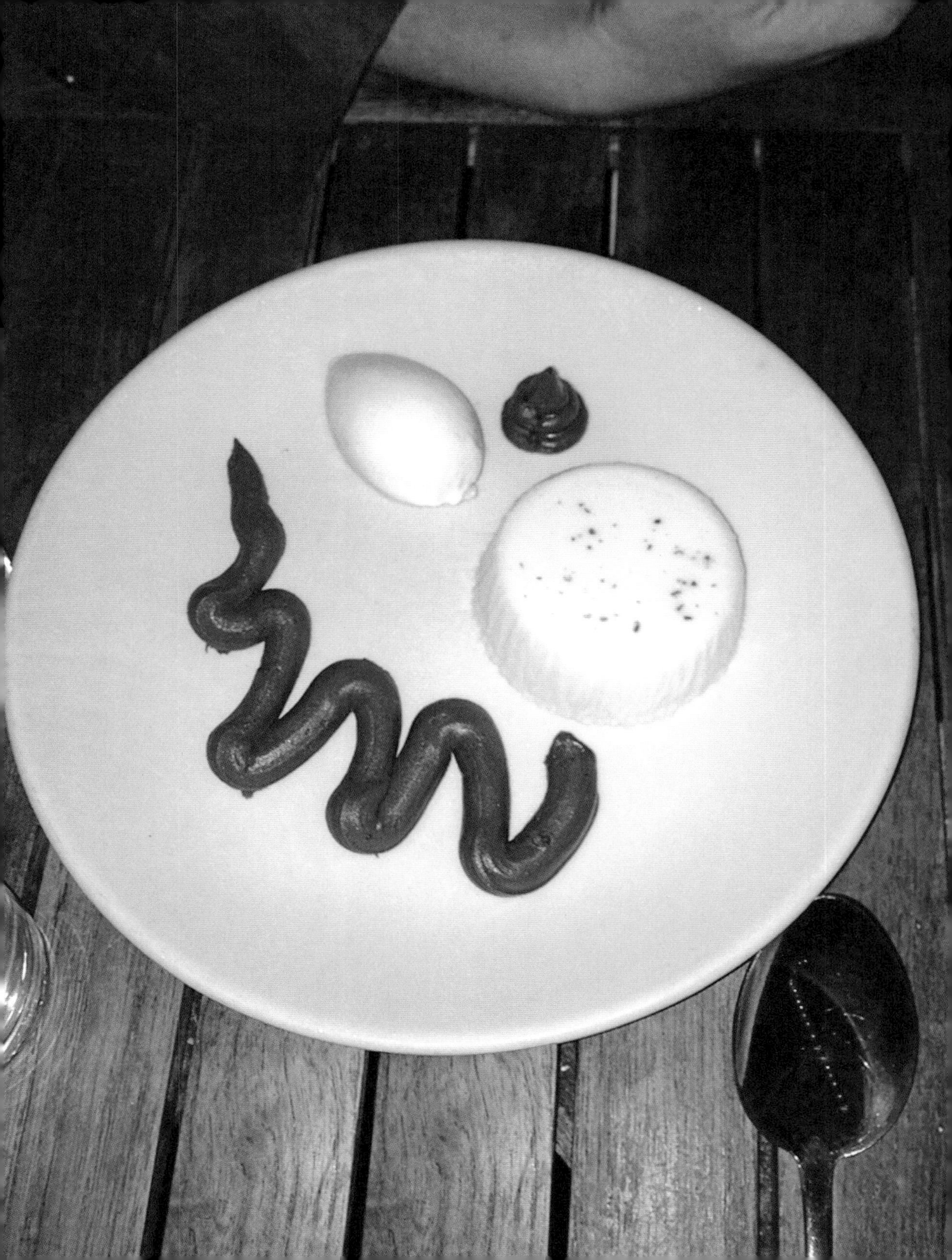

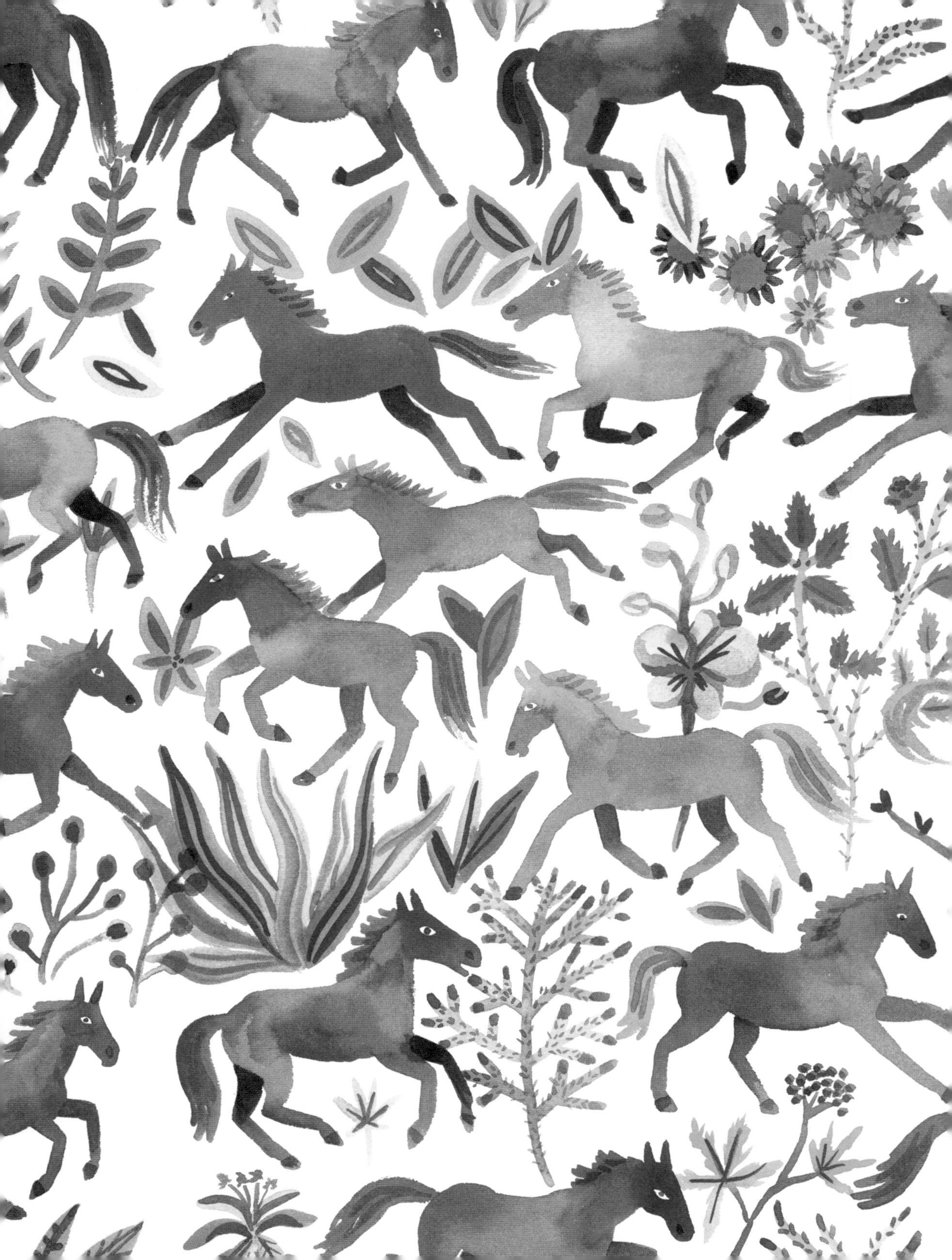

ARGENTINA TRAVEL DIARY

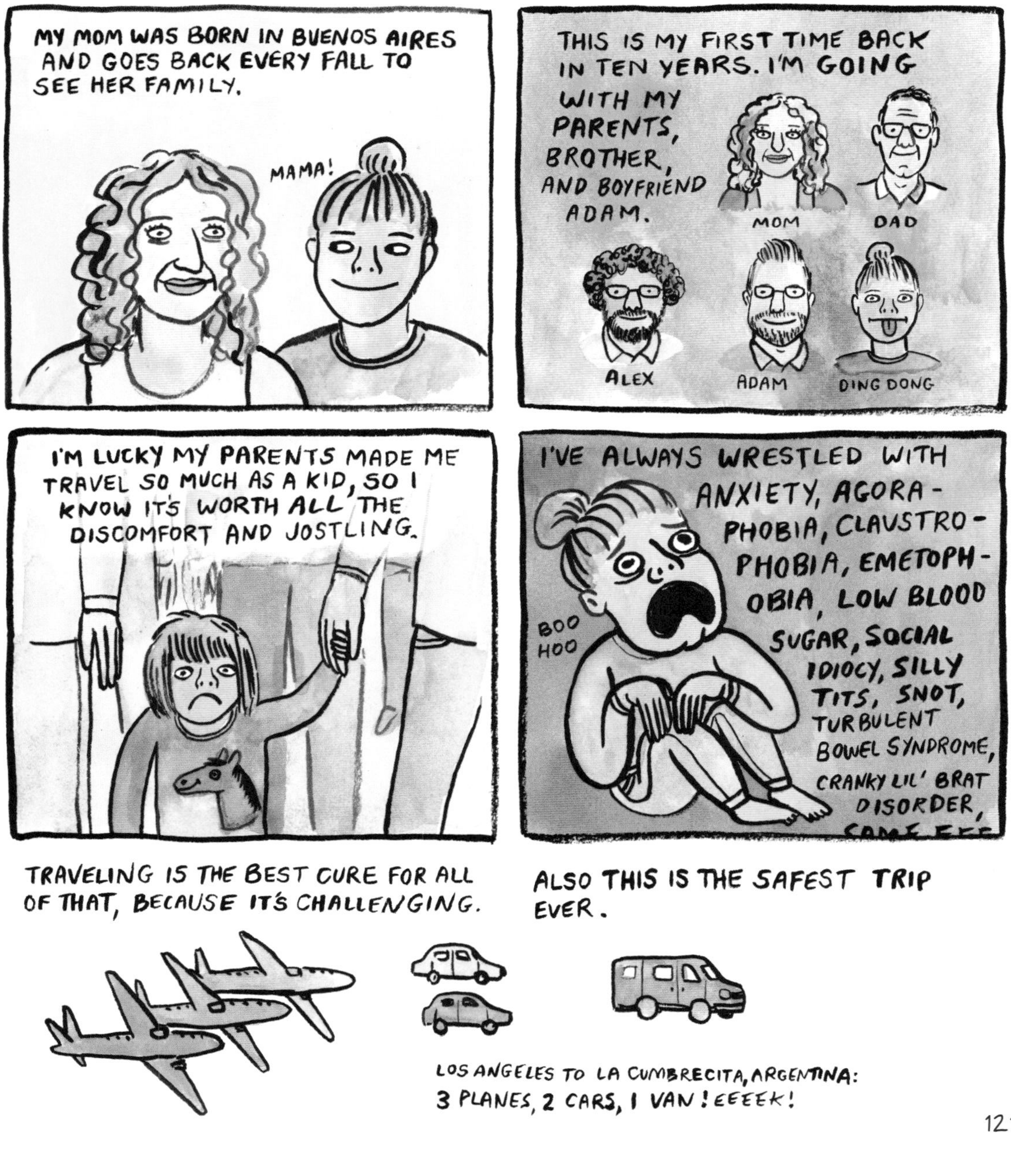

MY MOM WAS BORN IN BUENOS AIRES AND GOES BACK EVERY FALL TO SEE HER FAMILY.
MAMA!
THIS IS MY FIRST TIME BACK IN TEN YEARS. I'M GOING WITH MY PARENTS, BROTHER, AND BOYFRIEND ADAM.
MOM
DAD
ALEX
ADAM
DING DONG
I'M LUCKY MY PARENTS MADE ME TRAVEL SO MUCH AS A KID, SO I KNOW IT'S WORTH ALL THE DISCOMFORT AND JOSTLING.
I'VE ALWAYS WRESTLED WITH ANXIETY, AGORA-PHOBIA, CLAUSTRO-PHOBIA, EMETOPH-OBIA, LOW BLOOD SUGAR, SOCIAL IDIOCY, SILLY TITS, SNOT, TURBULENT BOWEL SYNDROME, CRANKY LIL' BRAT DISORDER,
BOO HOO
TRAVELING IS THE BEST CURE FOR ALL OF THAT, BECAUSE IT'S CHALLENGING.
ALSO THIS IS THE SAFEST TRIP EVER.
LOS ANGELES TO LA CUMBRECITA, ARGENTINA:
3 PLANES, 2 CARS, 1 VAN! EEEEK!

9/12 FLYING TO ARGENTINA

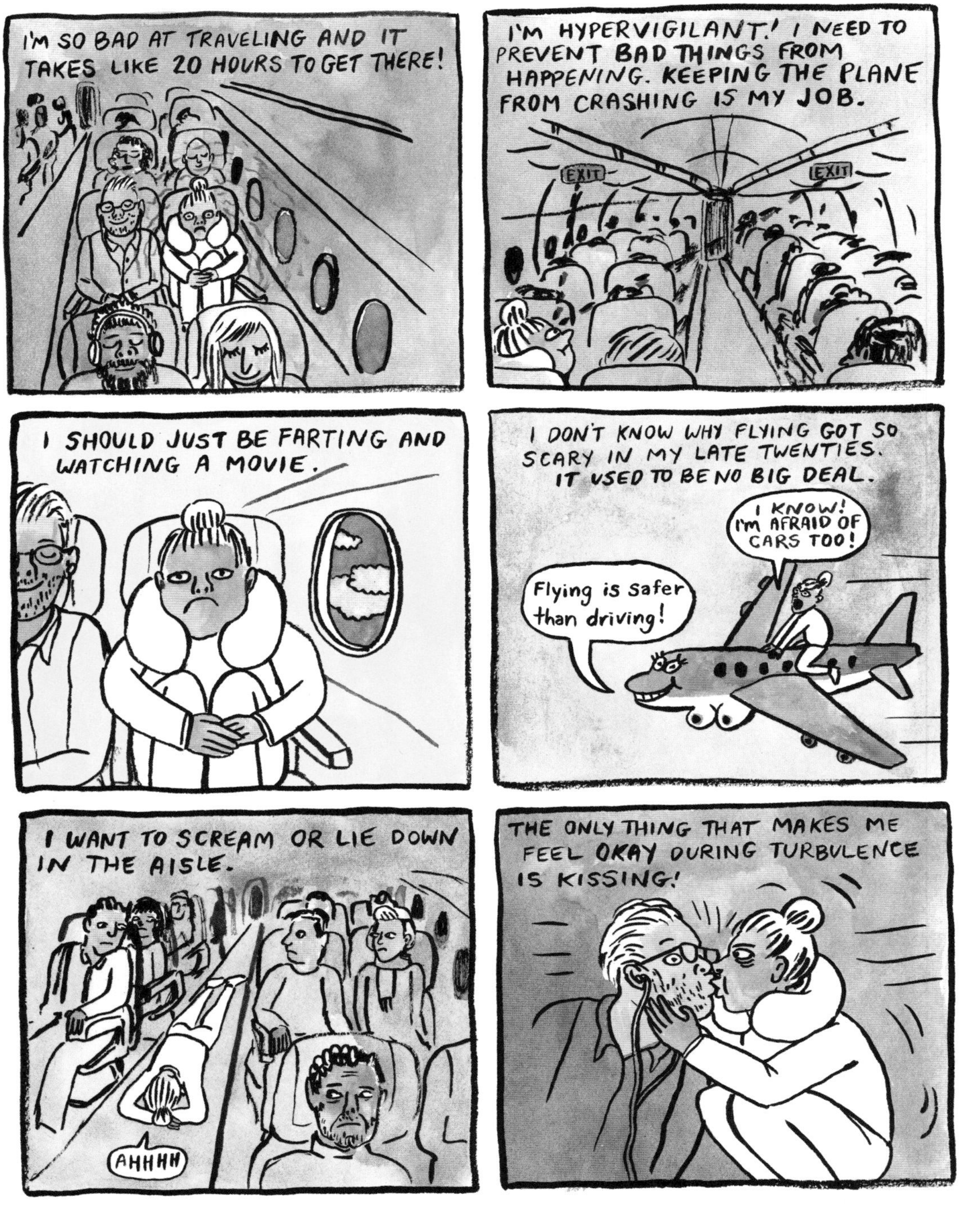

I'M SO BAD AT TRAVELING AND IT TAKES LIKE 20 HOURS TO GET THERE!
I'M HYPERVIGILANT! I NEED TO PREVENT BAD THINGS FROM HAPPENING. KEEPING THE PLANE FROM CRASHING IS MY JOB.
EXIT
EXIT
I SHOULD JUST BE FARTING AND WATCHING A MOVIE.
I DON'T KNOW WHY FLYING GOT SO SCARY IN MY LATE TWENTIES. IT USED TO BE NO BIG DEAL.
Flying is safer than driving!
I KNOW! I'M AFRAID OF CARS TOO!
I WANT TO SCREAM OR LIE DOWN IN THE AISLE.
AHHHH
THE ONLY THING THAT MAKES ME FEEL OKAY DURING TURBULENCE IS KISSING!

9/13 LA CUMBRECITA

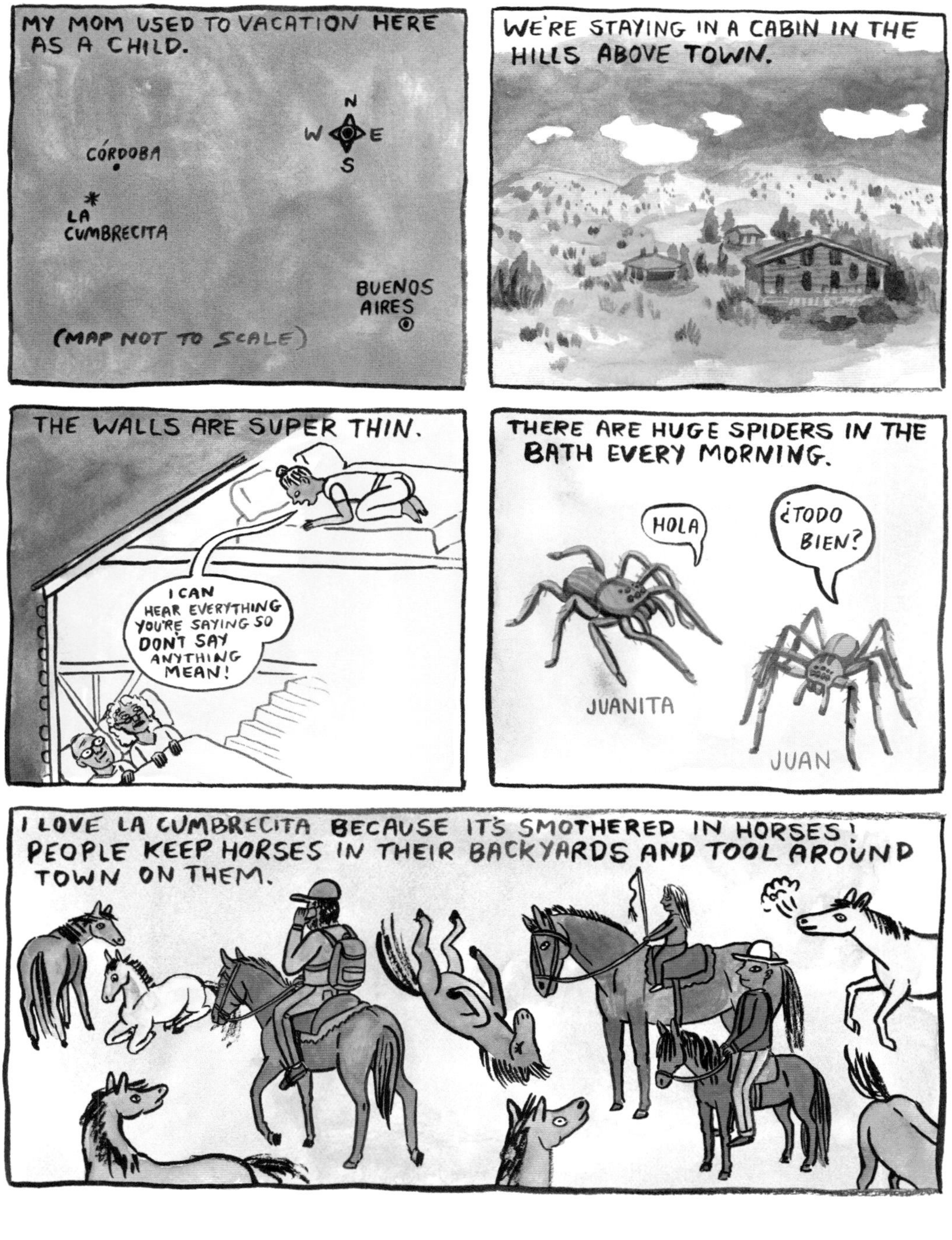
MY MOM USED TO VACATION HERE AS A CHILD.
N
W
E
S
CÓRDOBA
LA CUMBRECITA
BUENOS AIRES
(MAP NOT TO SCALE)
WE'RE STAYING IN A CABIN IN THE HILLS ABOVE TOWN.
THE WALLS ARE SUPER THIN.
I CAN HEAR EVERYTHING YOU'RE SAYING SO DON'T SAY ANYTHING MEAN!
THERE ARE HUGE SPIDERS IN THE BATH EVERY MORNING.
HOLA
¿TODO BIEN?
JUANITA
JUAN
I LOVE LA CUMBRECITA BECAUSE IT'S SMOTHERED IN HORSES! PEOPLE KEEP HORSES IN THEIR BACKYARDS AND TOOL AROUND TOWN ON THEM.

9/14 YOU'D THINK SOUTH AMERICAN FOOD WOULD BE SPICY BUT IT'S TOTALLY EUROPEAN. LOTS OF GERMAN/SWISS OPTIONS:

SPAETZLE + GOULASH

COMFORT SLOP

TRUCHE RÓQUEFORTE

"CHEESE FISH"

AND TONS OF ITALIAN FOOD:

MILANESA NAPOLITANA

CHEESE

HAM SLICE

BREADED MEAT CUTLET

TOMATO SAUCE

MY MOM USED TO MAKE THIS FOR DINNER EVERY WEEK

ÑOQUIS (GNOCCHI)

POTATO OR RICOTTA DUMPLINGS
BLISS PILLOWS

VIZCACHA IS THE STRANGEST THING YOU CAN EAT HERE. IT'S A BIG, CHINCHILLA-LIKE RODENT. ALEX AND I BOUGHT JARS OF PICKLED VIZCACHA AND STASHED THEM IN OUR LUGGAGE.

Vizcacha ESCABECHE

IT TASTES LIKE CHICKEN

AFTER DINNER, WE WATCHED BLADE II DUBBED IN SPANISH, WHILE I ATE TWO BAGS OF MEAT-FLAVORED CHIPS.

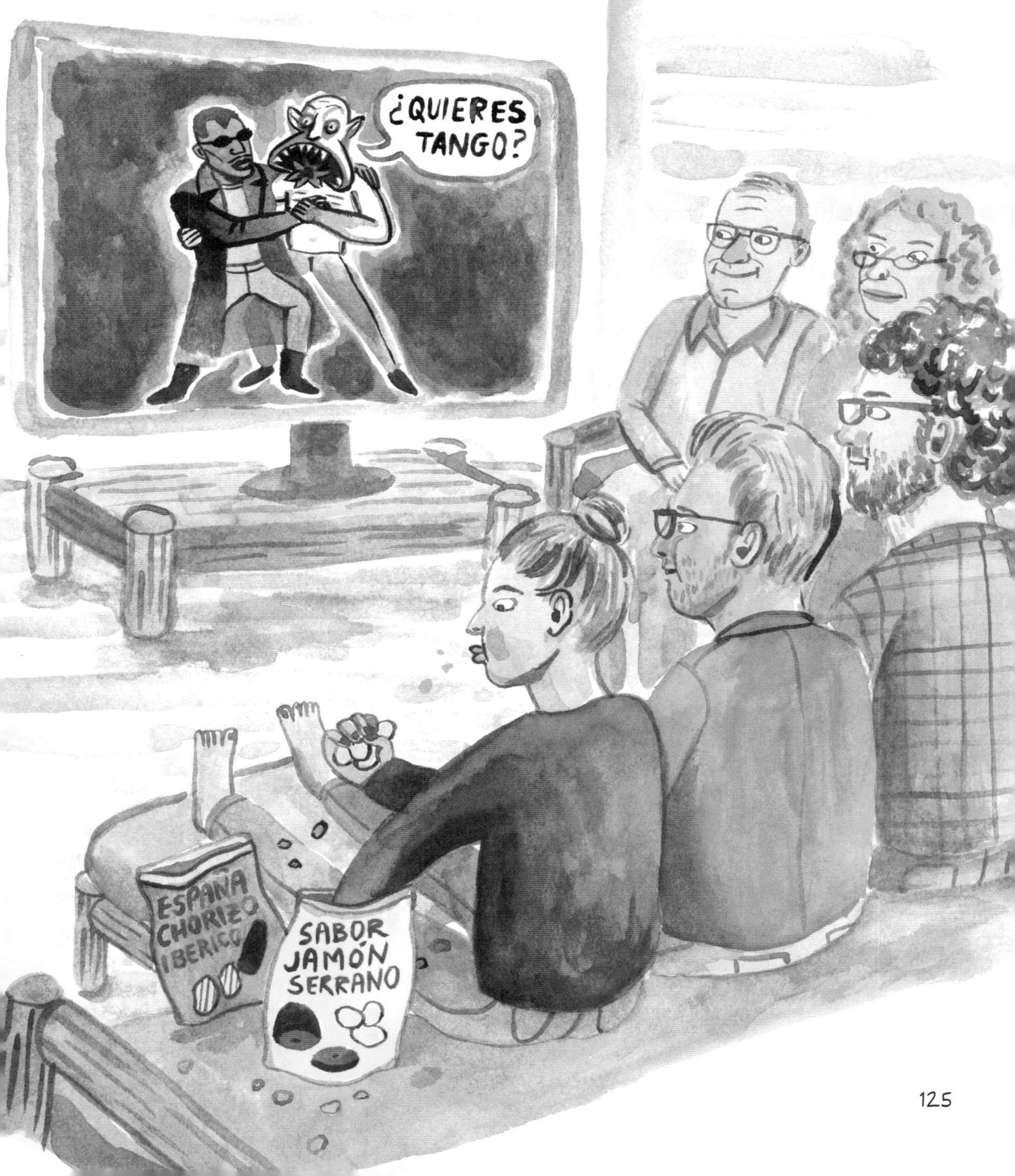
¿QUIERES TANGO?
ESPAÑA CHORIZO IBERICO
SABOR JAMÓN SERRANO

9/15 SOMETIMES IT'S OKAY TO WUSS OUT

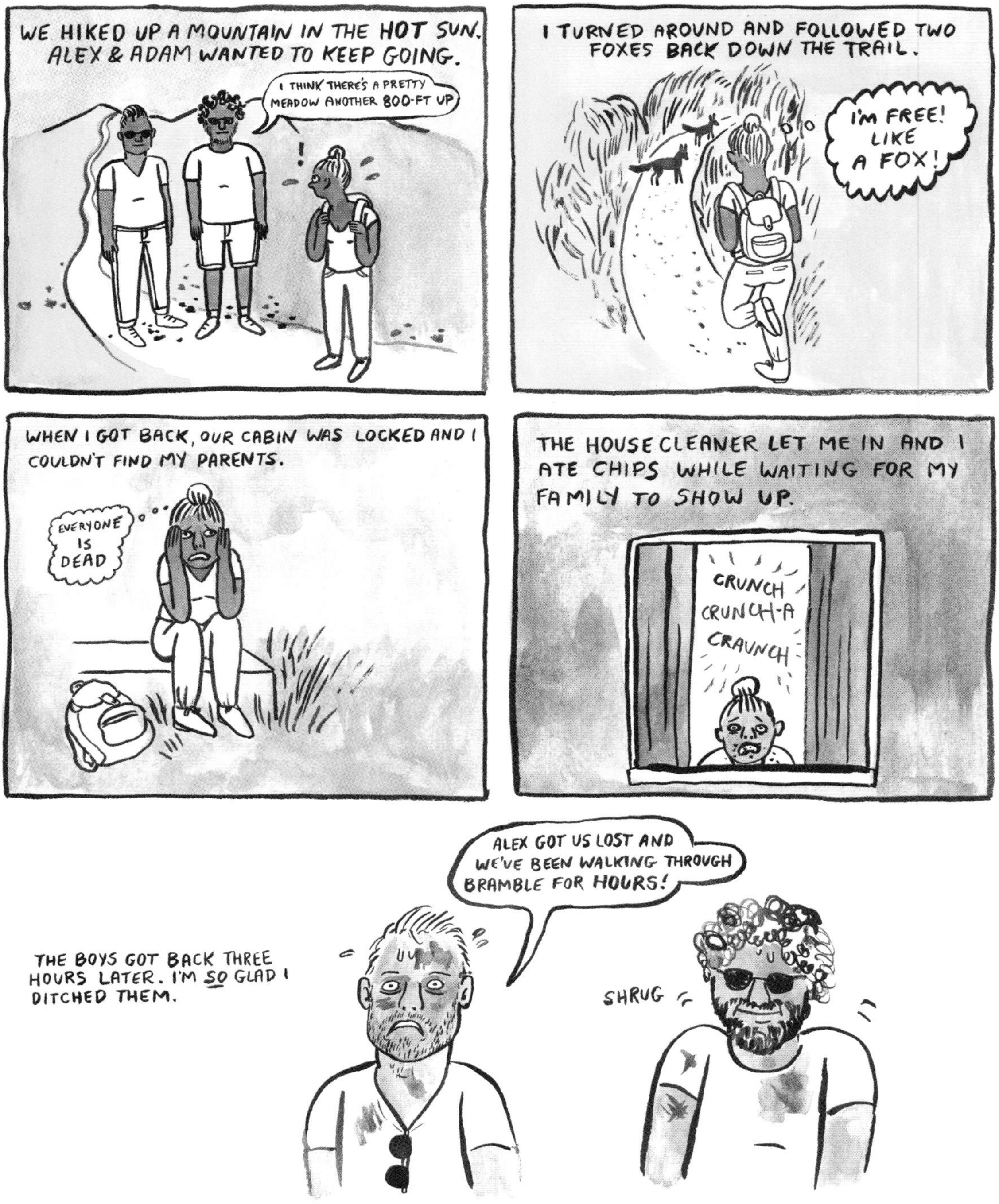
WE HIKED UP A MOUNTAIN IN THE HOT SUN. ALEX & ADAM WANTED TO KEEP GOING.
I THINK THERE'S A PRETTY MEADOW ANOTHER 800-FT UP
!
I TURNED AROUND AND FOLLOWED TWO FOXES BACK DOWN THE TRAIL.
I'M FREE! LIKE A FOX!
WHEN I GOT BACK, OUR CABIN WAS LOCKED AND I COULDN'T FIND MY PARENTS.
EVERYONE IS DEAD
THE HOUSE CLEANER LET ME IN AND I ATE CHIPS WHILE WAITING FOR MY FAMILY TO SHOW UP.
CRUNCH
CRUNCH-A
CRAUNCH
THE BOYS GOT BACK THREE HOURS LATER. I'M SO GLAD I DITCHED THEM.
ALEX GOT US LOST AND WE'VE BEEN WALKING THROUGH BRAMBLE FOR HOURS!
SHRUG

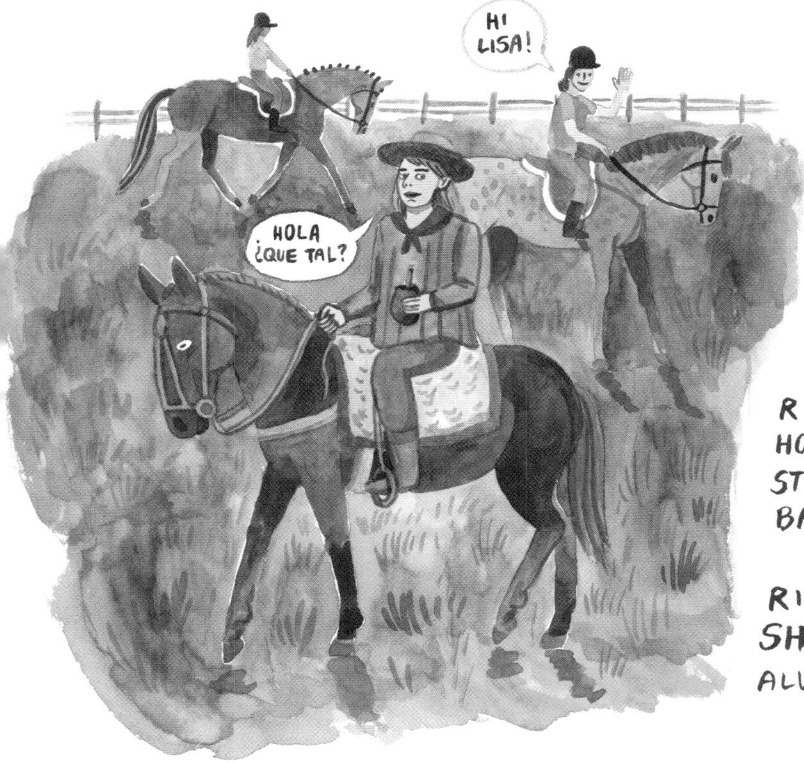
HI LISA!
HOLA ¿QUE TAL?

THIS EVENING ALEX AND I ARE RENTING HORSES AND I'M SO EXCITED AND SCARED I'LL FLY OFF AND CRACK MY SKULL. I'VE BEEN LOOKING FORWARDS TO THIS FOR MONTHS. I KEEP DAYDREAMING ABOUT RIDING A LITTLE CRIOLLO HORSE AROUND GAUCHO-STYLE AT THE ENGLISH BARN I RIDE AT IN L.A.

RIDING FEELS COOL AS SHIT BUT IT DOESN'T ALWAYS LOOK SEXY.

RIDING FEELS LIKE:

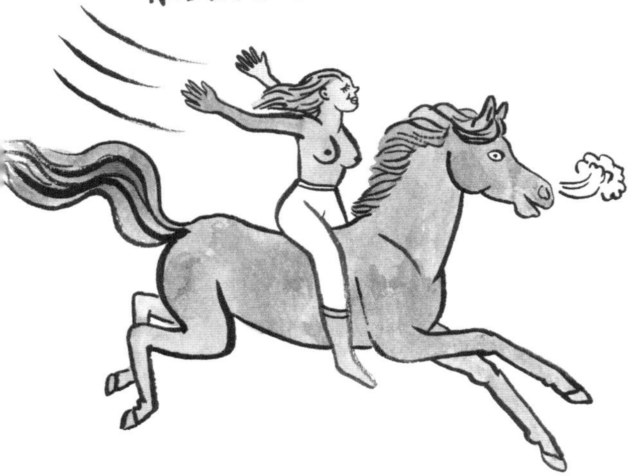

RIDING LOOKS LIKE:

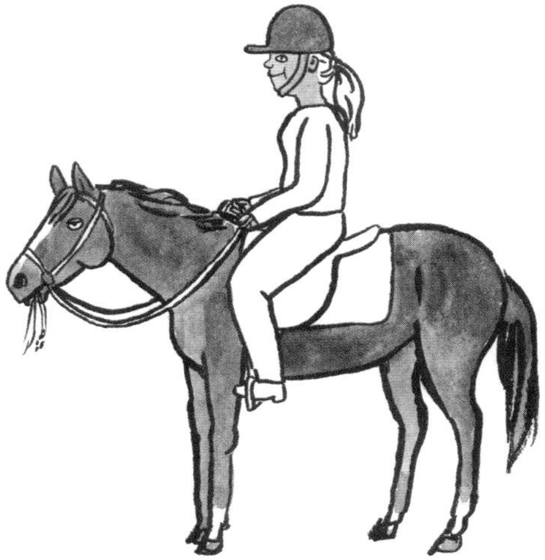

ONE TIME, ADAM SAID, "DON'T WORRY, EVERYONE LOOKS DORKY ON HORSEBACK!" AND I WAS SO UPSET, I COULDN'T SPEAK TO HIM FOR HALF A DAY.

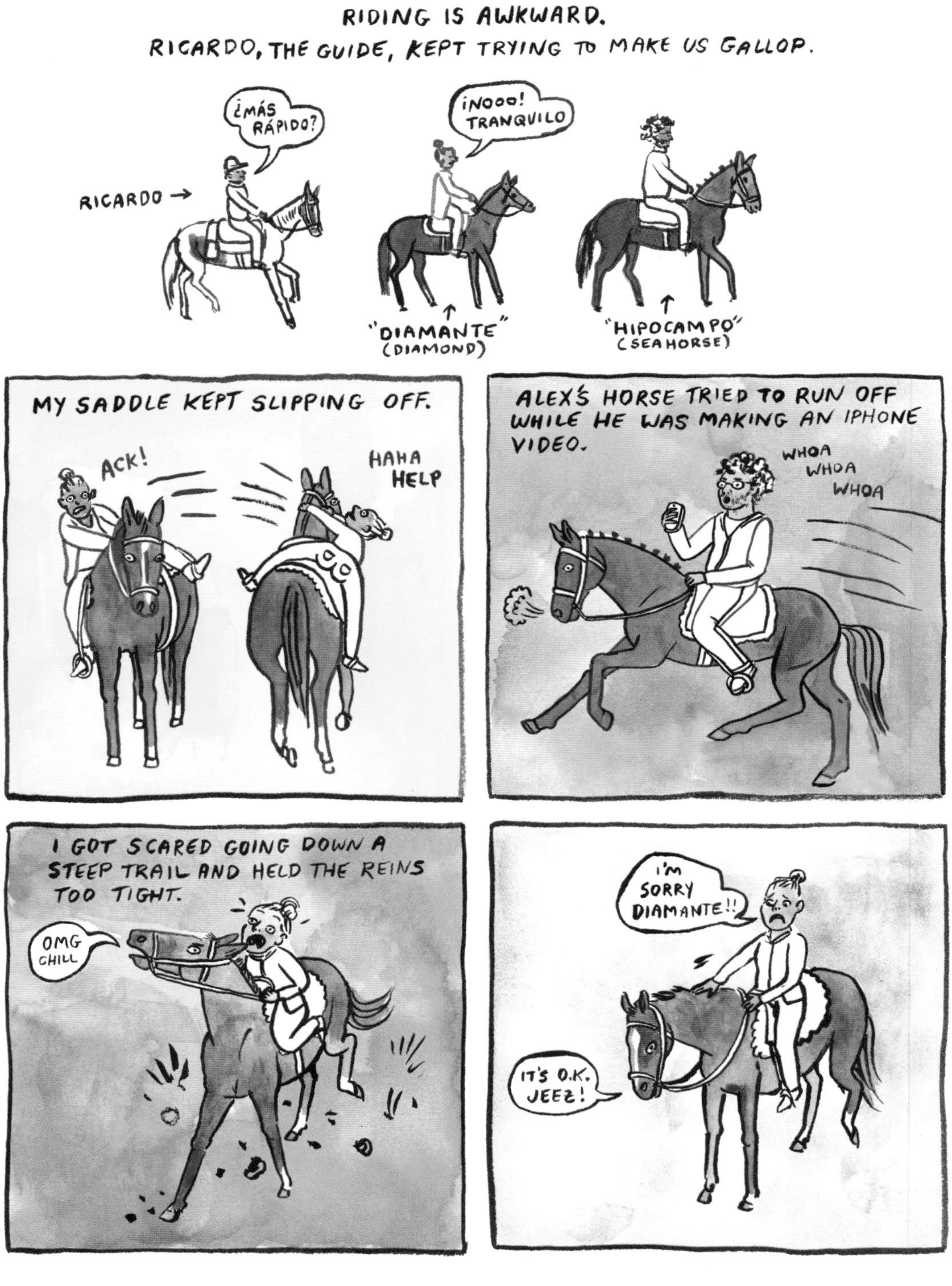
RIDING IS AWKWARD.
RICARDO, THE GUIDE, KEPT TRYING TO MAKE US GALLOP.
¿MÁS RÁPIDO?
¡NOOO! TRANQUILO
RICARDO →
"DIAMANTE" (DIAMOND)
"HIPOCAMPO" (SEAHORSE)
MY SADDLE KEPT SLIPPING OFF.
ACK!
HAHA HELP
ALEX'S HORSE TRIED TO RUN OFF WHILE HE WAS MAKING AN IPHONE VIDEO.
WHOA WHOA WHOA
I GOT SCARED GOING DOWN A STEEP TRAIL AND HELD THE REINS TOO TIGHT.
OMG CHILL
I'M SORRY DIAMANTE!!
IT'S O.K. JEEZ!

THIS IS A DIFFICULT THING TO WRITE ABOUT –
A YEAR AGO, ALEX'S GIRLFRIEND ROXY DIED.

SHE'S BEEN ON ALL OF OUR MINDS.
IT FEELS WEIRD THAT SHE ISN'T ON THIS TRIP WITH US.

AFTER SHE PASSED AWAY, I STARTED RIDING AGAIN FOR THE FIRST TIME IN TWO DECADES.

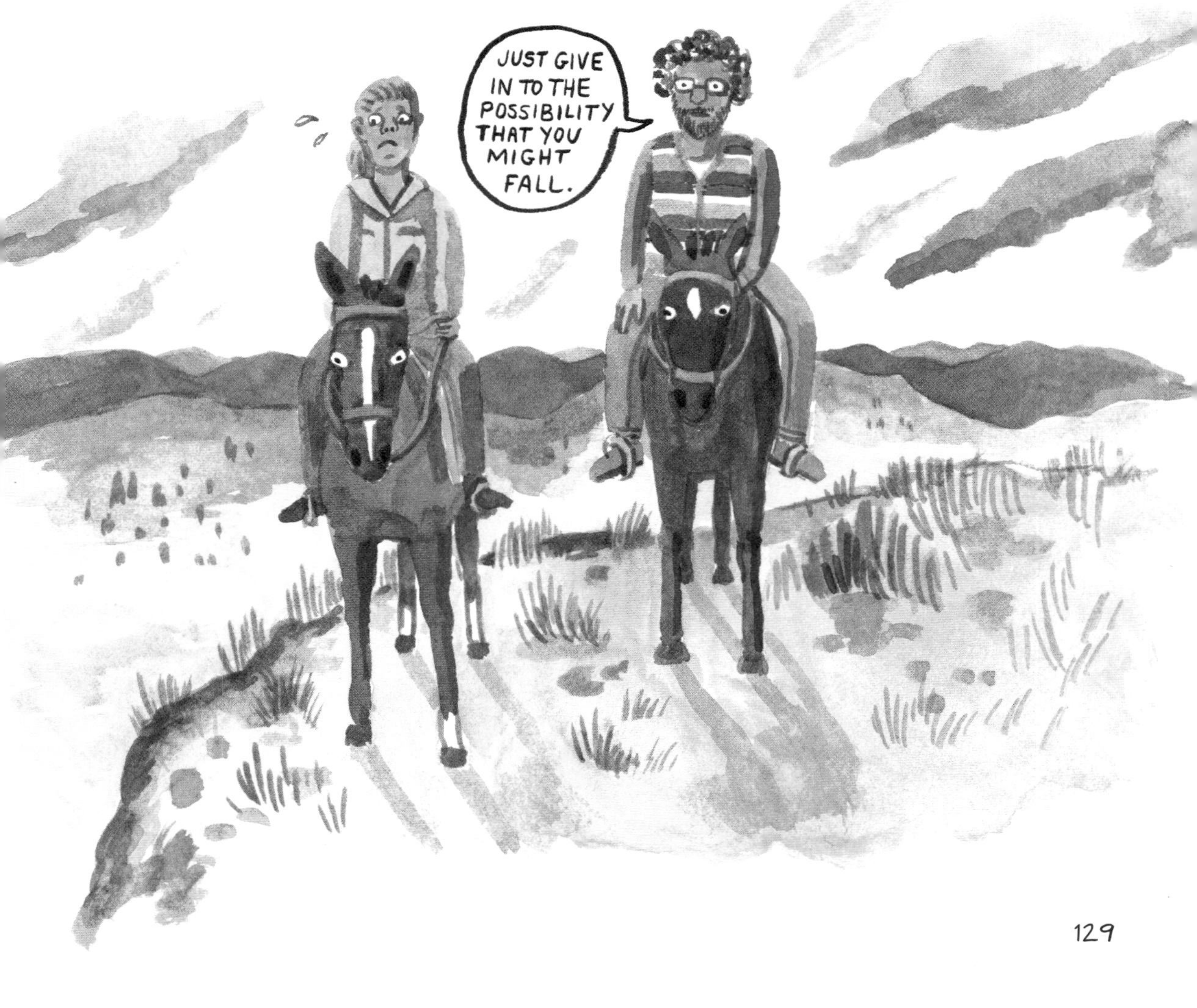
JUST GIVE IN TO THE POSSIBILITY THAT YOU MIGHT FALL.

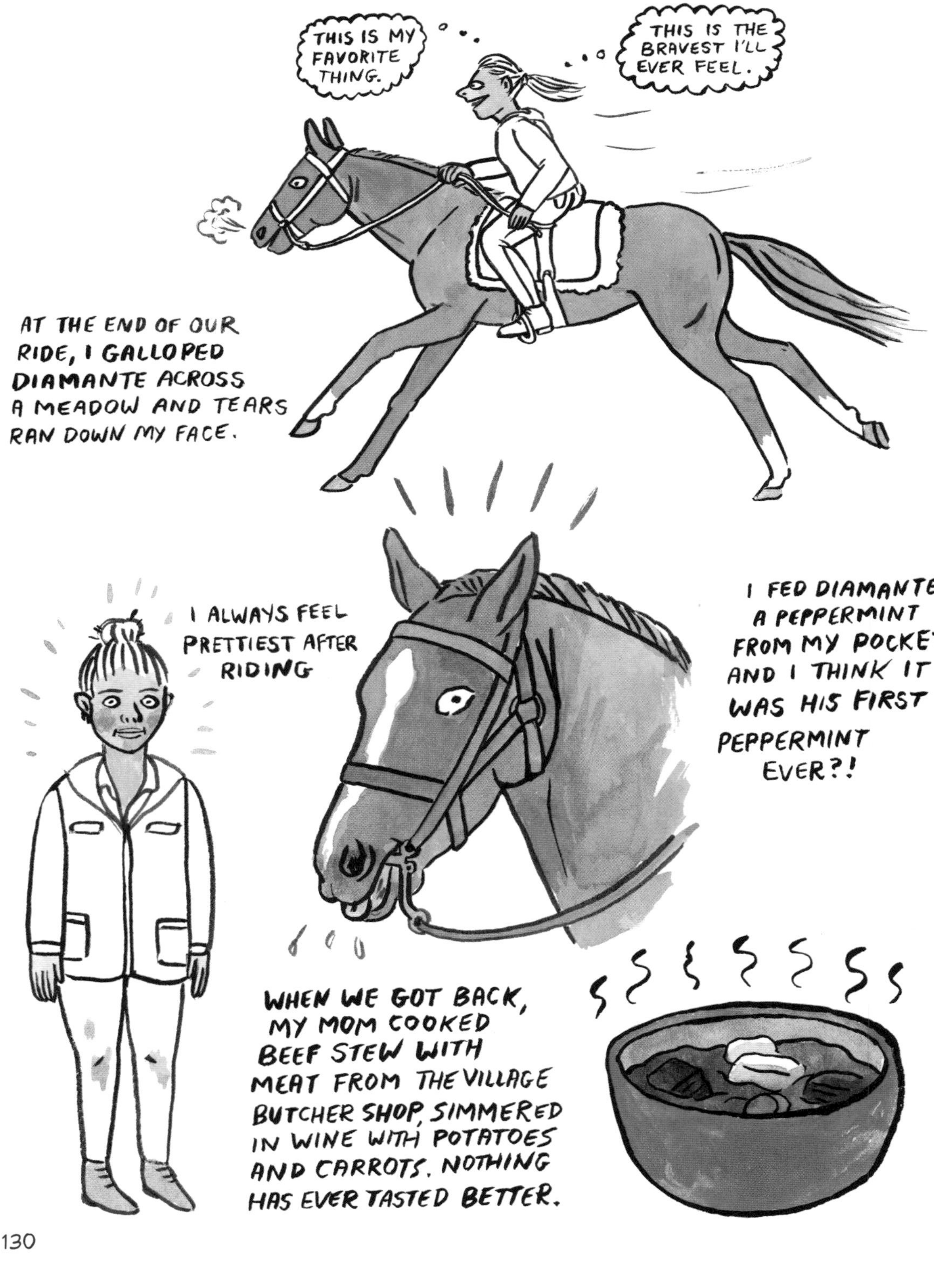
THIS IS MY FAVORITE THING.
THIS IS THE BRAVEST I'LL EVER FEEL.
AT THE END OF OUR RIDE, I GALLOPED DIAMANTE ACROSS A MEADOW AND TEARS RAN DOWN MY FACE.
I ALWAYS FEEL PRETTIEST AFTER RIDING
I FED DIAMANTE A PEPPERMINT FROM MY POCKET, AND I THINK IT WAS HIS FIRST PEPPERMINT EVER?!
WHEN WE GOT BACK, MY MOM COOKED BEEF STEW WITH MEAT FROM THE VILLAGE BUTCHER SHOP, SIMMERED IN WINE WITH POTATOES AND CARROTS. NOTHING HAS EVER TASTED BETTER.

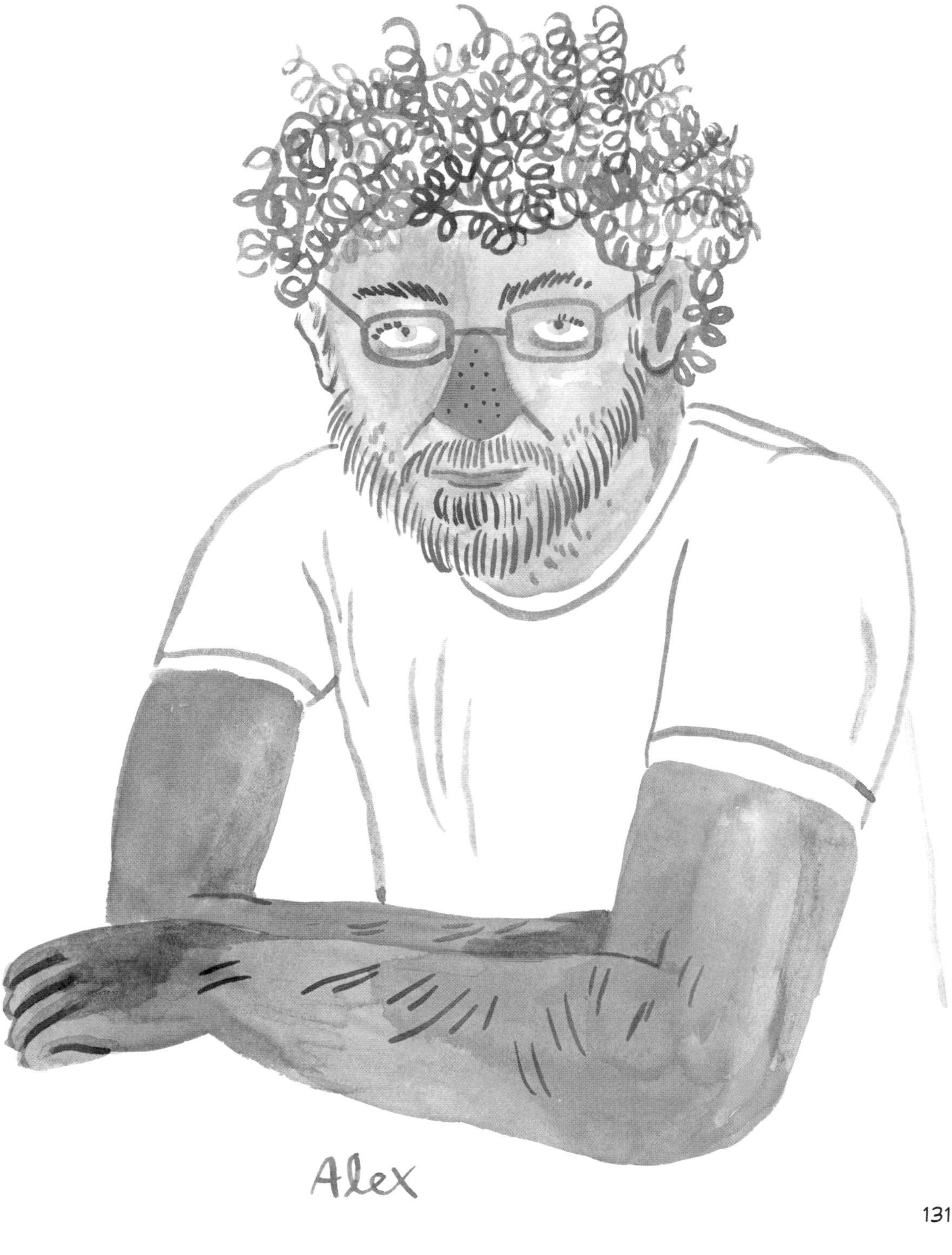
Alex

9/16 WE LEFT LA CUMBRECITA AND HEADED TO BUENOS AIRES TODAY. I MISS DIAMANTE ALREADY.

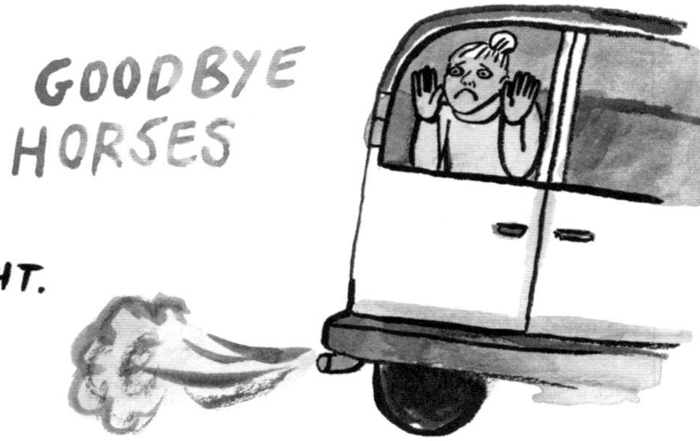
GOODBYE HORSES

WE DROVE BY SOME SWIMMING POOL DEALERSHIPS THAT DISPLAYED THE POOLS UPRIGHT.

IS THIS NORMAL? IT LOOKS INSANE.

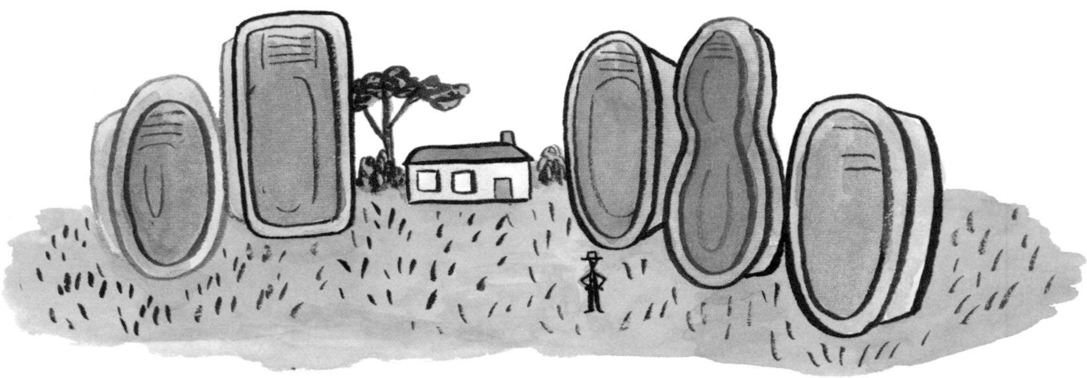

AT THE AIRPORT, A MAN PAID TWENTY PESOS TO CUT IN THE TAXI LINE AND MY MOM WENT FULL PORTEÑO AND CUSSED HIM OUT. GO MAMASITA!

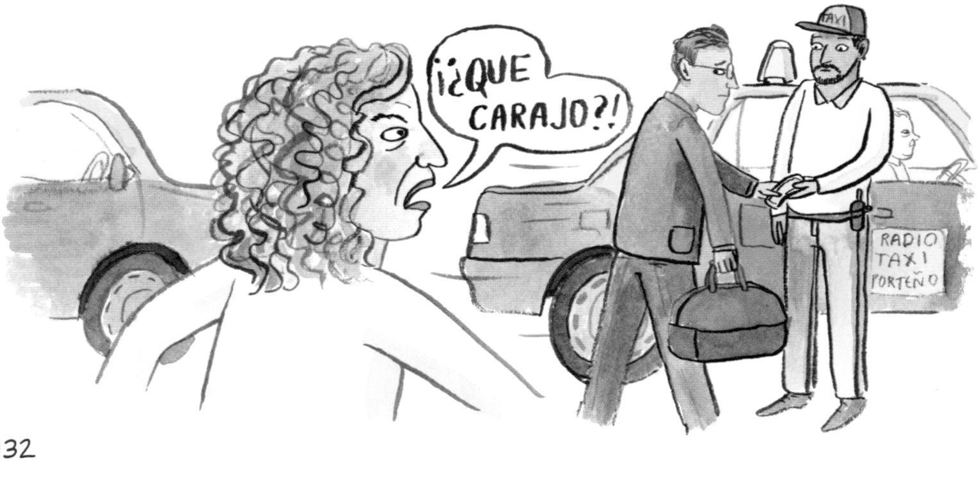
¡¿QUE CARAJO?!
TAXI
RADIO TAXI PORTEÑO

WE'RE STAYING AT AN APARTMENT IN RECOLETA CALLED "THE MASK."

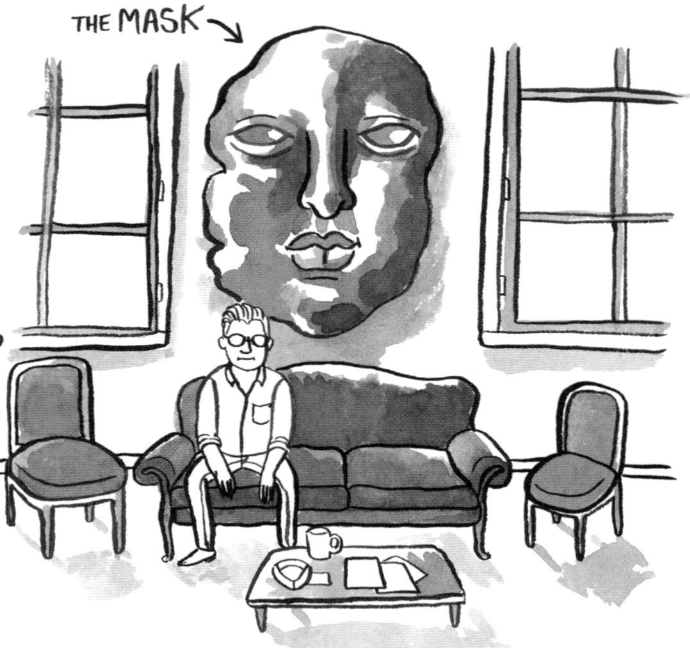
THE MASK

MY AUNT NORA CAME OVER TO EAT EMPANADAS AND FOR DESSERT WE SHARED A BLOCK OF CHEESE. WE PLAYED THIS GAME: KEEP SLICING THE BLOCK IN HALF AND EATING HALF BEFORE PASSING IT ALONG. WHOEVER CAN'T SPLIT IT ANYMORE LOSES THE GAME!

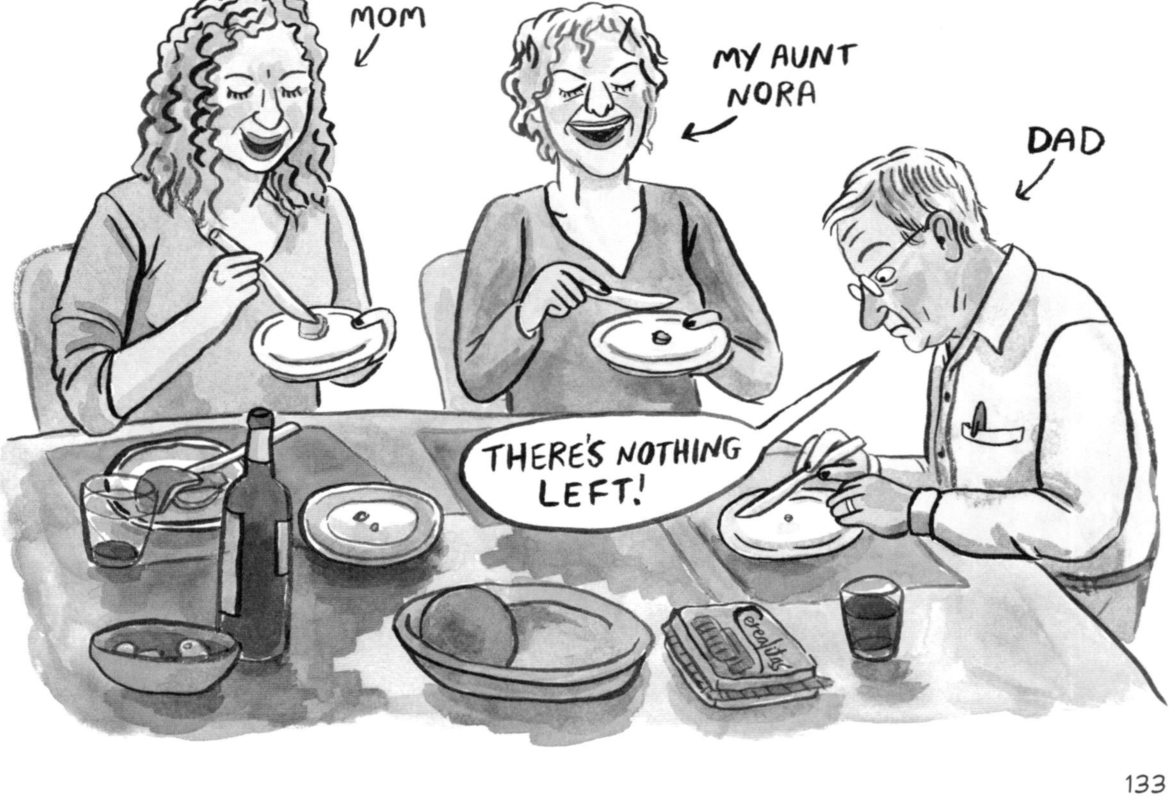
MOM
MY AUNT NORA
DAD
THERE'S NOTHING LEFT!
Cerealitas

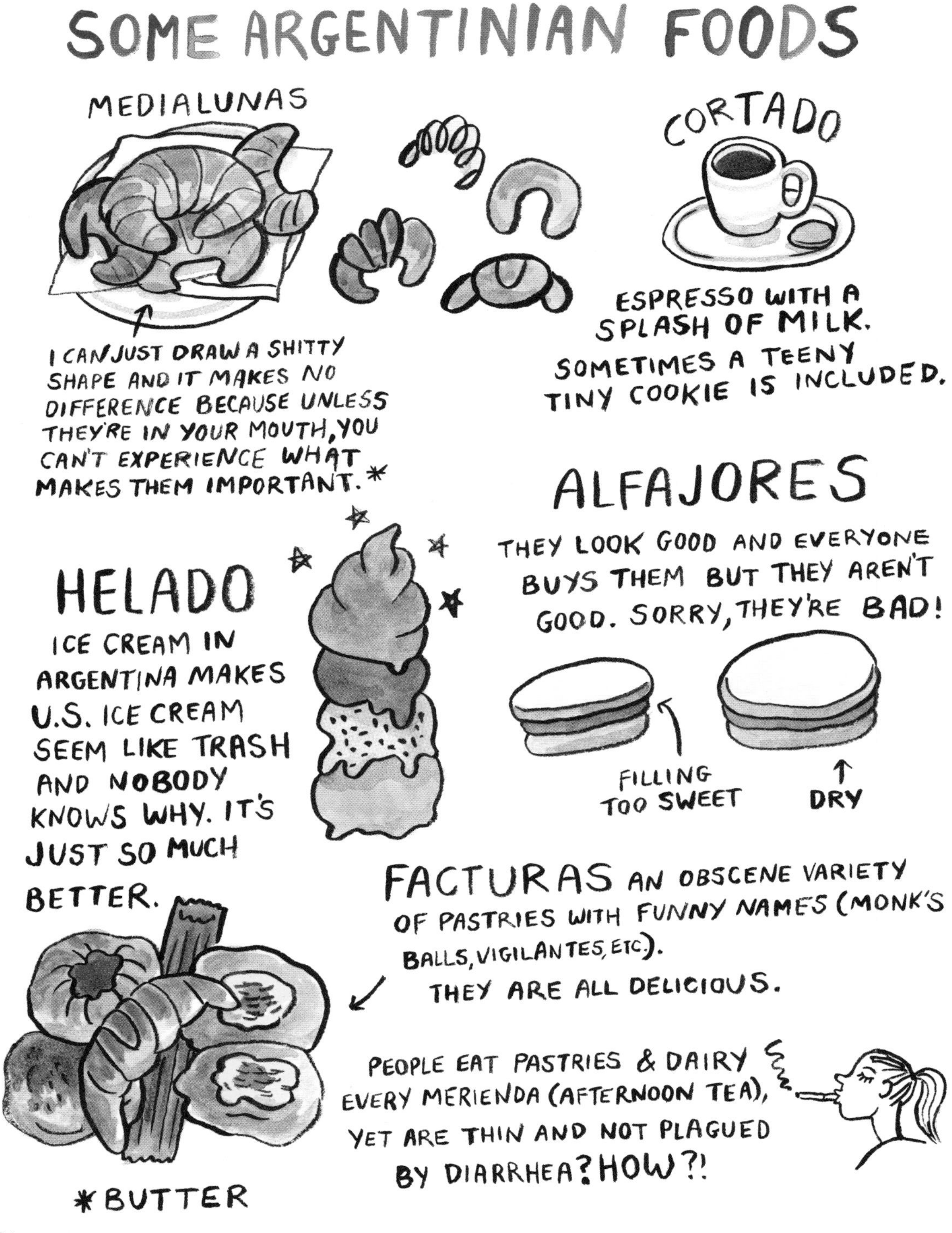
SOME ARGENTINIAN FOODS
MEDIALUNAS
I CAN JUST DRAW A SHITTY SHAPE AND IT MAKES NO DIFFERENCE BECAUSE UNLESS THEY'RE IN YOUR MOUTH, YOU CAN'T EXPERIENCE WHAT MAKES THEM IMPORTANT.*
CORTADO
ESPRESSO WITH A SPLASH OF MILK.
SOMETIMES A TEENY TINY COOKIE IS INCLUDED.
ALFAJORES
THEY LOOK GOOD AND EVERYONE BUYS THEM BUT THEY AREN'T GOOD. SORRY, THEY'RE BAD!
FILLING TOO SWEET
DRY
HELADO
ICE CREAM IN ARGENTINA MAKES U.S. ICE CREAM SEEM LIKE TRASH AND NOBODY KNOWS WHY. IT'S JUST SO MUCH BETTER.
FACTURAS AN OBSCENE VARIETY OF PASTRIES WITH FUNNY NAMES (MONK'S BALLS, VIGILANTES, ETC.).
THEY ARE ALL DELICIOUS.
PEOPLE EAT PASTRIES & DAIRY EVERY MERIENDA (AFTERNOON TEA), YET ARE THIN AND NOT PLAGUED BY DIARRHEA? HOW?!
*BUTTER

CHORIPAN

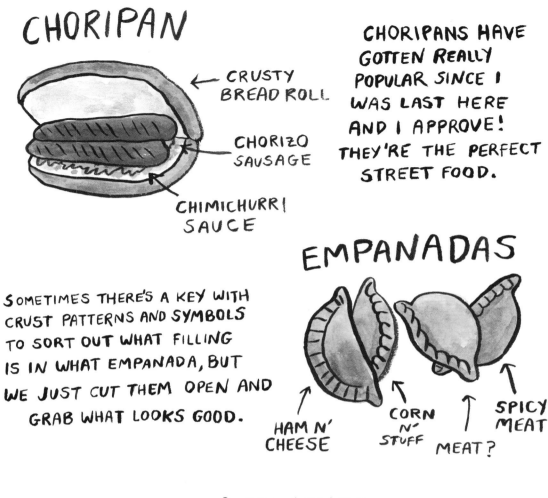

← CRUSTY BREAD ROLL

CHORIZO SAUSAGE

CHIMICHURRI SAUCE

CHORIPANS HAVE GOTTEN REALLY POPULAR SINCE I WAS LAST HERE AND I APPROVE! THEY'RE THE PERFECT STREET FOOD.

EMPANADAS

SOMETIMES THERE'S A KEY WITH CRUST PATTERNS AND SYMBOLS TO SORT OUT WHAT FILLING IS IN WHAT EMPANADA, BUT WE JUST CUT THEM OPEN AND GRAB WHAT LOOKS GOOD.

HAM N' CHEESE

CORN N' STUFF

MEAT?

SPICY MEAT

MEMBRILLO & MANCHEGO CHEESE

I USED TO THINK THIS WAS GROSS BUT NOW A LITTLE BIT TASTES EXQUISITE!

MEMBRILLO: FRUIT JELLY MADE OUT OF QUINCE.

THIS IS A QUINCE

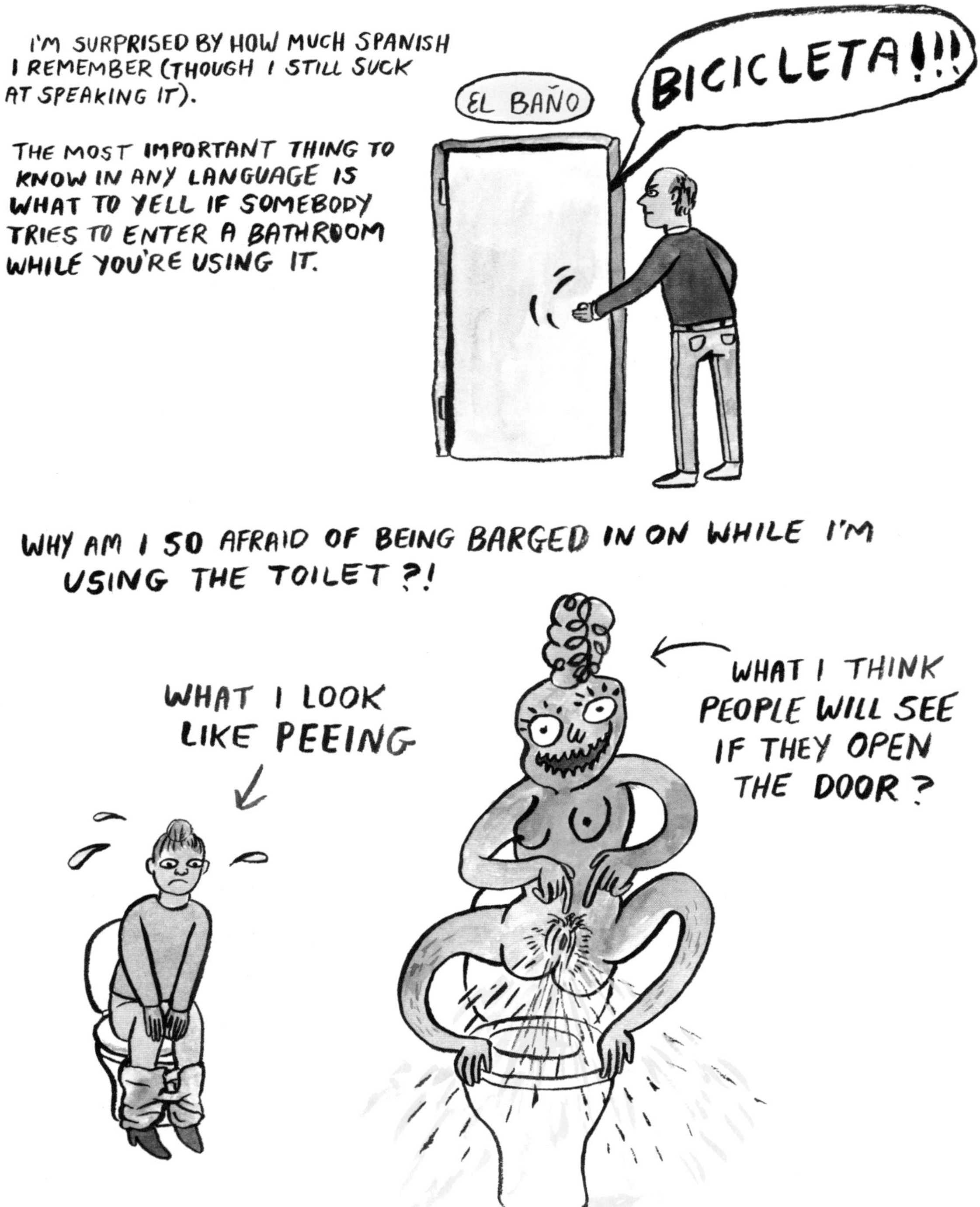
I'M SURPRISED BY HOW MUCH SPANISH I REMEMBER (THOUGH I STILL SUCK AT SPEAKING IT).
THE MOST IMPORTANT THING TO KNOW IN ANY LANGUAGE IS WHAT TO YELL IF SOMEBODY TRIES TO ENTER A BATHROOM WHILE YOU'RE USING IT.
EL BAÑO
BICICLETA!!!
WHY AM I SO AFRAID OF BEING BARGED IN ON WHILE I'M USING THE TOILET?!
WHAT I LOOK LIKE PEEING
WHAT I THINK PEOPLE WILL SEE IF THEY OPEN THE DOOR?

9/17 WE WENT ON A GUIDED TOUR OF "EL ZANJON," A TENEMENT BUILDING. NORMALLY I HATE TOURS! THEY'RE ALWAYS PACED TOO SLOWLY AND I FEEL TRAPPED. BUT OUR DOCENT TODAY KEPT ADDING UNEXPECTED DETAILS THAT KEPT ME VERY INTERESTED.

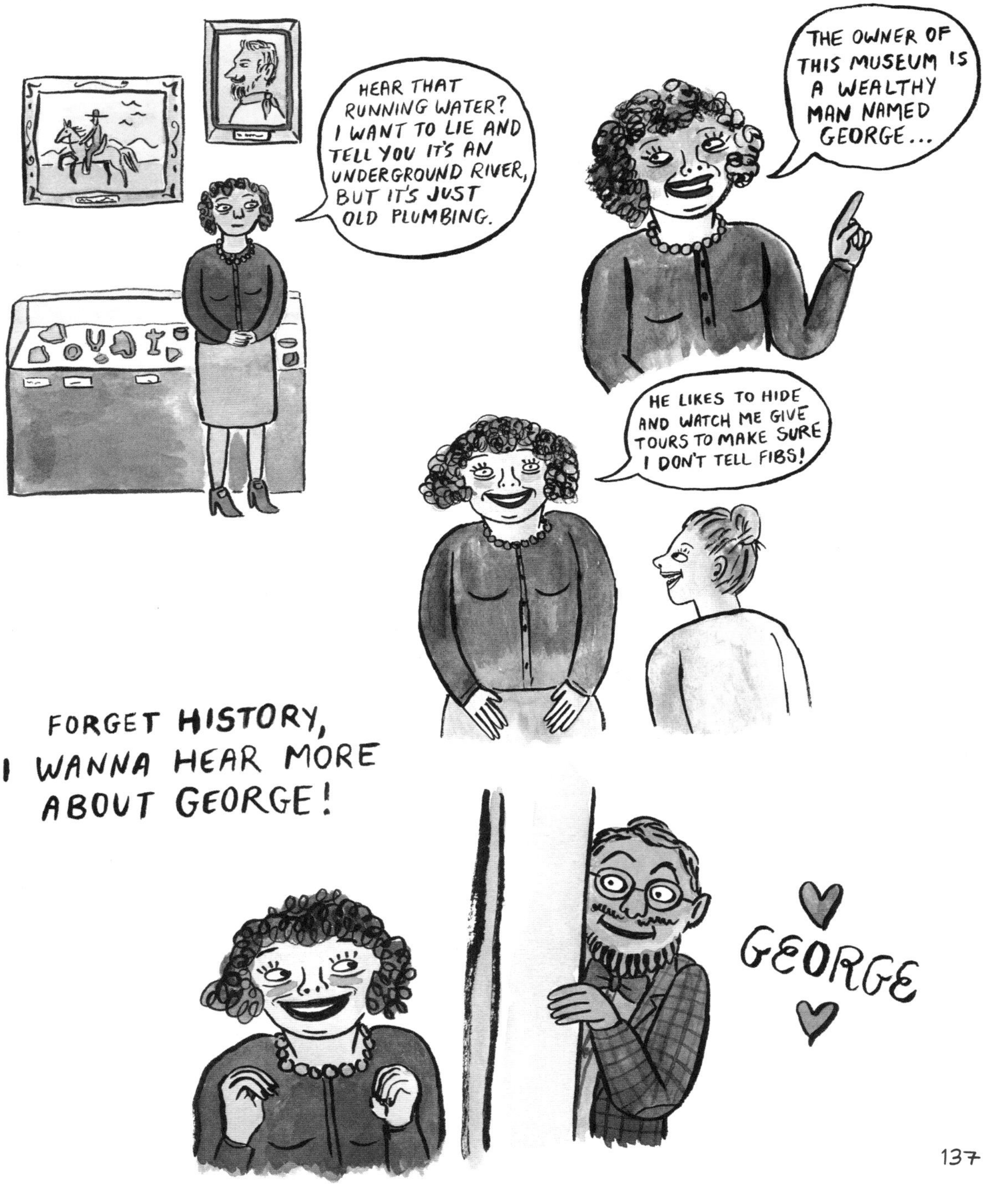

HEAR THAT RUNNING WATER? I WANT TO LIE AND TELL YOU IT'S AN UNDERGROUND RIVER, BUT IT'S JUST OLD PLUMBING.
THE OWNER OF THIS MUSEUM IS A WEALTHY MAN NAMED GEORGE...
HE LIKES TO HIDE AND WATCH ME GIVE TOURS TO MAKE SURE I DON'T TELL FIBS!
FORGET HISTORY, I WANNA HEAR MORE ABOUT GEORGE!
GEORGE

9/18 MY COUSIN PABLO TOOK US TO A **FUTBOL** GAME AT LA BOMBONERA STADIUM!

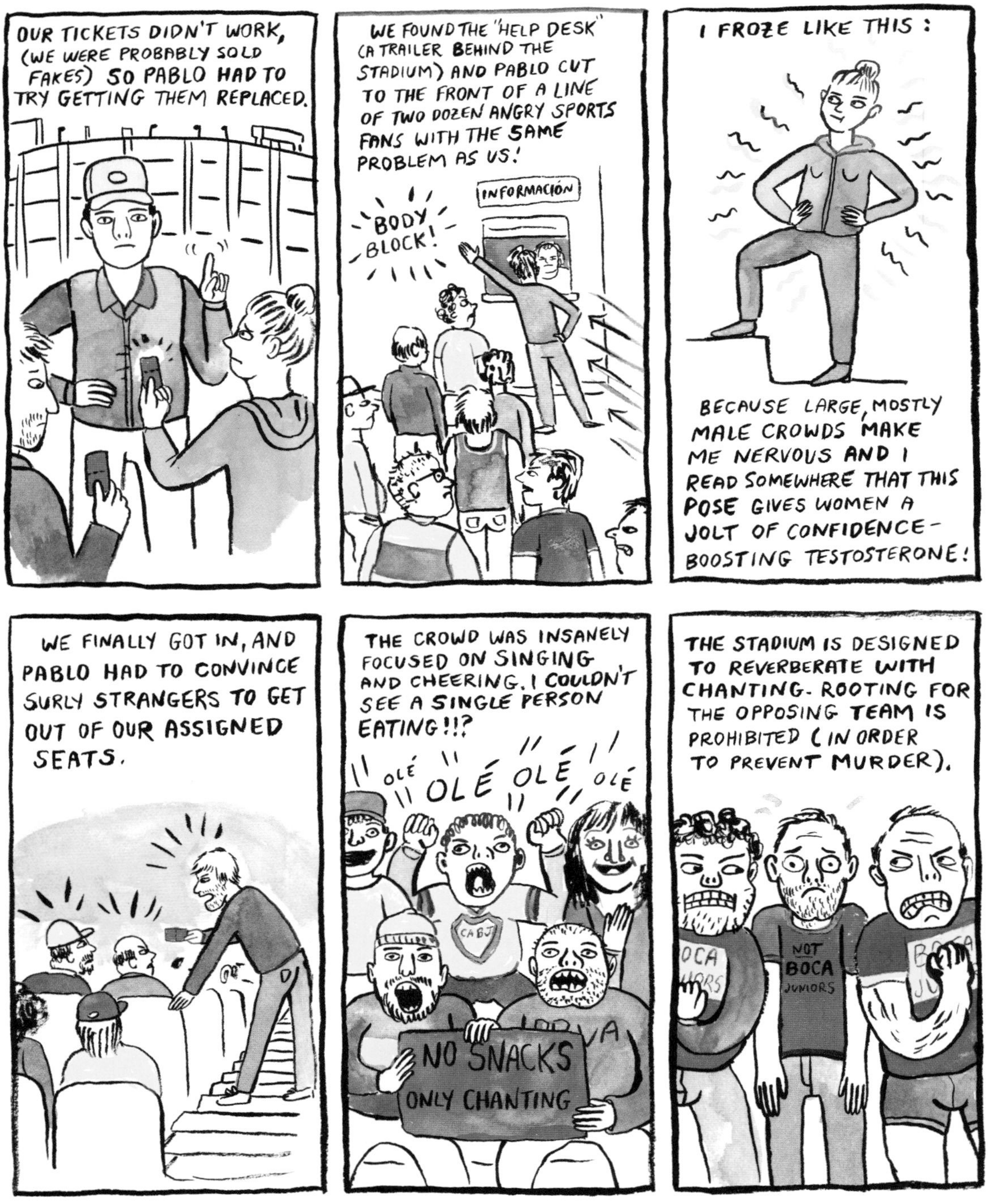

OUR TICKETS DIDN'T WORK, (WE WERE PROBABLY SOLD FAKES) SO PABLO HAD TO TRY GETTING THEM REPLACED.
WE FOUND THE "HELP DESK" (A TRAILER BEHIND THE STADIUM) AND PABLO CUT TO THE FRONT OF A LINE OF TWO DOZEN ANGRY SPORTS FANS WITH THE SAME PROBLEM AS US!
INFORMACIÓN
BODY BLOCK!
I FROZE LIKE THIS:
BECAUSE LARGE, MOSTLY MALE CROWDS MAKE ME NERVOUS AND I READ SOMEWHERE THAT THIS POSE GIVES WOMEN A JOLT OF CONFIDENCE-BOOSTING TESTOSTERONE!
WE FINALLY GOT IN, AND PABLO HAD TO CONVINCE SURLY STRANGERS TO GET OUT OF OUR ASSIGNED SEATS.
THE CROWD WAS INSANELY FOCUSED ON SINGING AND CHEERING. I COULDN'T SEE A SINGLE PERSON EATING!!?
OLÉ OLÉ OLÉ OLÉ
CABJ
NO SNACKS ONLY CHANTING
THE STADIUM IS DESIGNED TO REVERBERATE WITH CHANTING. ROOTING FOR THE OPPOSING TEAM IS PROHIBITED (IN ORDER TO PREVENT MURDER).
NOT BOCA JUNIORS

THE GAME IS *SUPER FUN* BUT HALF THE TIME I'M JUST WATCHING THE FANS.
EVERY TIME A GOAL GETS SCORED, A WAVE OF BODIES RUSHES TOWARDS THE FIELD, CLIMBS UP THE FENCE, AND A FEW PEOPLE GET CRUSHED AND NEED TO BE CARRIED OFF ON STRETCHERS.

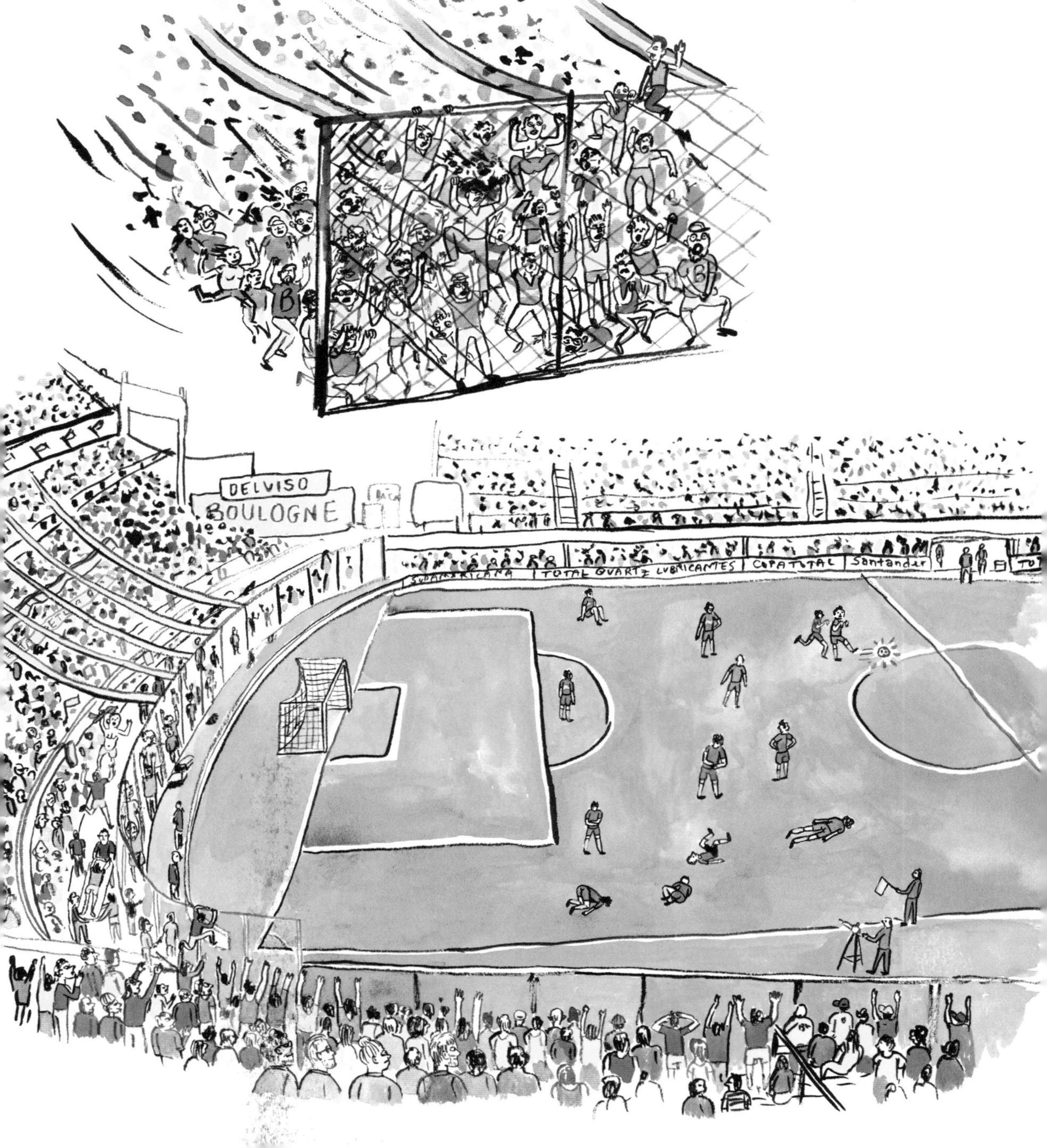
DELVISO
BOULOGNE
TOTAL QUARTZ LUBRICANTES
COPA TOTAL
Santander

9/19 WE WANDERED THROUGH LA RECOLETA CEMETERY. IT'S THE MOST COMPETITIVE GRAVEYARD I'VE EVER SEEN - EACH TOMB IS BUILT TO BE TALLER AND MORE DECADENT THAN THE ONE NEXT TO IT.

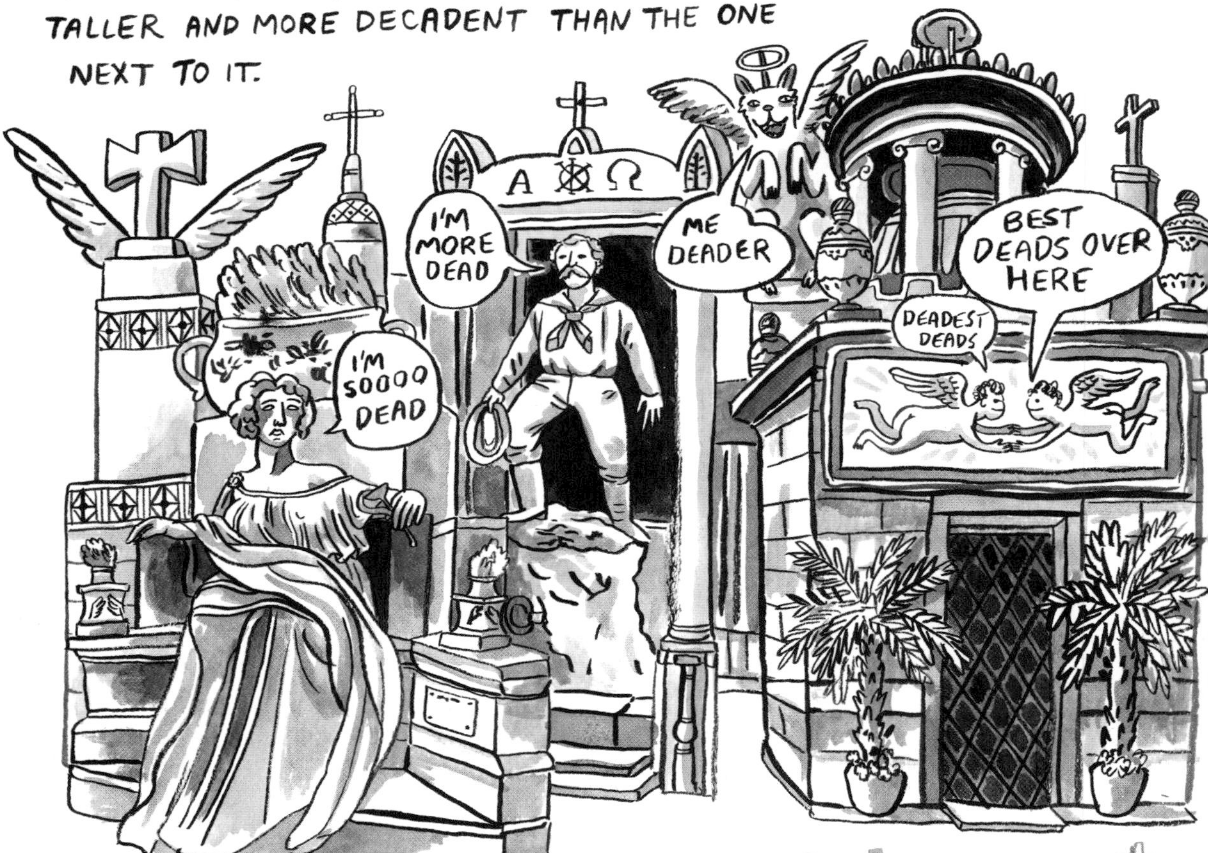

I'M SOOOO DEAD
I'M MORE DEAD
ME DEADER
DEADEST DEADS
BEST DEADS OVER HERE

MANY OF THE FAMILIES CAN NO LONGER AFFORD TO PAY RENT ON THEIR PLOTS, SO THE TOMBS HAVE FALLEN INTO DISREPAIR. THERE'S LOTS OF BROKEN GLASS AND HAUNTING ODORS.

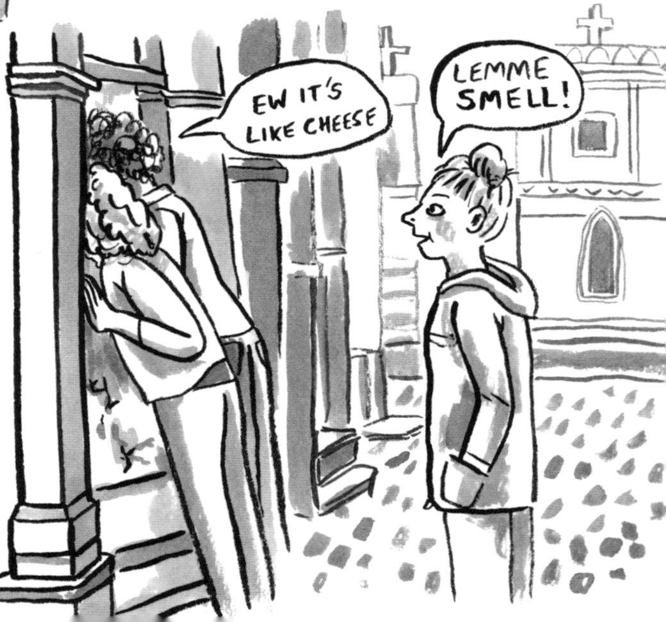

EW IT'S LIKE CHEESE
LEMME SMELL!

9/20 TODAY I'M SEEING MY COUSIN JULIETA. WHEN I WAS STRUGGLING IN COLLEGE, I TOOK A SEMESTER OFF TO LIVE WITH JULI IN BUENOS AIRES AND IT HELPED ME FIGURE THINGS OUT.

TRAVELING **ALWAYS** HELPS ME PULL MY HEAD OUT OF MY ASS (AND THEN RE-INSERTS IT FROM A NEW ANGLE).

I'M SHY, BUT WITHIN MINUTES SHE'S SHOWING ME HER NEW PAINTINGS AND I REMEMBER WHY WE FEEL CONNECTED DESPITE THE LANGUAGE BARRIER AND DISTANCE.

Julieta

I LOVE CHILDREN BUT...

...I DON'T WANT THEM

I FEEL LIKE I AM A CHILD

YES EXACTLY! I AM A CHILD!

WE'RE 30-YR-OLD BABIES!

JULI'S DOG

9/20 A BUNCH OF MY RELATIVES GATHERED AT MY AUNT'S BOYFRIEND'S HOUSE IN LOS CARDALES, A PEACEFUL VILLAGE IN THE COUNTRY JUST OUTSIDE OF BUENOS AIRES. WE SPEND HOURS DOING NOTHING, WAITING FOR THE BBQ TO START.

THINGS THAT MAKE ME FEEL SUPER OLD:

1. FALLING ASLEEP IN A CHAIR

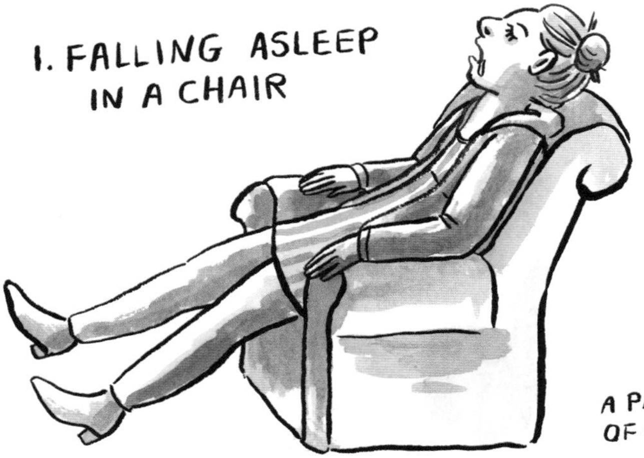

2. BIRD WATCHING

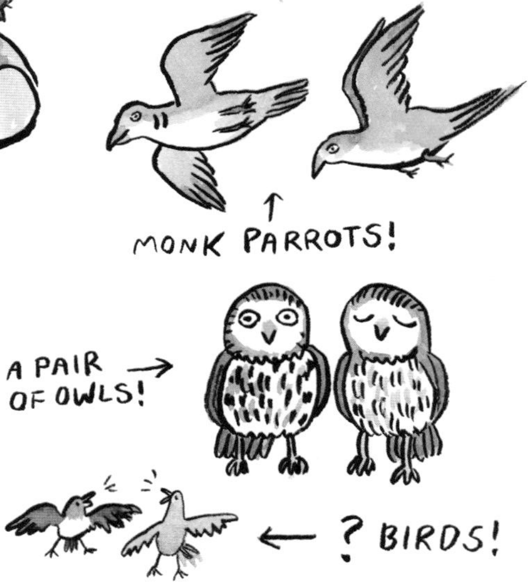
MONK PARROTS!
A PAIR OF OWLS!
? BIRDS!

3. RESTING MY EYES ON A SHELF OF CURIOS

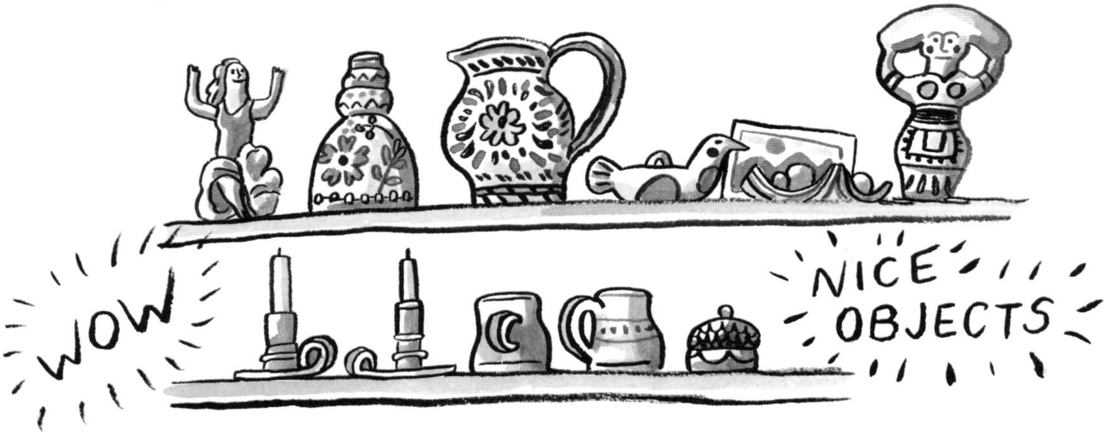
WOW
NICE OBJECTS

LOS CARDALES IS A GREAT PLACE TO DO ALL THESE THINGS!

BIRD ATTACK

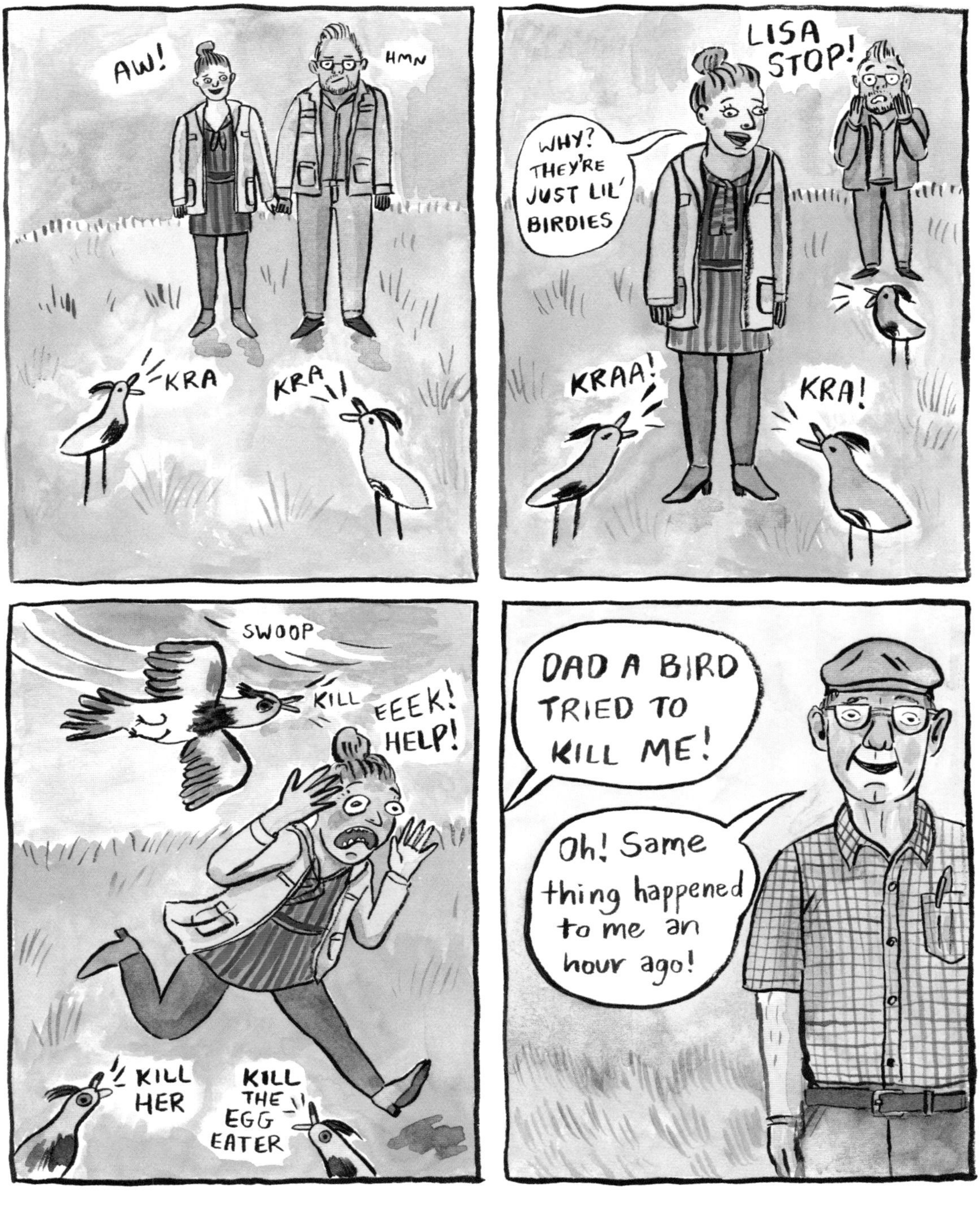
AW!
HMN
KRA
KRA
WHY? THEY'RE JUST LIL' BIRDIES
LISA STOP!
KRAA!
KRA!
SWOOP
KILL
EEEK! HELP!
KILL HER
KILL THE EGG EATER
DAD A BIRD TRIED TO KILL ME!
Oh! Same thing happened to me an hour ago!

IN THE EARLY 1900S, MY GREAT-GRANDPARENTS ESCAPED ANTI-JEWISH POGROMS (MASSACRE AND ETHNIC CLEANSING OF THEIR VILLAGES) IN THE UKRAINE.

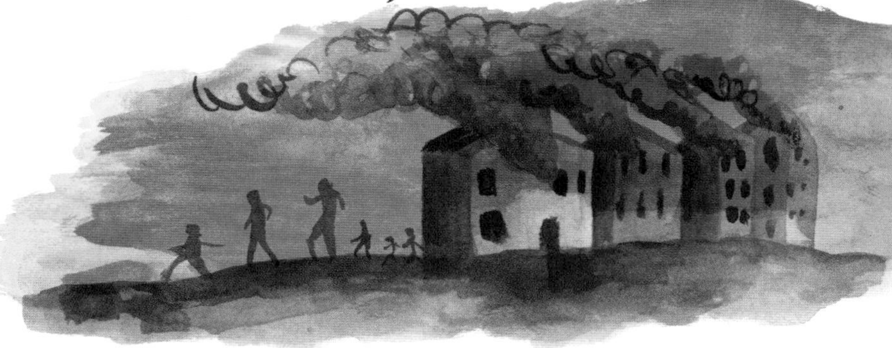

THEY MADE A HARROWING JOURNEY FROM ODESSA TO GENOA, ITALY.

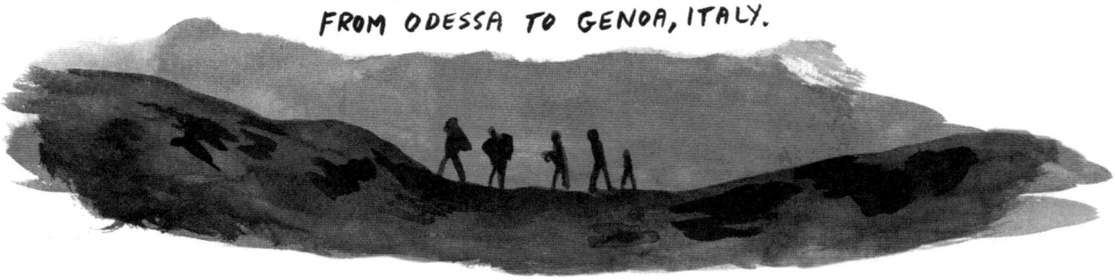

THEY INTENDED TO TRAVEL TO NEW YORK, BUT THE BOAT HAD ALREADY DEPARTED AND WOULDN'T RETURN FOR MONTHS.

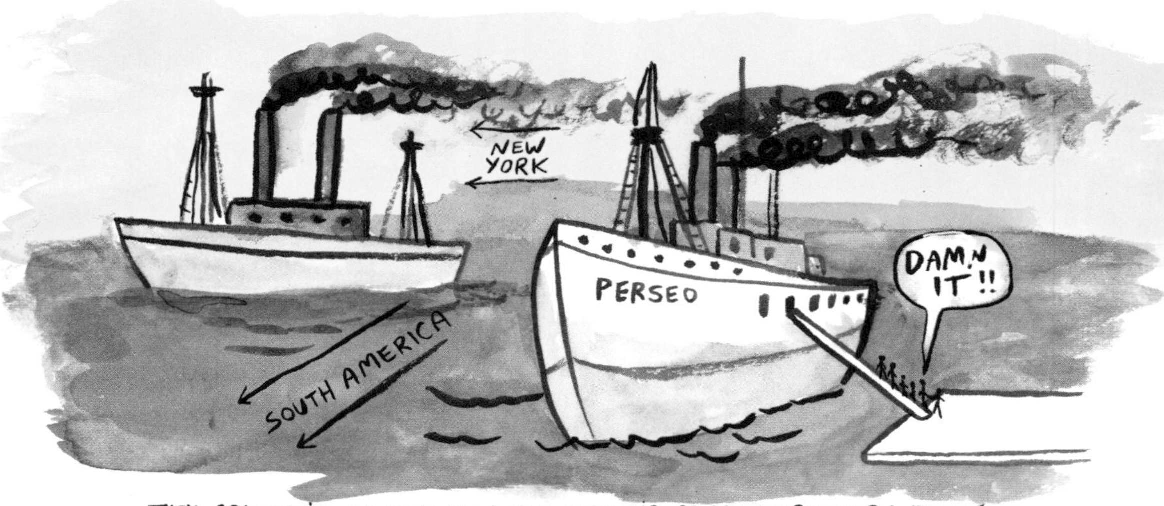
NEW YORK
PERSEO
SOUTH AMERICA
DAMN IT!!

THEY COULDN'T AFFORD TO WAIT AROUND, SO MY ANCESTORS TOOK THE NEXT BOAT OUT OF THE PORT, TO BUENOS AIRES.

IF THEY'D GOTTEN THERE JUST A LITTLE EARLIER, THEY WOULD HAVE SETTLED IN NEW YORK.

I'VE ALWAYS BEEN FASCINATED BY THIS STORY AND I MAKE MY MOM DESCRIBE IT OFTEN.

THERE ARE MILLIONS OF FAMILY HISTORIES LIKE THIS ONE. WHY DO I LIKE THINKING ABOUT IT SO MUCH?

WHEN I HEAR STORIES ABOUT MY ANCESTORS, I HAVE A FEELING OF REACHING BACK THROUGH TIME AND SECURING KINSHIP AND DEEPER PURPOSE.

— LIFE IS MOSTLY MEANINGLESS —

BUT THIS IS A CONNECTING STRAND AND GRASPING IT IS COMFORTING.

FOR OUR BIG FAMILY DINNER, MY COUSIN PABLO GRILLS ASADO: A HUGE VARIETY OF MEATS, INCLUDING STEAK, RIBS, CHORIZO, AND MORCILLA (BLOOD SAUSAGE).

AFTER FEASTING, THE WHOLE FAMILY SINGS AND DANCES WHILE MY COUSIN DIEGO PLAYS GUITAR.

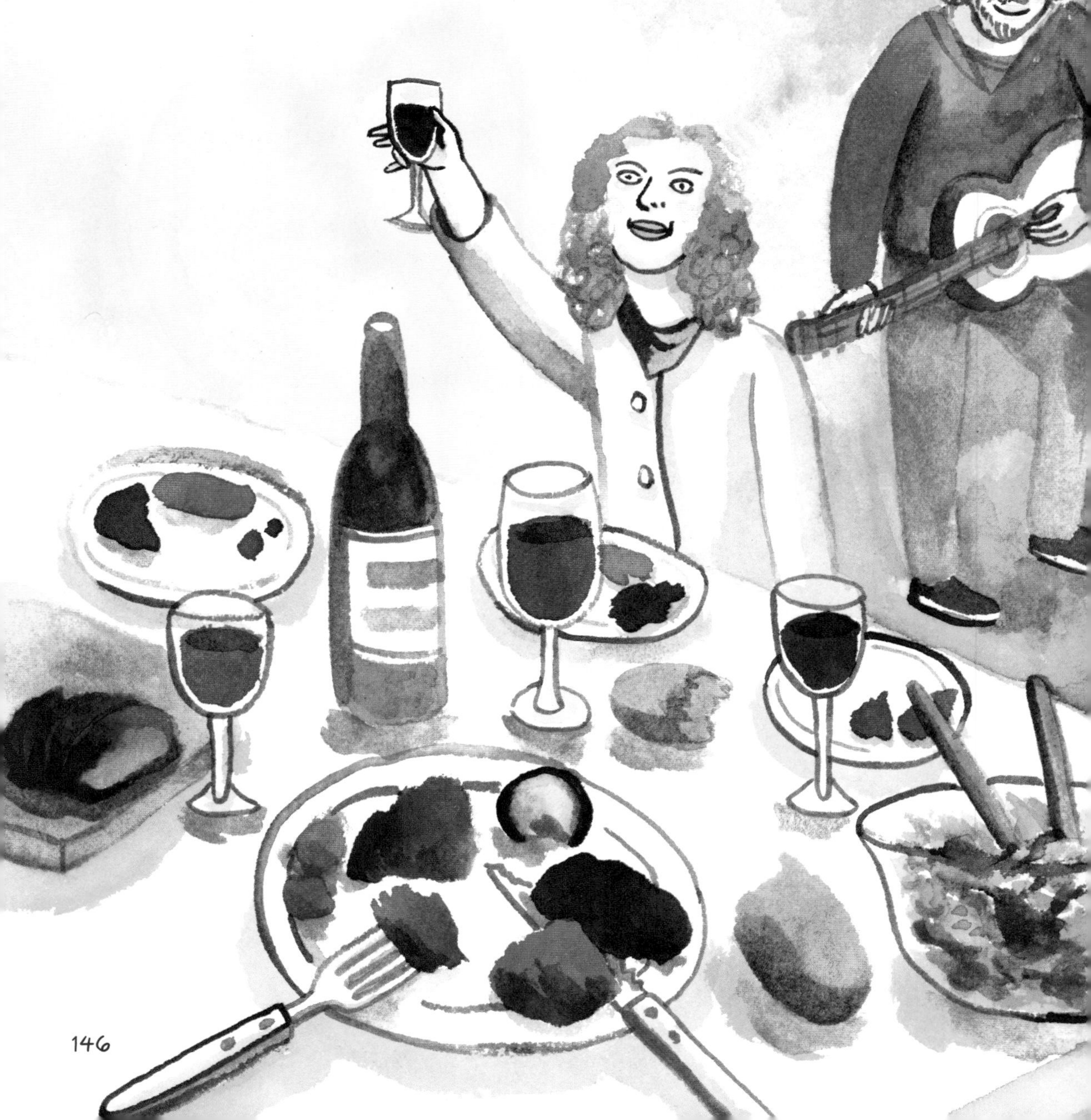

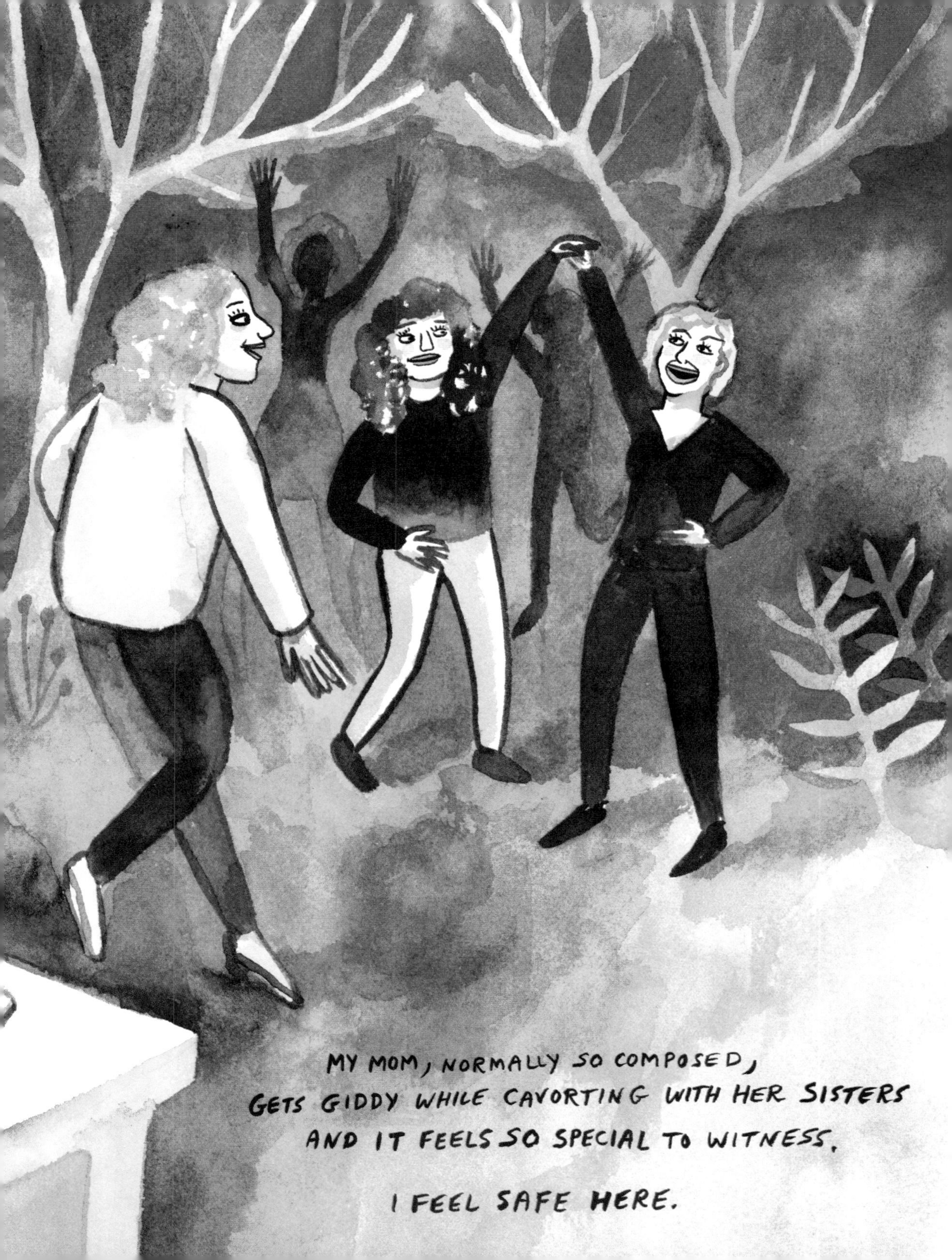
MY MOM, NORMALLY SO COMPOSED,
GETS GIDDY WHILE CAVORTING WITH HER SISTERS
AND IT FEELS SO SPECIAL TO WITNESS.
I FEEL SAFE HERE.

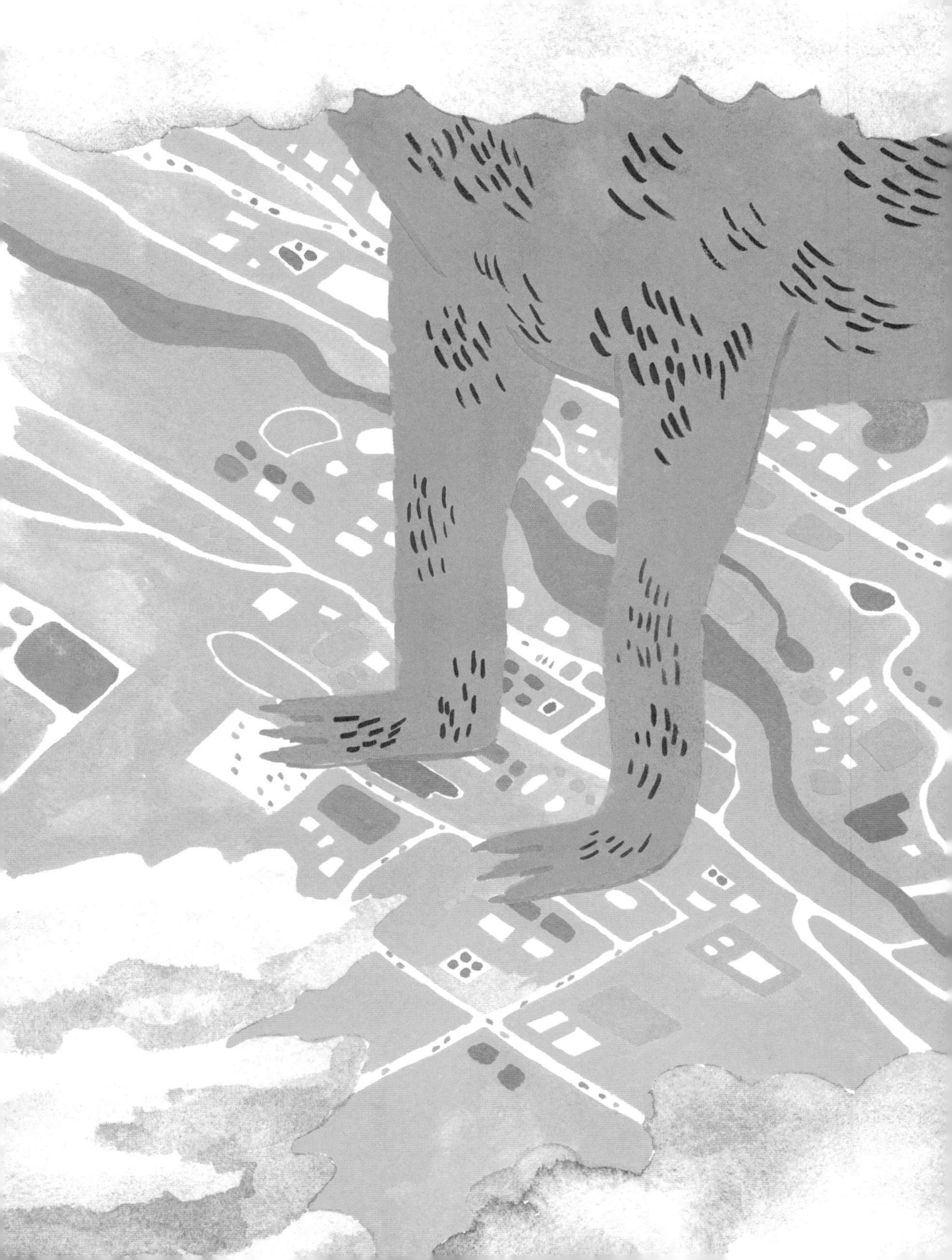

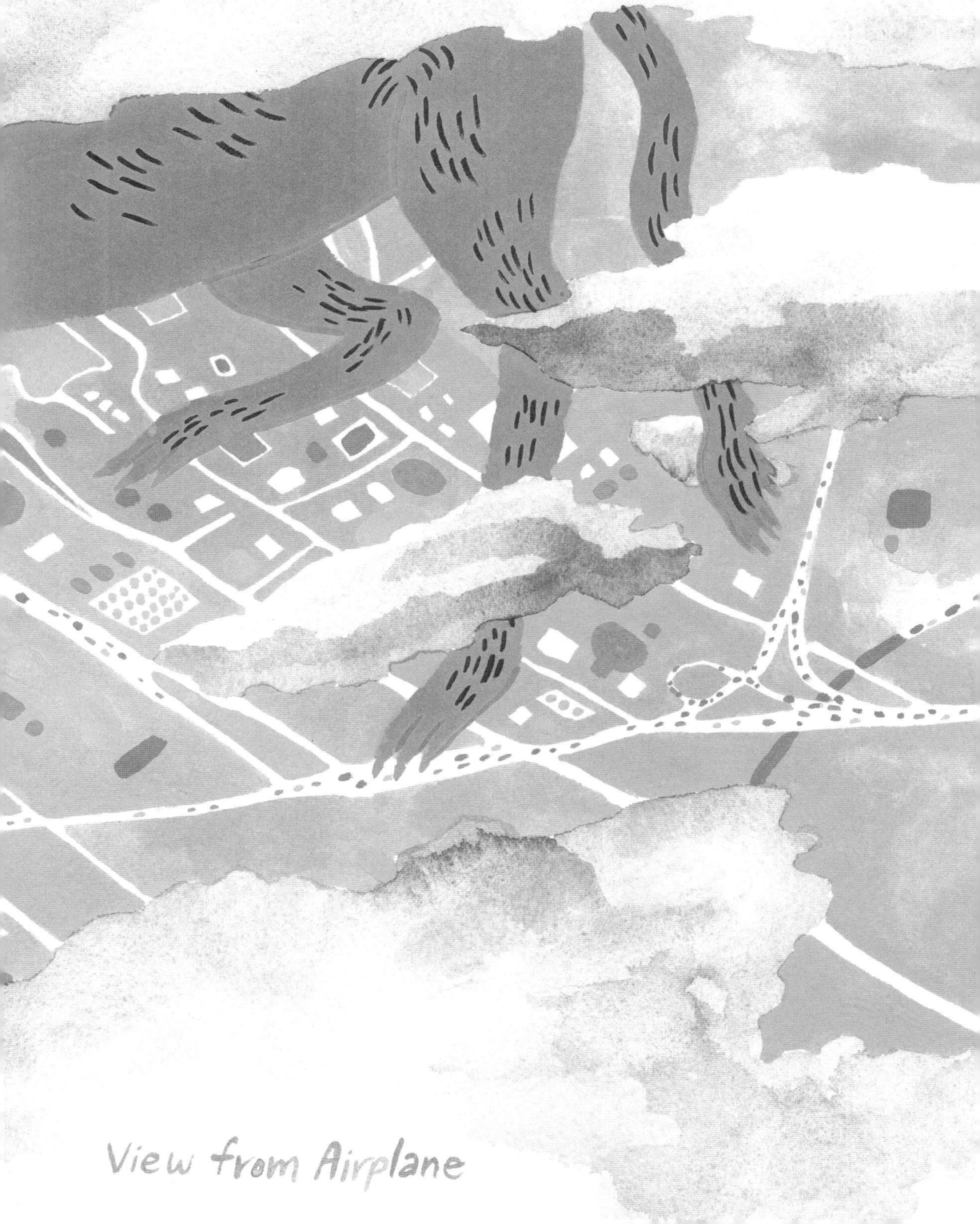

View from Airplane

WHAT WILL IT BE LIKE TO DIE?

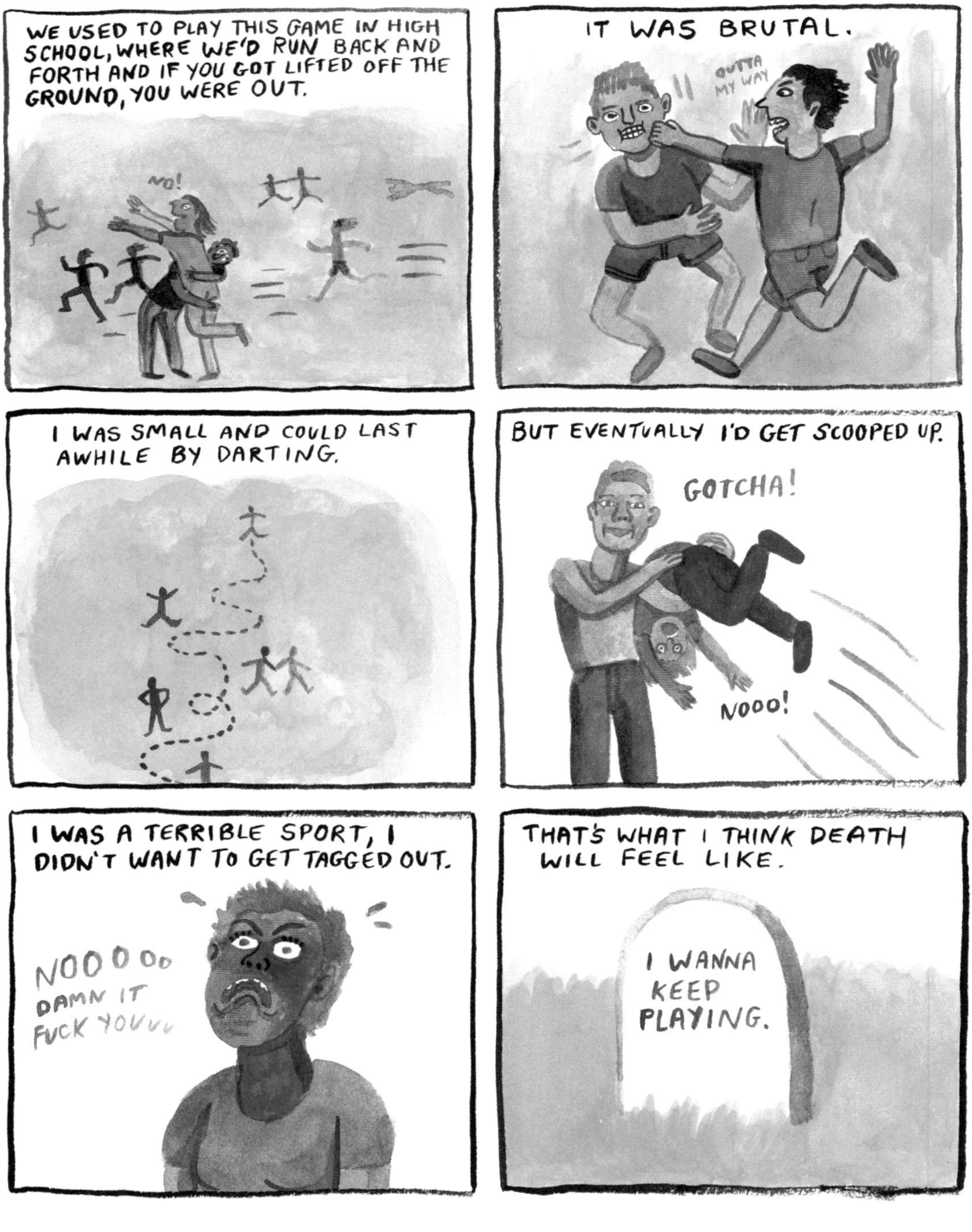
WE USED TO PLAY THIS GAME IN HIGH SCHOOL, WHERE WE'D RUN BACK AND FORTH AND IF YOU GOT LIFTED OFF THE GROUND, YOU WERE OUT.
NO!
IT WAS BRUTAL.
OUTTA MY WAY
I WAS SMALL AND COULD LAST AWHILE BY DARTING.
BUT EVENTUALLY I'D GET SCOOPED UP.
GOTCHA!
NOOO!
I WAS A TERRIBLE SPORT, I DIDN'T WANT TO GET TAGGED OUT.
NOOOOO
DAMN IT
FUCK YOUUU
THAT'S WHAT I THINK DEATH WILL FEEL LIKE.
I WANNA KEEP PLAYING.

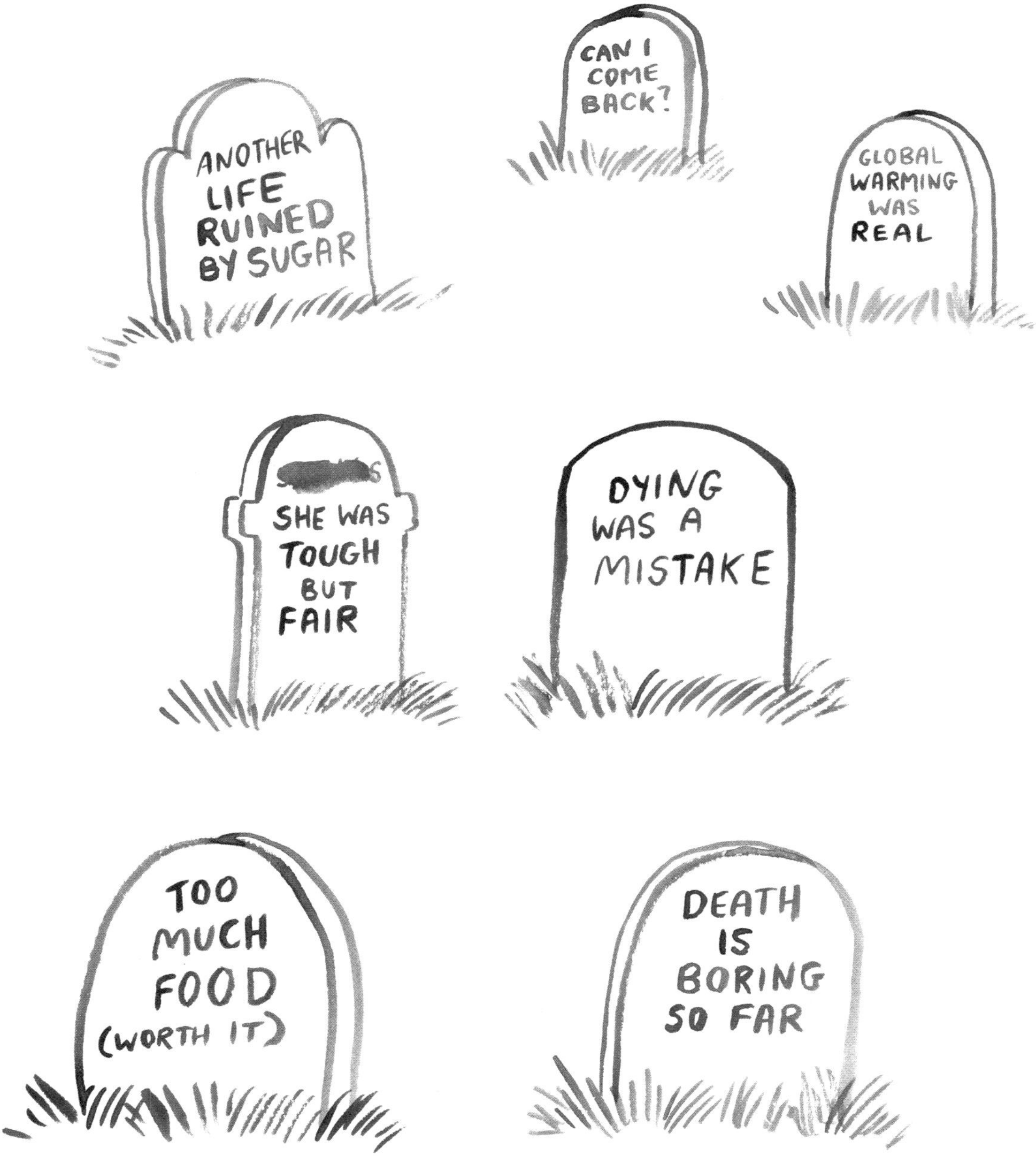
ANOTHER LIFE RUINED BY SUGAR
CAN I COME BACK?
GLOBAL WARMING WAS REAL
SHE WAS TOUGH BUT FAIR
DYING WAS A MISTAKE
TOO MUCH FOOD (WORTH IT)
DEATH IS BORING SO FAR

YOU CAN'T TAKE IT WITH YOU
WHEN YOU DIE

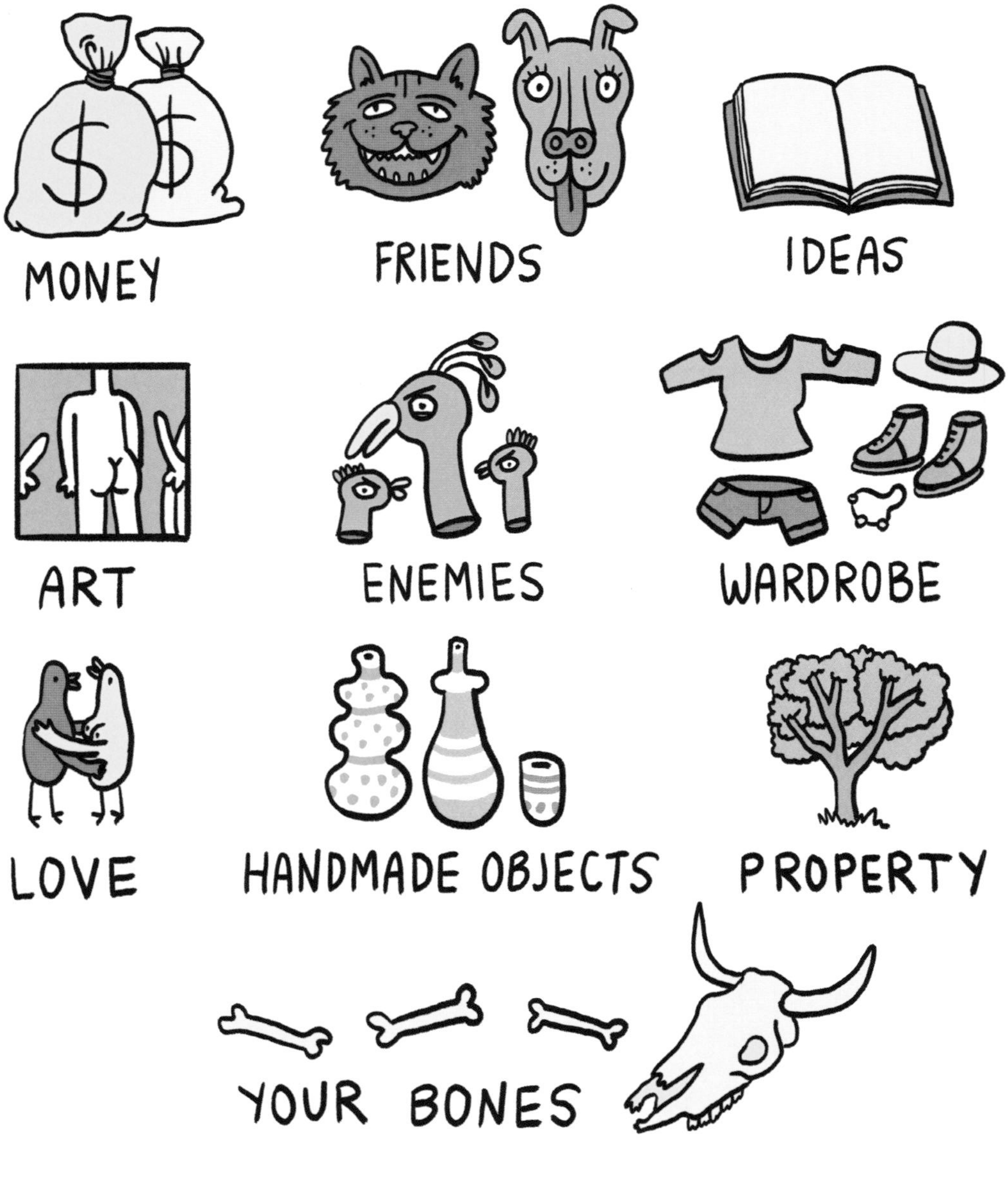
MONEY
FRIENDS
IDEAS
ART
ENEMIES
WARDROBE
LOVE
HANDMADE OBJECTS
PROPERTY
YOUR BONES

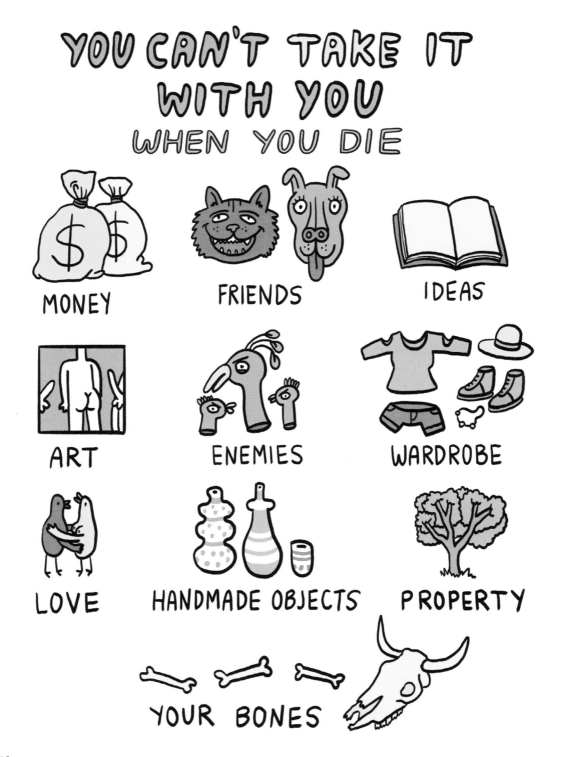

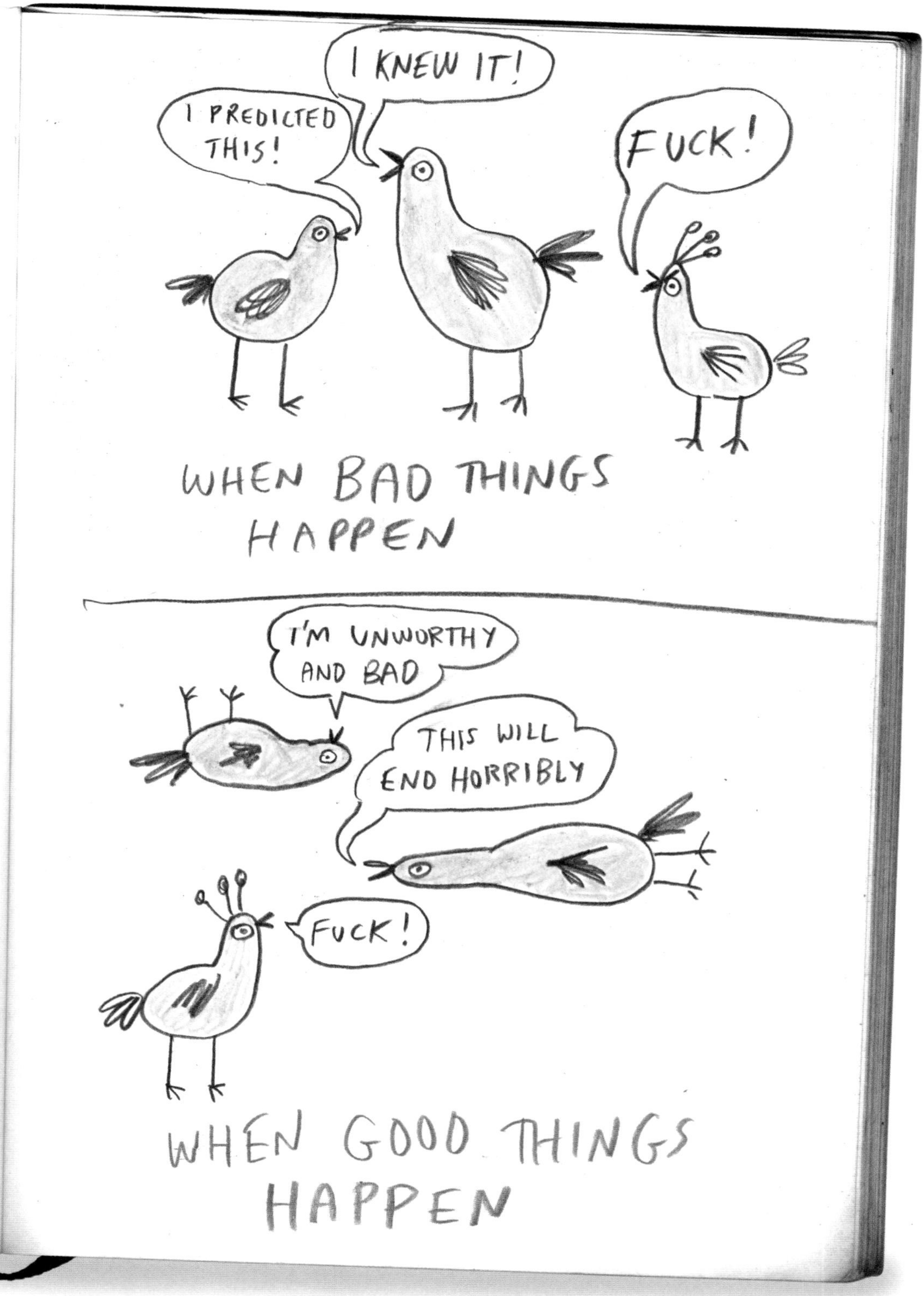
I PREDICTED THIS!
I KNEW IT!
FUCK!
WHEN BAD THINGS HAPPEN
I'M UNWORTHY AND BAD
THIS WILL END HORRIBLY
FUCK!
WHEN GOOD THINGS HAPPEN

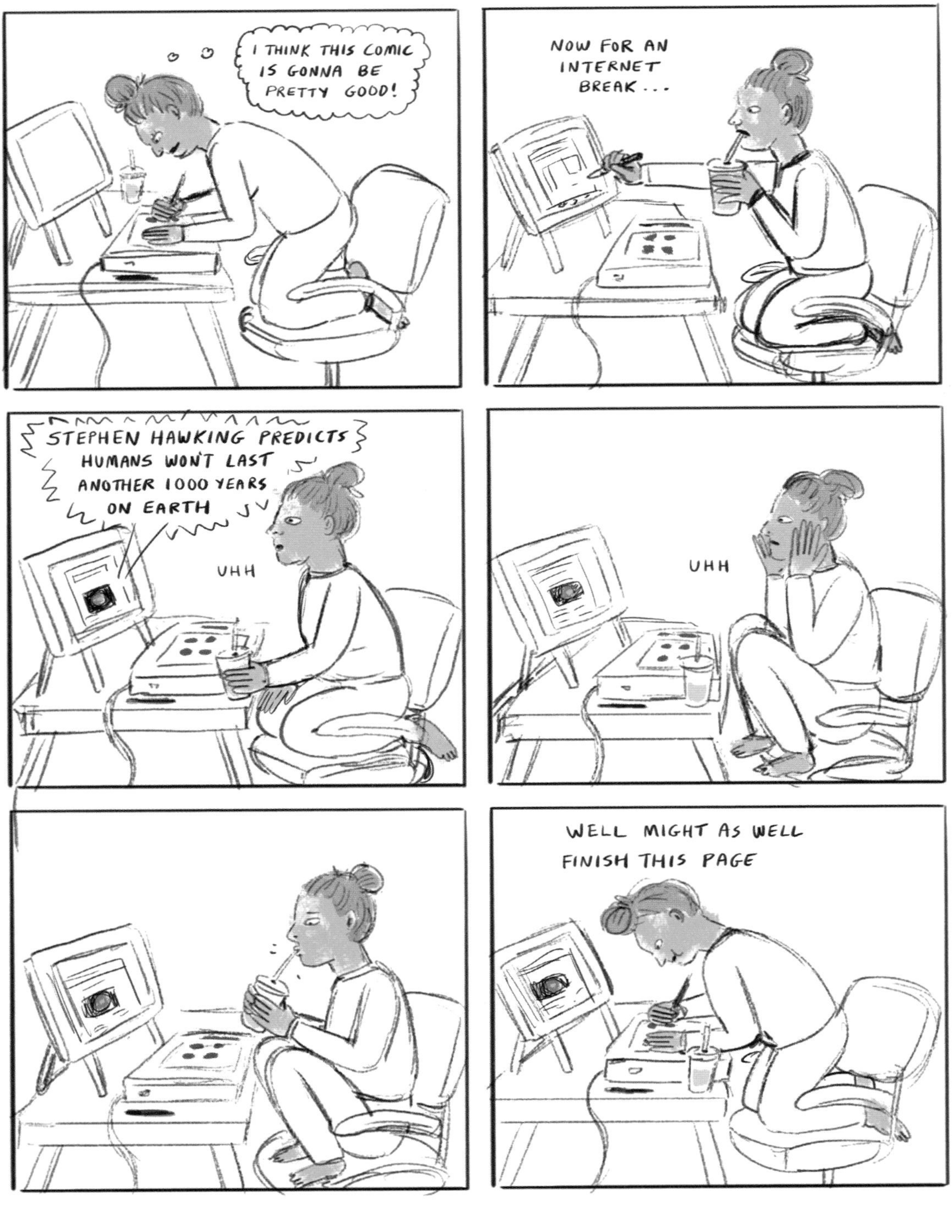
I THINK THIS COMIC IS GONNA BE PRETTY GOOD!
NOW FOR AN INTERNET BREAK...
STEPHEN HAWKING PREDICTS HUMANS WON'T LAST ANOTHER 1000 YEARS ON EARTH
UHH
UHH
WELL MIGHT AS WELL FINISH THIS PAGE

L.A. COMIC

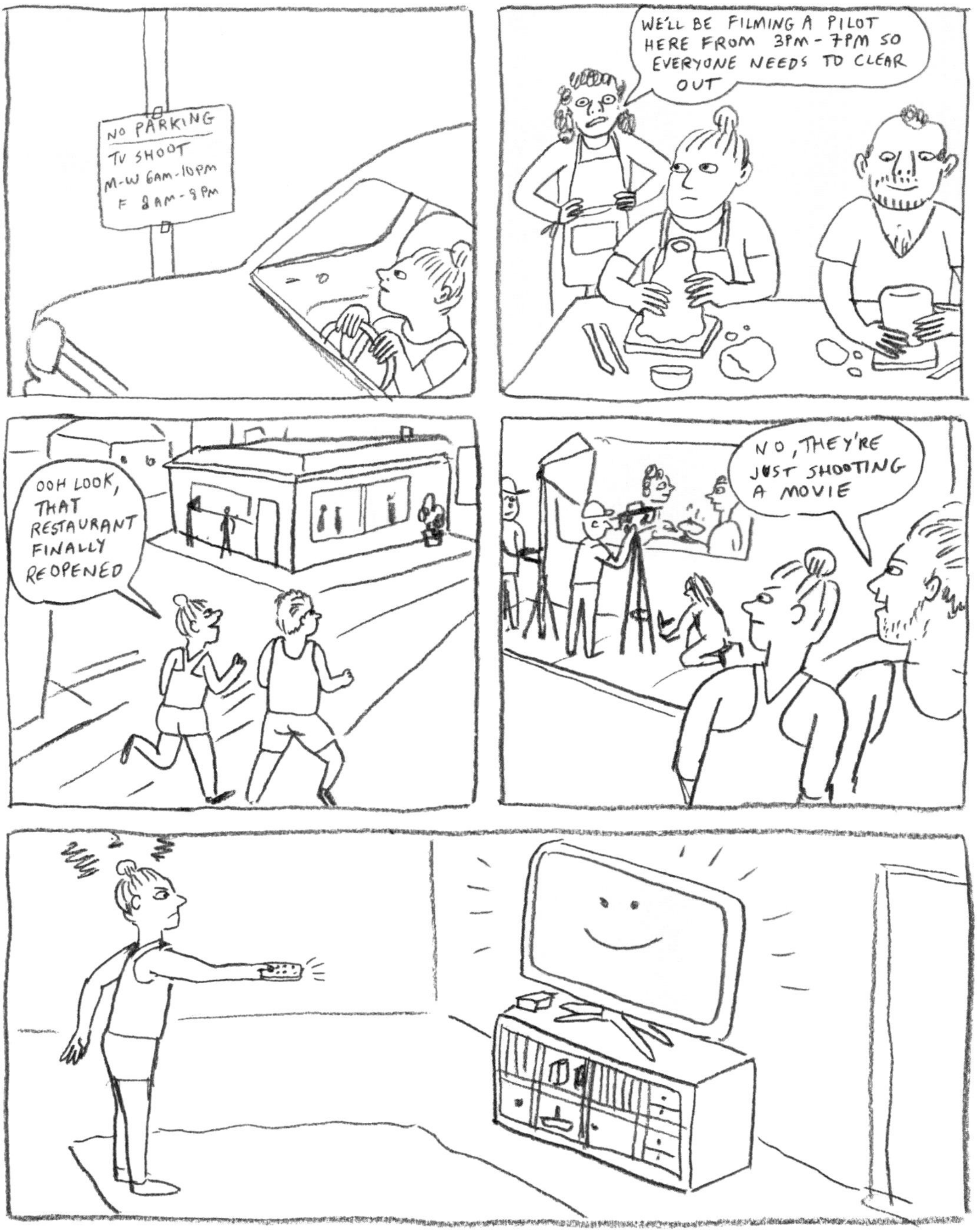
NO PARKING
TV SHOOT
M-W 6AM-10PM
F 8AM-8PM
WE'LL BE FILMING A PILOT HERE FROM 3PM-7PM SO EVERYONE NEEDS TO CLEAR OUT
OOH LOOK, THAT RESTAURANT FINALLY REOPENED
NO, THEY'RE JUST SHOOTING A MOVIE

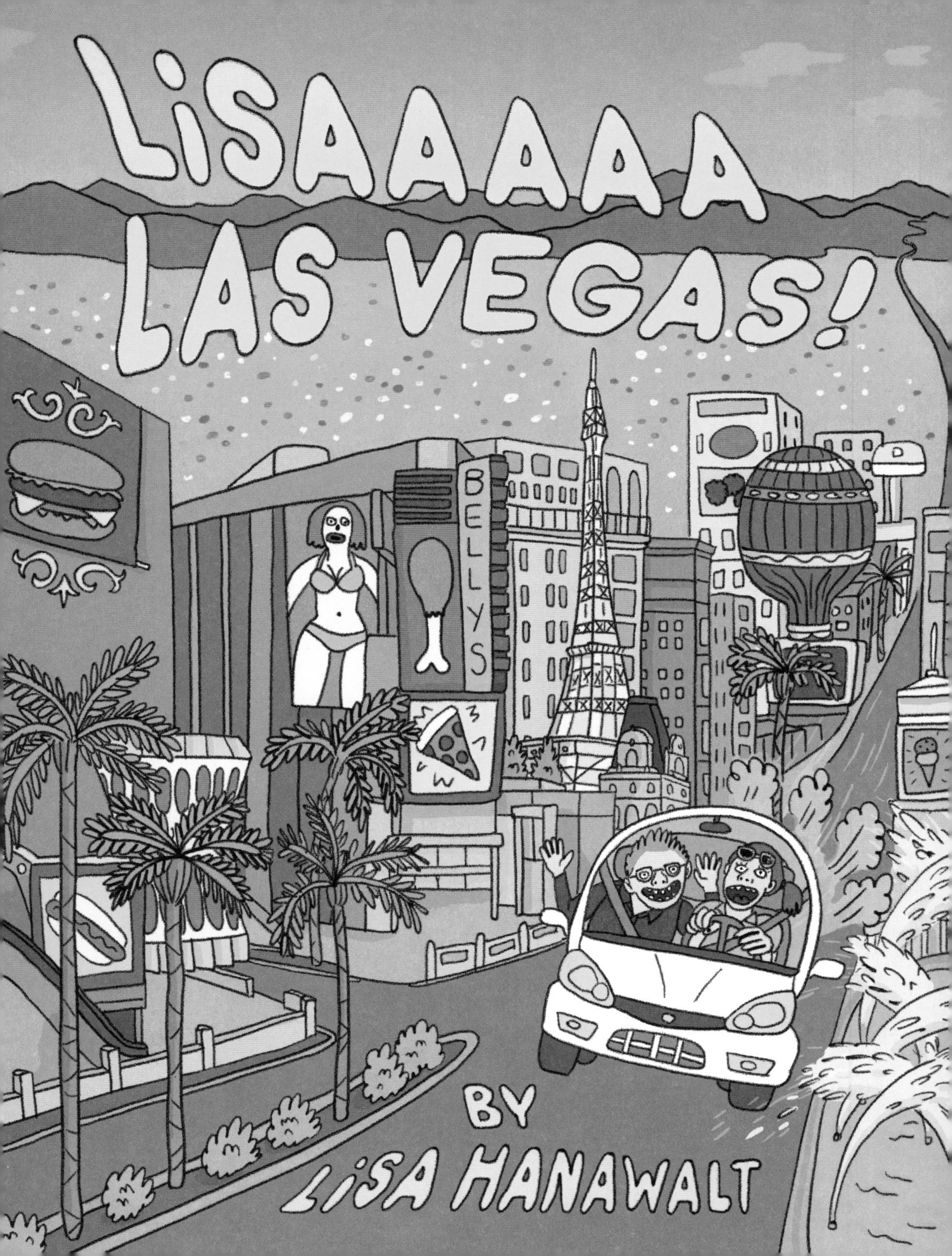
LiSAAAAA LAS VEGAS!
BELLYS
BY LiSA HANAWALT

LUCKY PEACH MAGAZINE BOOKED A HOTEL ROOM FOR ME AND MY BOYFRIEND AT THE COSMOPOLITAN ON THE VEGAS STRIP AND INSTRUCTED US TO GORGE OURSELVES AT ALL-YOU-CAN-EAT BUFFETS. EASY!

WE KNEW ABOUT THE COSMO BECAUSE WE'D SEEN THEIR INSANE AD PLAYING CONSTANTLY ON TV. IT'S A FLASHY MISHMASH OF MODELS AND MISBEHAVIOR SET TO A REMIX OF MAJOR LAZER'S "ORIGINAL DON," A SEXY, POUNDING, DANCE-PARTY SONG THAT MAKES YOU FEEL LIKE AN OBNOXIOUS AND MORALLY BEREFT PERSON FOR LISTENING TO IT. WE BLASTED IT ON REPEAT ON OUR WAY TO VEGAS, AND IT BECAME OUR ANTHEM OF EXCESS.

WE'RE SUCKING UP RESOURCES. WE'RE TREATING MONEY LIKE A TOY AND EATING TOO MUCH FOOD. WE'RE PLAYING THIS DUMB SONG TOO LOUD. WE'RE WOLF OF WALLSTREETING!!

SLOT MACHINE FULL OF MEAT, WHY NOT?!

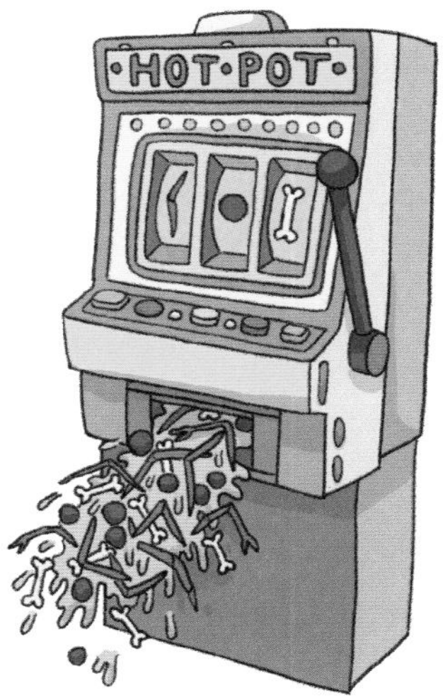
HOT·POT

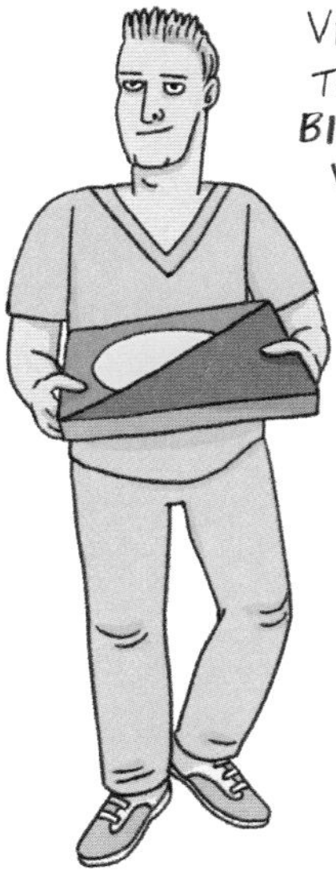

A PIZZA DOCTOR ??!!

VEGAS HOTELS USUALLY HAVE THEMES. CIRCUS CIRCUS IS A BIG TOP; THE PARIS AND THE VENETIAN ARE EUROPEAN. THE COSMOPOLITAN'S THEME IS MORE SUBTLE: "YOU'RE INTERESTING AND RICH!" IT'S PERFECT FOR YOUNG NARCISSISTS LIKE OURSELVES. THERE ARE CRYSTAL CHANDELIERS AND STRINGS OF SPARKLY GLASS BEADS DANGLING FROM THE CEILING. A FRANK SINATRA-TYPE GUY IS SINGING CLASSY JAZZY TUNES ON A STAGE WHILE PEOPLE MILL AROUND. FLAT-SCREENS IN THE ELEVATORS AND LOBBY SHOW ANIMATIONS OF BUGS MORPHING INTO STEAMPUNK GEARS. IT'S VERY EFFECTIVE AT MAKING THIS PLACE FEEL SPECIAL, BUT WITH A TOUCH OF OLD-SCHOOL VEGAS GLAMOUR. THERE ARE LITTLE HERDS OF BROS AND BACHELORETTES GRAZING AROUND, AND WE PASS A MAN IN SCRUBS CARRYING A LARGE PIZZA.

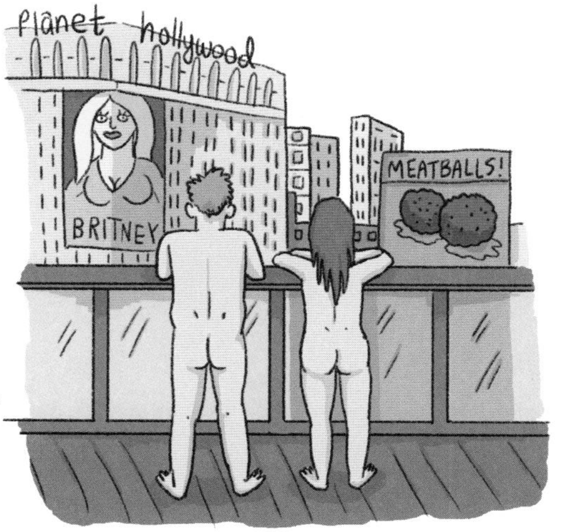
Planet hollywood
BRITNEY
MEATBALLS!

OUR HOTEL SUITE IS PALATIAL. IT TAKES EIGHT FULL SECONDS TO SPRINT FROM ONE SIDE TO THE OTHER AFTER REMOVING ALL YOUR CLOTHING, SWINGING YOUR PANTS ABOVE YOUR HEAD, AND YELLING, "GOODBYE FOREVER, PANTS!" PLUS THE BALCONY HAS AN AMAZING VIEW OF THE STRIP.

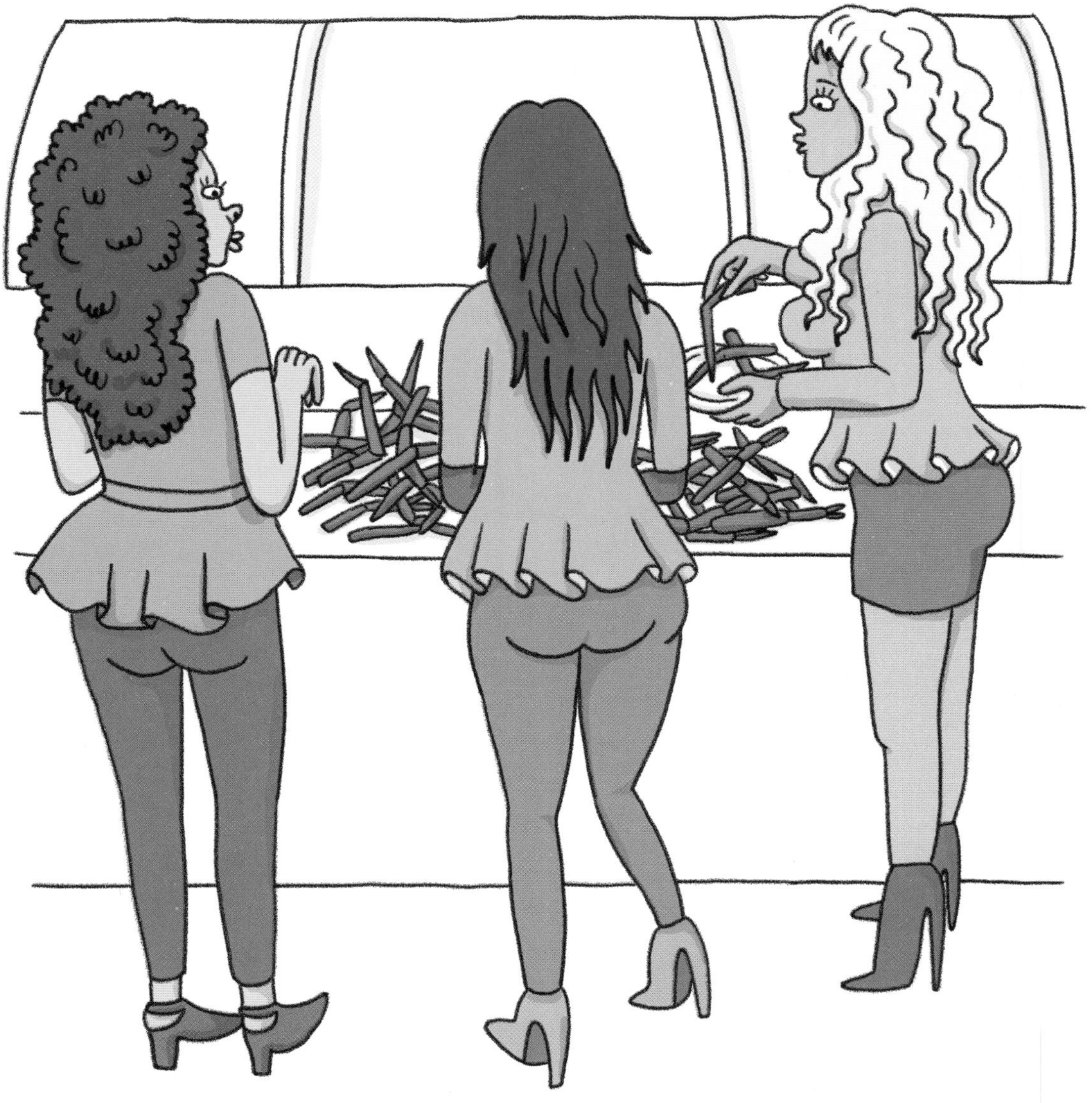

HOTTEST VEGAS TRENDS:
PEPLUM TOPS AND CRAB LEGS

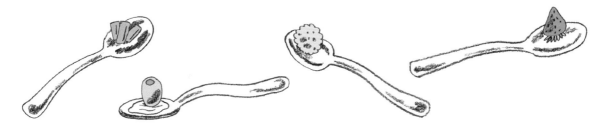

THE WICKED SPOON IS THE COSMO'S BUFFET, AND IT'S FANCIER THAN WHAT I'D IMAGINE FOR AN ALL-YOU-CAN-EAT VENUE. THERE ARE CLASSY AMUSE-BOUCHES AND TEENY-TINY PLATES THAT SUBLIMINALLY DISCOURAGE GUESTS FROM BEING HORRIBLE GORGE-BEASTS.

OH HO, BUT YOU CAN STILL GO SO GROSS HERE IF YOU WANT TO. THERE'S A MOUNTAIN OF CRAB LEGS THAT BACHELORETTES ARE GRABBING AT. THERE'S A FULL BUTCHER SHOP IN HOUSE— LIKE, THEY CHOP UP ENTIRE COWS AND PIGS IN THE CASINO—SO THE BUFFET HAS FRESHLY SMOKED PORK BELLY, STEAK, AND BONE-MARROW CHUNKS.

THERE'S A BIG, BEEFY CUSTOMER LOADING UP HIS PLATE WITH FRIED CHICKEN, PIZZA, MAC-N-CHEESE, SLIDERS, AND WHATEVER THE HELL ELSE, AND WHO CAN BLAME HIM FOR GOING A LITTLE NUTS? WHETHER YOU'RE THIS BIG GUY OR A SNOTTY FOODIE, YOU CAN FILL UP HERE. THERE'S SOMETHING FOR EVERYONE.

I START OUT KINDA HEAVY WITH A GIANT MEATBALL AND A MINI SHEPHERD'S PIE. THEN I GO REAL DAINTY WITH A DELICATE SHRIMP CEVICHE AND A MINI NICOISE SALAD WITH A QUAIL EGG. THEN I DON'T KNOW WHAT HAPPENS—MY PLATE IS A BLUR OF STEAK AND CRAB LEGS AND SOME BULGOGI THAT IS TOO CHEWY TO DO ANYTHING WITH BUT SUCK ON.

I TRY ONE SCOOP OF AN ARTICHOKE SALAD THAT IS PAST ITS PRIME AND NEEDS TO BE SPIT OUT, THEN QUICKLY ERASE THAT ERROR WITH A SAMPLING OF OLIVES AND CHEESES. BUFFET FOODS ARE HIT OR MISS AND OFTEN LUKEWARM, EVEN AT A FINE ESTABLISHMENT LIKE THIS, BUT THERE'S SO MUCH OF IT, AND IT'S CONSTANTLY REGENERATED SO THERE'S NO CHANCE FOR DISAPPOINTMENT TO TAKE HOLD.

EVERY DESSERT IS FANTASTIC. TWENTY DIFFERENT KINDS OF TART AND CAKE, PLUS INTERESTING GELATO FLAVORS. HEAVEN.

THE BUFFET STAFF ANTICIPATES HOARDING BEHAVIOR, SO THERE ARE NO PAPER NAPKINS ANYWHERE FOR CARRYING FOOD AWAY. I WANT TO SLIP A COFFEE-FLAVORED RICE KRISPIE TREAT INTO MY PURSE, BUT THE ONLY OPTION IS TOILET PAPER, WHICH... NOPE. DO I THINK ABOUT IT? YES. DO I BRING MY RICE KRISPIE TREAT ALL THE WAY INTO THE RESTROOM BEFORE SUMMONING A SCRAP OF DIGNITY? GET OFF MY BACK!

THE NEXT MORNING, WE GO TO THE OLDER BELLAGIO HOTEL FOR THEIR BRUNCH BUFFET AND HAVE TO WANDER THROUGH A CASINO TO FIND IT. ON THE WAY THERE, WE GET LOST IN AN ATRIUM DECKED OUT TO CELEBRATE THE CHINESE LUNAR NEW YEAR OF THE HORSE, AND IT'S MAGNIFICENT ENOUGH TO MAKE ME EXCLAIM, "OH F*****CK!" IN FRONT OF A BUNCH OF SURPRISED TOURISTS.

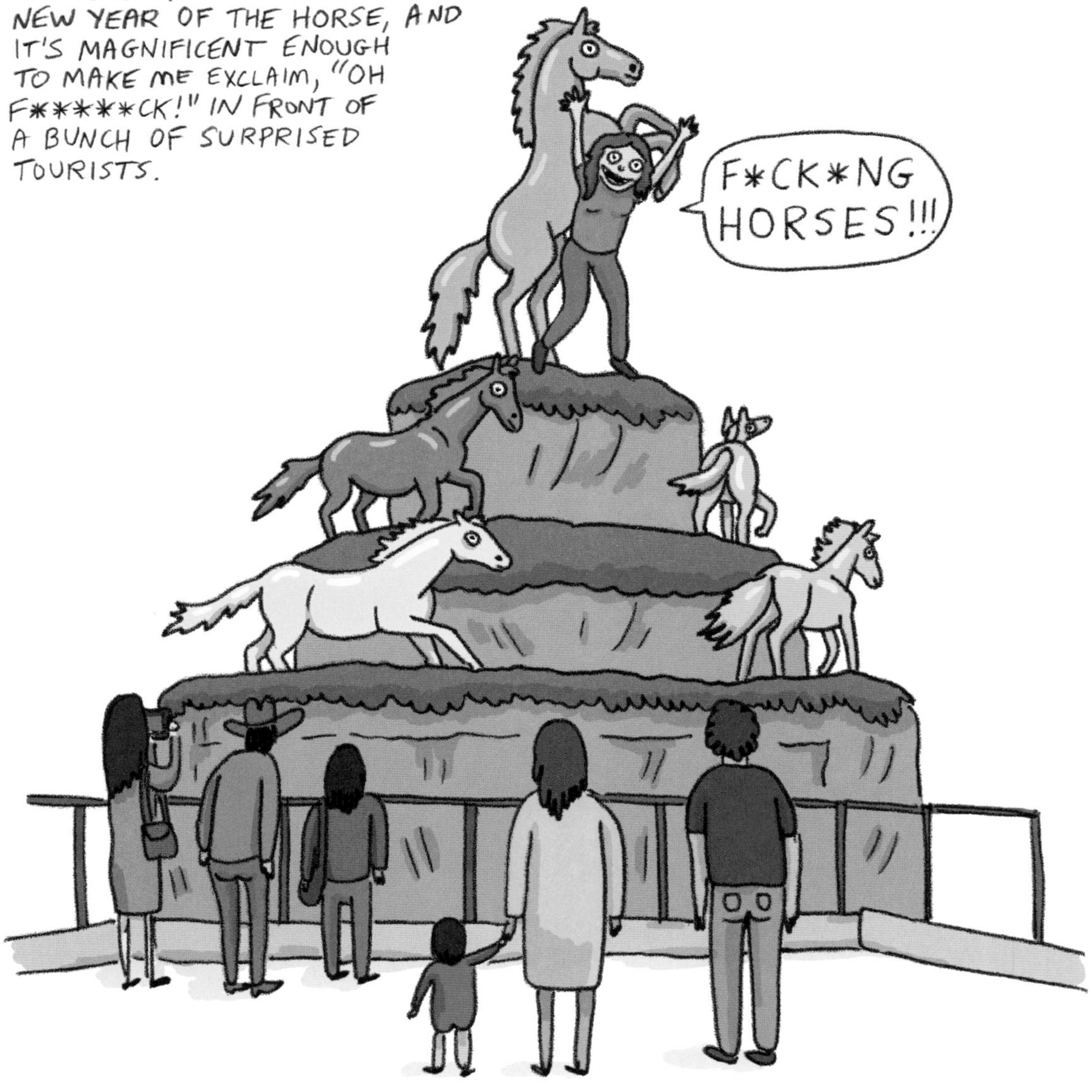
F*CK*NG HORSES!!!

THIS BUFFET HAS MUCH MORE STANDARD OFFERINGS THAN THE WICKED SPOON. THE MOST EXCITING THING IS THE CONGEE PORRIDGE. AND THERE'S AN OMELET STATION WITH CRAB OMELETS. WHY AM I SO CHARMED BY THE ABUNDANCE OF CRAB IN VEGAS?

I REALIZE ANOTHER BENEFIT OF BUFFETS. YOU CAN EAT LIKE A COMPLETE IDIOT HERE.

EVERYONE ELSE IS SO FOCUSED ON LOADING UP THEIR PLATES THAT NOBODY WILL STOP TO ASK YOU WHAT THE FUCK YOU'RE DOING LADLING SOUP DUMPLINGS ONTO PILES OF BACON. I DO THIS, AND NOBODY NOTICES. THEN I EAT IT, AND NOBODY STOPS ME.

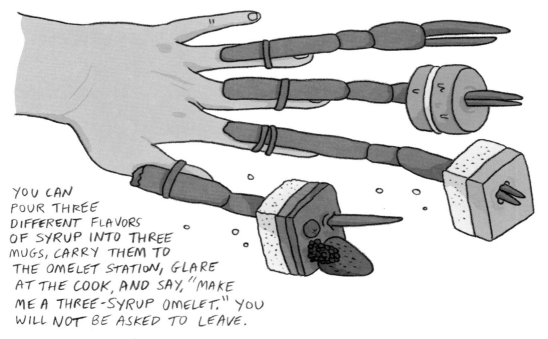

YOU CAN POUR THREE DIFFERENT FLAVORS OF SYRUP INTO THREE MUGS, CARRY THEM TO THE OMELET STATION, GLARE AT THE COOK, AND SAY, "MAKE ME A THREE-SYRUP OMELET." YOU WILL NOT BE ASKED TO LEAVE.

YOU CAN STICK PETIT FOURS ONTO THE ENDS OF CRAB LEGS, TIE THEM TO YOUR FINGERS, AND RUN AROUND CALLING YOURSELF EDWARD CAKECRABHANDS, AND YOU WILL SIMPLY BE OFFERED MORE CRAB. THERE ARE NO CONSEQUENCES TO MY ACTIONS HERE, AND IT'S INTOXICATING.

WE TRY TO WALK OFF OUR BRUNCH BY BROWSING HIGH-END SHOPS AT THE NEIGHBORING ARIA MALL, WHERE I DISCOVER THAT LUXURY GOODS HAVE A LAXATIVE EFFECT. I SEE A PRADA SKIRT WITH A HUMAN FACE PRINTED ON IT, AND MY GUTS CRAMP INSTANTLY.

WE HIT THE HOTEL GYM IN THE AFTERNOON, STILL FULL OF BUFFET, AND I SLOWLY PRANCE UP AND DOWN ON AN ELLIPTICAL TRAINER WHILE PLAYING MAHJONG ON THE ATTACHED SCREEN. LIFE IS GOOD HERE.

IN THE EVENING WE GO UPSTAIRS TO JOSÉ ANDRÉS'S RESTAURANT, JALEO, TO MEET RENATA, THE COSMO'S PUBLIC-RELATIONS MANAGER. JALEO ISN'T TECHNICALLY ALL YOU CAN EAT, BUT RENATA ORDERS US UNLIMITED COCKTAILS AND STUFFS US WITH A MILLION DIFFERENT DISHES OF INVENTIVE AND EXTRAVAGANT FOOD.

PRADARHEA

PORRÓN MORON

SHE ALSO ORDERS A PORRÓN PITCHER FULL OF BEER. IT'S A TRADITIONAL SPANISH THING AND THE RESTAURANT IS CLEARLY PROUD OF IT, BUT IT FEELS LIKE A FRATBOY STUNT. YOU HAVE TO HOLD IT ABOVE YOUR MOUTH AND POUR THE LIQUID DOWN YOUR THROAT IN AN ARC WITHOUT TOUCHING IT TO YOUR LIPS. IT'S VERY URINAL.

I RESENT HAVING TO TRY THIS FOR THE FIRST TIME IN PUBLIC BEFORE PRACTICING IT ALONE, AND OF COURSE I SPILL BEER DOWN THE FRONT OF MY BLOUSE. ONLY LATER, AFTER I'M ALREADY DRUNK, DO I TRY THE PORRÓN AGAIN AND DO WHAT I FEEL MUST BE A REALLY AWESOME JOB.

WE TALK TO RENATA FOR AN HOUR, WHICH IS TOO LONG BECAUSE I ONLY HAVE LIKE TWO QUESTIONS AND THEY'RE BOTH ABOUT GUESTS BEING ASSHOLES AT THE BUFFET.

I SHARE MY FANTASIES OF HOTEL GUESTS EXPLODING AFTER EATING TOO MUCH, WHICH I THOUGHT WE'D BE ON THE SAME PAGE ABOUT, BUT ACCORDING TO RENATA IT ISN'T AN ACTUAL PROBLEM!

I TRY A NEW ANGLE TO SEE BEHIND THE SCENES OF THE BUFFET KITCHEN, BUT RENATA INSISTS THAT ALL I'D SPY BACK THERE IS DISHWASHING. EITHER SHE'S TELLING THE DULL TRUTH, OR SHE'S HIDING SOMETHING.

DO GUESTS EVER OVER DO IT AND GET KICKED OUT?

WHAT DO YOU MEAN "OVER DO IT"?

UHHHH

WEE!

OOF!

MY PERSONAL GUESS? GUESTS WHO ATE SO MANY CRAB LEGS THEY TURNED INTO CRAB PEOPLE!! AND THEY ARE FORCED TO WORK IN THE CASINO KITCHEN. I'D BETTER GO EASY ON THE SEAFOOD.

WE SPEND OUR LAST FEW HOURS IN VEGAS GAMBLING AT THE SLOTS AND BLACKJACK TABLES.

LOOK, I WISH I COULD SAY WE WENT INSANE AND BLEW HUNDREDS OF DOLLARS AND THEN EARNED IT ALL BACK! BUT IN REALITY WE BET LOW, MADE MODEST WINNINGS, AND BASICALLY BROKE EVEN. EATING IS THE ONLY THING I LIKE TO DO TO EXCESS. I CHOOSE TO GAMBLE WITH MY GUTS!

163

CABALLOS CON CARNE

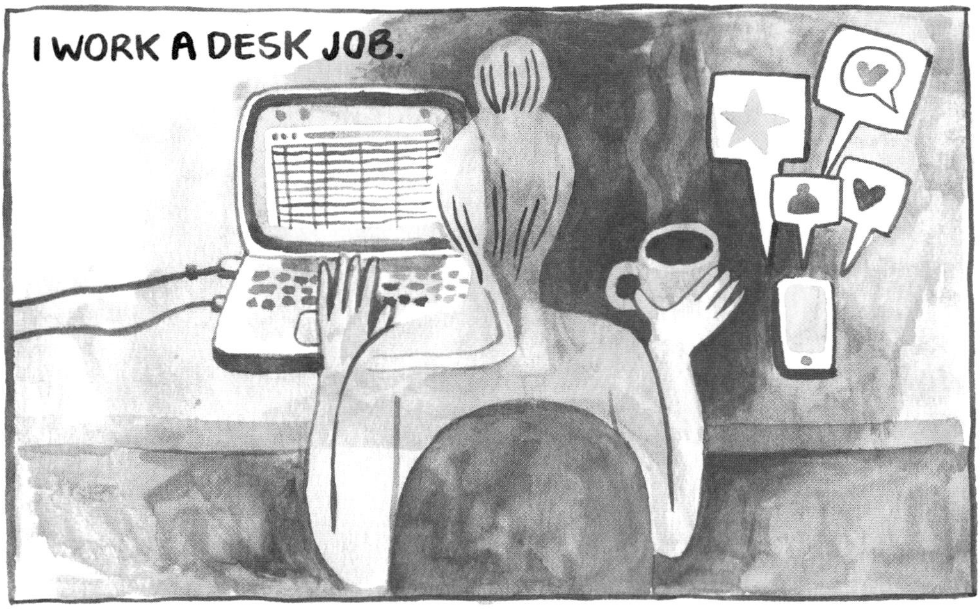
I WORK A DESK JOB.

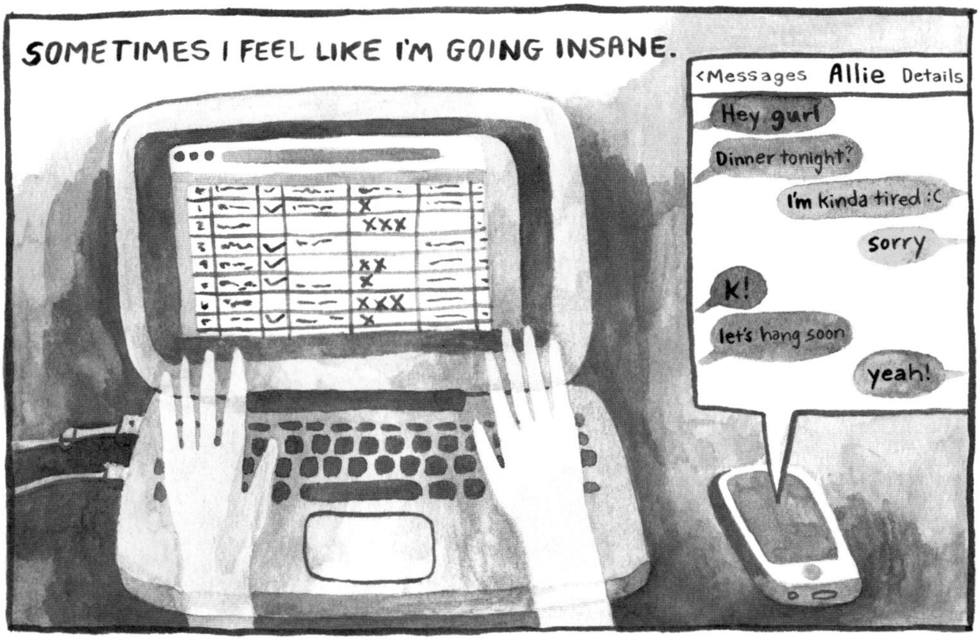
SOMETIMES I FEEL LIKE I'M GOING INSANE.
<Messages Allie Details
Hey gurl
Dinner tonight?
I'm kinda tired :C
sorry
K!
let's hang soon
yeah!

IT STARTED AS AN ESCAPIST THING. I NOTICED
PEOPLE DOING IT ONLINE.

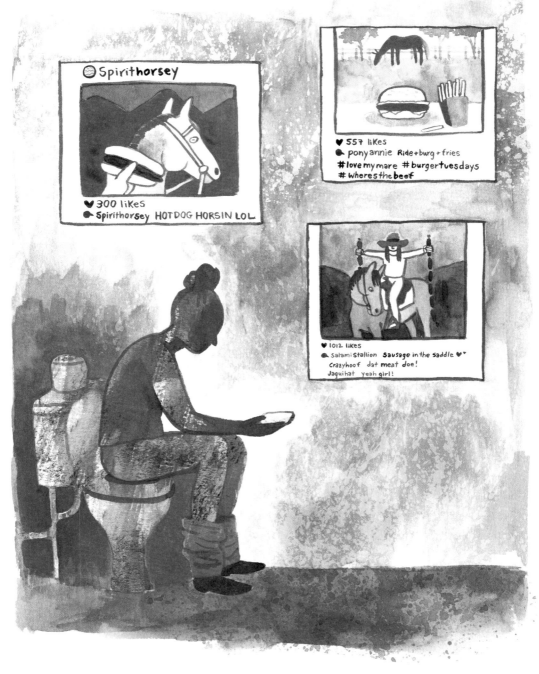

🌐 Spirithorsey

♥ 300 likes
🐴 Spirithorsey HOTDOG HORSIN LOL

♥ 557 likes
🐴 pony annie Ride+burg+fries
#love my mare #burgertuesdays
#wheres the beef

♥ 1012 likes
🐴 salami stallion Sausage in the saddle ♥
Crazyhoof dat meat doe!
Jaquihat yeah girl!

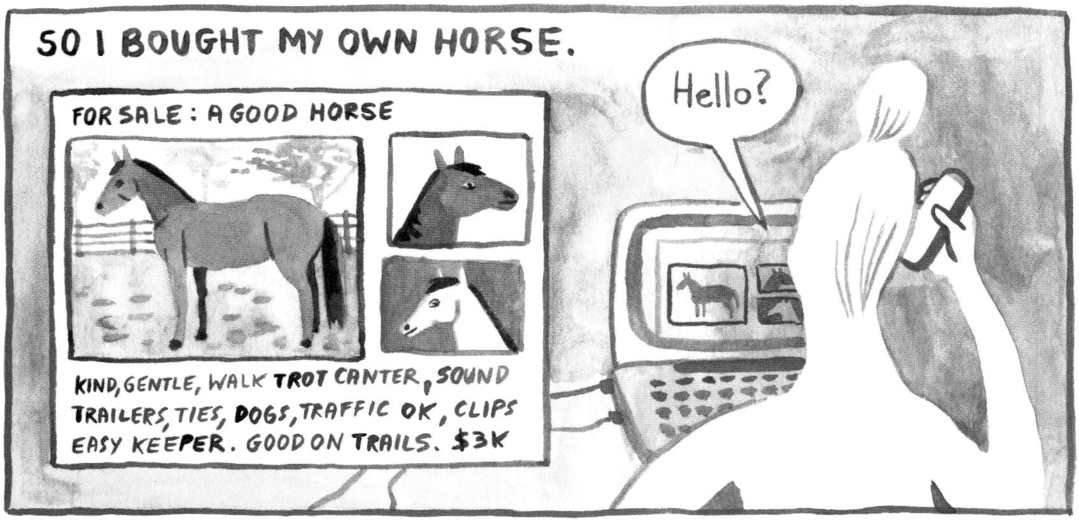
SO I BOUGHT MY OWN HORSE.
FOR SALE: A GOOD HORSE
KIND, GENTLE, WALK TROT CANTER, SOUND
TRAILERS, TIES, DOGS, TRAFFIC OK, CLIPS
EASY KEEPER. GOOD ON TRAILS. $3K
Hello?

THIS IS THE MOST IMPULSIVE THING I'VE EVER DONE.

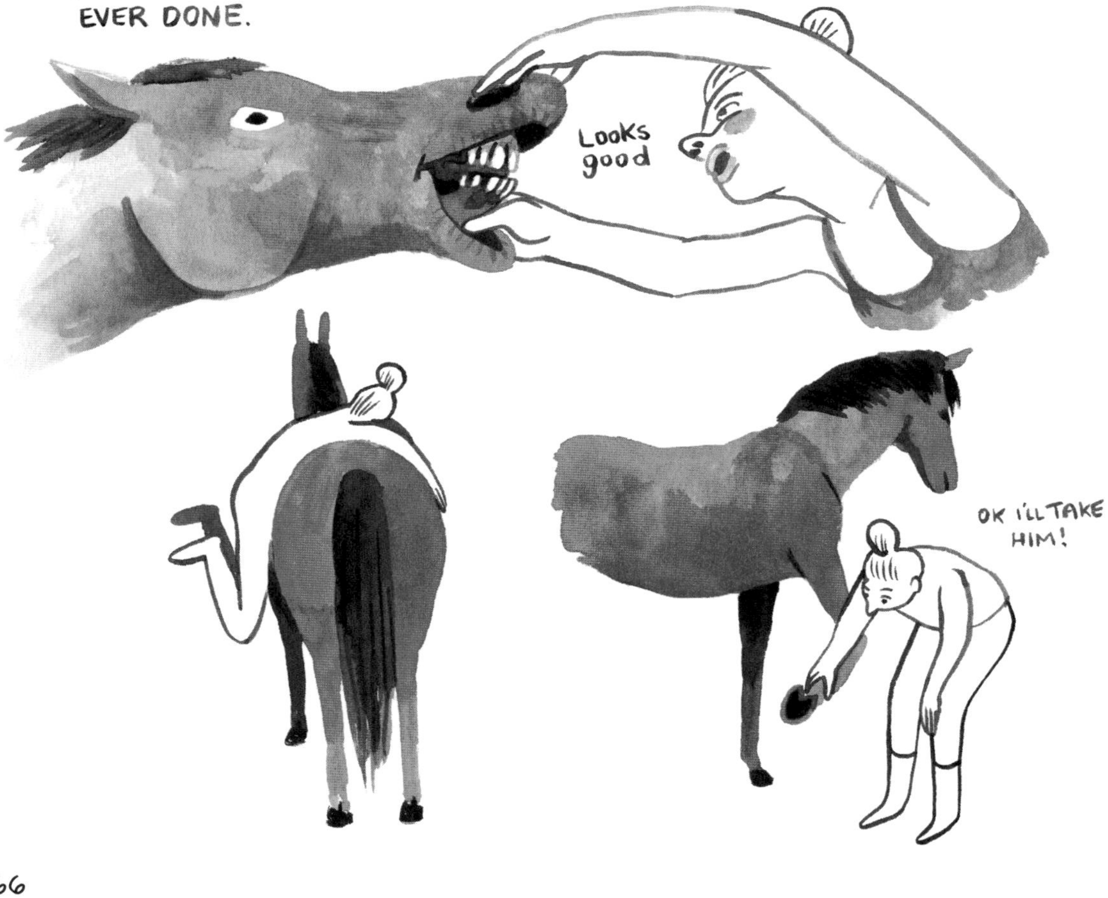
Looks good
OK I'LL TAKE HIM!

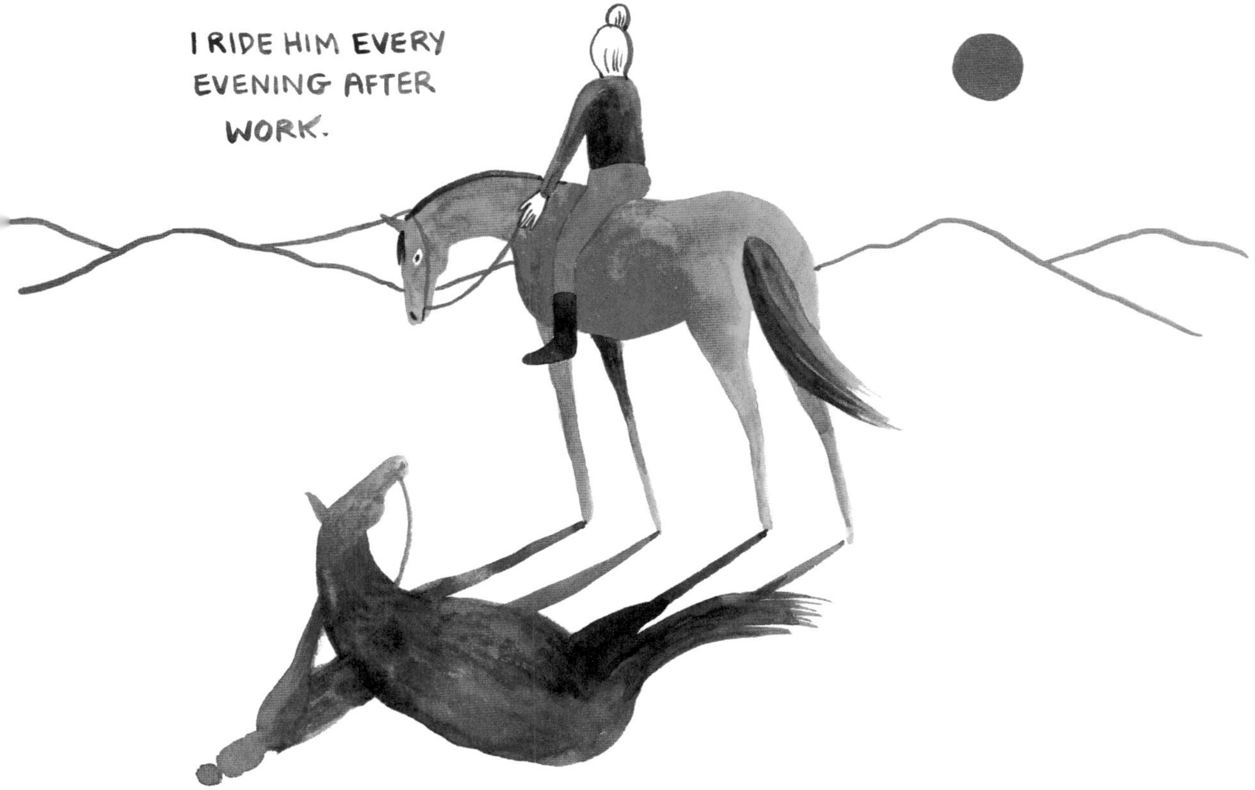
I RIDE HIM EVERY EVENING AFTER WORK.

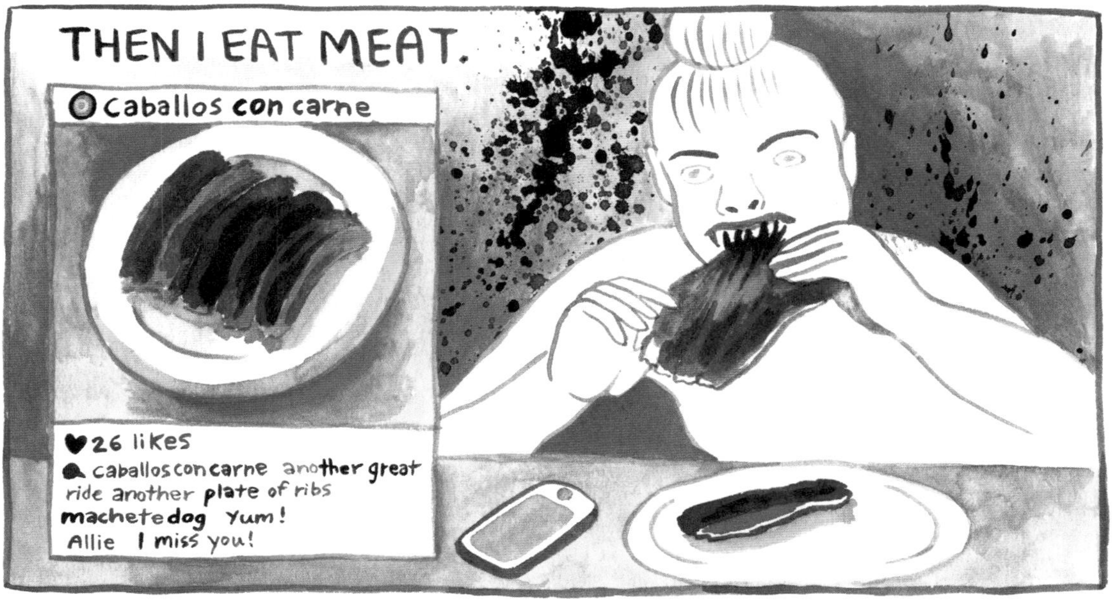
THEN I EAT MEAT.
Caballos con carne
26 likes
caballosconcarne another great ride another plate of ribs
machetedog Yum!
Allie I miss you!

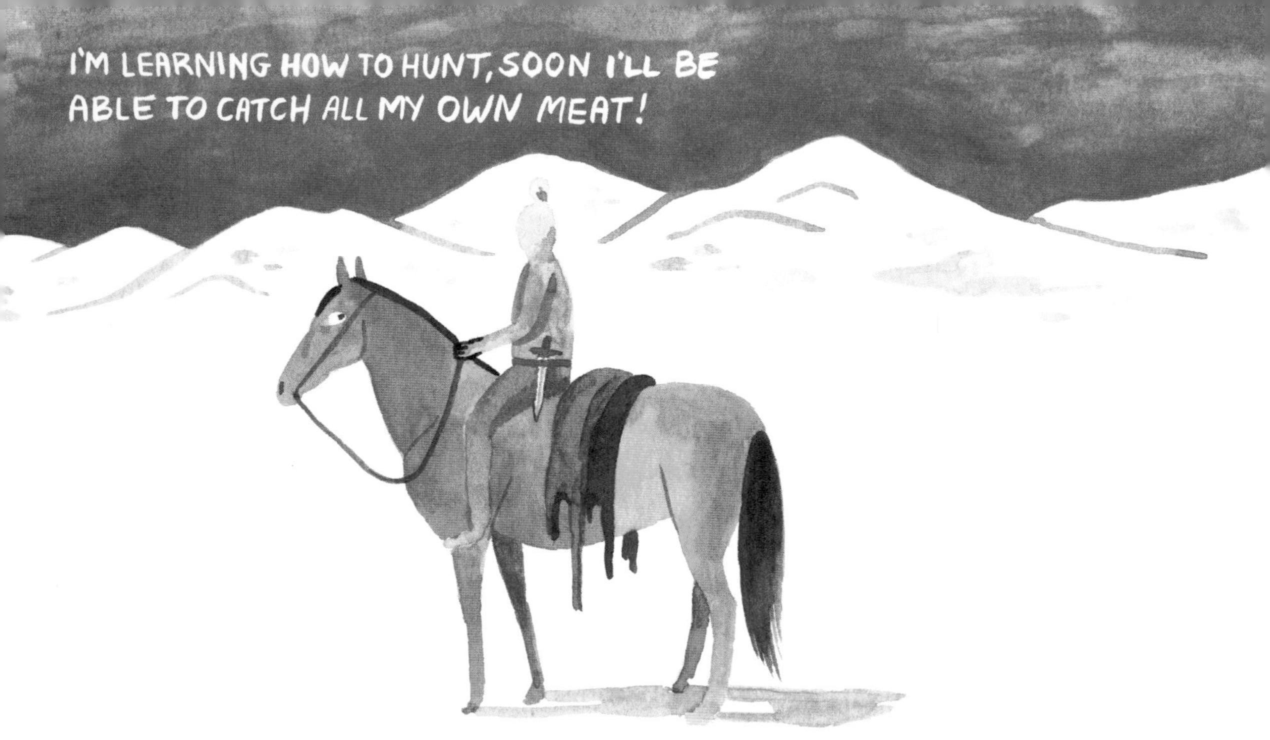
I'M LEARNING HOW TO HUNT, SOON I'LL BE ABLE TO CATCH ALL MY OWN MEAT!

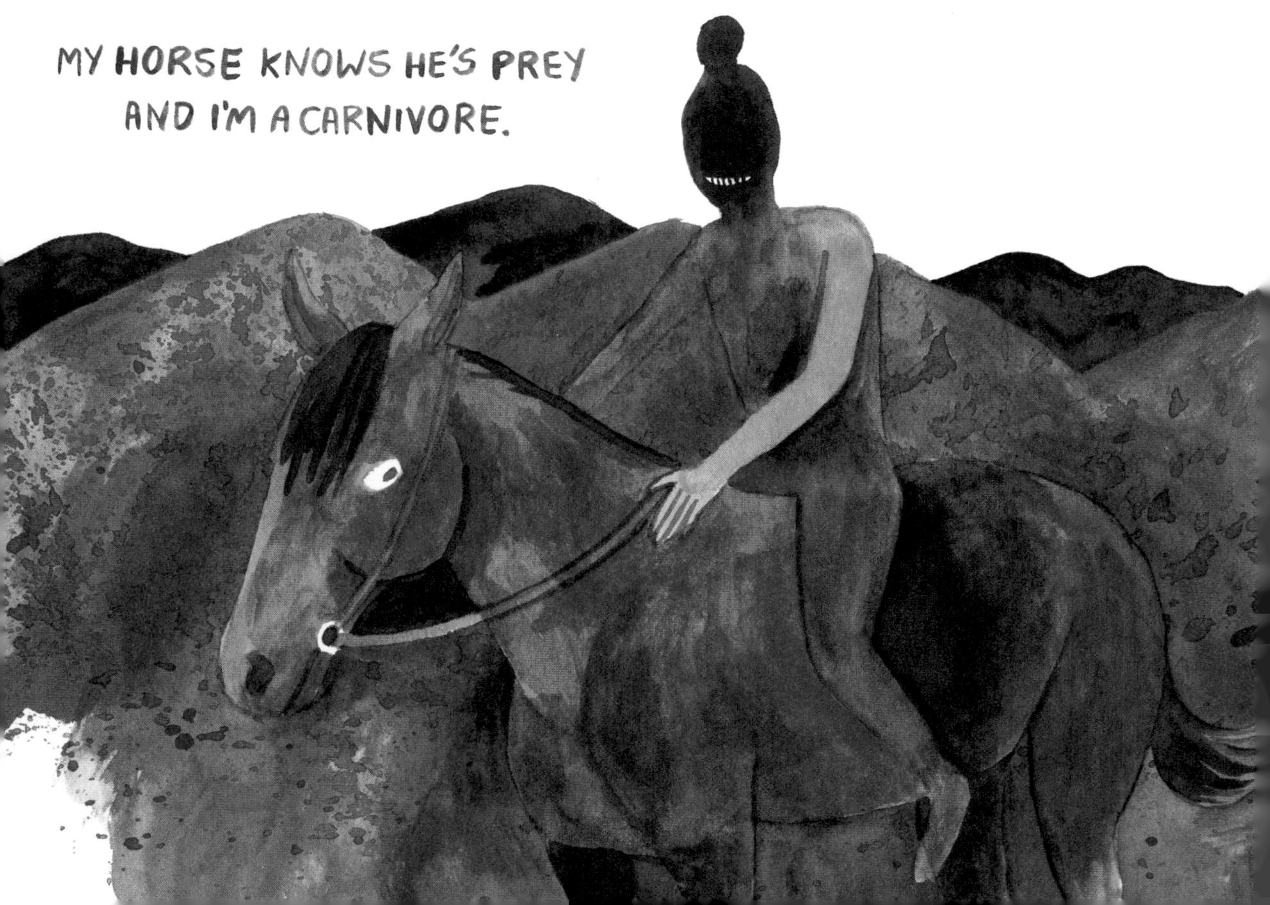
MY HORSE KNOWS HE'S PREY AND I'M A CARNIVORE.

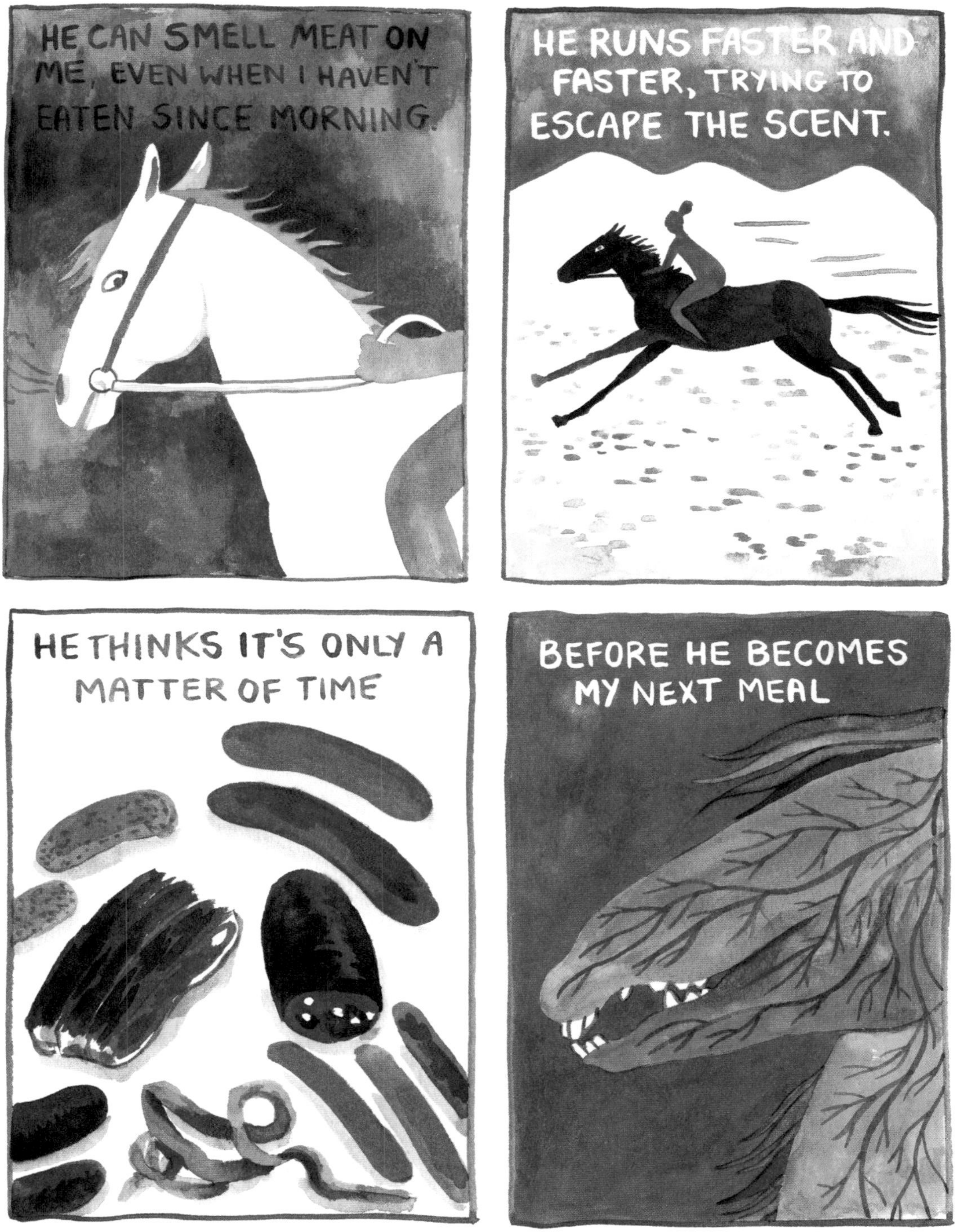
HE CAN SMELL MEAT ON ME, EVEN WHEN I HAVEN'T EATEN SINCE MORNING.
HE RUNS FASTER AND FASTER, TRYING TO ESCAPE THE SCENT.
HE THINKS IT'S ONLY A MATTER OF TIME
BEFORE HE BECOMES MY NEXT MEAL

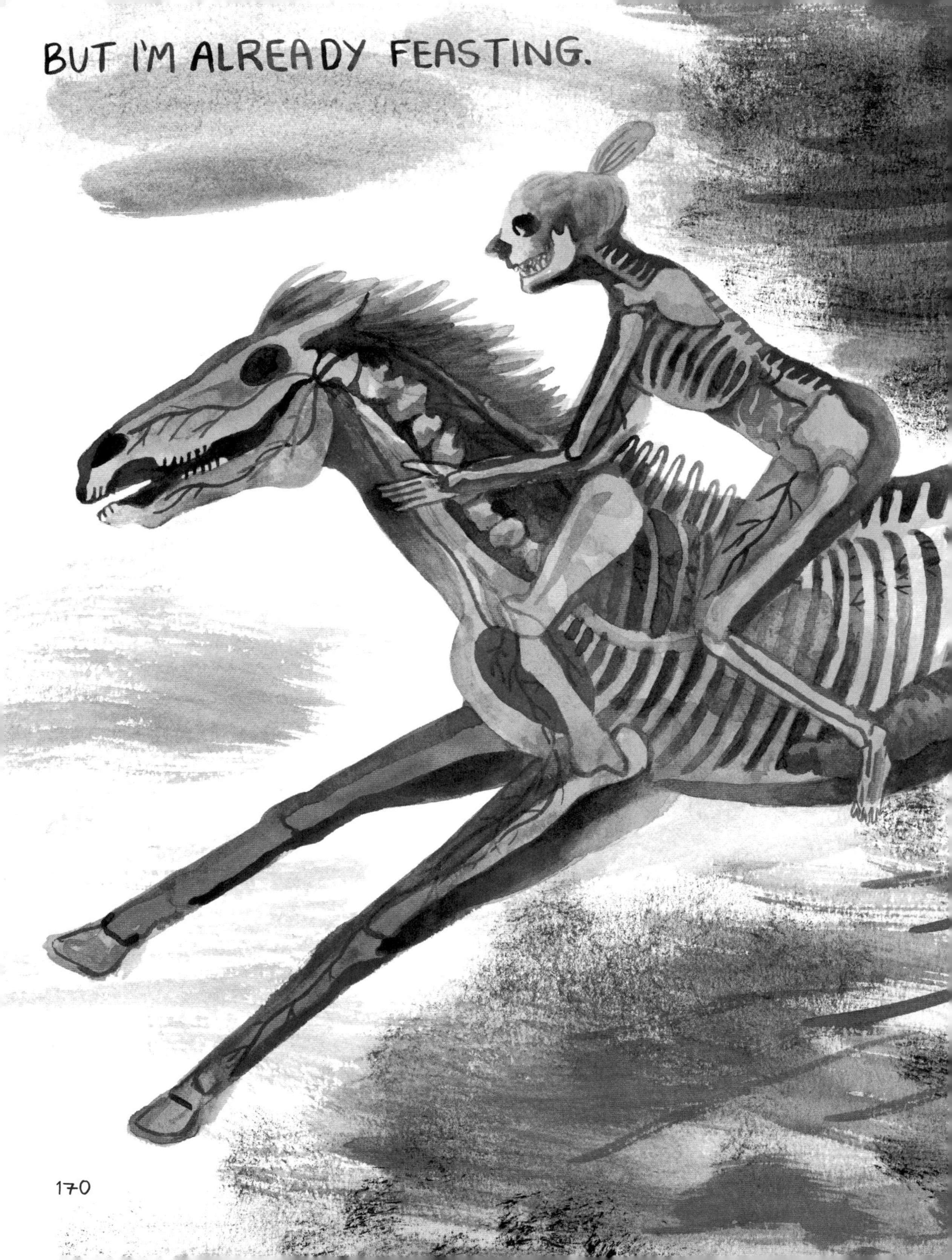
BUT I'M ALREADY FEASTING.

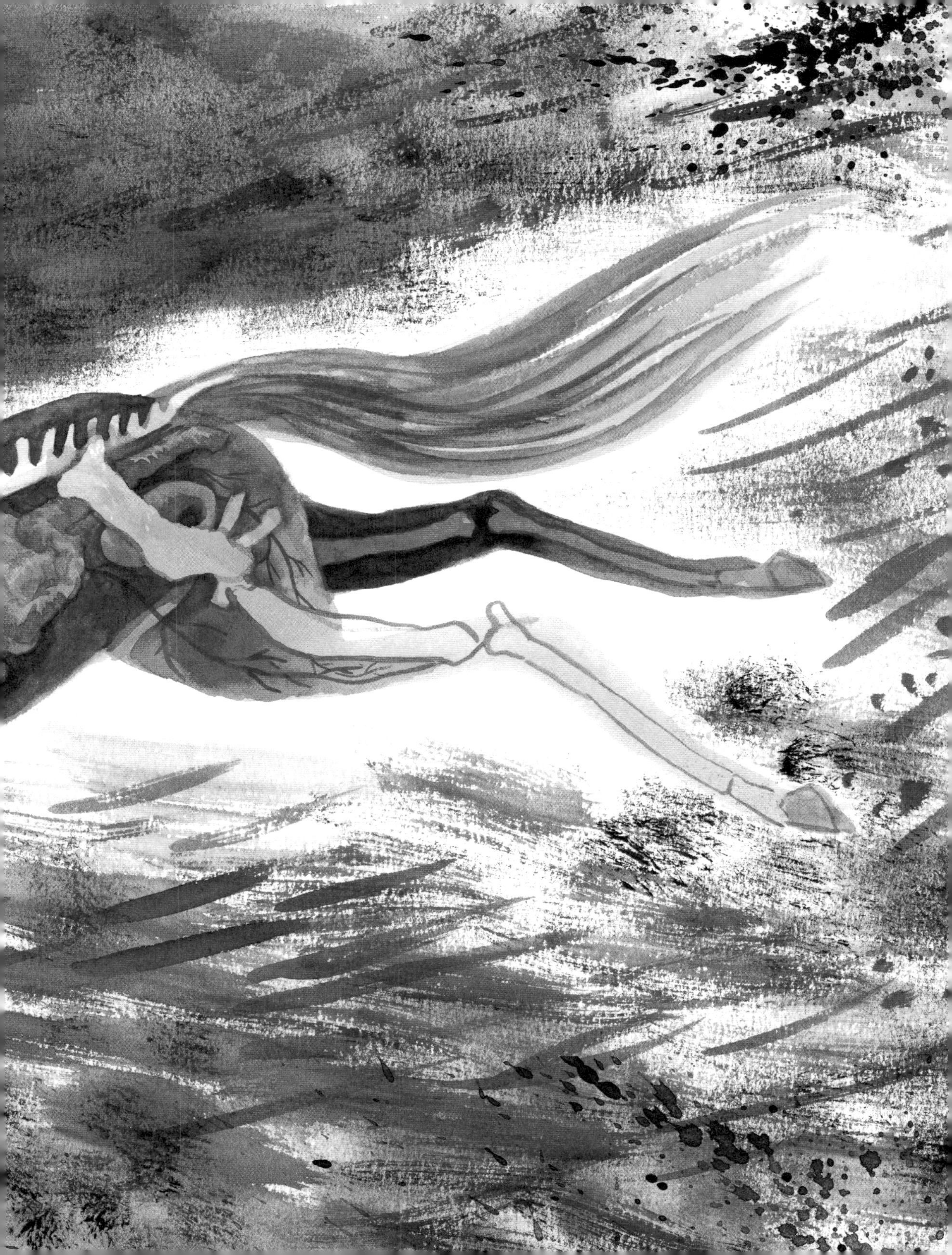

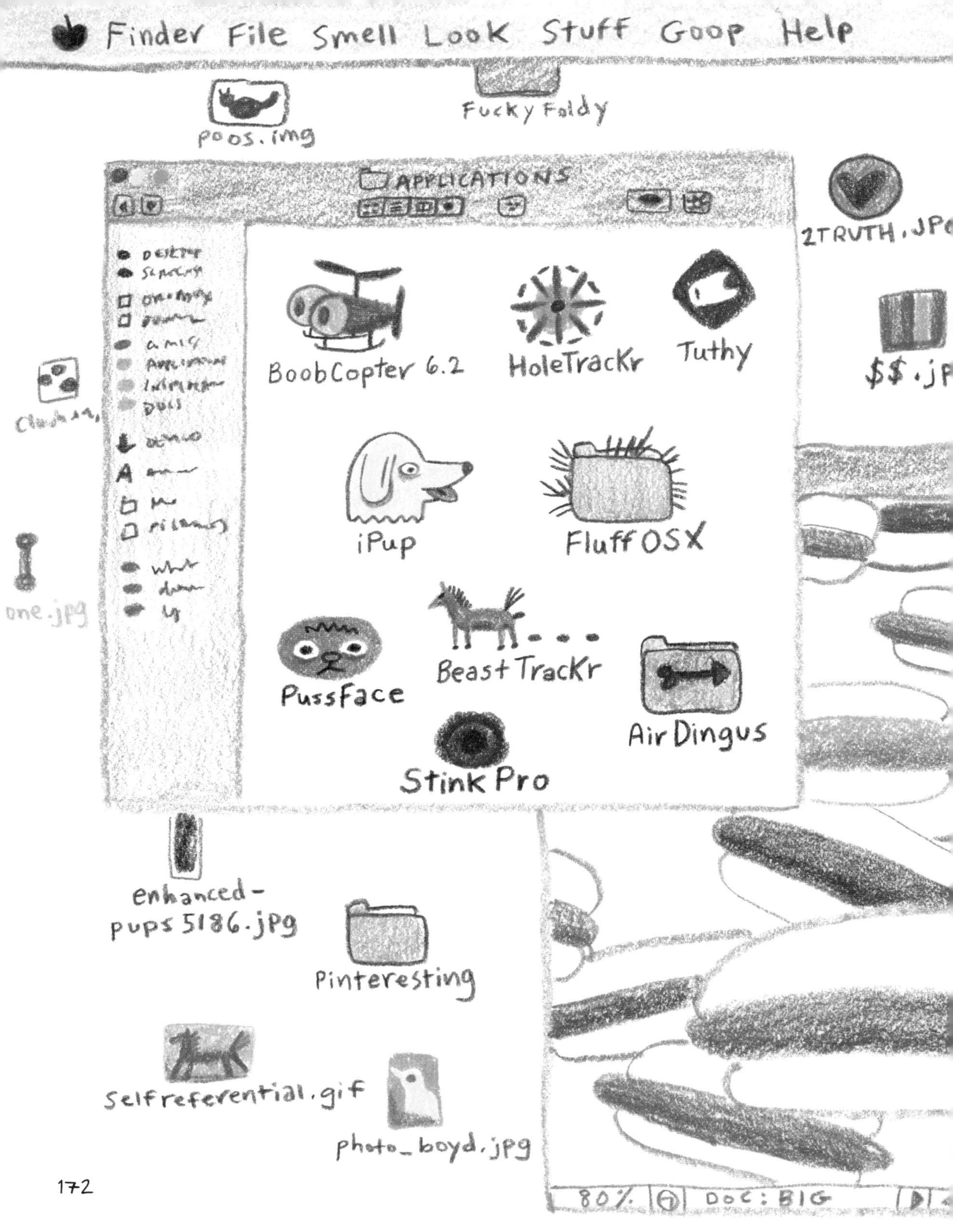

Finder File Smell Look Stuff Goop Help
poos.img
Fucky Foldy
APPLICATIONS
2TRUTH.JP
$$.jp
BoobCopter 6.2
HoleTrackr
Tuthy
iPup
FluffOSX
one.jpg
PussFace
BeastTrackr
AirDingus
Stink Pro
enhanced-
pups5186.jpg
Pinteresting
selfreferential.gif
photo_boyd.jpg
80%
DOC: BIG

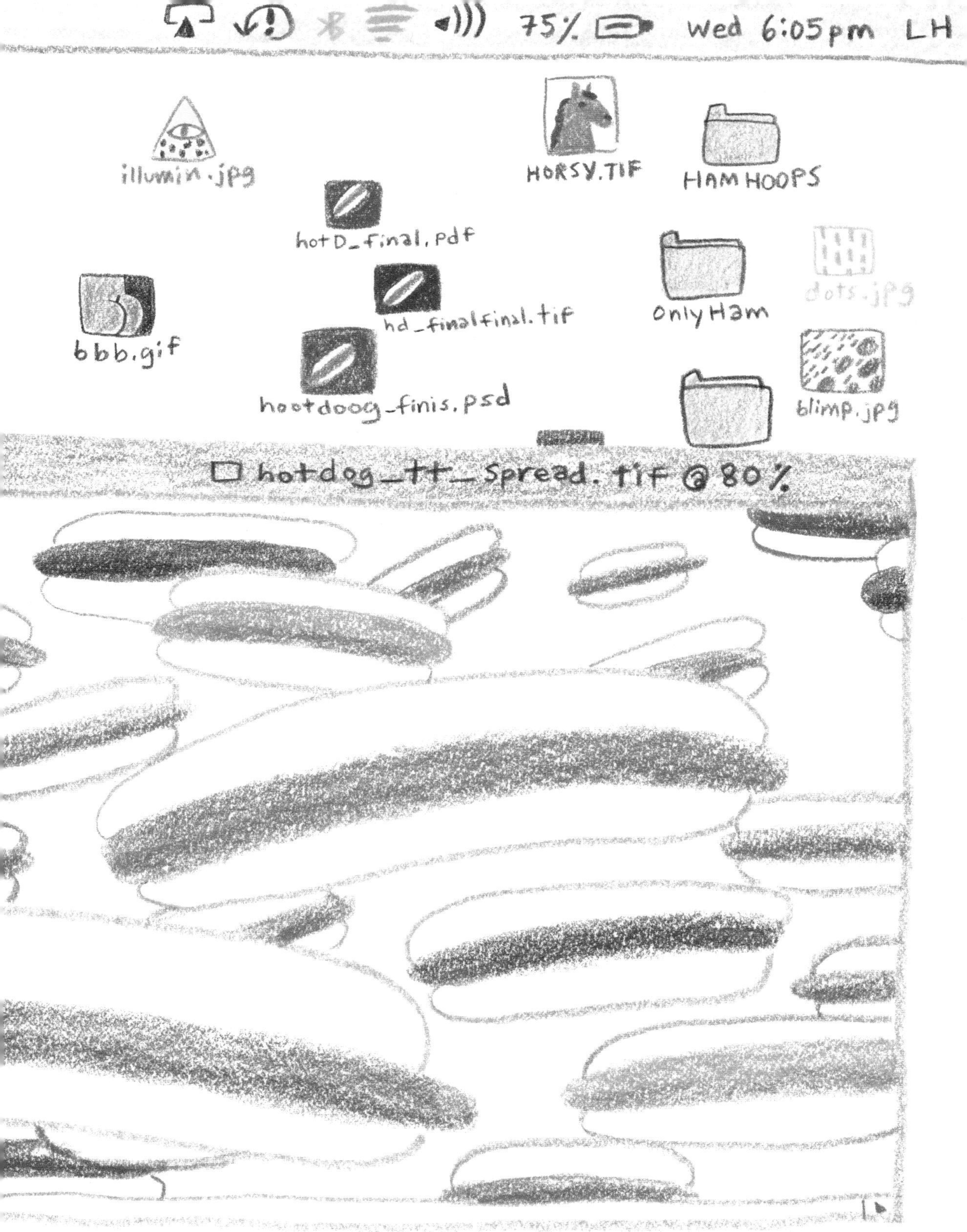
75% Wed 6:05pm LH
illumin.jpg
HORSY.TIF
HAM HOOPS
hotD_final.pdf
hd_finalfinal.tif
Only Ham
dots.jpg
bbb.gif
hootdoog_finis.psd
blimp.jpg
hotdog_tt_spread.tif @ 80%

DRAWNANDQUARTERLY.COM
LISAHANAWALT.COM

FIRST EDITION: JUNE 2016. PRINTED IN CHINA. 10 9 8 7 6 5 4 3 2 1
LIBRARY AND ARCHIVES CANADA CATALOGUING IN PUBLICATION:
HANAWALT, LISA, AUTHOR, ILLUSTRATOR. HOT DOG TASTE TEST/ LISA HANAWALT

ISBN 978-1-77046-237-3 (BOUND).
1. COMIC BOOKS, STRIPS, ETC.
I. TITLE. PN6727. H35H68 2016   741.5'973 C2015-906029-X

IT'S 65°F OUTSIDE RIGHT NOW.

PUBLISHED IN THE USA BY DRAWN & QUARTERLY, A CLIENT PUBLISHER OF FARRAR, STRAUS AND GIROUX.
ORDERS: 888.330.8477

THIS PART OF BOOKS IS SO BORING IT SHOULD BE ILLEGAL.

PUBLISHED IN CANADA BY DRAWN & QUARTERLY, A CLIENT PUBLISHER OF RAINCOAST BOOKS. ORDERS: 800.663.5714

ON THE NIGHT THE MOON ALIGNS WITH TALL TREE AND EGG MOUNTAIN, WE WILL GATHER TO FORM A MATRIARCHY AND COOK S'MORES.

PUBLISHED IN THE UNITED KINGDOM BY DRAWN & QUARTERLY, A CLIENT PUBLISHER OF PUBLISHERS GROUP UK.
ORDERS: INFO@PGUK.CO.UK

THANK YOU ALL MY DEAR FRIENDS.

THANK YOU ROXY. MISS YOU.

HUGE THANKS TO TRACY, JULIA, PEGGY, TOM, CHRIS, AND EVERYONE ELSE AT D&Q. THANK YOU MEREDITH KAFFEL.

MANY PIECES IN THIS BOOK, INCLUDING HOLIDAY FOOD DIARY, ON THE TRAIL WITH WYLIE, GOODBYE TO ALL THAT SUGAR..., LISAAAAA LAS VEGAS, BREAKFAST STUFF, OTTERS!, PLANTING, AND MORE WERE ORIGINALLY PUBLISHED IN LUCKY PEACH MAGAZINE.

SPECIAL THANKS TO PETER MEEHAN, RACHEL KHONG, WALTER GREEN, CHRIS YING, DAVID CHANG, AND EVERYONE ELSE AT LP.

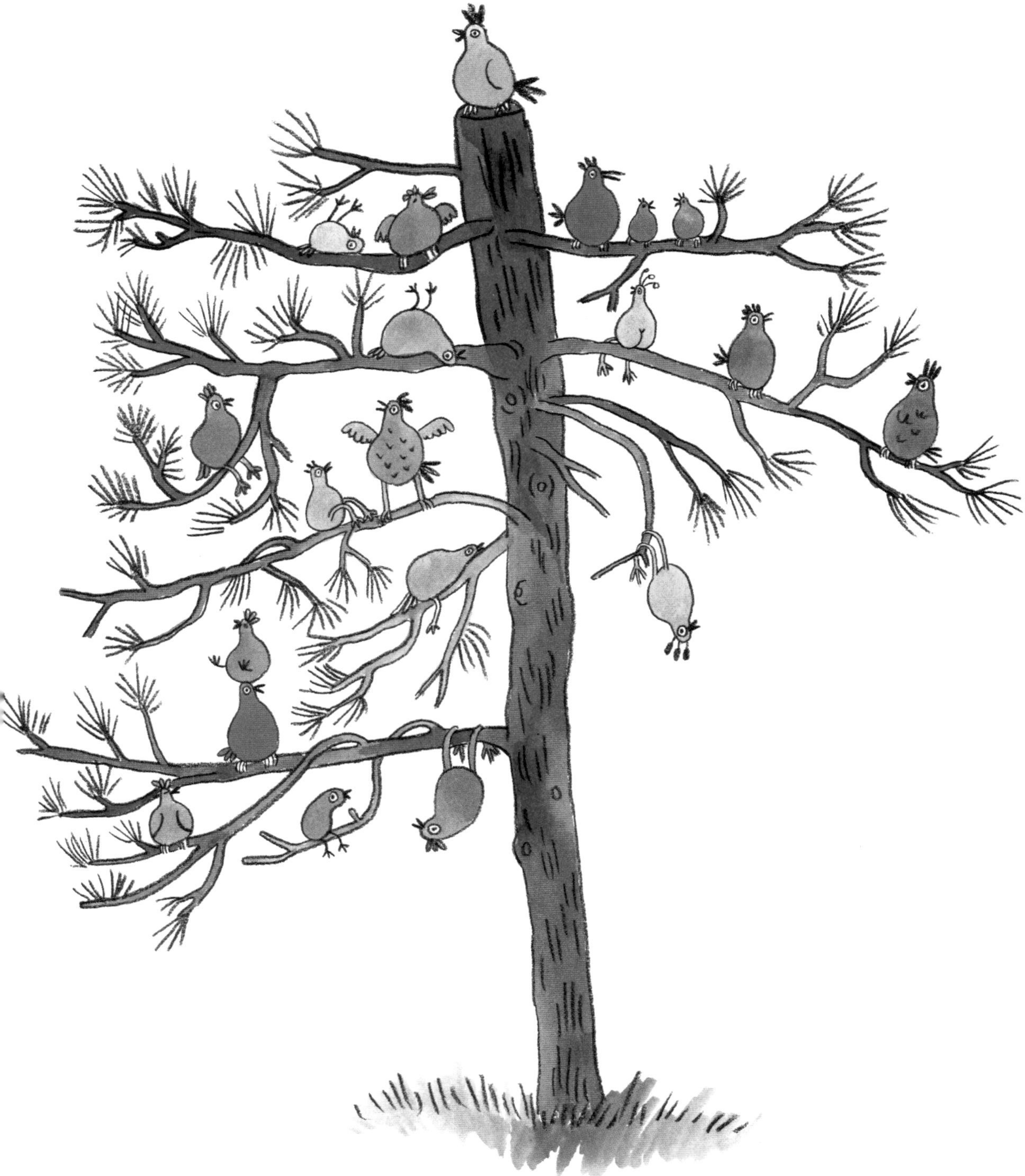

TREE FULLA IDIOTS

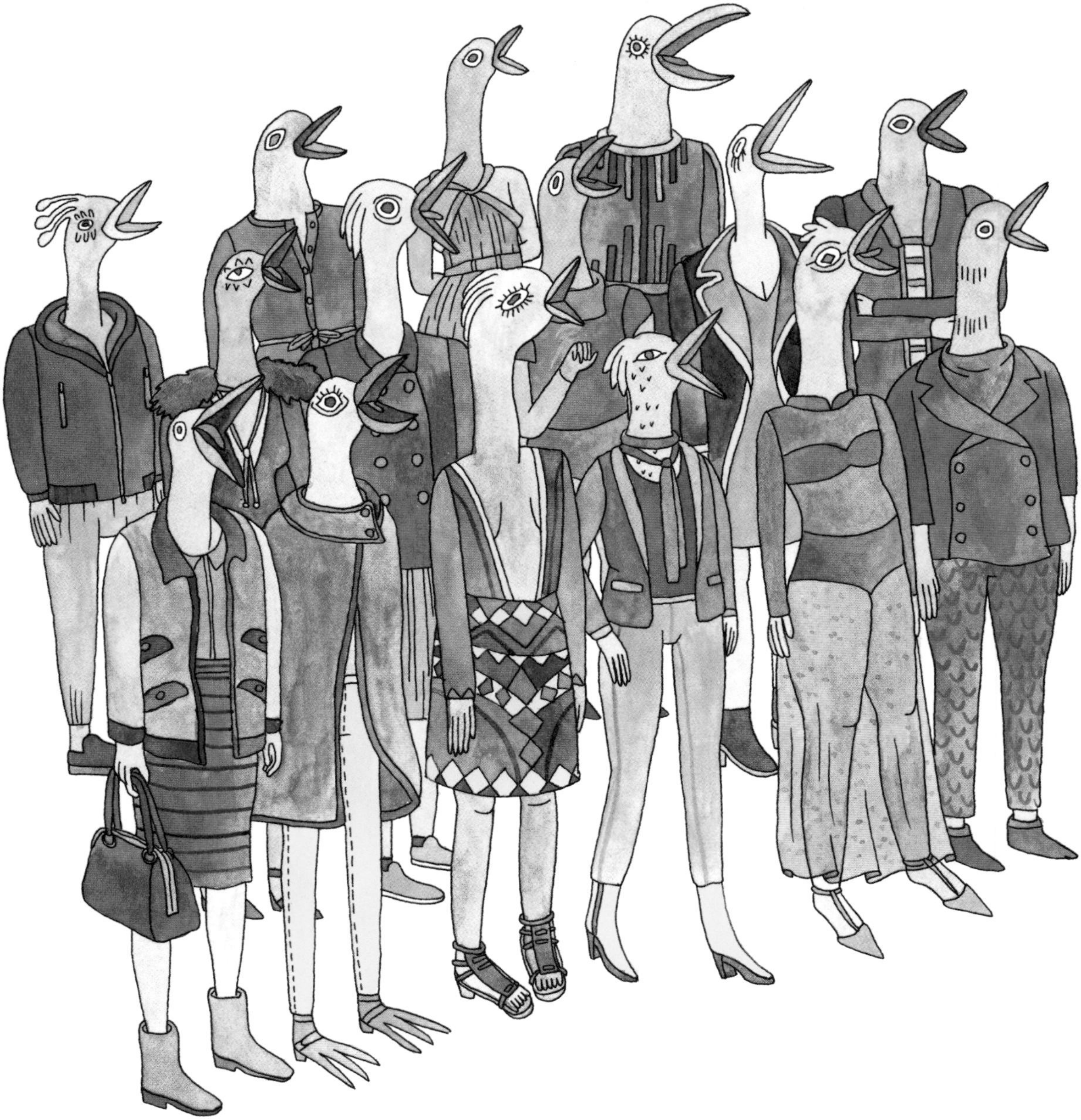

~~LISA HANAWALT IS A CARTOONIST~~

~~LISA HANAWALT IS AN ARTIST CURRENTLY~~

LISA HANAWALT IS AN ARTIST IN LOS ANGELES. LISA GREW UP IN PALO ALTO, CA AND GRADUATED FROM UCLA. LISA HAS A NERVOUS STOMACH AND A BRAVE BLADDER. HER WORK APPEARS ALL OVER THE PLACE, IN MANY DIFFERENT FORMS. SOMETIMES HER WORK IS JUST A FEELING YOU HAVE DEEP INSIDE. DRAWN & QUARTERLY PUBLISHED HER FIRST COLLECTION OF COMICS, MY DIRTY DUMB EYES, IN 2013.

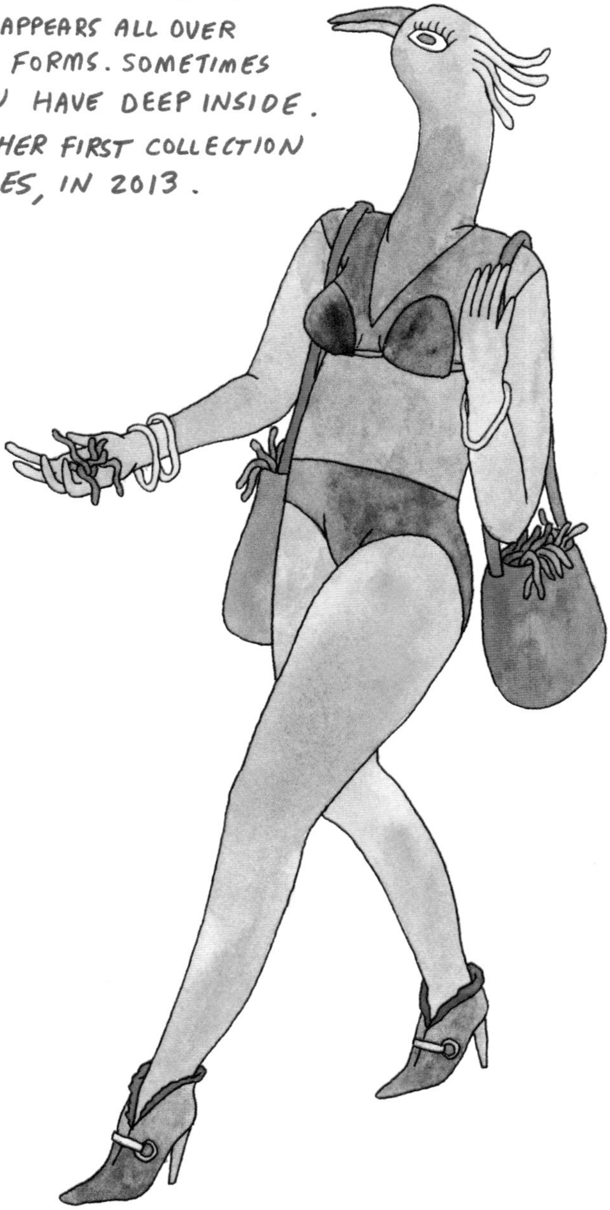

IN CONCLUSION:

- SPROUTS ARE FOOL'S NOODLES
- DON'T TRUST SMOOTH FOOD
- RAISINS MIGHT BE A CARCINOGEN
- I HAVE A HUNCH ABOUT CROISSANTS
- SHUT UP ABOUT FOOD FOR A MINUTE
- YOU DON'T HAVE TO LIKE FOOD BUT YOU DO HAVE TO TRY
- PEOPLE CAN'T TELL WHAT YOU ATE FOR LUNCH JUST BY LOOKING AT YOU.
- IT'S A MYTH THAT PEOPLE SMELL BURNT TOAST WHEN HAVING A STROKE, MOST PEOPLE SMELL BLOOD
- NEVER EAT A HOT DOG ON PURPOSE
- SHARE YOUR FOOD
- IF YOU'RE GOING TO A HOT DOG RESTAURANT, PRETEND YOU'RE ON YOUR WAY TO EAT SOMETHING ELSE

- ~~BANANAS ARE~~
- DON'T EAT YOUR OWN EGGS

WHERE TO GET ADDITIONAL FOOD HELP:

- BACK OF FRIDGE
- LUNCHETORIUM
- YOUR OWN ~~GODDAMN~~ KITCHEN